NONCANONICAL WRITINGS AND NEW TESTAMENT INTERPRETATION

CRAIG A. EVANS

HENDRICKSON PUBLISHERS
PEABODY, MASSACHUSETTS 01961-3473

ISBN 0–943575–95–8

Library of Congress Cataloging-in-Publication Data

Evans, Craig A.
   Noncanonical writings and New Testament interpretation   /
Craig A. Evans
      p.   cm.
   Includes bibliographical references and indexes.
   ISBN 0–943575–95–8
   1. Bible. N.T.—Extra-canonical parallels. 2. Apocryphal books—
Criticism, interpretation, etc. 3. Dead Sea Scrolls—Relation to the
New Testament. 4. Rabbinical literature—Relation to the New Testa-
ment. I. Title.
   BS2555.5.E83   1992
   229—dc20   92-31247
                                                                  CIP

On the cover: The 4th century C.E. Christian tombstone depicting the
Egyptian bird soul *rha* reflects the blending of Christian and Egyptian
ideas. Courtesy of Ikonenmuseum, Recklingshausen.

For James A. Sanders
Scholar, Mentor, Colleague

TABLE OF CONTENTS

APPENDIXES

INDEXES

PREFACE

This book is an introduction to the diverse bodies of literatures that are in various ways cognate to biblical literature, especially to the New Testament. It has been written to serve the needs of students who aspire to become New Testament interpreters. Although it is prepared primarily for the student, ministers, teachers, and biblical scholars alike will find it useful as well.

The last generation has witnessed the discovery and publication of a remarkable amount of ancient literature that in various ways is relevant to New Testament interpretation. Scholarly research has made it abundantly clear that much of this material proves to be exegetically helpful. But the sheer magnitude and diversity of this material has also proven to be intimidating to many students. Indeed, there are many teachers of biblical literature who are not sure exactly what makes up this literature and exactly how it is relevant. The purpose of this book is to arrange these diverse literatures into a comprehensible and manageable format. Not only will the various components of these literatures be listed and briefly described, specific examples will be offered to illustrate how they contribute to New Testament exegesis. Brief bibliographies will also be included with each section. A selected number of the major primary and secondary works will be cited. An index to the titles and authors of these writings will make it possible for the non-specialist to find them quickly.

I owe a word of thanks to the University's superb library staff, especially to Mr. Richard Wiebe, who prepared the Indexes to Ancient Sources and to Modern Authors, and to Mr. Ted Goshulak, who hunted down and ferreted out dozens of old, often out of print, and in some cases quite rare, books. Without his capable and prompt assistance, the writing of this book would have been infinitely more difficult and time-consuming.

Because this book is a tool designed to encourage students to make better use of the various primary literatures that are cognate to the writings of the Bible, I think that it is entirely fitting that it should be dedicated to James A. Sanders, Professor of Biblical Literature at the School of Theology at Claremont and Director of the Ancient Biblical Manuscript Center for Preservation and Research. From him I have learned much about Scripture and the communities of faith that studied and transmitted it.

C. A. Evans
Trinity Western University

ABBREVIATIONS

AB	Anchor Bible (Garden City: Doubleday)
ABRL	Anchor Bible Reference Library (New York: Doubleday)
AJSL	*American Journal of Semitic Languages and Literature*
ALGHJ	Arbeiten zur Literatur und Geschichte des hellenistischen Judentums
AnBib	Analecta biblica (Rome: Pontifical Biblical Institute)
ANRW	W. Haase, ed., *Aufstieg und Niedergang der römischen Welt* II (Berlin: de Gruyter)
AOS	American Oriental Series
APOT	R. H. Charles, ed., *The Apocrypha and Pseudepigrapha of the Old Testament* (2 vols.; Oxford: Clarendon, 1913)
ArBib	Aramaic Bible (Wilmington: Michael Glazier)
ASNU	Acta Seminarii Neotestamentici Uppsaliensis (Uppsala: Almqvist & Wiksells)
ASTI	*Annual of the Swedish Theological Institute in Jerusalem*
ATDan	Acta theologica danica
ATLA	American Theological Library Association
ATR	*Anglican Theological Review*
BA	*Biblical Archaeologist*
BASOR	*Bulletin of the American Schools of Oriental Research*
BASORSup	Bulletin of the American Schools of Oriental Research, Supplement Studies
BE	J. T. Milik, *The Books of Enoch: Aramaic Fragments of Qumrân Cave 4* (with M. Black; Oxford: Clarendon, 1976)
BETL	Bibliotheca ephemeridum theologicarum lovaniensum
Bib	*Biblica*
BibOr	Biblica et orientalia (Rome: Pontifical Biblical Institute)
BibRev	*Bible Review*

BIOSCS	*Bulletin of the International Organization for Septuagint and Cognate Studies*
BJS	Brown Judaic Studies
BJRL	*Bulletin of the John Rylands Library*
BR	*Biblical Research*
BST	Basel Studies in Theology
BTB	*Biblical Theology Bulletin*
BZ	*Biblische Zeitschrift*
BZAW	Beihefte zur Zeitschrift für die alttestamentliche Wissenschaft
CBQ	*Catholic Biblical Quarterly*
CBQMS	Catholic Biblical Quarterly Monograph Series
CH	Corpus Hermeticum
CNRS	Centre National de la Recherche Scientifique
CSEL	Corpus scriptorum ecclesiastorum latinorum
DJD	Discoveries in the Judaean Desert (Oxford: Clarendon)
DSSET	T. H. Gaster, *The Dead Sea Scriptures: In English Translation with Introduction and Notes* (Garden City: Doubleday, 1956; 3d ed., 1976)
DSS	Joseph A. Fitzmyer, *The Dead Sea Scrolls: Major Publications and Tools for Study* (rev. ed.; SBLRBS 20; Atlanta: Scholars, 1990)
EJMI	R. A. Kraft and G. W. E. Nickelsburg, *Early Judaism and Its Modern Interpreters* (Atlanta: Scholars, 1986)
EncJud	*Encyclopedia Judaica*
ESBNT	J. A. Fitzmyer, *Essays on the Semitic Background of the New Testament* (Missoula: Scholars, 1974)
ET	English Translation
EWQ	A. Dupont-Sommer, *The Essene Writings from Qumran* (trans. G. Vermes; Gloucester: Peter Smith, 1973)
ExpTim	*Expository Times*
GCS	Die Griechischen Christlichen Schriftsteller der ersten drei Jahrhundert (Leipzig: Hinrich; Berlin: Akademie)
GNS	Good News Studies (Wilmington: Michael Glazier)
GT	German Translation
HBD	P. J. Achtemeier, ed., *Harper's Bible Dictionary* (San Francisco: Harper & Row, 1985)
HDR	Harvard Dissertations in Religion
HeyJ	*Heythrop Journal*
HSM	Harvard Semitic Monograph
HSS	Harvard Semitic Studies
HTR	*Harvard Theological Review*
HTS	Harvard Theological Studies
HUCA	*Hebrew Union College Annual*

IA	Bruce M. Metzger, *An Introduction to the Apocrypha* (New York: Oxford University Press, 1957)
IDBSup	K. Crim, ed., *Interpreter's Dictionary of the Bible: Supplement* (Nashville: Abingdon, 1976)
IEJ	*Israel Exploration Journal*
IMJ	*Israel Museum Journal*
Int	*Interpretation*
IOS	*Israel Oriental Society*
ISBE	G. W. Bromiley et al., eds., *International Standard Bible Encyclopedia* (4 vols.; rev. ed.; Grand Rapids: Eerdmans, 1979–86)
JAL	Jewish Apocryphal Literature (New York: Harper & Brothers)
JAOS	*Journal of the American Oriental Society*
JBL	*Journal of Biblical Literature*
JBR	*Journal of Bible and Religion*
JETS	*Journal of the Evangelical Theological Society*
JewEnc	*Jewish Encyclopedia*
JJ	James H. Charlesworth, *Jesus within Judaism* (ABRL; New York: Doubleday, 1988)
JJS	*Journal of Jewish Studies*
JNES	*Journal of Near Eastern Studies*
JPS	The Jewish Publication Society of America (Philadelphia)
JQR	*Jewish Quarterly Review*
JQRMS	Jewish Quarterly Review Monograph Series
JR	*Journal of Religion*
JRS	*Journal of Roman Studies*
JSHRZ	Jüdische Schriften aus hellenistisch-römischer Zeit (Gütersloh: Mohn, 1973–)
JSJ	*Journal for the Study of Judaism*
JSNT	*Journal for the Study of the New Testament*
JSOTSup	Journal for the Study of the Old Testament, Supplements
JSPSup	Journal for the Study of the Pseudepigrapha, Supplements
JSS	*Journal of Semitic Studies*
JTS	*Journal of Theological Studies*
JTSA	Jewish Theological Seminary of America (New York)
JWSTP	M. E. Stone, ed., *Jewish Writings of the Second Temple Period* (Philadelphia: Fortress; Assen: Van Gorcum, 1984)
JZWL	*Jüdische Zeitschrift für Wissenschaft und Leben* (1862–75)
LCL	Loeb Classical Library (Cambridge: Harvard University Press)
LS	S. Safrai, ed., *The Literature of the Sages, Part 1* (Philadelphia: Fortress; Assen: Van Gorcum, 1987)
MGWJ	*Monatschrift für Geschichte und Wissenschaft des Judentums* (1851–1939)

MHUC	Monographs of the Hebrew Union College
Mikra	M. J. Mulder, ed., *Mikra: Text, Translation, Reading and Interpretation of the Hebrew Bible in Ancient Judaism and Early Christianity* (Philadelphia: Fortress; Assen: Van Gorcum, 1988)
NGP	Robert W. Funk, ed., *New Gospel Parallels* (2 vols.; Philadelphia: Fortress, 1985)
NHC	Nag Hammadi Codices
NHS	Nag Hammadi Studies (Leiden: Brill)
NIBC	New International Biblical Commentary (Peabody: Hendrickson)
NovT	*Novum Testamentum*
NovTSup	Novum Testamentum, Supplements (Leiden: Brill)
NTA	Edgar Hennecke and Wilhelm Schneemelcher, *New Testament Apocrypha* (2 vols.; Philadelphia: Westminster, 1963–65)
NTS	*New Testament Studies*
OAA	Bruce M. Metzger, ed., *Oxford Annotated Apocrypha: The Apocrypha of the Old Testament Revised Standard Version* (New York: Oxford University Press, 1977)
OBO	Orbis biblicus et orientalis
OCA	Orientalia Christiana Analecta (Rome: Pont Institutum Orientalium Studiorum, 1970)
OOT	M. de Jonge, ed., *Outside the Old Testament* (Cambridge: Cambridge University, 1985)
OTP	James H. Charlesworth, ed., *The Old Testament Pseudepigrapha* (2 vols.; Garden City: Doubleday, 1983–85)
PEQ	*Palestine Exploration Quarterly*
PIASH	*Proceedings of the Israel Academy of Sciences and Humanities*
PRS	*Perspectives in Religious Studies*
PVTG	Pseudepigrapha Veteris Testamenti Graece (Leiden: Brill)
RB	*Revue biblique*
RCB	*Revista de Cultura Biblica*
RelSRev	*Religious Studies Review*
RevQ	*Revue de Qumrân*
RSR	*Recherches de science religieuse*
SBL	Society of Biblical Literature
SBLAS	Society of Biblical Literature Aramaic Studies
SBLMS	Society of Biblical Literature Monograph Series
SBLTT	Society of Biblical Literature Texts and Translations
SBLRBS	Society of Biblical Literature Resources for Biblical Studies
SBLSP	*Society of Biblical Literature Seminar Papers*

SBT	Studies in Biblical Theology
SCHNT	Studia ad Corpus Hellenisticum Novi Testamenti (Leiden: Brill)
SCS	Septuagint and Cognate Studies
SE	*Studia Evangelica*
SJLA	Studies in Judaism in Late Antiquity (Leiden: Brill)
SJT	*Scottish Journal of Theology*
SP	Studia Patristica
SPB	Studia postbiblica (Leiden: Brill)
STDJ	Studies on the Texts of the Desert of Judah (Leiden: Brill)
STR-T	Studia Theologica Rheno-Traiectina (Utrecht: Kemink)
SUNT	Studien zum Umwelt des Neuen Testaments (Göttingen: Vandenhoeck & Ruprecht)
SVTP	Studia in Veteris Testamenti Pseudepigrapha (Leiden: Brill)
Textus	*Textus: Annual of the Hebrew University Bible Project* (Jerusalem)
TS	*Theological Studies*
TTij	*Theologisch Tijdschrift*
TU	Texte und Untersuchungen
VC	*Vigiliae christianae*
VTS	Vetus Testamentum Syriace
VTSup	Vetus Testamentum, Supplements (Leiden: Brill)
YJ	Yale Judaica (New Haven and London: Yale University)
ZAW	*Zeitschrift für die alttestamentliche Wissenschaft*
ZNW	*Zeitschrift für die neutestamentliche Wissenschaft*

INTRODUCTION

There are two principal difficulties that those who aspire to NT exegesis must face: learning the biblical languages and becoming familiar with the myriad of cognate literatures. The first difficulty is overcome through the study of Hebrew, Aramaic, and Greek. But the second difficulty is not so easily dealt with. Because these cognate literatures are so diverse and involve numerous difficulties of their own, many students and even a surprising number of teachers and professors are acquainted with very few of them. Perhaps another factor is knowing that there are scholars who have made it their lives' work to master certain of these literatures. It is understandable then that a beginning NT interpreter often hesitates to plunge into the Talmud or the Dead Sea Scrolls or some other body of writings.

Nevertheless, if one is to do competent NT exegesis, one must know something of these writings and of their relevance for the NT. Some of these writings are vital for understanding the NT, some much less so. But all are referred to by the major scholars. Thus, intelligent reading of the best of NT scholarship requires familiarity with these writings (just as it is necessary to know the biblical languages), if for no other reason.

AN OVERVIEW OF THE WRITINGS

1. *The Old Testament Apocrypha.* All of the writings of the OT Apocrypha (or Deutero-canonical books, as some call them) pre-date the NT (with the exception of portions of 2 Esdras). Most of these writings were written one or two centuries before the NT era. Most, if not all, were known to early Christians and to the writers of the NT. The OT Apocrypha forms, then, an indispensable bridge linking the worlds of the OT and the NT.

2. *The Old Testament Pseudepigrapha.* Many of the writings of the OT Pseudepigrapha, which represent the most diverse collection considered in this book, pre-date the NT; some are contemporaneous, and some post-date the NT. Many contain themes that are represented in the NT. In a few instances NT authors even quote pseudepigraphal writings.

3. *The Dead Sea Scrolls.* The Dead Sea Scrolls probably represent the most sensational twentieth-century archaeological and literary discovery in biblical studies. These writings, mostly in Hebrew, though some are in Aramaic and Greek, either pre-date the NT or are contemporaneous with the earliest NT writings (e.g., Paul's letters and perhaps one or two of the Synoptic Gospels). The authors of these writings (i.e., those found near Qumran) were probably members of the group that Josephus called the Essenes. They lived throughout Palestine, not just in the Dead Sea area where the caves are located, in which the scrolls were discovered. The scrolls provide significant parallels to NT vocabulary and ideas.

4. *Versions of the Old Testament.* The Greek OT, called the Septuagint, is also central for researching the NT for the simple reason that more than one half of the NT's quotations of the OT is from the Septuagint and not from the Hebrew. Three recensions of the Septuagint need to be mentioned. This chapter will also treat the Masoretic Text, the Old Latin, the Vulgate, and the Peshitta. The Aramaic tradition is treated in a chapter of its own.

5. *Philo and Josephus.* Two of the most noteworthy non-Christian Jewish authors of the first century are Philo and Josephus. Philo, who was born during the reign of Herod the Great, wrote several volumes in which he interprets various passages, institutions, and characters of the OT (primarily the Torah) in an allegorical manner. His allegorical interpretation parallels NT interpretation in a few places. Josephus, who lived a generation later, was raised in Palestine and became a participant in the Jews' bloody rebellion against Rome (66–70 C.E.). Befriended by the Roman conquerors, he wrote several works that describe the Jewish conflict and the biblical history of the Jewish people. His writings provide excellent background for NT interpretation, especially for the Gospels.

6. *The Targums.* The targums are Aramaic paraphrases of the Hebrew Bible. They originated in the synagogue, though how early is debated. Some targumic tradition can be traced to the first century and some of it is clearly relevant to certain NT passages.

7. *Rabbinic Literature.* The sayings and traditions of some of the tannaic rabbis may be traced back to the first century and may clarify certain aspects and passages of the NT. Here will be considered the Mishnah, Tosepta, and the early Midrashim. Although not from the early period, but containing some tannaic material, the Babylonian and Palestinian Talmuds and some of the later Midrashim will also be briefly discussed.

8. *The New Testament Pseudepigrapha.* The NT Pseudepigrapha (or Apocrypha) is made up of numerous pseudonymous gospels, books of acts, epistles, and apocalypses. Although most of this material is of no use for NT interpretation, there are some scholars who maintain that in a few instances (esp. in certain gospels) tradition has been preserved that may derive from the NT period and shed light on what is obscure in the NT itself.

9. *Early Church Fathers.* In addition to examining the so-called apostolic fathers (Ignatius, Polycarp, Clement of Rome, etc.) this chapter will survey some of the church's earliest exegetes and theologians, such as Origen, Clement of Alexandria, Tertullian, Cyprian, Eusebius, Jerome, and Augustine. Some of these writings may preserve traditions that derive from the NT period that could aid in exegesis.

10. *Gnostic Writings.* The Coptic Gnostic Codices from Nag Hammadi, Egypt, provide us with most of our gnostic primary materials. Many of these fourth-century Coptic writings are based on much earlier Greek writings that in some cases might date from the late first and early second centuries. Some scholars claim that they may even contain sayings of Jesus that are either authentic or at least more primitive than their counterparts in the Gospels of the NT. Some think that Johannine and Pauline Christology may owe its origin to ideas preserved in the gnostic writings. A few other gnostic writings will also be considered.

11. *Other Writings.* In this final chapter the Hermetic and Samaritan writings, among others, will be reviewed briefly. The former have been compared to Johannine theology, while the latter contain traditions that cohere with distinctive elements in Luke–Acts. A few of the most relevant pagan authors will be included.

THE VALUE

How is NT exegesis facilitated by studying these writings? These writings clarify the following areas of exegetical concern: (1) *The meaning of words.* In older commentaries the meaning of words is often defined by appeal to the classics (usually Greek, though sometimes Latin). It is not clear, however, how relevant these parallels are. (Is the way that Plato used a word in fourth-century B.C.E. Greece germane to the way the same word is used in the Gospel of Mark?) Perhaps in some cases, but parallels that are closer in time (first century B.C.E. to first century C.E.) and location (Palestine, eastern Mediterranean world) are more likely to be relevant. Appeal to the Septuagint, which contains the Apocrypha, is therefore quite appropriate. Although written mostly in Hebrew, Qumran documents often can be helpful in determining the meaning of certain words in the NT. Some of the Pseudepigrapha circulating in Palestine and the eastern Mediterranean can therefore be helpful in determining the meaning of words used in the NT. As an example, consider the word *episkopē* ("visitation"), which occurs a few times in the NT (Luke 19:44; 1 Pet 2:12; for the verb form see Luke 1:68, 78; 7:16; Acts 15:14). The NT's connotation of judgment, either for reward or for punishment, is clarified by OT usage (*episkopē* in the Septuagint, *pequddah* in the Hebrew; cf. Isa 10:3; Jer 8:12; 23:12; 50:27), not classical. Other words are not found in the Greek or Hebrew OT, but derive from the Targum (e.g., "Gehenna"; cf. Mark 9:47–48; *Tg. Isa* 66:24) or from pseudepigraphal writings (e.g., "Tartarus"; cf. 2 Pet 2:4; Ps.-Philo, *Bib. Ant.* 60:3).

(2) *Syntax.* The grammar of the NT is koine, not classical. It is also heavily influenced by the Semitic style of the Septuagint. This is seen by the NT's frequent use of *egeneto de* or *kai egeneto* ("and it came to pass"). This expression comes right out of the Septuagint. To "set one's face" and to go "before one's face" (cf. Luke 9:51–53) are idioms that derive from the Septuagint and whose meanings are clarified by the Greek OT. Other grammatical expressions reflect the Aramaic language of Palestine ("in truth" [Luke 4:25; 1QapGen 2:5]; "he was seen," meaning "he appeared" [Luke 24:34; 1QapGen 22:27]). Some of the NT's syntax seems to reflect Hebrew (preposition *en* with the articular infinitive meaning "while doing" [Luke 1:21; 2:6; 5:1]).

(3) *The meaning of concepts.* When Jesus tells his disciples that they have been given authority to "tread upon serpents [*ophis*] and scorpions" and that "the spirits are subject" to them (Luke 10:19–20), he may have alluded to Ps 91:13 ("You will tread upon lion and the adder, young lion and the serpent you will trample under foot"). Psalm 91 has nothing to do with Satan; but Jesus' words do (cf. Luke 10:17–18). Would a reference to treading upon serpents have been understood in first-century Palestine as a reference to Satan and demons? Very much so. Consider this eschatological hope expressed in one of the *Testaments of the Twelve Patriarchs*: "And Beliar [i.e., Satan] shall be bound by him [i.e., an agent of salvation on whom the Spirit of God shall rest; Isa 11:2]. And he shall grant to his children the authority to trample on wicked spirits" (*T. Levi* 18:12; cf. *T. Sim.* 6:6; *T. Zeb.* 9:8). Since Satan is represented as a serpent (*ophis*) in Gen 3:1–15 and the righteous will trample serpents under foot, it is not too difficult to see how the language of Psalm 91 could be adopted and applied to Satan and evil spirits as we find it in Luke 10 and the *Testament of Levi* 18. The targumic tradition also links serpents and scorpions with Satan and evil spirits (and Gen 3:15, which speaks of the woman's seed crushing the serpent's head, is understood in a messianic sense in the targums).

(4) *History.* Some of the writings that will be considered in this book contribute to what we know about the intertestamental and NT periods. 1 and 2 Maccabees are invaluable sources for our knowledge of the Jewish

revolt against Antiochus IV in 167 B.C.E. Josephus' *Jewish War* and *Antiquities of the Jews* reveal helpful information about Jewish politics and history at the turn of the era, especially with reference to Herod the Great and his family, and the time of Jesus and his earliest followers.

(5) *Historical, social, and religious context (i.e., Sitz im Leben)*. Following the death of Herod the Great Palestine went through a period of political instability and upheaval. Josephus cynically remarks, "Anyone might make himself a king" (*Ant.* 17.10.8 §285). Josephus has no sympathy for Jewish nationalists and would-be-liberators, calling them "brigands" (*lēstēs*). This is the very word that is used when Jesus is arrested and crucified (Mark 14:48; 15:27). In view of Josephus' description of these kingly claimants as *lestai*, some of whom may very well have thought of themselves as messiahs, it is possible that when *lēstēs* is used of Jesus, it meant "insurrectionist." Josephus also tells of false prophets who deluded the people by promising signs of deliverance, sometimes urging them to withdraw to the desert. The language that he uses (*Ant.* 17.10.7 §§278–284; 20.8.6 §168; 20.8.10 §188; *J.W.* 2.13.5 §§261–263; 6.5.4 §315) parallels, at places quite closely, the warnings that we read in the Gospels (cf. Matt 24:26; Mark 13:21–22).

(6) *Exegetical context*. Of major importance is the fact that the noncanonical writings quite often shed light on the interpretation of the OT passages quoted or alluded to in the NT. For example, parts of 2 Sam 7:12–16, the "Davidic Covenant," are quoted (Heb 1:5) or alluded to (Luke 1:32–33) in the NT as fulfilled in Jesus. Since Nathan's oracle originally spoke of Solomon the son of David, one wonders if early Christian interpretation would have been understood or accepted. Qumran has made it clear, however, that this oracle was interpreted in an eschatological sense, at least in some circles. The eschatological deliverer will be God's Son (4QFlor 1:11–12; 4QpsDan ar[a] 1:6–9; 2:1–4) and he will be seated on the throne of David (4QPBless 1–2), thus fulfilling the promise of 2 Samuel 7 in a way that Solomon and his descendants did not. As another example, the presentation of Jesus in the Prologue of the Fourth Gospel as the Logos ("word") is illumined by Philo and possibly by the targums. Philo describes the Logos as "God's first-born, the Word" (*On the Confusion of the Languages* 28 §146), through whom God created the world (*On the Cherubim* 35 §127). The targums say that God created humanity through the Memra ("word"): "The Memra of the Lord created man in his own image" (*Tg. Neof.* Gen 1:27; cf. *Tg. Isa* 45:12). The presence of "Word" as agent of creation in Genesis 1 is highly suggestive, since John 1 ("In the beginning . . .") echoes the language of the creation account.

(7) *Hermeneutical context (i.e., how Scripture could be interpreted, how it could applied, adapted)*. The literatures surveyed in this book help us understand how biblical literature was interpreted and what role it

played in the life of the Jewish and Christian communities of faith. Qumran affords us with examples of pesher interpretation whereby various prophetic details of Scripture were applied to contemporary events and events felt to be imminent. Rabbinic writings provide us with numerous examples in midrashic interpretation whereby Scripture was searched in an effort to find answers to the questions relating to how God's people should live and how they should understand their sacred tradition. Philo's writings illustrate allegorical interpretation. Do the details of Scripture point to meanings beyond the obvious and literal? The targums and some of the pseudepigraphal writings show how the biblical story can be paraphrased, expanded, and enriched. But perhaps more importantly, these various literatures aid us in understanding what role Scripture played in the life of the believing community. All of this sheds light on how early Christians understood their own sacred tradition.

(8) *Canonical context (i.e., what was regarded as Scripture and why).* The literatures surveyed in this book also help us understand what it meant to regard certain writings as authoritative. By what criteria were certain writings preserved and treated with reverence and respect not accorded to other writings? What was the understanding of the relationship between the OT and NT? In what sense is the NT part of the Bible? (And from a Christian point of view: In what sense is the OT part of the Bible?) In what sense did the "canonical" writings possess authority? What does the author of 2 Esdras mean when he says that whereas both the worthy and unworthy may read the twenty-four books (i.e., the OT), only the wise should be permitted to read the "seventy" books (i.e., the Apocrypha/Pseudepigrapha) that were written last (14:44–47; cf. 12:37–38)? The literatures surveyed in this book do not definitely answer these and related questions, but they provide much of the raw data that must be processed before we can begin to answer them responsibly.

THE METHOD

How are these writings put to use in doing NT exegesis? This is the principal concern of the present book. Comparative study of these writings constitutes an important step in the exegetical process.

In order to understand a given passage one must reconstruct as much as possible the world of thought in which the NT writer lived. Since the NT frequently quotes the OT (hundreds of times) or alludes to it (thousands of times) and everywhere presupposes its language, concepts, and theology, exegesis should be particularly sensitive to its presence and careful to reconstruct the exegetical-theological context of which a given OT quotation or allusion may have been a part. A comparative approach is essential. How was the OT passage quoted or alluded to understood by early Christians and Jews? To answer this question the interpreter should examine every occurrence of the passage. This involves studying the ancient versions and cognate literatures, the very writings treated in this book.

To assess properly the function of the OT in the NT the following questions must be raised:

(1) What OT text(s) is(are) being cited? Two or more passages may be conflated, and each may contribute insight.

(2) Which text-type is being followed (Hebrew, Greek, Aramaic)? What are the respective meanings of these versions? (Each may have an interpretive tradition of its own.) How does the version that the NT has followed contribute to the meaning of the quotation?

(3) Is the OT quotation part of a wider tradition or theology in the OT? If it is, the quotation may be alluding to a context much wider than the specific passage from which it has been taken.

(4) How did various Jewish and Christian groups and interpreters understand the passage? This question is vital, for often the greatest help comes from comparing the function of the OT in these sources.

(5) In what ways does the NT citation agree or disagree with the interpretations found in the versions and other ancient exegeses? Has the Jesus/Christian tradition distinctively shaped the OT quotation and its interpretation, or does the NT exegesis reflect interpretation current in pre-Christian Judaism?

(6) How does the function of the quotation compare to the function of other quotations in the NT writing under consideration. Has a different text-type been used? Has the OT been followed more closely or less so?

(7) Finally, how does the quotation contribute to the argument of the NT passage in which it is found?

If these questions are carefully considered, one's exegesis will be in large measure complete. Although the above steps have been applied to passages where the OT is present, either explicitly or implicitly, most of these steps are relevant for exegesis of any passage, for it is indeed a rare passage that alludes to or parallels no other. (For treatments concerned with other questions of exegesis consult the works listed in the bibliography below.)

In the chapters that follow the various literatures will be surveyed with the questions just considered kept in mind. In the final chapter a selection of passages from the NT will be studied and offered as examples of the benefits to be derived from addressing these questions and taking into account the various literatures of the biblical period.

GENERAL BIBLIOGRAPHY: R. Beckwith, *The Old Testament Canon of the New Testament Church and Its Background in Early Judaism* (Grand Rapids: Eerdmans, 1985); H. Conzelmann and A. Lindemann, *Arbeitsbuch zum Neuen Testament* (8th ed., Tübingen: Mohr [Siebeck], 1985); ET: *Interpreting the New Testament: An*

Introduction to the Principles and Methods of N.T. Exegesis (Peabody: Hendrickson, 1988); E. J. Epp and G. W. MacRae, eds., *The New Testament and Its Modern Interpreters* (Atlanta: Scholars, 1989) [for backgrounds see esp. pp. 1–71]; G. D. Fee, *New Testament Exegesis: A Handbook for Students and Pastors* (Philadelphia: Westminster, 1983); K. Froehlich, *Biblical Interpretation in the Early Church* (Philadelphia: Fortress, 1984); D. J. Harrington, *Interpreting the New Testament: A Practical Guide* (Wilmington: Michael Glazier, 1979); J. H. Hayes and C. R. Holladay, *Biblical Exegesis: A Beginner's Handbook* (Atlanta: John Knox, 1982); O. Kaiser and W. G. Kümmel, *Exegetical Method: A Student's Handbook* (New York: Seabury, 1981); J. L. Kugel and R. A. Greer, *Early Biblical Interpretation* (Philadelphia: Westminster, 1986); I. H. Marshall, ed., *New Testament Interpretation: Essays on Principles and Methods* (Grand Rapids: Eerdmans, 1977); L. M. McDonald, *The Formation of the Christian Biblical Canon* (Nashville: Abingdon, 1988); B. M. Metzger, *The Canon of the New Testament: Its Origin, Development, and Significance* (Oxford: Clarendon, 1987); J. A. Sanders, *Canon and Community* (Philadelphia: Fortress, 1984).

CHAPTER ONE

THE OLD TESTAMENT APOCRYPHA

1 Esdras	Susanna
2 Esdras	Bel and the Dragon
Tobit	Prayer of Manasseh
Judith	1 Maccabees
Additions to Esther	2 Maccabees
Wisdom of Solomon	3 Maccabees (see Old Testament
Ecclesiasticus (Sirach)	Pseudepigrapha)
Baruch	4 Maccabees (see Old Testament
Letter of Jeremiah	Pseudepigrapha)
Prayer of Azariah and the Song of	Psalm 151 (see Old Testament
the Three Children	Pseudepigrapha)

Fifteen books make up the OT Apocrypha (or Deutero-canonical books). Some editions of the Bible incorporate the Letter of Jeremiah into Baruch as its sixth and final chapter. These editions, therefore, have fourteen books. Whereas Protestants do not regard the books of the Apocrypha as inspired or as canonical, the Roman Catholic, Greek Orthodox, Russian Orthodox, and Coptic Churches accept most of them. (For a listing of their respective canons of the Apocrypha see Appendix 1.)

The word "apocrypha" is a Greek word literally meaning "hidden away." Why "hidden"? Over the centuries those who appreciated and approved of these books as authoritative thought of them as hidden from the uninitiated and simple. They were reserved for the wise and learned. On the other hand, those who viewed these books as spurious and as possessing no authority have understood them as hidden because of perceived heretical tendencies. It is probably for this reason that the word "apocrypha" has come to mean "false." For example, when a story about a well-known person is suspected of being untrue we say that it is "apocryphal."

The Apocrypha (the word is actually plural—the singular is apocryphon—but people often think of it as singular) represents several types of writing. Some of the writings are historical (e.g., 1 Esdras, 1 and 2 Maccabees), some are romantic (e.g., Tobit, Judith, Susanna, Additions to Esther), some are didactic (e.g., Wisdom of Solomon, Ecclesiasticus), some are moralistic (e.g., Baruch, Letter of Jeremiah, Bel and the Dragon), and some are devotional (e.g., Prayer of Azariah and the Song of the Three Children, Prayer of Manasseh). One is apocalyptic (2 Esdras).

The Greek text of the Apocrypha is found in the Septuagint (see chap. 4). The best ET is that edited by B. M. Metzger, *The Apocrypha of the Old Testament, Revised Standard Version* (New York: Oxford University, 1977) [= *OAA*]. This edition contains several helpful notes and tables. Metzger has also edited *A Concordance to the Apocryphal/Deuterocanonical Books of the Revised Standard Version* (London: Collins; Grand Rapids: Eerdmans, 1983). See also the ET edition of the Apocrypha in the *New Revised Standard Version* (New York: Oxford, 1989).

SUMMARIES

1 Esdras. 1 Esdras is not accepted as canonical by the Roman Catholic Church. (It was rejected by the Council of Trent, 8 April 1546.) The Roman Bible includes it in an appendix. (In the Vulgate it is called 3 Esdras.) It is, however, accepted by the Greek Orthodox and Russian Orthodox Churches. It is a historical writing based upon 2 Chr 35:1–36:23, Ezra, and Neh 7:38–8:12. However, the story of the three men in the court of Darius (3:1–5:6), which has no parallel in the OT, may represent the author's chief concern (Metzger, *IA*, 18). The book follows neither the Masoretic Text nor the LXX. The unknown author apparently intended to emphasize the religious reforms of Josiah (1:1–24), Zerubbabel (5:47–6:34), and Ezra (8:1–9:55). It was written probably in the second century B.C.E.

Text: R. Hanhart, *Esdrae liber 1* (Septuaginta 8/1; Göttingen: Vandenhoeck & Ruprecht, 1974). *Commentary:* J. M. Myers, *I & II Esdras* (AB 42; Garden City: Doubleday, 1964) 1–104. *Critical Studies:* H. W. Attridge, "Historiography," *JWSTP,* 157–60; G. W. E. Nickelsburg, "Stories of Biblical and Early Post-Biblical Times," *JWSTP,* 131–35.

2 Esdras. 2 Esdras also is not accepted by the Roman Church, although it is included in an appendix with 1 Esdras. It is, however, accepted by the Russian Orthodox Church. In the Vulgate it is 4 Esdras. (The book is also known as 4 Ezra and is sometimes included in the OT Pseudepigrapha. On the confusing Esdras-Ezra nomenclature see the tables below.)

2 Esdras does not resume the historical narrative of 1 Esdras, as one might suppose, but is called "2 Esdras" because of the opening verse: "The second book of the prophet Ezra. . . ." The book is an apocalypse consisting largely of seven revelations (3:1–5:20; 5:21–6:34; 6:35–9:25; 9:38–10:59; 11:1–12:51; 13:1–58; 14:1–48) which are primarily concerned with moral themes. Apparently, at least three authors are responsible for 2 Esdras. The original author was probably a first-century Palestinian Jew who, writing in Aramaic or Hebrew, produced chaps. 3–14 (the original 4 Ezra). It was subsequently translated into Greek. A second-century Christian added a Greek introduction (chaps. 1–2). Finally, a third-century Christian added the last two chapters (15–16) in Greek. The Semitic original is lost, and only a fragment of the Greek has survived (15:57–59). The purpose of the original author was to show that God is just, despite the evil of the Rome of his day and the calamities that had befallen Jerusalem (Metzger, *IA*, 30).

TABLE OF ESDRAS NOMENCLATURE

Hebrew Bible	Septuagint	Vulgate	English Apocrypha
Ezra	2 Esdras	1 Esdras	
Nehemiah	3 Esdras	2 Esdras	
	1 Esdras	3 Esdras	1 Esdras
	4 Esdras	2 Esdras	

TABLE OF EZRA NOMENCLATURE

1 Ezra	Ezra-Nehemiah of the Hebrew Bible
2 Ezra	4 Esdras (Vulgate) = 2 Esdras (English Apocrypha) chaps. 1–2
3 Ezra	1 Esdras (Septuagint) = 3 Esdras (Vulgate) = 1 Esdras (English Apocrypha)
4 Ezra	4 Esdras (Vulgate) = 2 Esdras (English Apocrypha) chaps. 3–14
5 Ezra	4 Esdras (Vulgate) = 2 Esdras (English Apocrypha) chaps. 15–16

(adapted from H. W. Attridge, "Historiography," *JWSTP*, 158)

Text: R. L. Bensly, *The Fourth Book of Ezra, the Latin Version Edited from the MSS* (Cambridge: Cambridge University, 1895); B. Violet, *Die Esra-Apokalypse (IV. Ezra)* vol. 1: *Die Überlieferung* (GCS 18; Leipzig: Hinrich, 1910). *Commentary:* J. M. Myers, *I & II Esdras* (AB 42; Garden City: Doubleday, 1964) 107–354. *Critical Studies:* G. K. Beale, "The Problem of the Man from the Sea in IV Ezra 13 and Its Relation to the Messianic Concept in John's Apocalypse," *NovT* 25 (1983) 182–88; M. E. Stone, "Apocalyptic Literature," *JWSTP*, 412–14; A. L. Thompson, *Responsibility for Evil in the Theodicy of IV Ezra* (SBLDS 29; Missoula: Scholars, 1977).

Tobit. Tobit is accepted by the Roman Catholic, Greek Orthodox, and Russian Orthodox Churches. The book tells a romantic, moralistic story of the adventures of Tobit and his son Tobias in Nineveh shortly after the exile of the northern kingdom (2 Kgs 17:1–6). It was originally written in Aramaic or Hebrew sometime in the second century B.C.E. by an unknown author. Subsequently it was translated into Greek. Tobit's prophecy of the rebuilding of the temple (14:5–7) has received attention in recent scholarship concerned with the place of the temple in first-century eschatological expectations.

Text: R. Hanhart, Tobit (Septuaginta 8/5; Göttingen: Vandenhoeck & Ruprecht, 1983). Commentaries: C. A. Moore, Tobit (AB 40A; Garden City: Doubleday, forthcoming); F. Zimmermann, The Book of Tobit (JAL; New York: Harper, 1958). Critical Studies: R. Doran, "Narrative Literature," EJMI, 296–99; G. W. E. Nickelsburg, "Stories of Biblical and Early Post-Biblical Times," JWSTP, 40–46.

Judith. Judith is accepted by the Roman Catholic, Greek Orthodox, and Russian Orthodox Churches. Notwithstanding several serious anachronisms and historical blunders, the book tells a heroic tale of the beautiful Judith whose courage and faith in God saved her village from destruction at the hands of one of Nebuchadnezzar's generals. In many ways the book stands in the tradition of the heroes in Judges (see 4:4–22). Originally a second-century B.C.E. Hebrew composition, probably reflecting the tensions and fears of the Maccabean struggle (Metzger, IA, 43), the work survives in Greek, Latin, Syriac, and several later Hebrew recensions. Nothing is known of the author.

Text: R. Hanhart, Iudith (Septuaginta 8/4; Göttingen: Vandenhoeck & Ruprecht, 1979). Commentary: C. A. Moore, Judith (AB 40; Garden City: Doubleday, 1985). Critical Studies: R. Doran, "Narrative Literature," EJMI, 302–4; M. S. Enslin and S. Zeitlin, The Book of Judith (Leiden: Brill, 1972); G. W. E. Nickelsburg, "Stories of Biblical and Early Post-Biblical Times," JWSTP, 46–52.

Additions to Esther. Six additions to Esther, comprising 107 verses, have been accepted by the Roman Catholic, Greek Orthodox, and Russian Orthodox Churches. When translating the Hebrew, Jerome collected these additions, which are found only in the Greek version (the LXX), and placed them at the end of the original Hebrew Esther as 10:4–16:24 (which is followed by the Rheims and Douay edition), thus confusing the chronological sequence. The order of the LXX, which contains the translation of the original Hebrew, as well as the Greek additions, is as follows: (1) Addition 1 (11:2–12:6); (2) Hebrew 1:1–3:13; (3) Addition 2 (13:1–7); (4) Hebrew 3:14–4:17; (5) Addition 3 (13:8–14:19); (6) Hebrew 5:1–2 (=Addition 4 [15:1–2]); (7) Addition 4 (15:1–16); (8) Hebrew 5:3–8:12; (9) Addition 5 (16:1–24); (10) Hebrew 8:13–10:3; (11) Addition 6 (10:4–11:1). Esther may have been translated into Greek by "Lysimachus the son of Ptolemy" (11:1), who claims that the entire document, additions and all, is genuine. The purpose of the additions is to introduce God and religion into a book which originally did not once mention the name of God.

Text: R. Hanhart, *Esther* (Septuaginta 8/3; Göttingen: Vandenhoeck & Ruprecht, 1966; 2d ed., 1983). *Commentary:* C. A. Moore, *Daniel, Esther and Jeremiah: The Additions* (AB 44; Garden City: Doubleday, 1987) 153–252. *Critical Studies:* W. H. Brownlee, "Le livre grec d'Esther et la royauté divine. Corrections orthodoxes au livre d'Esther," *RB* 73 (1966) 161–85; G. W. E. Nickelsburg, "The Bible Rewritten and Expanded," *JWSTP,* 135–38, 155.

Wisdom of Solomon. The Wisdom of Solomon is accepted by the Roman Catholic, Greek Orthodox, and Russian Orthodox Churches. It is a pseudepigraphon that claims to have been written by Israel's celebrated monarch (see 7:1–14; 8:17–9:18; compare 1 Kgs 3:6–9; 2 Chr 1:8–10). This book is part of the late wisdom tradition and is comparable to Sirach (see below) and parts of Proverbs. It was originally written in Greek and probably derives from Alexandria of the first century B.C.E. It warns the wicked, praises wisdom, provides examples of God's mighty acts in history, and ridicules idolatry.

Text: J. Ziegler, *Sapientia Salomonis* (Septuaginta 12/1; Göttingen: Vandenhoeck & Ruprecht, 1962; 2d ed., 1980). *Commentaries:* D. Winston, *The Wisdom of Solomon* (AB 43; Garden City: Doubleday, 1979); J. Reider, *The Book of Wisdom* (JAL; New York: Harper, 1957). *Critical Studies:* M. Gilbert, "Wisdom Literature," *JWSTP,* 301–13; B. L. Mack and R. E. Murphy, "Wisdom Literature," *EJMI,* 380–87.

Ecclesiasticus. Commonly called (Jesus ben) Sira, or the Wisdom of Jesus the son of Sirach, though in the Latin tradition it is known as Ecclesiasticus (i.e., the "church book"). Sirach is accepted by the Roman Catholic, Greek Orthodox, and Russian Orthodox Churches. The original document was written in Hebrew by Joshua ben Sira (ca. 180 B.C.E.) and was later introduced and translated into Greek by his grandson around 132 B.C.E. Only fragments of the Hebrew text remain, most of which date from the Middle Ages. Sirach is probably intended to be two volumes, consisting of chaps. 1–23 and 24–51, with each volume beginning with an encomium on wisdom (see 1:1–10; 24:1–34). In many respects the book resembles Proverbs. It is, as Bruce Metzger has remarked, "the first specimen of that form of Judaism which subsequently developed into the rabbinical schools of the Pharisees and the Sadducees" (*OAA,* 128). Sirach 24 is of special interest for the interpretation of John 1:1–18.

Text: J. Ziegler, *Sapientia Iesu filii Sirach* (Septuaginta 12/2; Göttingen: Vandenhoeck & Ruprecht, 1965; 2d ed., 1980). *Commentary:* P. W. Skehan and A. A. Di Lella, *The Wisdom of Ben Sira* (AB 39; New York: Doubleday, 1987). *Critical Studies:* M. Gilbert, "Wisdom Literature," *JWSTP,* 290–301; B. L. Mack, *Wisdom and the Hebrew Epic: Ben Sira's Hymn in Praise of the Fathers* (Chicago and London: University of Chicago, 1985); idem and R. E. Murphy, "Wisdom Literature," *EJMI,* 373–77.

Baruch. Baruch, or 1 Baruch, purports to be the work of Baruch, friend and secretary of the prophet Jeremiah (see Jer 32:12; 36:4). Originally a Hebrew writing, it has survived in Greek, Latin, Syriac, and other languages of the Mediterranean. It appears to have at least two parts, the first consisting of prose (1:1–3:8), the second poetry (3:9–5:9). The purpose of the first part is to bring an awareness of sin and the need for repentance, while the purpose of the second part is to offer praise to wisdom and comfort to an oppressed Jerusalem. The two parts were probably brought together ca. 100 B.C.E.

Text: J. Ziegler, *Jeremias, Baruch, Threni, Epistula Jeremiae* (Septuaginta 15; Göttingen: Vandenhoeck & Ruprecht, 1957; 2d ed., 1976). *Commentary:* C. A. Moore, *Daniel, Esther and Jeremiah: The Additions* (AB 44; Garden City: Doubleday, 1987) 255–316. *Critical Studies:* B. L. Mack and R. E. Murphy, "Wisdom Literature," *EJMI*, 377–78 [on Bar 3:9–4:4]; G. W. E. Nickelsburg, "The Bible Rewritten and Expanded," *JWSTP*, 140–46; E. Tov, *The Book of Baruch also called 1 Baruch* (SBLTT 8; Missoula: Scholars, 1975) [on Bar 1:1–3:8].

Letter of Jeremiah. The Letter of Jeremiah (or Jeremy) appears as chapter 6 of Baruch in the LXX, which is followed by the Vulgate (and the Rheims and Douay version). The letter is accepted by the Roman Catholic, Greek Orthodox, and Russian Orthodox Churches. The document purports to be a letter from the prophet Jeremiah, exhorting the Jewish exiles to eschew idolatry. The apocryphal letter may have been inspired by Jer 10:11, an Aramaic verse which reads: "The gods who did not make the heavens and the earth shall perish from the earth and from under the heavens" (Metzger, *IA*, 96). Several OT passages have been drawn upon (Isa 40:18–20; 41:6–7; Jer 10:3–9, 14; Ps 115:4–8). The letter was probably originally written in Greek, perhaps as early as 300 B.C.E.

Text: J. Ziegler, *Jeremias, Baruch, Threni, Epistula Jeremiae* (Septuaginta 15; Göttingen: Vandenhoeck & Ruprecht, 1957; 2d ed., 1976). *Commentary.* C. A. Moore, *Daniel, Esther and Jeremiah: The Additions* (AB 44; Garden City: Doubleday, 1987) 317–58. *Critical Studies:* C. J. Ball, "The Epistle of Jeremy," *APOT*, 1.526–611; G. W. E. Nickelsburg, "The Bible Rewritten and Expanded," *JWSTP*, 146–49, 156.

Prayer of Azariah and the Song of the Three Children. The Prayer of Azariah and the Song of the Three Children is an addition inserted between Dan 3:23 and 3:24. It is accepted by the Roman Catholic, Greek Orthodox, and Russian Orthodox Churches. There are several additions to Daniel, the three major ones being the Prayer of Azariah and the Song of the Three Children (or Young Men), Susanna, and Bel and the Dragon. These additions were probably composed in Greek, although Aramaic is possible. In the case of the addition under consideration, the original language of composition may have been Hebrew. The Prayer of Azariah and the Song of the Three Children itself probably represents a combination of two additions. The Prayer of Azariah is uttered by one of the young men in the furnace (Abednego; cf. Dan 1:7). It confesses Israel's sin and petitions God that Israel's enemies be put to shame. It is followed by a song of praise and exhortation to praise. It owes much of its inspiration to Ps 148:1–2, 7–12 (Metzger, *IA*, 103).

Text: J. Ziegler, *Susanna, Daniel, Bel et Draco* (16/2; Göttingen: Vandenhoeck & Ruprecht, 1954). *Commentary:* C. A. Moore, *Daniel, Esther and Jeremiah: The Additions* (AB 44; Garden City: Doubleday, 1987) 39–76. *Critical Studies:* C. Kuhl, *Die drei Männer im Feuer (Daniel, Kapitel 3 und seine Zusätze): Ein Beitrag zur israelitisch-jüdischen Literaturgeschichte* (BZAW 55; Giessen: Töpelmann, 1930); G. W. E. Nickelsburg, "The Bible Rewritten and Expanded," *JWSTP,* 149–52.

Susanna. Susanna is accepted by the Roman Catholic, Greek Orthodox, and Russian Orthodox Churches. In the LXX and Vulgate Susanna is chap. 13 of Daniel. In other versions, however, Susanna appears as an introduction to chap. 1 (perhaps because in v. 45 Daniel is referred to as a "young lad" and according to v. 64 it was "from that day onward" that Daniel enjoyed a great reputation). Susanna is the story of a beautiful woman who is pursued by two lustful elders. When wrongly accused, she is defended by the wise Daniel. The lesson of Susanna is that virtue and faith will ultimately be vindicated. It is likely that the story was originally composed in Greek, as is especially seen in the Greek word-plays in vv. 54–59 (Metzger, *IA,* 110–11).

Text: J. Ziegler, *Susanna, Daniel, Bel et Draco* (16/2; Göttingen: Vandenhoeck & Ruprecht, 1954). *Commentary:* C. A. Moore, *Daniel, Esther and Jeremiah: The Additions* (AB 44; Garden City: Doubleday, 1987) 77–116. *Critical Studies:* R. Doran, "Narrative Literature," *EJMI,* 299–301; G. W. E. Nickelsburg, "Stories of Biblical and Early Post-Biblical Times," *JWSTP,* 37–38.

Bel and the Dragon. Bel and the Dragon is accepted by the Roman Catholic, Greek Orthodox, and Russian Orthodox Churches. This addition is made up of two stories designed to demonstrate the foolishness of idolatry and the dishonesty of the heathen priesthood. Like the other additions to Daniel, these stories teach that God's people will persevere, if they have faith. It may have been inspired by biblical traditions that speak of God's slaying Leviathan (Metzger, *IA,* 120). In the LXX, Bel and the Dragon is added to Daniel 12, while in the Vulgate it makes up chap. 14.

Text: J. Ziegler, *Susanna, Daniel, Bel et Draco* (16/2; Göttingen: Vandenhoeck & Ruprecht, 1954). *Commentary:* C. A. Moore, *Daniel, Esther and Jeremiah: The Additions* (AB 44; Garden City: Doubleday, 1987) 117–49. *Critical Studies:* R. Doran, "Narrative Literature," *EJMI,* 301–2; G. W. E. Nickelsburg, "Stories of Biblical and Early Post-Biblical Times," *JWSTP,* 38–40.

Prayer of Manasseh. The Prayer of Manasseh is accepted by the Greek Orthodox Church. Inspired by 2 Chr 33:11–13, this document purports to be King Manasseh's prayer of repentance after being exiled. Moreover, the reference to two works that contain Manasseh's prayer (2 Chr 33:18–20), which are lost, may very well have prompted our unknown writer to compose this piece (Metzger, *IA,* 124–25). See comments in chapter 2.

Text: A. Rahlfs, *Psalmi cum Odis* (Septuaginta 10; Göttingen: Vandenhoeck & Ruprecht, 1967; 2d ed., 1979). *Commentary:* J. H. Charlesworth, "Prayer of Manasseh," *OTP*, 2.625–37; H. E. Ryle, "Prayer of Manasses," *APOT*, 1.612–24. *Critical Studies:* W. Baars and H. Schneider, "Prayer of Manasseh," in Baars and Schneider, *The Old Testament in Syriac According to the Peshitta Version* (VTS 4/6; Leiden: Brill, 1972) i–vii, 1–9; D. Flusser, "Psalms, Hymns and Prayers," *JWSTP*, 555.

1 Maccabees. 1 Maccabees is accepted by the Roman Catholic, Greek Orthodox, and Russian Orthodox Churches. The book tells of the events surrounding the Jewish uprising against Antiochus IV Epiphanes. 1 Maccabees describes the courage of Mattathias the priest and his sons, especially Judas Maccabeus, after whom the book and the period of time are named. The book is probably an apology for the Hasmonean dynasty which, not too many years after Israel had regained its independence, had fallen into disfavor among many of the strictest observers of Judaism. Originally written in Hebrew, probably sometime late in the second century B.C.E. (though some scholars place chaps. 14–16 after 70 C.E.), the history of 1 Maccabees is for the most part trustworthy (though at times it is at variance with 2 Maccabees—and it is not always certain which account is to be preferred). Unlike 2 Maccabees, 1 Maccabees contains no miraculous accounts. Solomon Zeitlin thinks that the book which the Yosippon (see chap. 5) refers to as *Sepher Bet Hasmanaim* ("The Book of the House of the Hasmoneans") is the Hebrew 1 Maccabees.

Text: W. Kappler, *Maccabaeorum liber I* (Septuaginta 9/1; Göttingen: Vandenhoeck & Ruprecht, 1967). *Commentary:* J. A. Goldstein, *I Maccabees* (AB 41; Garden City: Doubleday, 1976). *Critical Studies:* H. W. Attridge, "Historiography," *JWSTP*, 171–76; idem, "Jewish Historiography," *EJMI*, 316–23; S. Zeitlin, "Josippon," *JQR* 53 (1962–63) 277–97, esp. 290.

2 Maccabees. 2 Maccabees is accepted by the Roman Catholic, Greek Orthodox, and Russian Orthodox Churches. The book is not a sequel to 1 Maccabees; rather it covers approximately the same events and period of time (=1 Macc 1:10–7:50). According to 2:23–28, 2 Maccabees is an abridgement of a five-volume work by one "Jason of Cyrene." This larger history is now lost. Most suspect that 2 Maccabees is historically less trustworthy. Its purpose is to enhance the theological dimensions of the Jerusalem temple and the Jewish struggle for independence. See also its seventh chapter for a defense of the resurrection. 2 Maccabees was probably written originally in Greek in the first century B.C.E.

Text: R. Hanhart, *Maccabaeorum liber II* (Septuaginta 9/2; Göttingen: Vandenhoeck & Ruprecht, 1959). *Commentary:* J. A. Goldstein, *II Maccabees* (AB 41A; Garden City: Doubleday, 1983). *Critical Studies:* H. W. Attridge, "Historiography," *JWSTP*, 176–83; idem, "Jewish Historiography," *EJMI*, 316–23; R. Doran, *Temple Propaganda: The Purpose and Character of 2 Maccabees* (CBQMS 12; Washington: Catholic Biblical Association, 1981).

THEMES

The writings that make up the OT Apocrypha contribute much to NT background. There are several political and theological themes that may be reviewed briefly.

God. 2 Maccabees 7:28 may be the first to teach that God created the universe out of nothing. In Sir 43:27 God is called "the All." God is called "Father" (Tob 13:4), "Judge" (Sir 17:15–24), and "King" (Jdt 9:12; 2 Macc 7:9). Wisdom 11:22–12:2 teaches that God's love is universal. God is all-knowing and all-powerful (Sir 42:15–25).

Piety and Martyrdom. In 1 Esdr 4:13–47 the pious wisdom of Zerubbabel is cited as an important factor in reminding the Persian king Darius of his vow to have Jerusalem and the temple rebuilt. The wickedness of God's people is cited in 2 Esdras as the major cause of Israel's misfortunes. The book of Tobit revolves around the piety of Tobit and his son Tobias. Tobit tithed, kept the dietary laws, gave food and clothing to the poor, and greatest of all, buried the dead. (According to Sir 3:30; 7:10, almsgiving atones for sin.) The book of Judith tells the story of a beautiful woman who risked her life, but kept herself from being dishonored by Holofernes. In 9:1 she humbles herself and prays. In Add Esth 14:1–19 Queen Esther humbles herself (v. 2) and prays fervently to God. In Bar 1:5–14 the penitent weep, fast, pray, and send money to Jerusalem to reestablish worship in Jerusalem. The Prayer of Azariah and the Song of the Three Young Men greatly enhances the theme of piety found in Daniel. In Susanna the piety of Susanna and the wisdom of the young man Daniel are vindicated. The Prayer of Manasseh is a classic in pious penitence. Perhaps the greatest example of piety in the face of persecution occurs in 2 Maccabees 7 where a mother and her seven sons are put to death for refusing to eat pork (v. 1; cf. 4 Macc 8–17; *b. Giṭ.* 57b; *Lam. Rab.* 1:16 §50).

Salvation History. A frequent theme is that of Israel's obduracy (1 Esdr 1:47–52; 2 Esdr 3:20–22; 4:30; Tob 1:5; Jdt 5:17–21; Bar 1:15–2:10; Add Esth 14:6–7; PrAzar 4–7, 14; Sus 52–53; Pr Man 9–10, 12) and return from the exile (1 Esdr 2:1–15; Bar 5:1–9).

Zionism. Much of 2 Esdras is concerned with the fate of "Zion" (i.e., Jerusalem). In 13:29–50 the Messiah is seen standing on the top of Mount Zion (v. 35), with Zion now sitting in judgment upon the nations (vv. 36–38). In Tob 14:5b the aged Tobit prophesies that Jerusalem and the temple, having been destroyed, will be rebuilt "in splendor." Sirach recounts the recent glories of the temple (Sir 49:11–13; 50:1–21). Baruch 1:10–14 is concerned with the reestablishment of worship in Jerusalem.

Defense of Hasmonean dynasty. 1 Maccabees probably affords the best examples (14:25–15:9; 16:1–3; 2 Macc 15:7–24; see also Sir 50:1–24 [praise of Simon]).

Messiah. The Messiah is kept by the Most High until the last days (2 Esdr 12:32; 13:26; 14:9). He will judge the wicked and rescue God's remnant (12:33–35). He is described in terms of Dan 7:13 (cf. Mark 14:62). The Messiah will set up a kingdom that will last 400 years (2 Esdr 7:26–30), after which time he and all people will die. After seven days of silence there will be a general resurrection and judgment (7:31–44). Elsewhere hope is expressed that a prophet will arise (1 Macc 4:46; 9:27; 14:41). This hope is probably based on Deut 18:15–18.

Resurrection. According to 2 Macc 7:9: "The King of the universe will raise us up to an everlasting renewal of life, because we have died for his laws" (see vv. 11, 14, 23, 29). Also, in 2 Macc 12:44 we read: ". . . those who had fallen would rise again. . . ." (see also 14:46). Also, in 2 Esdr 7:32: "And the earth shall give up those who are asleep in it, and the dust those who dwell silently in it; and the chambers shall give up the souls which have been committed to them." Wisdom 3:1–9 teaches immortality, if not resurrection (see also 6:17–20).

Eschatology. "Signs of the End" include terror, unrighteousness, the sun shining at night, the moon during the day, blood dripping from wood, talking stones, and falling stars (2 Esdr 5:1–13; see also 6:21–24; 15:12–27). The End will involve salvation for the righteous and judgment for the wicked (2 Esdr 5:56–6:6, 25–28; 7:26–44; 8:63–9:13).

Intercession of the Saints. According to 2 Macc 15:11–16, dead saints intercede for the living. (Onias the high priest and Jeremiah the prophet intercede for Judas.) Furthermore, according to 12:43–45, the living may pray and offer sacrifices for the dead (does this relate to 1 Cor 15:29?).

The Canon of Scripture. In Sir 39:1 the OT is referred to as "law" and "prophecies." In 2 Esdr 14:44 "ninety-four" books are mentioned. The reference is to the "twenty-four books" of the OT (v. 45) and, most likely, the seventy of the Apocrypha and Pseudepigrapha. Both the seventy and the twenty-four are restored miraculously by Ezra and five others (vv. 37–48), a legend that parallels the translation of the LXX (*Ep. Arist.* §307b). Whereas the twenty-four are to be read by all, the seventy are to be read only by the wise (2 Esdr 14:45–46). There are at least fifty-one apocryphal writings among the scrolls and fragments of Qumran (M. McNamara, *Palestinian Judaism and the New Testament* [GNS 4; Wilmington: Glazier, 1983] 121–24). More than sixty writings are found in J. H. Charlesworth, ed., *OTP.* The OT itself refers to books which are now lost: Book of the Wars of Yahweh (Num 21:14), Book of Jasher (Josh 10:13; 2 Sam 1:18), Book of the Acts of Solomon (1 Kgs 11:41), Book of the Annals of the Kings of Israel (1 Kgs 14:19; 2 Chr 33:18), Book of the Annals of the Kings of Judah (1 Kgs 14:29; 15:7), Annals of Samuel the Seer and Annals of Gad the Seer (1 Chr 29:29), Words of Nathan the Prophet (2 Chr 9:29), Prophecy of Ahijah the Shilonite (2 Chr 9:29), Annals of Shemaiah the Prophet and of Iddo the Seer (2 Chr 12:15),

Annals of Jehu son of Hanani (2 Chr 20:34), an untitled writing of Isaiah (2 Chr 26:22), Annals of Hozai (2 Chr 33:18), a lament for Josiah by Jeremiah (2 Chr 35:25). 1 Maccabees 16:24 refers to the Annals of John Hyrcanus. Various lost writings are mentioned in the Pseudepigrapha (*T. Job* 40:14 ["Omissions"]; 41:6 ["Omissions of Eliphas"]; 49:3 ["Hymns of Kasia"]; 50:3 ["The Prayers of Amaltheia's Horn"]). In *Eccl. Hist.* 6.13.6 Eusebius refers to several "disputed books" (*antilegomena*): Sirach and Wisdom of Solomon (of the OT Apocrypha), Hebrews and Jude (of the NT), and Barnabas and Clement (of the apostolic fathers).

GENERAL BIBLIOGRAPHY: *Text:* A. Rahlfs, *Septuaginta* (2 vols.; Stuttgart: Würt-tembergische Bibelanstalt, 1935); J. Ziegler et al., *Septuaginta: Vetus Testamentum Graecum* (16 vols.; Göttingen: Vandenhoeck & Ruprecht, 1939–86). *Translation:* B. M. Metzger, ed., *OAA. Introduction:* G. W. Anderson, "Canonical and Non-canonical," in P. R. Ackroyd and C. F. Evans, eds., *The Cambridge History of the Bible* (3 vols.; Cambridge: Cambridge University, 1963–70) 1.113–59; R. H. Charles, ed., *APOT*, vol. 1: *Apocrypha*; N. De Lange, *Apocrypha: Jewish Literature of the Hellenistic Age* (New York: Viking, 1978); B. M. Metzger, *IA*; G. W. E. Nickelsburg, *Faith and Piety in Early Judaism: Texts and Documents* (Philadelphia: Fortress, 1983); idem, *Jewish Literature between the Bible and the Mishnah* (Philadelphia: Fortress, 1981); W. O. E. Oesterley, *An Introduction to the Books of the Apocrypha* (New York: Macmillan, 1935); L. Rost, *Judaism Outside the Hebrew Canon: An Introduction to the Documents* (Nashville: Abingdon, 1976) 21–99; H. F. D. Sparks, *The Apocryphal Old Testament* (Oxford: Clarendon, 1984); M. E. Stone, ed., *JWSTP*, 33–184, 283–324, 412–14; D. W. Suter, "Old Testament Apocrypha," *HBD*, 36–38; C. C. Torrey, *The Apocryphal Literature: A Brief Introduction* (New Haven: Yale University Press, 1945); L. T. Whitelocke, ed., *An Analytical Concordance of the Books of the Apocrypha* (Washington: University Press of America, 1978).

CHAPTER TWO

THE OLD TESTAMENT PSEUDEPIGRAPHA

1 Enoch
2 Enoch
3 Enoch
Sibylline Oracles
Treatise of Shem
Apocryphon of Ezekiel
Apocalypse of Zephaniah
Fourth Book of Ezra (=2 Esdras
  3–14)
Greek Apocalypse of Ezra
Vision of Ezra
Questions of Ezra
Revelation of Ezra
Apocalypse of Sedrach
2 Baruch
3 Baruch
Apocalypse of Abraham
Apocalypse of Adam (see NHC)
Apocalypse of Elijah
Apocalypse of Daniel
Testaments of the Twelve
  Patriarchs
  Testament of Reuben
  Testament of Simeon
  Testament of Levi
  Testament of Judah
  Testament of Issachar
  Testament of Zebulon
  Testament of Dan
  Testament of Naphtali

Testament of Gad
Testament of Asher
Testament of Joseph
Testament of Benjamin
Testament of Job
Testaments of the Three Patriarchs
  Testament of Abraham
  Testament of Isaac
  Testament of Jacob
Testament (Assumption) of Moses
Testament of Solomon
Testament of Adam
Letter of Aristeas
Jubilees
Martyrdom and Ascension of
  Isaiah [3:13–4:22 = Testament of
  Hezekiah]
Joseph and Aseneth
Life of Adam and Eve
Pseudo-Philo, *Biblical Antiquities*
Lives of the Prophets
Ladder of Jacob
4 Baruch [= Omissions of
  Jeremiah]
Jannes and Jambres
History of the Rechabites
Eldad and Modad
History of Joseph
Ahiqar

(continued on next page)

Pseudo-Phocylides	Orphica
3 Maccabees	Ezekiel the Tragedian
4 Maccabees	Fragments of Pseudo-Greek Poets
The Sentences of the Syriac	Pseudo-Hesiod
Menander	Pseudo-Pythagoras
More Psalms of David	Pseudo-Aeschylus
Psalm 151 (see OT Apocrypha)	Pseudo-Sophocles
Psalm 152	Pseudo-Euripides
Psalm 153	Pseudo-Philemon
Psalm 154	Pseudo-Diphilus
Psalm 155	Pseudo-Menander
Prayer of Manasseh (see OT	Aristobulus
Apocrypha)	Demetrius the Chronographer
Psalms of Solomon	Aristeas the Exegete
Hellenistic Synagogal Prayers	Eupolemus
Prayer of Joseph	Pseudo-Eupolemus
Prayer of Jacob	Cleodemus Malchus
Odes of Solomon	Artapanus
Philo the Epic Poet	Pseudo-Hecataeus
Theodotus	5 Maccabees

The writings of the OT Pseudepigrapha are numerous and diverse. Several literary genres are represented in this amorphous collection. Their dates of composition also cover a broad period of time, with *Ahiqar* being the oldest at ca. seventh or sixth century B.C.E. and the Apocalypse of Daniel the youngest at ca. ninth century C.E. Many of these books were among those to which 4 Ezra refers: "Ninety-four books were written. And . . . the Most High spoke to me, saying, 'Make public the twenty-four books that you wrote first and let the worthy and unworthy read them; but keep the seventy that were written last, in order to give them to the wise among your people. For in them is the spring of understanding, the fountain of wisdom, and the river of knowledge' " (14:44–47). The "twenty-four" books are the books that make up the Jewish Bible or what Christians call the OT. The seventy books are the books of the Apocrypha (see chap. 1) and the books of the Pseudepigrapha. The author of 4 Ezra was probably very close to the truth. In addition to the sixty-six books treated in this chapter (many of which did not exist when 4 Ezra was written) some fifty more apocryphal and pseudepigraphal writings were found among the scrolls of Qumran (see chap. 3). Thus, in the time of the writing of 4 Ezra there were probably more than seventy books in this category of those "written last."

The word pseudepigrapha is a Greek word meaning "falsely super-scribed," or what we moderns might call writing under a pen name. The classification, "OT Pseudepigrapha," is a label that scholars have given to these writings. Although some of them have been grouped together or associated in one way or another, most never had any connection to one another. James Charlesworth and a team of scholars wrestled for a decade or longer with the definition of this category called "Pseudepig-rapha." They decided to retain the word because of its widespread and long-time usage, but they have carefully defined what the word means and what the criteria are for inclusion in this category. According to Charlesworth:

> The present description of the Pseudepigrapha is as follows: Those writings 1) that, with the exception of Ahiqar, are Jewish or Christian; 2) that are often attributed to ideal figures in Israel's past; 3) that customarily claim to contain God's word or message; 4) that frequently build upon ideas and narratives present in the OT; 5) and that almost always were composed either during the period 200 B.C. to A.D. 200 or, though late, apparently preserve, albeit in an edited form, Jewish traditions that date from that period. (J. H. Charlesworth, OTP, 1.xxv)

Charlesworth further notes that the following pseudepigraphal items were not included "because they were far removed from the Old Testament in date and character" (OTP, 1.xxvi):

Vision of Daniel
Death of Abraham
Hebrew Apocalypse of Elijah
Book of Jasher
Conflict of Adam and Eve with Satan
Cave of Treasures
Book of the Rolls
Sin of Solomon
Pirqe de Rabbi Eliezer (see chap. 8)
Syriac Apocalypse of Ezra
Book of the Bee
Questions Addressed by the Queen [of Sheba], and Answers Given by Solomon

The line that divides the OT Apocrypha from the OT Pseudepigrapha is not clearly drawn. Two writings found in the Apocrypha, the Prayer of Manasseh and 4 Ezra (contained within 2 Esdras), belong in the Pseudepigrapha. Three writings found in the Pseudepigrapha, 3 Maccabees, 4 Maccabees, and Psalm 151, appear in some canons of Scripture as part of the Apocrypha (see Appendix 1).

The OT Pseudepigrapha greatly enhance our study into the background of early Judaism and Christianity. These writings shed light on various doctrines, including how Scripture was interpreted.

SUMMARIES

To simplify reference to the following summaries the pseudepigraphal books have been subdivided according to the categories and order found in *OTP:* (1) Apocalyptic Literature, (2) Testaments, (3) Old Testament Expansions, (4) Wisdom and Philosophical Literature, (5) Prayers, Psalms, and Odes, and (6) Fragments, with an appendix.

Part One: Apocalyptic Literature

1 Enoch. *1 Enoch,* also known as the *Ethiopic Apocalypse of Enoch,* is the oldest of the three pseudepigraphal books attributed to Enoch, the man who apparently did not die, but was taken up to heaven (Gen 5:24). The book was originally written in either Hebrew or Aramaic, perhaps both, but it survives in complete form only in Ethiopic (*Geʻez*), and in fragmentary form in Aramaic, Greek (1:1–32:6; 6:1–10:14; 15:8–16:1; 89:42–49; 97:6–104), and Latin (106:1–18). As it now stands, *1 Enoch* appears to consist of the following five major divisions: (1) The Book of the Watchers (chaps. 1–36); (2) The Book of the Similitudes (chaps. 37–71); (3) The Book of Astronomical Writings (chaps. 72–82); (4) The Book of Dream Visions (chaps. 83–90); and (5) The Book of the Epistle of Enoch (chaps. 91–107). The materials in *1 Enoch* range in date from 200 B.C.E. to 50 C.E. *1 Enoch* contributes much to intertestamental views of angels, heaven, judgment, resurrection, and the Messiah. This book has left its stamp upon many of the NT writers, especially the author of Revelation. *1 Enoch's* "Son of Man" is important for Jesus research.

Bibliography: E. Isaac, "1 (Ethiopic Apocalypse of) Enoch," *OTP,* 1.5–89; M. A. Knibb, *The Ethiopic Book of Enoch* (Oxford: Clarendon, 1978); idem, "The Ethiopic Book of Enoch," *OOT,* 26–55; J. T. Milik, *BE;* C. D. Osburn, "The Christological Use of 1 Enoch I.9 in Jude 14, 15," *NTS* 23 (1977) 334–41; M. E. Stone, "Apocalyptic Literature," *JWSTP,* 395–406; idem, "The Bible Rewritten and Expanded," *JWSTP,* 90–97; D. W. Suter, "Weighed in the Balance: The Similitudes of Enoch in Recent Research," *RelSRev* 7 (1981) 217–21.

2 Enoch. *2 Enoch,* or the *Slavonic Apocalypse of Enoch,* was written late first century C.E. in Egypt by a Jew. It survives only in late Old Slavonic manuscripts. It may have been composed originally in Aramaic or Hebrew, later being translated into Greek, and later still being translated into Old Slavonic. It is an amplification of Gen 5:21–32 (from Enoch to the Flood). Major theological themes include: (1) God created the world "out of nothing" (24:2); (2) seven heavens (30:2–3) and angelic hosts; (3) God created the souls of men before the foundation of the earth (23:5); (4) abodes of heaven and hell are already prepared for righteous and sinners; and (5) ethical teachings, which at times parallel those of the NT and Proverbs.

Bibliography: F. I. Andersen, "2 (Slavonic Apocalypse of) Enoch," *OTP,* 1.91–221; M. E. Stone, "Apocalyptic Literature," *JWSTP,* 406–8; S. Pines, "Eschatology and the Concept of Time in the Slavonic Book of Enoch," in R. J. Z. Werblowsky and C. J. Bleeker, eds., *Types of Redemption* (Leiden: Brill, 1970) 72–87.

3 Enoch. 3 Enoch, or the *Hebrew Apocalypse of Enoch,* was supposedly written by Rabbi Ishmael the "high priest" after his visionary ascension into heaven (d. 132 C.E.). Although it contains a few Greek and Latin loan words, there is no reason to suspect that the original language of *3 Enoch* was anything other than Hebrew. Whereas some of the traditions of *3 Enoch* may be traced back to the time of Rabbi Ishmael, and even earlier, the date of composition is probably closer to the fifth or sixth centuries. It was probably written in or near Babylon. The book may be divided into the following four major parts: (1) The ascension of Ishmael (chaps. 1–2); (2) Ishmael meets the exalted Enoch (chaps. 3–16); (3) a description of the heavenly household (chaps. 17–40); and (4) the marvels of heaven (chaps. 41–48). *3 Enoch* sheds some light on Merkabah mysticism. In the book there appears to be present a tendency to minimize the powers of Metatron (= Enoch).

Bibliography: P. S. Alexander, "3 (Hebrew Apocalypse of) Enoch," *OTP,* 1.223–315; idem, "The Historical Setting of the Hebrew Book of Enoch," *JJS* 28 (1977) 156–80; H. Odeberg, *3 Enoch* (Cambridge: Cambridge University, 1928; repr. New York: Ktav, 1973).

Sibylline Oracles. Called the "Sibylline Oracles" because of an association with the legendary "Sibyls" of antiquity, who were aged women who uttered prophecies in poetic form. Scholars are unsure if there ever really was a "Sibyl" who inaugurated this tradition. Collections of "Sibylline" oracles appeared in a variety of centers in the ancient world. These collections enjoyed considerable prestige in the Roman Empire and allowed Jews and Christians to communicate their religious views. These oracles, consisting of fourteen books, range in date from the second century B.C.E. to the seventh century C.E. Both Jews and Christians contributed to the collection that now makes up part of the Pseudepigrapha. For NT study Oracles 3–5 are the most significant.

Bibliography: J. J. Collins, "Sibylline Oracles," *OTP,* 1.317–472; idem, *The Sibylline Oracles of Egyptian Judaism* (SBLDS 13; Missoula: Scholars, 1974) [studies Oracles 3–5].

Treatise of Shem. The *Treatise of Shem* was originally written in the first century B.C.E. in either Hebrew or Aramaic, but is now preserved in a fifteenth-century Syriac manuscript. It comprises twelve chapters that correspond to the twelve signs of the zodiac, with the last two, due to a scribal error, in reverse order. The interest in stars in this book may shed some light on Matt 2:1–12.

Bibliography: J. H. Charlesworth, "Rylands Syriac MS 44 and a New Addition to the Pseudepigrapha: The Treatise of Shem," *BJRL* 60 (1978) 376–403; idem, "Treatise of Shem," *OTP*, 1.473–86.

Apocryphon of Ezekiel. The *Apocryphon of Ezekiel* was probably written in either Hebrew or Greek between 50 B.C.E. and 50 C.E. The text survives in fragmentary form only (chiefly in the form of quotations) in Greek, Latin, and Aramaic (i.e., the Talmud). Although the original document was of Jewish origin, there is evidence of Christian redaction. Its main contribution concerns the doctrines of resurrection and final judgment.

Bibliography: K.-G. Eckart, "Das Apokryphon Ezechiel," *JSHRZ* 5.1 (1974) 45–54; J. R. Mueller, *The Five Fragments of the 'Apocryphon of Ezekiel': A Critical Study* (JSPSup 5; Sheffield: JSOT, forthcoming); idem and S. E. Robinson, "Apocryphon of Ezekiel," *OTP*, 1.487–95.

Apocalypse of Zephaniah. The *Apocalypse of Zephaniah*, originally composed in Greek sometime between 100 B.C.E. and 70 C.E., survives in a Greek quotation by Clement of Alexandria and in twenty pages of Coptic. One scholar conjectures that three-quarters of the original document are lost. This book is typical of the heavenly journey theme in which the seer witnesses the judgment and punishment of sinners and the vindication of the righteous.

Bibliography: O. S. Wintermute, "Apocalypse of Zephaniah," *OTP*, 1.497–515.

Fourth Book of Ezra. 4 Ezra comprises chaps. 3–14 of an expanded book that is part of the Apocrypha and is known as 2 Esdras. 4 Ezra, a late first-century Jewish writing, contains seven visions that God gave to Ezra the scribe/prophet. The Christian Greek additions (chaps. 1–2 and 15–16) were added in the second and third centuries. The purpose of 4 Ezra is to denounce the evil of Rome and to lament the misfortunes of Jerusalem. See 2 Esdras in chapter 1.

Bibliography: G. H. Box, *The Ezra-Apocalypse* (London: Pitman, 1912); M. A. Knibb, "Apocalyptic and Wisdom in 4 Ezra," *JSJ* 13 (1982) 56–74; B. M. Metzger, "The Fourth Book of Ezra," *OTP*, 1.516–79; T. W. Willett, *Eschatology in the Theodicies of 2 Baruch and 4 Ezra* (JSPSup 4; Sheffield: JSOT, 1989). See bibliography on 2 Esdras in chapter 1.

Greek Apocalypse of Ezra. The *Greek Apocalypse of Ezra* depicts a vision that Ezra received concerning sin and the punishment of the wicked. Ezra descends into hell where he sees Herod and other infamous characters tormented for their sin. The book was likely written in Greek by a Christian sometime between the second and ninth centuries.

Bibliography: M. E. Stone, "Greek Apocalypse of Ezra," *OTP*, 1.561–79; O. Wahl, *Apocalypsis Esdrae, Apocalypsis Sedrach, Visio Beati Esdrae* (PVTG 4; Leiden: Brill, 1977).

Vision of Ezra. The *Vision of Ezra* is an account of Ezra's journey into the regions of hell to witness the punishment of the wicked. Whereas the righteous are able to pass by the gates of hell untouched, the wicked are ripped apart by dogs (or lions) and are burned. After descending into the deeper regions of hell, Ezra witnesses the torture of various types of sinners (e.g., "the angels of hell were pricking their eyes with thorns" [40]). The book was originally written in Greek by a Christian between the fourth and seventh centuries, but survives only in Latin.

Bibliography: J. R. Mueller and G. A. Robbins, "Vision of Ezra," *OTP,* 1.581–90; O. Wahl, *Apocalypsis Esdrae, Apocalypsis Sedrach, Visio Beati Esdrae* (PVTG 4; Leiden: Brill, 1977).

Questions of Ezra. The *Questions of Ezra* is extant in Armenian, but scholars are uncertain if it originated in that language. Beyond the fact that the book is Christian and is modeled on Jewish apocalyptic, nothing can be said with certainty about its date or place of writing. Like the Ezra writings above, the *Questions of Ezra* is concerned with the fate of the righteous and the wicked.

Bibliography: M. E. Stone, "The Apocryphal Literature in the Armenian Tradition," *PIASH* 4 (1971) 59–77, 371–72; idem, "Questions of Ezra," *OTP,* 1.591–99.

Revelation of Ezra. The *Revelation of Ezra* was probably originally written in Latin by a Christian sometime before the ninth century (though how much earlier is unknown). This pseudepigraphon comprises only seven verses. "The author believed that the nature of the year was predetermined by the day of the week on which it began" (Fiensy, *OTP,* 1.603).

Bibliography: D. A. Fiensy, "Revelation of Ezra," *OTP,* 1.601–4.

Apocalypse of Sedrach. The *Apocalypse of Sedrach,* a Christian writing, is an account of one Sedrach, who, after the delivery of a sermon, is taken up into heaven where he questions the Lord concerning the fate of sinners. He begs the Lord to be more lenient with the wicked. When finally satisfied, he allows the Lord to take his soul to Paradise. The text was originally written in Greek sometime between the second and fifth centuries and now survives in a fifteenth-century manuscript.

Bibliography: S. Agourides, "Apocalypse of Sedrach," *OTP,* 1.605–13; O. Wahl, *Apocalypsis Esdrae, Apocalypsis Sedrach, Visio Beati Esdrae* (PVTG 4; Leiden: Brill, 1977).

2 Baruch (Syriac Apocalypse). *2 Baruch,* or the *Syriac Apocalypse of Baruch,* was composed early in the second century C.E. by a Jew who wished to encourage fellow Jews in the Dispersion. Originally written in Hebrew, the document was later translated into Greek and still later into

Syriac. Only a fragment of the Greek survives. The theme of the book revolves around the end of the age and the appearance of the Messiah. Although the book ostensibly is concerned with the first destruction of Jerusalem, its real concern is with Jerusalem's second destruction in 70 C.E.

Bibliography: R. H. Charles, *The Apocalypse of Baruch Translated from the Syriac* (London: Adam and Charles Black, 1896); S. Dedering, *Apocalypse of Baruch* (Leiden: Brill, 1973); A. F. J. Klijn, "2 (Syriac Apocalypse of) Baruch," *OTP,* 1.615–52; idem, "The Syriac Apocalypse of Baruch," *OOT,* 193–212; M. E. Stone, "Apocalyptic Literature," *JWSTP,* 408–10; T. W. Willett, *Eschatology in the Theodicies of 2 Baruch and 4 Ezra* (JSPSup 4; Sheffield: JSOT, 1989).

3 Baruch (Greek Apocalypse). 3 Baruch, or the *Greek Apocalypse of Baruch,* was composed sometime between the first and third centuries in Greek and today survives in Greek and Slavonic. The book may originally have been a Jewish writing that has undergone Christian redaction, or it may have been a Christian writing that relied heavily upon Jewish traditions. The account tells of a weeping Baruch, secretary of the prophet Jeremiah, who is told by an angel of the Lord the "mysteries" of what has happened and what will happen.

Bibliography: H. E. Gaylord, "3 (Greek Apocalypse of) Baruch," *OTP,* 1.653–79; J.-C. Picard, *Apocalypsis Baruchi Graeca* (PVTG 2; Leiden: Brill, 1967); M. E. Stone, "Apocalyptic Literature," *JWSTP,* 410–12.

Apocalypse of Abraham. The *Apocalypse of Abraham* was composed by a Jew sometime in the first or second centuries C.E. possibly in Hebrew, but it now survives only in Old Slavonic. If originally Hebrew, then in all probability the *Apocalypse* was composed in Palestine. Although a Jewish work, there are some Christian and gnostic interpolations. The book tells of Abraham's rejection of idolatry, of his request to know the true, living God (chaps. 1–8), and of Abraham's journey to heaven, where heaven and the future of the world are revealed to him (chaps. 9–32).

Bibliography: G. H. Box and J. I. Landsman, *The Apocalypse of Abraham* (London: Macmillan, 1918); R. Rubinkiewicz, "Apocalypse of Abraham," *OTP,* 1.681–705; M. E. Stone, "Apocalyptic Literature," *JWSTP,* 415–18.

Apocalypse of Adam. The *Apocalypse of Adam* is a gnostic revelation that dates from sometime between the first and fourth centuries. It is preserved in Sahidic Coptic as tractate five in Codex V (64.1–85.32) of the Nag Hammadi library (see chap. 10 below). It is likely that the original document was Greek. Although clearly dependent upon Genesis, the *Apocalypse* never quotes this biblical book in its retelling of the creation story.

Bibliography: C. W. Hedrick, *The Apocalypse of Adam* (SBLDS 46; Chico: Scholars, 1980); G. MacRae, "Apocalypse of Adam," *OTP,* 1.707–19; idem, "The Apocalypse of Adam," in D. M. Parrott, ed., *Nag Hammadi Codices V, 2–5 and VI with Papyrus Berolinensis 8502, 1 and 4* (NHS 11; Leiden: Brill, 1979) 151–95; B. A. Pearson, "Jewish Sources in Gnostic Literature," *JWSTP*, 470–74.

Apocalypse of Elijah. The *Apocalypse of Elijah*, a Christian writing from sometime between the first and fourth centuries, is an eschatological work that describes the coming of the Antichrist, martyrdom of the righteous, and the coming of Christ and the establishment of the millennial kingdom. The *Apocalypse* survives in Coptic (Akhmimic and Sahidic) and in a Greek fragment. In all likelihood the original language was Greek.

Bibliography: A. Pietersma, S. T. Comstock, and H. W. Attridge, *The Apocalypse of Elijah: Based on Pap. Chester Beatty 2018* (SBLTT 19; Pseudepigrapha Series 9; Chico: Scholars, 1981); O. S. Wintermute, "Apocalypse of Elijah," *OTP*, 1.721–53.

Apocalypse of Daniel. The *Apocalypse of Daniel* is a ninth-century Christian apocalypse in which Daniel is purported to have predicted the Byzantine-Arab wars of the eighth century (chaps. 1–7). In the second half of the *Apocalypse* (chaps. 8–14) Daniel describes the end of the age, the Antichrist, the day of judgment, and the appearance of Christ. The book survives in Greek, the language in which it was originally written.

Bibliography: G. T. Zervos, "Apocalypse of Daniel," *OTP*, 1.755–70.

Part Two: Testaments

Testaments of the Twelve Patriarchs. The *Testaments of the Twelve Patriarchs* were written between 109 and 106 B.C.E. by a Pharisee who greatly admired John Hyrcanus at the zenith of the Maccabean (or Hasmonean) dynasty. The conviction was that Hyrcanus and his Levite family constituted the messianic line. Later revisions condemn the apostate Hasmonean line and expect Messiah to come from the tribe of Judah. The *Testaments* are inspired by Jacob's testament in Genesis 49 and typically follow this form: (1) Introduction in which scene is set; (2) narrative from patriarch's life; (3) ethical exhortation; (4) prediction of future; (5) second exhortation; and (6) patriarch's burial. Major theological themes would include: (1) forgiveness and grace, freely given to those of contrite spirit; (2) exhortation to love God and neighbor (*T. Dan* 5:3; Mark 12:30–31); (3) ethical teachings that frequently parallel the NT; (4) universalism, even Gentiles can be saved through Israel (*T. Levi* 14:4; *T. Benj.* 9:2); (5) Messiah (alternating between Levi and Judah) is free from sin; he is righteous, establishes new priesthood, mediator for Gentiles; (6) resurrection; and (7) demonology and doctrines about Antichrist. Although some scholars have argued for Aramaic (cf. CTLevi ar; 1QTLevi ar; 4QTJos ar; 4QTJud ar; 4QTLevi ar[a,b,c]) or Hebrew (3QTJud?; 4QTJud?; 4QTNaph) as the original language of the *Testaments*, it is more likely that Greek, one of the languages in which the *Testaments* have survived, was the original. The *Testaments* are very important for NT studies.

Bibliography: R. H. Charles, *The Greek Versions of the Testaments of the Twelve Patriarchs* (London: Oxford University, 1908; repr. Hildesheim: Olms, 1960); J. J. Collins, "Testaments," *JWSTP,* 331–44; idem, "The Testamentary Literature in Recent Scholarship," *EJMI,* 268–76; M. de Jong, ed., *Studies on the Testaments of the Twelve Patriarchs* (Leiden: Brill, 1975); idem, "The Testaments of the Twelve Patriarchs and the NT," *SE* 1 (1957) 546–56; H. W. Hollander, "The Testaments of the Twelve Patriarchs," *OOT,* 71–91; H. C. Kee, "Testaments of the Twelve Patriarchs," *OTP,* 1.775–828; G. W. E. Nickelsburg, ed., *Studies on the Testament of Joseph* (SCS 5; Missoula: Scholars, 1975).

Testament of Job. The *Testament of Job* is an embellishment of the biblical book of Job, originally written in Greek, perhaps as early as the first century B.C.E., but no later than the first century C.E. The book contributes much to our knowledge of early Jewish and Christian beliefs about Satan. The book emphasizes Job's piety (seen especially in his rejection of idolatry) and patient endurance.

Bibliography: S. P. Brock, *Testamentum Iobi* (PVTG 2; Leiden: Brill, 1967); J. J. Collins, "Testaments," *JWSTP,* 349–54; idem, "The Testamentary Literature in Recent Scholarship," *EJMI,* 276–77; R. A. Kraft, *The Testament of Job* (SBLTT 5; Pseudepigrapha Series 4; Missoula: Scholars, 1974); R. P. Spittler, "Testament of Job," *OTP,* 1.829–68; idem, "The Testament of Job," *OOT,* 231–47.

Testaments of the Three Patriarchs. The *Testaments of the Three Patriarchs* (Abraham, Isaac, and Jacob) probably derive from an original first-century Greek Testament of Abraham which later was expanded (second to third century) to include Testaments of Isaac and Jacob. The expanded version was eventually adopted by the church and was read with great interest. Christian interpolations occur chiefly in the Testaments of Isaac and Jacob. The *Testaments* greatly embellish details in the lives of the patriarchs and describe the judgment of humanity.

Bibliography: G. H. Box, *The Testament of Abraham* (London: Macmillan, 1927); J. J. Collins, "The Testamentary Literature in Recent Scholarship," *EJMI,* 277–78; R. Doran, "Narrative Literature," *EJMI,* 287–89; G. W. E. Nickelsburg, ed., *Studies on the Testament of Abraham* (rev. ed. SCS 6; Missoula: Scholars, 1976); idem, "Stories of Biblical and Early Post-Biblical Times," *JWSTP,* 60–64; E. P. Sanders, "Testament of Abraham," *OTP,* 1.871–902; idem, "The Testament of Abraham," *OOT,* 56–70; W. F. Stinespring, "Testament of Isaac," *OTP,* 1.903–11; idem, "Testament of Jacob," *OTP,* 1.913–18; M. E. Stone, "Apocalyptic Literature," *JWSTP,* 420–21; idem, *Testament of Abraham* (SBLTT 2; Pseudepigrapha Series 2; Missoula: Scholars, 1972).

Testament (Assumption) of Moses. The *Testament* (or *Assumption*) *of Moses* was composed by a Jew in the first century C.E. in either Aramaic or Hebrew. The original author may have been a Pharisee or an Essene. The only extant manuscript is in Latin and apparently is a translation of a Greek version. At least one-third of the original work is lost. Some scholars assume that part of the lost portion is the so-called *Assumption of Moses* to which Jude 9 apparently refers. R. H. Charles thought that originally there were two books, a Testament and an Assumption, that were later combined (*APOT*, 2.208). The book tells of the prophecy that Moses gave to Joshua before the former died. This is a highly useful writing for NT studies.

Bibliography: R. H. Charles, *The Assumption of Moses* (London: Adam and Charles Black, 1897) [Latin text]; J. J. Collins, "The Testament (Assumption) of Moses," *OOT*, 145–58; idem, "The Testamentary Literature in Recent Scholarship," *EJMI*, 277; idem, "Testaments," *JWSTP*, 344–49; A.-M. Denis, *Fragmenta pseude-pigraphorum quae supersunt graeca* (PVTG 3; Leiden: Brill, 1970) 63–67 [Greek fragments]; G. W. E. Nickelsburg, ed., *Studies on the Testament of Moses* (SCS 4; Cambridge: SBL, 1973); J. Priest, "Testament of Moses," *OTP*, 1.919–34; idem, "Some Reflections on the Assumption of Moses," *PRS* 4 (1977) 92–111.

Testament of Solomon. The *Testament of Solomon* was composed in Greek sometime between the first and third centuries by a Christian. The book "is a haggadic-type folktale about Solomon's building the temple of Jerusalem combined with ancient lore about magic, astrology, angelology, demonology, and primitive medicine" (Duling, *OTP*, 1.935). The book stresses God's power over the demons, by whom humankind is often oppressed, links demonology with astrology (i.e., demons reside in the stars), and is keenly interested in medicine. See the discussion concerning Eleazar the exorcist in Appendix 5.

Bibliography: D. C. Duling, "Solomon, Exorcism, and the Son of David," *HTR* 68 (1975) 235–52; idem, "Testament of Solomon," *OTP*, 1.935–87; C. C. McCown, *The Testament of Solomon* (Leipzig: J. C. Hinrichs, 1922).

Testament of Adam. The *Testament of Adam* was composed sometime between the second and fifth centuries by a Jew, although it now contains several Christian additions. It exists in several languages, and Hebrew, Greek, and Syriac have all been proposed as the original. It seems likely, however, that since virtually no evidence exists for a Hebrew original, and since the Greek appears to be dependent on the Syriac, the book was originally written in Syriac. The book teaches that God originally intended Adam to evolve into a god (3:2, 4), but because of the Fall this did not take place. The book is also greatly interested in angelology.

Bibliography: S. E. Robinson, "Testament of Adam," *OTP*, 1.990–95; idem, *The Testament of Adam: An Examination of the Syriac and Greek Traditions* (SBLDS 52; Chico: Scholars, 1982).

Part Three: Old Testament Expansions

Letter of Aristeas. The *Letter* (or *Epistle*) *of Aristeas* claims to be an eyewitness account of Aristeas, an officer of the court of Ptolemy

Philadelphus (285–247 B.C.E.), written to brother Philocrates. It purports to explain the translation of the LXX (see §§10–11), and to defend Alexandrian Judaism (Jewish wisdom, moral insight, value of Torah, political rights). Several historical blunders suggest that it is pseudonymous. Written in Greek, probably between 130 and 70 B.C.E., with additions as late as first century C.E., *Aristeas* was used by Josephus (*Ant.* 12.2.1 §11–12.2.15 §118).

Bibliography: M. Hadas, *Aristeas to Philocrates* (JAL; New York: Harper, 1951); S. Jellicoe, "The Occasion and Purpose of the Letter of Aristeas: a Re-examination," *NTS* 12 (1964) 144–50; B. L. Mack, "Wisdom Literature," *EJMI*, 378–79; G. W. E. Nickelsburg, "Stories of Biblical and Early Post-Biblical Times," *JWSTP*, 75–80; R. J. H. Shutt, "Letter of Aristeas," *OTP*, 2.7–34; idem, "Notes on the Letter of Aristeas," *BIOSCS* 10 (1977) 22–30.

Jubilees. Written in Hebrew by a Pharisee between 135 and 105 B.C.E., *Jubilees* is a midrashic rewriting of Genesis-Exodus, from creation to the giving of the law on Sinai, given to Moses while on the Mount (Exod 24:12).

The author has freely condensed (e.g. the story of plagues on Pharaoh, Ex 7–10 = Jub 48:4–11), omitted (e.g. the blessing of Ephraim and Manasseh, Gen 48:1–20), expurgated (e.g. the notice of Abraham's presenting his wife to foreign rulers as his sister, Gen 12:10–20; 20:2–7), explained (e.g. Reuben's apparent incest, Gen 35:22 = Jub 33:2–20), supplemented (e.g. tales of Abraham's youth, Jub 12:1–9, 12f., 16–21, 25–27), and sometimes radically recast the biblical episodes (e.g. Isaac's covenant with Abimelech, Gen 26:23–33 = Jub 24:21–33) (Wintermute, *OTP*, 2.35).

Jubilees may be outlined: (1) Introduction (chap. 1); (2) Creation and Adam stories (chaps. 2–4); (3) Noah stories (chaps. 5–10); (4) Abraham stories (chaps. 11–23); (5) Jacob and his family (chaps. 24–45); and (5) Moses stories (chaps. 46–50). The purpose of *Jubilees* is to call the Jewish reader to a more faithful obedience to the law. The author is interested in the question of evil. He believes that evil derives from the demonic world and that Adam is not to be blamed for its continuing effects. Whereas the author believes that God will be gracious and forgiving toward Israel, he entertains no hope for Gentiles. Only the Ethiopic version is complete (or nearly so), with a few Greek, Latin, Syriac, and Hebrew (cf. Qumran, caves 1, 2, 3, 4, and 11) fragments extant. Because of the latter, it is believed that *Jubilees* was originally written in Hebrew. Studying the method in which *Jubilees* retells biblical narratives, coloring respective episodes with otherwise unrelated biblical texts, is very helpful for understanding early biblical interpretation.

Bibliography: R. H. Charles, *The Ethiopic Version of the Hebrew Book of Jubilees* (Oxford: Clarendon, 1895); A.-M. Denis, *Fragmenta pseudepigraphorum quae supersunt graeca* (PVTG 3; Leiden: Brill, 1970) 70–102; J. C. Endres, *Biblical Interpretation in the Book of Jubilees* (CBQMS 18; Washington: Catholic Biblical Association, 1987); G. W. E. Nickelsburg, "The Bible Rewritten and Expanded," *JWSTP*, 97–104; J. C. VanderKam, "The Book of Jubilees," *OOT*, 111–44; idem, *Textual and Historical Studies in the Book of Jubilees* (HSM 14; Missoula: Scholars, 1977) [Hebrew fragments]; O. S. Wintermute, "Jubilees," *OTP*, 2.35–142.

Martyrdom and Ascension of Isaiah. The *Martyrdom and Ascension of Isaiah* is made up of two documents: (1) the Martyrdom (chaps. 1–5) and (2) the Ascension (chaps. 6–11). The first part (esp. 1:1–3:12; 5:1–16) is a Jewish work that tells of the prophet's martyrdom by order of Manasseh and is probably to be dated to the second century B.C.E. It was probably written in Hebrew. In 5:12–14 we are told that Isaiah was sawed in two. The Babylonian Talmud (*Yebam.* 49b) tells of Isaiah being swallowed up by a cedar, which Manasseh ordered cut in two. According to the Palestinian Talmud (*Sanh.* 10.2), Isaiah attempted to flee from Manasseh by hiding in a cedar. Unfortunately the hem of his garment betrayed the prophet's hiding place, so Manasseh ordered the tree cut down. This tradition is probably echoed in Heb 11:37, where the author tells us that the righteous have been stoned and "sawed in two." *Martyrdom and Ascension of Isaiah* 3:13–4:22 is a later Christian addition, sometimes called the Testament of Hezekiah; it describes Isaiah's vision. The second half of the book (chaps. 6–11) is also a Christian addition describing Isaiah's visionary ascension into heaven. The Christian additions were originally composed in Greek and may date as late as the fourth century.

Bibliography: R. H. Charles, *The Ascension of Isaiah* (London: Adam and Charles Black, 1900); R. Doran, "Narrative Literature," *EJMI*, 293–94; A. K. Helmbold, "Gnostic Elements in the 'Ascension of Isaiah,' " *NTS* 18 (1972) 222–27; M. A. Knibb, "Martyrdom and Ascension of Isaiah," *OTP*, 2.143–76; idem, "The Martyrdom of Isaiah," *OOT*, 178–92; G. W. E. Nickelsburg, "Stories of Biblical and Early Post-Biblical Times," *JWSTP*, 52–56.

Joseph and Aseneth. *Joseph and Aseneth* was composed in Greek (though one scholar has suggested Hebrew), probably in Egypt sometime between the first century B.C.E. and early second century C.E. Although Jewish in origin, the book contains a few Christian interpolations. The book attempts to explain how it was that Joseph, the most righteous of all of the sons of Jacob, married Aseneth, the daughter of a heathen priest (cf. Gen 41:45). The reason that this book gives is that Aseneth rejected the idolatry of her father and people and came to place her faith in the God of the Hebrews. The book narrates an exciting story of intrigue and adventure. After Pharaoh's son dies in an unsuccessful coup attempt (in which he had solicited the support of Dan and Gad), from which Pharaoh himself dies out of grief, Joseph becomes the ruler of Egypt and reigns 48 years.

Bibliography: C. Burchard, "The Importance of Joseph and Aseneth for the Study of the NT," *NTS* 32 (1986) 102–34; idem, "Joseph and Aseneth," *OTP*, 2.177–247; idem, "Joseph and Aseneth," *OOT*, 92–110; R. Doran, "Narrative

Literature," *EJMI*, 290–93; G. W. E. Nickelsburg, "Stories of Biblical and Early Post-Biblical Times," *JWSTP*, 65–71; M. Philonenko, *Joseph et Asénath* (SPB 13; Leiden: Brill, 1968).

Life of Adam and Eve. The *Life of Adam and Eve* was composed in all probability in Hebrew, from which a Greek "Apocalypse of Moses" and a Latin "Life" were translated. These two versions contain differing materials and so probably should be understood as products of independent development. Since the so-called *Apocalypse of Moses* is really an account of the life of Adam and Eve, it is printed along with the Latin "Life" in *OTP.* The original Hebrew probably dates from first century B.C.E. or C.E., while the Greek and Latin versions derive from sometime between the second and fourth centuries.

Bibliography: M. D. Johnson, "Life of Adam and Eve," *OTP,* 2.249–95; G. W. E. Nickelsburg, "The Bible Rewritten and Expanded," *JWSTP,* 107–18; J. L. Sharp, "The Second Adam in the Apocalypse of Moses," *CBQ* 35 (1973) 35–46 [draws comparisons between Paul and *Apocalypse of Moses*].

Pseudo-Philo. Pseudo-Philo's *Biblical Antiquities* (or *Liber Antiquitatum Biblicarum*) is a midrashic retelling of biblical history from Adam to David. Probably originally composed in Hebrew and later translated into Greek, the text survives in several Latin manuscripts. Pseudo-Philo may have been written as early as the first or even second century B.C.E., but most scholars favor a date toward the end of the first century C.E. Somewhere along the line this book came to be assigned to Philo Judaeus of Alexandria (see chap. 5), but there is little chance that he was its author; hence the title, "Pseudo-Philo." As with most haggadic midrash, Pseudo-Philo wishes to answer questions raised in the biblical narratives and to take the opportunities to put the various doctrines of early Judaism into the mouths of ancient biblical worthies. Comparing the author's method in retelling the biblical narratives is important for NT studies, particularly in Gospel studies.

Bibliography: D. J. Harrington, *The Hebrew Fragments of Pseudo-Philo's* Liber Antiquitatum Biblicarum *Preserved in the Chronicles of Jerahmeel* (SBLTT 3; Pseudepigrapha Series 3; Missoula and Cambridge: SBL, 1974); idem, "Pseudo-Philo," *OTP,* 2.297–377; idem, "Pseudo-Philo, *Liber Antiquitatum Biblicarum*," *OOT,* 6–25; G. W. E. Nickelsburg, "The Bible Rewritten and Expanded," *JWSTP,* 107–10.

Lives of the Prophets. The *Lives of the Prophets* is a first-century C.E. document that summarizes the key teachings and events in the lives of most of Israel's prophets: Isaiah, Jeremiah, Ezekiel, Daniel, Hosea, Micah, Amos, Joel, Obadiah, Jonah, Nahum, Habakkuk, Zephaniah, Haggai, Zechariah, Malachi, Nathan (2 Sam 7, 11), Ahijah (1 Kgs 11–12), Joad (1 Kgs 13), Azariah (2 Chr 15), Elijah (1 Kgs 17; 2 Kgs 1–2), Elisha (1 Kgs 19; 2 Kgs 2, 4–6, 13), Zechariah (2 Chr 24). The four "major prophets" receive the greatest attention, while Jonah (who is the youth saved by

Elijah!), Habakkuk (cf. Bel 33–39), Elijah, and Elisha also figure promi-
nently. Much of the material is legendary and midrashic in nature.
Although many once believed that *Lives* was originally composed in
Hebrew, the evidence now seems to point to Greek. The designation of
Moses as "God's chosen one" (2:14) could be significant, for that is a
messianic designation in Luke (23:35) as well.

Bibliography: D. R. A. Hare, "The Lives of the Prophets," *OTP*, 2.379–99; D.
Satran, "Lives of the Prophets," *JWSTP*, 56–60; C. C. Torrey, *The Lives of the
Prophets: Greek Text and Translation* (Philadelphia: SBL, 1946).

Ladder of Jacob. The *Ladder of Jacob* was composed by a Jew in the first
century C.E., but now survives only in Slavonic. It is possible that it was
originally Hebrew, but it is more likely that it was written in Greek by a
Jew who also knew Hebrew and assumed that readers would also know
Hebrew. The purpose of the book is to emphasize the sovereignty of God.
The story has been inspired by Gen 28:12–14, esp. v. 13.

Bibliography: H. G. Lunt, "Ladder of Jacob," *OTP*, 2.401–11.

4 Baruch. 4 Baruch, or *Omissions* [or *Paraleipomena*] *of Jeremiah*, was
composed in either the first or second century C.E. Extant in several
versions, *4 Baruch* probably was originally composed in Hebrew. The
original author was Jewish, but the text contains at least one lengthy
Christian interpolation (8:12–9:32). Other interpolations probably include
6:7, 13, 25. In the story the righteous Abimelech falls asleep after
gathering figs. Upon waking (a feature that the author interprets as
evidence for the resurrection) he discovers that 66 years have elapsed.
Babylon has destroyed Jerusalem and has carried off its inhabitants into
captivity. He learns, however, that soon God's people will be able to
return. *4 Baruch* teaches that the holy vessels from the temple survived
the temple's destruction and that someday they will be used again when
the temple is restored.

Bibliography: R. Doran, "Narrative Literature," *EJMI*, 294–96; R. A. Kraft and
A.-E. Purintun, *Paraleipomena Jeremiou* (SBLTT 1; Pseudepigrapha Series 1; Mis-
soula: SBL, 1972); G. W. E. Nickelsburg, "Stories of Biblical and Early Post-Biblical
Times," *JWSTP*, 72–75; J. Riaud, *"Paraleipomena Jeremiou," OOT*, 213–30; S. E.
Robinson, "4 Baruch," *OTP*, 2.413–25.

Jannes and Jambres. Jannes and Jambres was composed in Greek by a
Jew sometime in the first or second century. The legendary figures Jannes
and Jambres were thought to have been two of Pharaoh's magicians who
opposed Moses. This tradition is alluded to in 2 Tim 3:8–9. In *Targum
Pseudo-Jonathan* they interpret a dream of Pharaoh in which Moses' birth
is predicted (*Tg. Ps.-J.* Exod 1:15), and they later reappear as Balaam's
helpers (*Tg. Ps.-J.* Num 22:22). In his commentary on Matthew (on 27:9)

Origen (third century) refers to an apocryphal book entitled the Book of Jannes and Jambres. Other ancient authors knew of these magicians. It seems clear that there was such a book in late antiquity, but only Greek and Latin fragments of it have survived. Of interest is Jannes' return from the dead through necromancy to warn his brother Jambres of the consequences of evil.

Bibliography: A.-M. Denis, *Fragmenta Pseudepigraphorum quae supersunt graeca* (PVTG 3; Leiden: Brill, 1970) 69; M. McNamara, *The New Testament and the Palestinian Targum to the Pentateuch* (AnBib 27A; Rome: Pontifical Biblical Institute, 1978) 82–96; A. Pietersma and R. T. Lutz, "Jannes and Jambres," *OTP*, 2.427–36.

History of the Rechabites. The *History of the Rechabites* was probably composed in Hebrew or Aramaic, with Greek being the oldest translation. The original author was probably Jewish, writing (chaps. 3–15) sometime in the first or second centuries, while later Christians added to it (chaps. 1–2, 16, 19–23) in the third and fourth (and possibly later) centuries. The book is a story of a righteous man named Zosimus whose request to visit the abode of the "Blessed Ones" is finally granted. He is transported over the ocean to an island that resembles Paradise where the Blessed Ones live. They identify themselves as the Rechabites who had left Jerusalem in the time of Jeremiah (Jer 35) and describe to the visitor the secrets of death and soul ascent.

Bibliography: J. H. Charlesworth, *The History of the Rechabites: Volume I: The Greek Recension* (SBLTT 17; Pseudepigrapha Series 10; Chico: Scholars, 1982); idem, "History of the Rechabites," *OTP*, 2.443–61; B. McNeil, "The Narrative of Zosimus," *JSJ* 9 (1978) 68–82.

Eldad and Modad. *Eldad and Modad* (or Medad) was probably composed in either Hebrew or Greek before the writing of the *Shepherd of Hermas* (second century). Whether it is Jewish or Christian is impossible to determine. All that survives is one sentence, quoted in Hermas (*Herm. Vis.* 2.3.4): " 'The Lord is near to those who turn [to him],' as it is written in the [book of] Eldad and Modad, who prophesied in the desert to the people." The book apparently was based on Num 11:26–29 which tells of two prophets, Eldad and Medad. "According to rabbinic sources, the contents of the Book of Eldad and Modad apparently contained references to Gog and Magog, the end of time, and the coming of a royal Messiah" (Martin, *OTP*, 2.463). This is certainly the case in the *Fragment Targum* to Num 11:26, in which the prophecy of Eldad and Modad is recast as an apocalypse predicting Messiah's victory at the end of time: "At the end of days Gog and Magog will ascend against Jerusalem and by the hands of Messiah they will fall."

Bibliography: A.-M. Denis, *Fragmenta pseudepigraphorum quae supersunt graeca* (PVTG 3; Leiden: Brill, 1970) 68; E. G. Martin, "Eldad and Modad," *OTP*, 2.463–65;

M. McNamara, *The New Testament and the Palestinian Targum to the Pentateuch* (AnBib 27A; Rome: Pontifical Biblical Institute, 1978) 235–37.

History of Joseph. The *History of Joseph* was composed originally in Greek, probably before 400 C.E., and seems to be a midrashic expansion of Gen 41:39–42:36. The text is preserved only in fragments. As in *Joseph and Aseneth* (29:9), Joseph is referred to as "king" of Egypt.

Bibliography: A.-M. Denis, *Fragmenta pseudepigraphorum quae supersunt graeca* (PVTG 3; Leiden: Brill, 1970) 235–36; G. T. Zervos, "History of Joseph," *OTP,* 2.467–75.

Part Four: Wisdom and Philosophical Literature

Ahiqar. The story (or "Words") of *Ahiqar* was composed originally in Aramaic sometime in the seventh or sixth century B.C.E. Thus it is by far the oldest item in the Pseudepigrapha. It is an instance of the wisdom genre and teaches that the guilty will be found out and the righteous will be vindicated. The story tells of Ahiqar the sage who adopts his nephew Nadin and raises him as his own son. When Nadin succeeds his adopted father as counselor to King Esarhaddon, the young man falsely accuses the aged sage of a plot to overthrow the king. Nadin's scheme, however, is foiled, Ahiqar is reconciled to the king, and Nadin is put in irons and sternly lectured, after which he swells up and bursts.

Bibliography: J. M. Lindenberger, "Ahiqar," *OTP,* 2.479–507; idem, *The Aramaic Proverbs of Ahiqar* (Baltimore and London: Johns Hopkins University, 1983).

3 Maccabees. 3 Maccabees was written originally in Greek in the first century C.E. It is a Jewish composition that tells of Ptolemy IV Philopator's (221–204 B.C.E.) persecution of the Jews in Alexandria (out of anger of his being refused entry into the Holy Place of the temple of Jerusalem), a persecution that is thwarted by divine intervention. The prayers of the devout Eleazar finally bring about a change in the king, who now orders an end to the persecutions and a seven-day feast of celebration at his expense. Since the book has nothing to do with the Maccabean period, its title is really a misnomer. The purpose of the writing is probably to encourage Jews to remain faithful to their religious customs.

Bibliography: H. Anderson, "3 Maccabees," *OTP,* 2.509–29; M. Hadas, *The Third and Fourth Books of Maccabees* (JAL; New York: Harper, 1953); R. Hanhart, *Maccabaeorum liber II* (Septuaginta 9/3; Göttingen: Vandenhoeck & Ruprecht, 1960); B. M. Metzger, "The Third Book of the Maccabees," *OAA,* 294–308; G. W. E. Nickelsburg, "Stories of Biblical and Early Post-Biblical Times," *JWSTP,* 80–84.

4 Maccabees. 4 Maccabees was composed originally in Greek in the first century C.E. Like 3 Maccabees, its name is a misnomer, for it has nothing to do with the Maccabean period (though reference to the martyrdoms of Eleazar and the seven sons and their mother [2 Macc

6:18–7:42] is no doubt what gave the book its title). Instead, it is a philosophical treatise that attempts to show in terms of Greek philosophy that the Jewish faith is the true religion. The book teaches that martyrdom is a substitutionary atonement that expiates the sins of the nation (1:11; 6:27–29 ["Make my blood their purification, and take my life in exchange for theirs"]; 17:21; 18:14).

Bibliography: H. Anderson, "4 Maccabees," *OTP*, 2.531–64; M. Gilbert, "Wisdom Literature," *JWSTP*, 316–19; M. Hadas, *The Third and Fourth Books of Maccabees* (New York: Harper, 1953); B. L. Mack, "Wisdom Literature," *EJMI*, 396–98; B. M. Metzger, "The Fourth Book of the Maccabees," *OAA*, 309–29.

Pseudo-Phocylides. Pseudo-Phocylides was originally composed in Greek sometime in either the first century B.C.E. or C.E. The author of this poem claims to be Phocylides, an Ionic poet who lived in Miletus in the sixth century B.C.E. The real author was likely a Jew who wished to show that Jewish ethics had been taught long ago by a respected gentile ethicist.

Bibliography: M. Gilbert, "Wisdom Literature," *JWSTP*, 313–16; B. L. Mack, "Wisdom Literature," *EJMI*, 395–96; P. W. van der Horst, "Pseudo-Phocylides," *OTP*, 2.565–82; idem, "Pseudo-Phocylides and the New Testament," *ZNW* 69 (1978) 187–202; idem, *The Sentences of Pseudo-Phocylides: Introduction, Translation and Commentary* (SVTP 4; Leiden: Brill, 1978).

The Sentences of the Syriac Menander. The *Sentences of the Syriac Menander* was originally composed in Syriac in the third century C.E. However, it is quite likely that the author availed himself of a Greek anthology of sayings. It is a wisdom work that seeks to give people practical guidance for living. The author holds to a high view of God and is thus a monotheist, possibly a Jew.

Bibliography: T. Baarda, "The Sentences of the Syriac Menander," *OTP*, 2.583–606.

Part Five: Prayers, Psalms, and Odes

More Psalms of David. There are extant five whole Psalms and a fragment of a sixth beyond the canonical 150. Since they are of separate origin, they should be treated separately. Psalm 151 was originally written in Hebrew, possibly at Qumran (=11QPs^a). There are two versions of this Psalm (151A and 151B, of which most of the second is lost). It tells of David's defeat of Goliath. Psalm 152 is extant only in Syriac, but may have been composed originally in Hebrew by a Palestinian Jew sometime in the first two or three centuries B.C.E. It describes David's cry for help in fighting the lion and wolf. Psalm 153 is also extant only in Syriac, but probably was originally composed in Hebrew by a Palestinian Jew sometime in the last two or three centuries B.C.E. It describes David's thanks for being delivered from the lion and wolf. Psalm 154 was written originally in Hebrew, a version of which is preserved at Qumran (11QPs[a]). It is also extant in Syriac. It is probably second century B.C.E. It is a call to praise God. Psalm 155 was composed in Hebrew and is also extant in 11QPs[a] and in Syriac. It purports to be Hezekiah's cry for help when the Assyrians had surrounded Jerusalem.

Bibliography: J. H. Charlesworth and J. A. Sanders, "More Psalms of David," OTP, 2.609–24; B. M. Metzger, "Psalm 151," OAA, 330–31; J. A. Sanders, The Dead Sea Psalms Scroll (Ithaca: Cornell University, 1967); idem, The Psalms Scroll of Qumran Cave 11 (11QPs[a]) (DJD 4; Oxford: Clarendon, 1965); idem, "Two Non-Canonical Psalms in 11QPs[a]," ZAW 76 (1964) 57–75.

Prayer of Manasseh. Although part of the Apocrypha—that part that did not gain entry into the Catholic Bible at Trent in 1546—OTP places the Prayer of Manasseh in the Pseudepigrapha because of its pseudonymity. Inspired by 2 Chr 33:11–13, this document purports to be the prayer of repentance uttered by King Manasseh after his exile. It was probably composed originally in Greek (though several scholars are convinced that the original was Semitic) sometime in the first or second century B.C.E. See comments and bibliography in chapter 1.

Psalms of Solomon. The Psalms of Solomon is a collection of eighteen Hebrew psalms written around 50 B.C.E., probably in response to the Roman takeover a few years earlier. They are now extant in several Greek and Syriac manuscripts. The Psalms have had little influence on the NT. Major themes would include: (1) anticipation of fulfillment of promises (12:7), the coming of Messiah/King (17:21–18:9), who would rule by the power of God (17:37); (2) the "Conqueror" who is probably Pompey (63 B.C.E.; 17:14; 8:18–21); (3) sexual sin, which is viewed as particularly offensive; and (4) the "righteous" who are the Pharisees, while the "sinners" are the Sadducees. Traditionally it has been believed that the Psalms were composed by a Pharisee or Pharisaic group. Wright ("Psalms," 1972), however, has called this conclusion into question.

Bibliography: J. H. Charlesworth, "Jewish Hymns, Odes, and Prayers," EJMI, 415–16; M. de Jonge, "The Psalms of Solomon," OOT, 159–77; D. Flusser, "Psalms, Hymns and Prayers," JWSTP, 573–74; J. L. Trafton, The Syriac Version of the Psalms of Solomon: A Critical Evaluation (SCS 11; Atlanta: Scholars, 1985); R. B. Wright, "Psalms of Solomon," OTP, 2.639–70; idem, "The Psalms of Solomon, the Pharisees, and the Essenes," in R. A. Kraft, ed., 1972 Proceedings: International Organization for Septuagint and Cognate Studies and the Society of Biblical Literature Pseudepigrapha Seminar (SCS 2; Missoula: SBL, 1972) 136–47.

Hellenistic Synagogal Prayers. Sixteen Hellenistic Synagogal Prayers are found "scattered among the Christian liturgy Books Seven and Eight of the Apostolic Constitutions" (Fiensy, OTP, 2.671). There is no evidence that would suggest that these prayers were written in any language other than Greek, the language of the Constitutions. Because many of these prayers contain nothing distinctively Christian, or when they do, it usually has the appearance of an interpolation, it seems likely that these prayers are indeed Jewish and were composed sometime in the second or third century C.E. The prayers reflect the "orthodoxy" of emerging Judaism. The Christian interpolations are christological (e.g., Christ born of virgin, of line of David [6:2]; the divine Word [1:8; 5:20]; mediator [4:22; 6:13]).

Bibliography: J. H. Charlesworth, "Jewish Hymns, Odes, and Prayers," *EJMI*, 416–17 [for a convenient list of ancient prayers see p. 424]; D. A. Fiensy and D. R. Darnell, "Hellenistic Synagogal Prayers," *OTP*, 2.671–97.

Prayer of Joseph. The *Prayer of Joseph* was composed either in Aramaic (if Jewish) or in Greek (if Christian) in the first century C.E. The book teaches that Jacob was the incarnation of the angel "Israel" who competed with the angel Uriel over their respective rank in heaven. Jonathan Smith (*OTP*, 2.699) believes that "the text was most likely an extended testament developed out of Jacob's blessing of Joseph's sons in Genesis 48." "Israel" is understood to mean "one who sees God" (v. 3), rather than "prince of God." Only fragments are extant, amounting to no more than nine verses.

Bibliography: A.-M. Denis, *Fragmenta pseudepigraphorum quae supersunt graeca* (PVTG 3; Leiden: Brill, 1970) 61–63; J. Z. Smith, "Prayer of Joseph," *OTP*, 2.699–714; idem, "The Prayer of Joseph," in J. Neusner, ed., *Religions in Antiquity: Essays in Memory of Erwin Ramsdell Goodenough* (Supplements to Numen 14; Leiden: Brill, 1968) 253–94.

Prayer of Jacob. The *Prayer of Jacob* was probably originally composed in Greek sometime between the first and fourth centuries C.E. by a Jew apparently interested in magic. The author requests wisdom from God, perhaps even immortality.

Bibliography: J. H. Charlesworth, "Prayer of Jacob," *OTP*, 2.715–23.

Odes of Solomon. The *Odes of Solomon* were originally written in either Syriac or Aramaic in the late first or early second century C.E. Contrary to older opinion the *Odes* are no longer viewed as gnostic or as Jewish, but as early Christian. It is therefore highly unlikely that the *Odes* themselves or the traditions they presuppose were drawn upon by the Fourth Evangelist. The theme of the *Odes* is one of thanksgiving for the advent of the promised Messiah. Dualism, the hypostatic and mediatorial role of the Word, and the concept of salvation are similar to the ideas in the Fourth Gospel. James Brownson has recently argued that the *Odes* may very well have been composed by a community that broke from the Johannine community. For evidence of this he cites several parallels between *Odes* and the Johannine Epistles.

Bibliography: J. Brownson, "The Odes of Solomon and the Gospel of John," *JSP* 2 (1988) 46–69; J. H. Charlesworth, "Odes of Solomon," *OTP*, 2.725–71; idem,

The Odes of Solomon: The Syriac Texts (SBLTT 13; Pseudepigrapha Series 7; Missoula: Scholars, 1978); idem, "The Odes of Solomon—Not Gnostic," *CBQ* 31 (1969) 357–69; idem, "Qumran, John and the Odes of Solomon," in Charlesworth, ed., *John and Qumran* (London: Geoffrey Chapman, 1972; repr. as *John and the Dead Sea Scrolls* [New York: Crossroad, 1990]) 107–36; idem and R. A. Culpepper, "The Odes of Solomon and the Gospel of John," *CBQ* 35 (1973) 298–322; J. T. Sanders, "Nag Hammadi, Odes of Solomon, and NT Christological Hymns," in J. E. Goehring et al., eds., *Gnosticism & the Early Christian World* (J. M. Robinson Festschrift; Sonoma: Polebridge, 1990) 51–66.

Part Six: Fragments

Philo the Epic Poet. Philo the Epic Poet was a Jew who may have lived in Alexandria and who composed in Greek in the third or second century B.C.E. All that has survived are fragments of his *On Jerusalem* quoted in Eusebius, *Praeparatio Evangelica* 9.20.1; 9.24.1; and 9.37.1–3. Imitating the classic style of Greek poets, the author lauds the patriarchs and the city of Jerusalem.

Bibliography: H. W. Attridge, "Philo the Epic Poet," *OTP*, 2.781–84.

Theodotus. Theodotus, who was either Jewish or Samaritan, composed a piece of epic poetry probably entitled *On the Jews* in either the first or second century B.C.E. Written in Greek, it tells of the rape of Jacob's daughter Dinah (Gen 34) and the slaughter of the men of Shechem.

Bibliography: F. Fallon, "Theodotus," *OTP*, 2.785–89.

Orphica. Orphica purports to be an oracle by one Orphaeus to his son and pupil Musaeus. Written by a Jew in archaizing Greek, probably in the first century B.C.E. or C.E., it describes the attributes of God.

Bibliography: M. LaFargue, "Orphica," *OTP*, 2.795–801.

Ezekiel the Tragedian. Ezekiel the Tragedian (as he is called by Eusebius in *Praeparatio Evangelica* 9.28.1) composed a drama in Greek entitled the *Exagoge* ("Leading Out") in the second century B.C.E. Centering around the character of Moses, the drama is based on Exodus 1–15.

Bibliography: R. G. Robertson, "Ezekiel the Tragedian," *OTP*, 2.803–19.

Fragments of Pseudo-Greek Poets. The *Fragments of Pseudo-Greek Poets* is a collection of poetic compositions by Jews in deliberate imitation of classical Greek poetry. These imitations were often combined with authentic materials. The purpose of these poems was to support Jewish thought by showing that it was paralleled by the best in the Greek tradition. Hesiod, Pythagoras, Aeschylus, Sophocles, Euripides, Philemon, Diphilus, and Menander are imitated. God, judgment, and the folly of the Greek myths are the main items of interest. Most of these second-

or third-century B.C.E. fragments are preserved by Clement of Alexandria, a second-century Greek church father.

Bibliography: H. W. Attridge, "Fragments of Pseudo-Greek Poets," *OTP*, 2.821–30.

Aristobulus. Aristobulus was originally composed in Greek, probably some time in the second century B.C.E., perhaps during the reign of Ptolemy VI Philometor (155–145 B.C.E.). Five fragments have survived: (1) Frg. 1 is concerned with the astronomical features of the Passover. (2) Frg. 2 is concerned with the nature of God, in which Aristobulus attempts to explain OT anthropomorphisms. (3) Frg. 3 claims that Plato and Pythagoras had borrowed from Jewish law in articulating their ethical theories. (4) Frg. 4, like Frg. 2, discusses God's nature and, like Frg. 3, suggests that various Greek poets had ideas similar to those of Moses. (5) Frg. 5 argues cosmologically for the holiness of the sabbath and cites Homer, Hesiod, and (the mythical) Linus for evidence that even the Greeks regarded the sabbath as holy.

Bibliography: A. Yarbro Collins, "Aristobulus," *OTP*, 2.831–42; B. L. Mack, "Wisdom Literature," *EJMI*, 379–80.

Demetrius the Chronographer. Six fragments from *Demetrius the Chronographer* are all that survive this third-century B.C.E. work. The fragments deal with various periods in Israel's history. (1) Frg. 1 retells the story of the sacrifice of Isaac (Gen 22). (2) Frg. 2 retells the story of Jacob, his sons, and Joseph. It also provides part of Moses' genealogy. (3) Frg. 3 supplies the genealogies of Moses and his wife Zipporah. (4) Frag, 4 retells the story of making the bitter waters sweet (Exod 15:22–27). (5) Frg. 5 tells how the wandering Israelites obtained their weapons (from the drowned Egyptians). (6) Frg. 6 is supposedly from a work entitled *On the Kings in Judaea* in which a chronology from the deportations of Israel and Judah to the time of Demetrius is given.

Bibliography: H. W. Attridge, "Historiography," *JWSTP*, 161–62; J. Hanson, "Demetrius the Chronographer," *OTP*, 2.843–54.

Aristeas the Exegete. Aristeas the Exegete is a late second- or early first-century B.C.E. retelling of the book of Job. Since the account depends upon the LXX throughout, it is likely that Greek was the language of its original composition. In this account Job is a descendant of Esau. Because of a reference in the *Letter of Aristeas* (§6) to a previous work concerning the Jews, it has been suggested that both works bearing the name Aristeas were authored by the same person. However, the scholarly consensus now is that the works derive from two persons. All that survives of the text are four verses quoted in Eusebius, *Praeparatio Evangelica* 9.25.1–4.

Bibliography: R. Doran, "Aristeas the Exegete," *OTP*, 2.855–59.

Eupolemus. Eupolemus is a late second- or early first-century B.C.E. Jewish author whose work, perhaps originally entitled *On the Kings of Judea,* survives as only five fragments. The first four fragments are preserved in Eusebius, *Praeparatio Evangelica* 9.26.1; 9.30.1–34.18; 9.34.20; and 9.39.2–5. The fifth fragment is preserved in Clement of Alexandria, *Stromateis* 1.141.4. The fragments deal with various persons and events in Israel's history. (1) Frg. 1 identifies Moses as the world's first sage, who invented the alphabet and wrote laws. (2) Frg. 2, the longest of all, traces the history of Israel from Moses to Solomon and the building of the temple. (3) Frg. 4 concerns King Jonachim (by which is probably meant King Joachim [=Jehoiakim]) and the destruction by Nebuchadnezzar.

Bibliography: H. W. Attridge, "Historiography," *JWSTP,* 162–65; idem, "Jewish Historiography," *EJMI,* 313–15; A.-M. Denis, *Fragmenta pseudepigraphorum quae supersunt graeca* (PVTG 3; Leiden: Brill, 1970) 179–86; F. Fallon, "Eupolemus," *OTP,* 2.861–72; Ben Zion Wacholder, *Eupolemus: A Study of Judaeo-Greek Literature* (MHUC 3; Cincinnati: HUC, 1974).

Pseudo-Eupolemus. In Eusebius' *Preparatio Evangelica* there are two quotations, one supposedly from Eupolemus and another given as anonymous. Scholars assign both quotations to first-century B.C.E. *Pseudo-Eupolemus.* The first fragment (9.17.2–9) describes Abraham as a master astrologer. The second fragment (9.18.2) traces Abraham's ancestry to the giants and claims that the patriarch taught astrology to the Phoenicians and later to the Egyptians. The language of the original fragments was very likely Greek.

Bibliography: H. W. Attridge, "Historiography," *JWSTP,* 165–66; A.-M. Denis, *Fragmenta pseudepigraphorum quae supersunt graeca* (PVTG 3; Leiden: Brill, 1970) 179–86; R. Doran, "Pseudo-Eupolemus," *OTP,* 2.873–82.

Cleodemus Malchus. Cleodemus Malchus' work survives only as a single Greek fragment quoted by Josephus (*Ant.* 1.15.1 §§239–241) and then later by Eusebius (*Praeparatio Evangelica* 9.20.2–4). In all likelihood the original text was Greek. In the fragment we are told that one "Keturah bore Abraham mighty sons" (*Ant.* 1.15.1 §240) named Surim, after whom Assyria was named, and Afera and Iafra, after whom Africa was named.

Bibliography: R. Doran, "Cleodemus Malchus," *OTP,* 2.883–86.

Artapanus. Only three fragments of the second- or third-century B.C.E. work of *Artapanus* survive. These fragments tell of the cultural contributions of Abraham, Joseph, and Moses while they were in Egypt. Abraham taught astrology (frg. 1: Eusebius, *Praeparatio Evangelica* 9.18.1). Joseph excelled as manager and surveyor (frg. 2: *Praep. Ev.* 9.23.1–4). Moses was mighty in magic and military strategy (frg. 3: *Praep. Ev.* 9.27.1–37). An interesting feature in the story about Moses is that Chenephres, one of the several "kings" over Egypt, out of envy sought to do away with Moses by sending him out on a very dangerous military campaign. Much to everyone's surprise, Moses is victorious. When he returns to Egypt he demands the release of the Hebrews.

Bibliography: H. W. Attridge, "Historiography," *JWSTP,* 166–68; J. J. Collins, "Artapanus," *OTP,* 2.889–903.

Pseudo-Hecataeus. There are four fragments attributed to Hecataeus of Abdera, a historian who wrote ca. 300 B.C.E. Of these only one is likely the work of Pseudo-Hecataeus (according to R. Doran, *OTP* 2.905–16). (1) Frg. 1, probably authentic, refers to Hecataeus' description of the Jewish Scriptures as "holy and reverent" (*Ep. Arist.* §31). (2) Frg. 2 claims that Hecataeus quoted Sophocles in his book, *On Abraham and the Egyptians* (Clement of Alexandria, *Stromateis* 5.113). This fragment probably derives from Pseudo-Hecataeus (second century B.C.E.). (3) Frg. 3 reports Alexander the Great's tribute-free gift of Samaria to the Jews. Since the reference may very well be to the Samaritan revolt in 331 B.C.E., Doran judges this fragment to be genuine. (4) Frg. 4, by far the longest, reports some of the events in the years following the death of Alexander the Great, especially those concerning the Jews (Josephus, *Ag. Ap.* 1.22 §§183–205).

Bibliography: H. W. Attridge, "Historiography," *JWSTP,* 169–71; R. Doran, "Pseudo-Hecataeus," *OTP,* 2.905–19.

Appendix (not treated in *OTP*)

5 Maccabees. 5 Maccabees is extant in Arabic, though it is thought that it may have been written originally in Hebrew. (It is not to be confused with the "5 Maccabees" of the Syriac Codex Ambrosianus, which is no more than an excerpt from Josephus, *J.W.* 6.) It covers the period 184–6 B.C.E. (from the attempt on the treasury by Heliodorus to Herod's final brutal murders), and it is the longest of the books of Maccabees (59 chapters). It was written after 70 C.E., for there are allusions to a "third captivity" (9:5) and to the "destruction of the second house" (21:30). Because the writing does not appear in earlier collections of Scripture (such as the major codices of the LXX), scholars have assumed that 5 Maccabees is nothing more than a late (possibly medieval) conflation of parts of the other books of Maccabees, Josephus' *Antiquities,* and the Hebrew chronicle of Jewish history called Yosippon. Some scholars have in fact suggested that 5 Maccabees is an epitome of Yosippon. J. H. Charlesworth, however, does not think so. He believes that the book, utilizing some sources common to the books of Maccabees and Yosippon, may actually derive from the late first century. On Yosippon see chap. 5.

Bibliography: W. Grudem, "Alphabetical List for Old Testament Apocrypha and Pseudepigrapha," *JETS* 19 (1976) 297–313, esp. 308; J. H. Charlesworth, *The Pseudepigrapha and Modern Research, With a Supplement* (2d ed.; SCS 7; Chico: Scholars, 1981) 153–56. For Arabic text see B. Walton, ed., *Biblia Sacra Polyglotta* (London: Roycroft, 1657) 4.112–59 (where it is called "Arabic 2 Maccabees"). Text was taken from Paris Polyglot of 1645. A Latin translation is provided by Gabriel Sionita. The Latin has been translated into English by Henry Cotton, *The Five Books of Maccabees* (Oxford: Oxford University, 1832) 278–446. Cotton (p. xxx) believes that 5 *Maccabees* had been written in Hebrew and translated into Greek, of which nothing now survives.

THEMES

Because of the quantity and diversity of the materials that make up the OT Pseudepigrapha, it is difficult to speak of themes that are common to very many of them. For a convenient survey see Charlesworth, *OTP,* 1.xxi–xxxiv. There are four aspects of the Pseudepigrapha that have relevance for NT study.

1. *Pseudepigraphy.* Considering the literary convention of pseudepigraphy in the case of so many of the writings that make up the OT Pseudepigrapha might help us understand the presence and meaning of pseudonymity in the NT itself. For years scholars have suspected that the Pastorals, James, the Petrines, Jude, and sometimes other books are pseudepigraphal. How do the alleged pseudepigrapha of the NT compare to the numerous pseudepigraphal writings of the period? What were the purposes of pseudepigraphy? Was the early church aware of pseudepigraphy and, if so, what was its attitude toward it? The church of the second and third centuries certainly was aware of pseudepigraphy and apparently took a dim view of it. According to the *Apostolic Constitutions:* "Among the ancients also some have written apocryphal books of Moses, and Enoch, and Adam, and Isaiah, and David, and Elijah, and of the three patriarchs, pernicious and repugnant to the truth" (6:16). Tertullian (*On Baptism* 17) defrocked an elder for authoring the Acts of Paul (see chap. 7). But does this mean that the early church believed that pseudepigraphy was in itself wrong? Recently David Meade has concluded that the early church condemned pseudepigraphy when it was used to promote heretical ideas. He notes, for example, that initially no one objected to the use of the Gospel of Peter, until it was discovered to contained heresy (Eusebius, *Eccl. Hist.* 6.12.15). Even the Muratorian Canon's rejection of forged Pauline epistles to the Laodiceans and to the Alexandrians seems motivated by concerns over Marcionite heresy (cf. Meade, 203–7).

Some scholars think that pseudepigraphy was motivated by the search for authority (cf. Collins). Others suspect that it had something to do with the effort to establish claims over against rivals (cf. Beckwith). I think that both views are correct and that in many cases they complement one another. Just as the demise of the spirit of prophecy occasioned intertestamental pseudepigraphy, so the passing of the apostolic age occasioned the emergence of Christian pseudepigraphy (see chap. 8). The gnostic codices of Nag Hammadi also illustrate this phenomenon (see chap. 10). Writing in the names of various apostolic figures, diverse gnostic sects vie with one another for doctrinal legitimacy. In any case, understanding pseudepigraphy should significantly be aided by study of the OT Pseudepigrapha.

Bibliography: R. Beckwith, "The Earliest Enoch Literature and its Calendar: Marks of their Origin, Date and Motivation," *RevQ* 10 (1981) 365–403; J. H. Charlesworth, "Pseudepigraphy," in E. Ferguson, ed., *Encyclopedia of Early Christianity* (New York: Garland, 1990) 775–78; J. J. Collins, "Pseudonymity, Historical Reviews and the Genre of the Revelation of John," *CBQ* 39 (1977) 329–43, esp. 331–32; A. B. Kolenkow, "The Literary Genre 'Testament,' " *EJMI*, 264–66; D. G. Meade, *Pseudonymity and Canon: An Investigation into the Relationship of Authorship and Authority in Jewish and Earliest Christian Tradition* (Grand Rapids: Eerdmans, 1987); B. M. Metzger, "Literary Forgeries and Canonical Pseudepigrapha," *JBL* 91 (1972) 3–24; D. S. Russell, *The Method and Message of Jewish Apocalyptic* (London: SCM; Philadelphia: Westminster, 1964) 127–39 for summary of approaches; M. E. Stone, "Apocalyptic Literature," *JWSTP*, 427–33.

2. *Idealization of the Past.* Related to the first point, there is a tendency in the Pseudepigrapha to glorify the biblical characters of long ago. Biblical heroes of the past become models of piety and faithfulness for later generations. Past events too are special, for future events will parallel them. Lying behind this concern is typological thinking where it is assumed that what has taken place in the past foreshadows what is happening in the present or what will happen in the future. For example, several writings allegedly speak of the first destruction of Jerusalem and the temple, while in reality they are speaking of the second destruction in 70 C.E. It is assumed that the horrible events of 70 are explained by the sad events of 586 B.C.E.

Bibliography: G. W. E. Nickelsburg, *Faith and Piety in Early Judaism: Texts and Documents* (Philadelphia: Fortress, 1983); D. Patte, *Early Jewish Hermeneutic in Palestine* (SBLDS 22; Missoula: Scholars, 1975) 159–67.

3. *Apocalyptic.* The Apocalypses and the Testaments chiefly contain apocalyptic material. Even in the writings placed in "OT expansions," such as *Jubilees* or *Biblical Antiquities*, apocalyptic material is present. These writings describe visions of the future (most of which is biblical history usually presented in symbolic language). There is great interest in eschatology, that is, the events that culminate in the end of human history and of earth as we know it. There is great interest in resurrection, judgment, hell, and paradise. Messianic interest in those writings that are clearly Jewish (as opposed to Christian) is limited to five pseudepig-

rapha (*Psalms of Solomon, 2 Baruch, 4* Ezra [=2 Esdras 3–14], *1 Enoch* 37–71, *3 Enoch*).

Bibliography: J. J. Collins, "Apocalyptic Literature," *EJMI*, 345–70; D. S. Russell, *The Method and Message of Jewish Apocalyptic* (London: SCM; Philadelphia: Westminster, 1964); M. E. Stone, "Apocalyptic Literature," *JWSTP*, 383–427, 433–41.

4. *Rewritten Bible.* A phenomenon that is common in the OT Pseudepigrapha, but one that is not limited to it, is something that scholars call "rewritten Bible." Rewritten Bible refers to the retelling, usually with omissions, supplements, and loose paraphrases, of biblical narratives. What is left unclear, or unsaid, in the biblical narratives is explained either in narrative form, or with the insertion of a speech, prophecy, or hymn. Rewritten Bible is found in the Targums (see chap. 6), in some of the writings of Qumran (see chap. 3), and even in the NT itself (as seen in the relationship of Matthew and Luke to Mark). There are two principal features involved. First, there is the question of what relationship the rewritten narratives have to the biblical writings. J. H. Charlesworth has addressed this question. He rightly claims that most of the OT Pseudepigrapha, even those writings which are not obvious examples of rewritten Bible, have drawn upon and interpreted the OT in important ways. He finds four categories: (1) *inspiration,* where the OT inspires in the pseudepigraphal writer a given theme or style (e.g., *Prayer of Manasseh* and Pss 151–155); (2) *framework,* where the OT provides the basis, or framework, for a new story (e.g., *4 Ezra, 2 Baruch, Testaments of the Twelve Patriarchs, Testament of Job*); (3) *launching,* where the OT narrative provides the point of departure for a continuation of the story (e.g., *1 Enoch,* which is in part launched by Gen 5:23–24); and (4) *inconsequential,* where pseudepigraphal writings are influenced by the OT in only the slightest way, often doing nothing more than borrowing the name and reputation of an ancient worthy (e.g., *Apocalypse of Adam* and *Treatise of Shem*). Other writings are obvious examples of rewritten Bible (e.g., *Jubilees* and *Pseudo-Philo* [within the Pseudepigrapha], Josephus' *Jewish Antiquities* and 1QapGenesis [outside the Pseudepigrapha]). Charlesworth believes that ultimately the motivation behind the Pseudepigrapha, especially those that can be classified as instances of rewritten Bible, is to interpret Scripture.

This leads to the second question: What methods do these writings employ in their attempts to interpret Scripture? Reviewing *Jubilees* and *Pseudo-Philo* we find condensation, omission, supplementation, and reshaping. Names and genealogies are added, problems are explained, discrepancies are resolved, new connections or associations are offered, speeches and prayers are rewritten, speeches, prayers, and hymns are added, biblical language is modernized, and biblical narratives are often enriched with details from similar biblical accounts. This last feature is one of the most striking aspects of the rewritten Bible: the tendency to utilize Scripture from elsewhere in the Bible to elaborate on the biblical story at hand. Not only is this genre valuable as a source of exegetical tradition for comparative purposes, but it sheds valuable light on the editorial techniques of the hagiographers (i.e., the authors of "sacred writings") of the intertestamental and NT periods. These editorial techniques could, for example, teach us much about the evangelists' use of their sources (cf. Bauckham and Evans).

Bibliography: P. S. Alexander, "Retelling the Old Testament," in D. A. Carson and H. G. M. Williamson, eds., *It is Written: Scripture Citing Scripture* (B. Lindars Festschrift; Cambridge and New York: Cambridge University, 1988) 99–121; R. Bauckham, "The Liber Antiquitatum Biblicarum of Pseudo-Philo and the Gospels as 'Midrash,'" in R. T. France and D. Wenham, eds., *Studies in Midrash and Historiography* (Gospel Perspectives 3; Sheffield: JSOT, 1983) 33–76; J. H. Charlesworth, "The Pseudepigrapha as Biblical Exegesis," in C. A. Evans and W. F. Stinespring, eds., *Early Jewish and Christian Exegesis* (W. H. Brownlee Festschrift; Homage 10; Atlanta: Scholars, 1987) 139–52; D. Dimant, "Use and Interpretation of Mikra in the Apocrypha and Pseudepigrapha," *Mikra*, 379–419; C. A. Evans, "The Genesis Apocryphon and the Rewritten Bible," *RevQ* 13 (1988) 153–65; idem, "Luke and the Rewritten Bible: Aspects of Lucan Hagiography," in J. H. Charlesworth and C. A. Evans, eds., *The Pseudepigrapha and Biblical Interpretation* (JSPSup; Sheffield: JSOT) forthcoming; G. W. E. Nickelsburg, "The Bible Rewritten and Expanded," *JWSTP,* 89–156.

GENERAL BIBLIOGRAPHY: *Principal Studies:* R. H. Charles, ed., *APOT* (2 vols.); J. H. Charlesworth, "The Concept of the Messiah in the Pseudepigrapha," *ANRW* 2.19.1 (1979) 188–218; idem, ed., *OTP* (2 vols.); idem, *The Pseudepigrapha and Modern Research, with a Supplement* (2d ed.; SCS 7; Chico: Scholars, 1981); A.-M. Denis, *Concordance grecque des pseudépigraphes d'Ancien Testament* (Louvain-la-Neuve: Université Catholique de Louvain, 1987); idem, *Introduction aux pseudépigraphes grecs d'Ancien Testament* (SVTP; Leiden: Brill, 1970); M. de Jonge, ed., *OOT;* R. A. Kraft and G. W. E. Nickelsburg, eds., *EJMI;* M. E. Stone, ed., *JWSTP. Related Studies:* J. H. Charlesworth, *The Old Testament Pseudepigrapha and the New Testament* (SNTSMS 54; Cambridge: Cambridge University, 1985); idem, "Pseudepigrapha," *HBD,* 836–40; idem and C. A. Evans, *The Pseudepigrapha and Biblical Interpretation* (JSPSup; Sheffield: JSOT, forthcoming); G. E. Ladd, "Pseudepigrapha," *ISBE* 4.1040–43; G. W. E. Nickelsburg, *Faith and Piety in Early Judaism: Texts and Documents* (Philadelphia: Fortress, 1983); idem, *Jewish Literature between the Bible and the Mishnah* (Philadelphia: Fortress, 1981); L. Rost, *Judaism Outside the Hebrew Canon: An Introduction to the Documents* (Nashville: Abingdon, 1976) 100–154, 191–97.

CHAPTER THREE

THE DEAD SEA SCROLLS

1QapGen (*Genesis Apocryphon*)
1QDM (*Sayings of Moses*)
1QH (*Thanksgiving Hymns*)
1QIsa^{a,b} (Isaiah, copies a and b)
1QJN (*New Jerusalem*)
1QJub^{a,b} (*Jubilees*, copies a and b)
1QLitPr^{a,b} (*Liturgical Prayers*, a and b)
1QM (*War Scroll*)
1QMyst (*Book of Mysteries*)
1QNoah (*Book of Noah*)
1QpHab (*Commentary on Habakkuk*)
1QS (*Manual of Discipline*)
1QTLevi ar (Aramaic *Testament of Levi*)
2QapDavid (*Apocryphon of David*)
2QEnGiants (*Enoch's Book of Giants*)
2QapMoses (*Apocryphon of Moses*)
2QapProph (apocryphal prophetic text)
3QHym (*Hymn of Praise*)
3QTreasure (*Copper Scroll*)
4QAgesCreat (*Ages of Creation*)
4QAmram^{b-e} (*Testament of Amram*)
4QapLam (apocryphal *Lamentations*)
4QapPs (apocryphal Psalms)
4QCatena^{a,b}
4QD^{b,e} (*Melchizedek and Melkiresha*)
4QDibHam^{a,b} (*Words of the Luminaries*)

4QFlor (*Florilegium*) or 4QEschMidr (*Eschatological Midrashim*)
4QMess ar (Aramaic messianic text)
4QMMT (*Miqsat Ma'aseh Torah*)
4QOrd^{a,b,c} (*Ordinances*)
4QPBless (*Patriarchal Blessings*)
4QPrNab (*Prayer of Nabonidus*)
4QPsAp^{a-c} (apocryphal Psalms)
4QpsDan ar^{a,b,c} (pseudo-Daniel)
4QPsJosh (*Psalms of Joshua*)
pap4QRitMar (*Ritual of Marriage Papyrus*)
4QSam^a (Samuel)
4QShirShabb (*Song of the Sabbath*)
4QTanh (*Tanhumim*)
4QTestim (*Testimonia*)
4QtgLev (*Targum of Leviticus*)
4QtgJob (*Targum of Job*)
4QTJos ar (Aramaic *Testament of Joseph*)
4QTQahat (*Testament of Qahat*)
4QVisSam (*Vision of Samuel*)
4QWiles (*Wiles of the Harlot*)
5QapMal (*Apocryphon of Malachi*)
5QCurses (*Curses*)
5QRègle (*Rule*)

(continued on next page)

6QAllegory (*Allegory of the Vine*)	11QPs[a] (*Psalms Scroll*)
6QApoc ar (Aramaic apocalypse)	11QTemple[a,b] (*Temple Scroll*)
6QapSam/Kgs (*Samuel-Kings* Apocryphon)	11QtgJob (*Targum to Job*)
	Masada
6QD (*Damascus Document*)	Murabba'at
6QPriestProph (*Priestly Prophecy*)	Nahal Hever
6QProph (*Prophecy Text*)	8HevXIIgr
8QHym (hymnic passage=8Q5)	Nahal Se'elim
11QBer (*Benediction*)	Nahal Mishmar
11QHalakah	Khirbet Mird
11QMelch (*Melchizedek Text*)	Cairo Genizah

The Dead Sea Scrolls probably constitute the single most important biblically related literary discovery of the twentieth century. Many of the mss remained unpublished until the Huntington Library of San Marino, California, made its collection of photographs of the Dead Sea Scrolls available to all qualified scholars. Shortly thereafter the Institute for Antiquity and Christianity of Claremont, California, announced the imminent publication of photographs of all the scrolls that had not been published before. James M. Robinson and Robert H. Eisenman have prepared a two-volume work that contains photographs of all of the unpublished manuscripts and fragments: *A Facsimile Edition of the Dead Sea Scrolls* (Washington: Biblical Archaeology Society, 1991).

The Dead Sea Scrolls have contributed significantly to biblical scholarship in several fields: (1) the study of ancient writing and making of books/scrolls; (2) textual criticism of the OT; (3) linguistic studies in Hebrew and Aramaic; (4) apocryphal and pseudepigraphal studies; (5) the study of sects and groups, particularly the Essenes, within Palestinian Jewry; (6) ancient methods of biblical interpretation; (7) intertestamental history; (8) first-century doctrines and religious ideas; and (9) NT background studies.

There is debate over the origin of the Qumran community and its relationship to the group that Philo, Josephus, and others called the "Essenes." Philo mentions the group in two places. In *Quod Omnis Probus Liber sit* (*That Every Good Man Is Free*) 12 §§75–91 he describes the "Essaioi" as persons of high moral standards, who are "especially devout in the service of God, not by offering sacrifices of animals, but by resolving to sanctify their minds." They live communally in villages, they avoid cities, they are frugal, modest, peaceful, egalitarian, and respectful of elders. They are called Essaioi, Philo thinks, because the word is related to *hosiotēs* ("holiness"). In *Apologia pro Judaeis,* a work that is lost but quoted by Eusebius (*Praeparatio Evangelica* 8.11.1–18), Philo repeats many of the things related in *Quod Omnis* and adds that the Essaioi are made up mostly of older men ("there are no children of younger years among the Essaioi, nor even adolescents or young men"), who are farmers, shepherds, keepers of bees, and craftsmen of every sort. They constitute a self-sufficient community. They hold all things common. They care for the sick.

Josephus mentions the Essenes many times; twice he dwells upon them at length. In the *Jewish War* (2.8.2–11 §§119–158) Josephus calls the group "Essenoi." He tells us that they renounce pleasure, disdain marriage, and adopt young children in order to instruct them in their ways. They wear white garments. They live communally. They are sober and taciturn. Josephus also describes their requirements for membership and their strict regulations for daily life. The Essenes believe in the eternal soul, which after death will either join the abode of the righteous or the pit of Hades. Josephus then describes another order of Essenes which believes that marriage is proper and necessary, not for pleasure, but for the propagation of the human race. This passage is closely paralleled by Hippolytus, *Refutation of All Heresies* 9.18–28, and may even be dependent upon the *Jewish War.* Josephus discusses the Essenes in a briefer account in *Jewish Antiquities* 18.1.5 §§18–22. One important comment should be noted. He says that "they send offerings to the Temple, but offer no sacrifices there since the purifications to which they are accustomed are different. For this reason, they refrain from entering into the common enclosure, but offer sacrifices among themselves" (*Ant.* 18.1.5 §19). This is in essential agreement with what Philo had said (*Quod Omnis* 12 §75). What Josephus meant when he said "offer sacrifices among themselves" is a matter of scholarly debate.

Pliny the Elder (ca. 75 C.E.) provides some useful information regarding the location of the Essenes (*Natural History* 5.17.4). According to him, the Essenes were situated west of the Dead Sea and north of Engedi and Masada. This is the same location where the Dead Sea Scrolls have been found. He goes on to say that although the Essenes did not practice marriage, their numbers grew because throngs of people sought to join them, having "repented" for their past lives. Probably drawing on the same source, Dio Chrysostom (ca. 100 C.E.), according to his biographer, Synesius, "praises the Essenes, who form an entire and prosperous city near the Dead Sea, in the center of Palestine, not far from Sodom" (Dio Chrysostom §5).

Because of the similarities of doctrine and practice between the Essenes and the writers of the Dead Sea Scrolls and because of the location of this group near the Dead Sea, most scholars today have concluded that the scrolls were once part of the library of the Essenes. But what of the origin of this community? Here there is less agreement among scholars. Among the most plausible reconstructions is the hypothesis that the community was founded by the "Teacher of Righteousness," who criticized and was opposed by Jewish high priest and King Jannaeus (ca. 104–103 B.C.E.) and perhaps was put to death by Jannaeus' son Hyrcanus II (ca. 64 B.C.E.), the "Wicked Priest" (cf. 1QpHab 8:8–13; 9:9–12). Moreover, it has been suggested by R. Goossens that the Teacher of Righteousness was Onias the Righteous, a pious man remembered for his answered prayer (m. Ta'an. 3:8; Josephus, Ant. 14.2.1 §22; see Appendix 5). But this identification is not without difficulties and so has not won many followers. J. H. Charlesworth has suggested that the Wicked Priest was Jonathan, the younger brother of Judas Maccabeus and Simon. But it may be, as W. H. Brownlee argued, that the Wicked Priest was a technical term that referred to more than one Hasmonean high priest. I am inclined to agree. Like the Teacher of Righteousness, which probably came to be viewed as a title of office, so the Wicked Priest came to be understood as the title of the opposing office. Most scholars do agree, however, that the frequently appearing word "Kittim" refers to the Romans, which supports seeing the community as originating in the late second century B.C.E. and thriving on through the first century B.C.E. and into the first century C.E.

Bibliography: W. H. Brownlee, "A Comparison of the Covenanters of the Dead Sea Scrolls with pre-Christian Jewish Sects," BA 13 (1950) 50–72; idem, "The Historical Allusions of the Dead Sea Habakkuk Midrash," BASOR 126 (1952) 10–20; idem, "The Wicked Priest, the Man of Lies, and the Righteous Teacher— The Problem of Identity," JQR 73 (1982) 1–37; P. R. Callaway, The History of the Qumran Community: An Investigation (JSPSup 3; Sheffield: JSOT, 1988); J. H. Charlesworth, "The Origin and Subsequent History of the Authors of the Dead Sea Scrolls: Four Transitional Phases among the Qumran Essenes," RevQ 10 (1980) 213–33; D. Dimant, "Qumran Sectarian Literature," JWSTP, 542–47; A. Dupont-Sommer, EWQ, 1–67, 339–67; idem, The Jewish Sect of Qumran and the Essenes (London: Vallentine, Mitchell, 1954); C. T. Fritsch, "Herod the Great and the Qumran Community," JBL 74 (1955) 175–81; R. Goossens, "Onias le Juste, le Messie de a Nouvelle Alliance, lapidé à Jérusalem en 65 av. J.-C.," La Nouvelle Clio 7 (1950) 336–53; idem, "Les Kittim du Commentaire d'Habacuc," La Nouvelle Clio 9 (1952) 138–70; G. Jeremias, Der Lehrer der Gerechtigkeit (SUNT 2; Göttingen: Vandenhoeck & Ruprecht, 1963); J. Murphy-O'Connor, "Demetrius I and the Teacher of Righteousness (I Macc. x, 25–45)," RB 83 (1976) 400–420; idem, "Judean Desert," EJMI, 139–43; L. H. Schiffman, ed., Archaeology and History in the Dead Sea Scrolls (Y. Yadin Festschrift; JSPSup 8; Sheffield: JSOT, 1990); G. Vermes, "The Essenes and History," JJS 32 (1981) 18–31; A. S. van der Woude, "Wicked Priest or Wicked Priests? Reflections on the Identification of the Wicked Priest in the Habakkuk Commentary," JJS 33 (1982) 349–59.

The Dead Sea Scrolls constitute a vast and diverse body of written materials. These materials have been categorized according to the geographical regions in which they have been found. Of all the regions "Qumran" (from the gulch called Wadi Qumran) is best known. Recovered from eleven caves, the writings of Qumran number more than 800 documents. Many of these are in fragments (some 15,000 fragments in all). J. H. Charlesworth (*JJ*, 184–86) subdivides the principal writings as "Qumran Rules" (ten documents), "Qumran Hymns and Prayers" (23 documents), "Qumran Commentaries" (21 documents), "Qumran Apocryphal and Other Works" (33 documents), and "Other" (nine documents). In many cases there are two or more fragmentary copies of these documents scattered among the caves. Counting the biblical books and the duplicates, the eleven caves of Qumran have yielded hundreds of documents (more than 700 from Cave 4 alone). The several regions are as follows:

Qumran
Masada
Murabba'at
Naḥal Ḥever (Wadi Khabra)
Naḥal Se'elim (Wadi Seuyal)
Naḥal Mishmar (Wadi Mahras)
Khirbet Mird
Cairo Genizah

The chief finds of these regions will be summarized below, with most of the attention given to Qumran. Emphasis has been placed on the sectarian and apocryphal documents.

SUMMARIES OF QUMRAN DOCUMENTS

1. 1QapGen (*Genesis Apocryphon*). The *Genesis Apocryphon* of Cave 1 is written in Aramaic and is a first-person retelling of some of the narratives of Genesis concerning the patriarchs. Lamech suspects that the birth of his son Noah was in some ways supernatural, so he goes to his father Methuselah. Methuselah, however, takes the matter to his father Enoch for an explanation. Enoch explains that sin had taken place in the days of his father Jared involving the sons of God (Gen 6:1–3). Therefore, God was about to bring upon the earth a fearful judgment. The Noah story is then retold with embellishments. The next hero is Abraham who is warned in a dream that men will try to kill him in order to take his wife. When Pharaoh learns of Sarah's beauty he takes her and tries to kill Abraham. Sarah saves his life by claiming that he was only her kinsman. (This is perhaps an attempt to justify the biblical account of Abraham's deceit.) The story continues with the adventures of Lot and the promise of a son to Abraham. The *Genesis Apocryphon* is quite similar in style to *Jubilees*.

Bibliography: C. A. Evans, "The Genesis Apocryphon and the Rewritten Bible," *RevQ* 13 (1988) 153–65; A. Dupont-Sommer, *EWQ*, 284–94; J. A. Fitzmyer,

DSS, 137–40; idem, *The Genesis Apocryphon of Qumran Cave I: A Commentary* (2d ed.; BibOr 18A; Rome: Pontifical Biblical Institute, 1971) [Aramaic text, ET, commentary, bibliography, and response to reviews of 1966 edition]; T. H. Gaster, *DSSET*, 358–72, 377–81.

2. 1QDM (*Dibre Moshe* = 1Q22). The *Sayings of Moses* purports to be Moses' farewell address to Israel. Moses exhorts the people to remain loyal to Yahweh and to abhor the idolatry of the pagans that they will encounter in the promised land. He reminds them to observe the Year of Release (every seventh year). The fragment ends with instructions regarding the day of Atonement.

Bibliography: A. Dupont-Sommer, *EWQ*, 307–9; T. H. Gaster, *DSSET*, 373–76.

3. 1QH (*Hôdāyôt* [*Thanksgiving Hymns*]). The *Thanksgiving Hymns* of Cave 1 powerfully describe the frame of mind of the covenanters of Qumran. Their separation from the corrupt world, their spiritual ascents into the heavens, and their pain at being opposed and rebuffed by non-believers constitute the main themes of these hymns. Some have suggested (T. H. Gaster thinks incorrectly) that hymn 8 was written by the Teacher of Righteousness himself, since the hymn concerns one whose insights have been rejected by "garblers of the truth." There are nineteen complete hymns and fragments of several others.

Bibliography: D. Dimant, "Qumran Sectarian Literature," *JWSTP*, 522–24; A. Dupont-Sommer, *EWQ*, 198–54; T. H. Gaster, *DSSET*, 144–216, 236–57; B. Kittel, *The Hymns of Qumran: Translation and Commentary* (SBLDS 50; Chico: Scholars, 1981); M. Mansoor, *The Thanksgiving Hymns* (STDJ 3; Leiden: Brill; Grand Rapids: Eerdmans, 1961); E. H. Merrill, *Qumran and Predestination: A Theological Study of the Thanksgiving Hymns* (STDJ 8; Leiden: Brill, 1975); J. Murphy-O'Connor, "The Judean Desert," *EJMI*, 130–32.

4. 1QIsa[a,b] (Isaiah, first and second copies). Two copies of Isaiah were discovered among the contents of Cave 1. Copy "a," also known as the Great Isaiah Scroll, is complete, while copy "b" is fragmentary (fragments of chaps. 7–66). Whereas copy "a" follows the Hebrew preserved in the Masoretic tradition closely, copy "b" takes liberties with the text, almost to the point that it could be regarded as a sort of Hebrew targum to Isaiah. One interesting example in "a" is its rendering of Isaiah 6:9–10 and 13, where the prophet's word no longer is to bring about further obduracy, but is transformed into an exhortation to guard against impiety. "Go on hearing, but don't hear" (v. 9) is transformed into "Go on hearing *because* you will hear." "Make the heart of this people fat . . . lest it understand" (v. 10) becomes "Make the heart of this people *appalled* [at evil] . . . *Let* it understand." Later in v. 13 "A holy seed is its stump" becomes "*How* can the holy seed be its stump?," implying that the Jerusalem establishment cannot be the holy seed, for the Qumran com-

munity is the holy seed. Numerous other modifications can be detected in copy "a."

Bibliography: W. H. Brownlee, *The Meaning of the Qumran Scrolls for the Bible* (New York: Oxford University, 1964) 155–259; M. Burrows, ed., *The Dead Sea Scrolls of St. Mark's Monastery* (2 vols.; New Haven: American Schools of Oriental Research, 1950) vol. 1 [*The Isaiah Manuscript and the Habakkuk Commentary*], plates I–LIV [photographs of 1QIsa[a]]; C. A. Evans, "1QIsaiah[a] and the Absence of Prophetic Critique at Qumran," *RevQ* 11 (1984) 560–70; E. Y. Kutscher, *The Language and Linguistic Background of the Isaiah Scroll (1 QIsa[a])* (indexed and corrected by E. Qimron; STDJ 6A; Leiden: Brill, 1979); J. C. Trever, *Scrolls from Qumran Cave I* (Jerusalem: The Albright Institute of Archaeological Research and The Shrine of the Book, 1972) 13–123 [black and white photograph on left hand side, color photograph on right].

5. 1QJN (*New Jerusalem* = 1Q32). *New Jerusalem* is extant in Hebrew and Aramaic fragments discovered in several of the caves (cf. 2QJN ar; 4QJN ar; 4QJN; 5QJN ar; 11QJN ar). The document describes the future temple of the New Jerusalem of restored Israel. Modeled after Ezekiel 40–47, it is presented as a vision in which precise measurements and liturgical practices for the new temple are clarified.

Bibliography: D. Dimant, "Qumran Sectarian Literature," *JWSTP,* 531–32; A. Dupont-Sommer, *EWQ,* 307–9.

6. 1QJub[a], 1QJub[b] (*Jubilees,* copies a and b = 1Q17–18). 1QJub[a], 1QJub[b] = *Jub.* 27:19–21; 35:8–10; 36:12[?]. Several fragments of the pseudepigraphal work *Jubilees* have also been recovered in caves 2, 3, 4, and 11 (cf. 2QJub[a] [= *Jub.* 3:7–8]; 2QJub[b] [= *Jub.* 46:1–3]; 3QJub[= *Jub.* 23:6–7, 12–13, 23(?)]; 4QJub [= *Jub.* 21:22–24; 23:21–23, 30–31]; 11QJub [= *Jub.* 3:25–27; 4:7–11, 13–14, 16–17, 29–30; 5:1–2; 6:12(?); 12:15–17, 28–29]). Many of these identifications are tentative.

Bibliography: A. Dupont-Sommer, *EWQ,* 298–300; J. C. VanderKam and J. T. Milik, "The First *Jubilees* Manuscript from Qumran Cave 4: A Preliminary Publication," *JBL* 110 (1991) 243–70.

7. 1QLitPr[a,b] (*Liturgical Prayers* = 1Q34). These liturgical prayers may be related to 4QPrFêtes[a–c], perhaps also to 4QPrLit[b]. André Dupont-Sommer thinks that one of them may have had something to do with Pentecost. There are prayers that the righteous enjoy God's blessing, while the wicked suffer "pains in their bones." There is also a petition that God renew his covenant with his people.

Bibliography: A. Dupont-Sommer, *EWQ,* 335–36; T. H. Gaster, *DSSET,* 437–38.

8. 1QM (*Milḥāmāh* [*War Scroll*]). The *War Scroll* describes the great and final eschatological battle between the sons of light and the sons of darkness. In this battle the evil Prince of Darkness, also known as Belial (or Beliar), and his corrupt minions will be annihilated. The scroll

provides detailed instructions for proper battle formations, formations which appear to reflect Roman military tactics. The righteous priests of the Qumran community play prominent rolls in the anticipated eschatological battle. Only those who are ritually pure may participate. The scroll also contains the thanksgiving hymn that is to be sung when the battle is won. There are several fragments of this text in Cave 4 (cf. 4QM^{a-e}; pap4QM$^{f,g?}$). 6QHym may be related to the *War Scroll*.

Bibliography: D. Dimant, "Qumran Sectarian Literature," *JWSTP*, 515–17; A. Dupont-Sommer, *EWQ*, 164–97; J. A. Fitzmyer, *DSS*, 141–43; T. H. Gaster, *DSSET*, 399–423, 452–57; J. Murphy-O'Connor, "The Judean Desert," *EJMI*, 132–33; J. P. M. van der Ploeg, *Le rouleau de la guerre* (STDJ 2; Leiden: Brill, 1959); Y. Yadin, *The Scroll of the War of the Sons of Light against the Sons of Darkness* (Oxford: Oxford University, 1962).

9. 1QMyst (*Book of Mysteries* = 1Q27). The *Book of Mysteries* is a short fragment that warns of the certainty of the day of judgment when evil will at last be purged from the earth. It begins by noting that most people do not know what is coming, and it concludes by noting that most people recognize that sin is wrong.

Bibliography: A. Dupont-Sommer, *EWQ*, 326–27; T. H. Gaster, *DSSET*, 429.

10. 1QNoah (= 1Q19). The *Book of Noah* is related to *1 Enoch* 8:4–9:4; 106:9–10, in which the sins of the earth and the birth of Noah are described.

Bibliography: J. T. Milik, *BE*, 55–60.

11. 1QpHab (*Pesher* or *Commentary on Habakkuk*). Of all the pesharim (or "commentaries") on Scripture discovered at Qumran the pesher on Habakkuk of Cave 1 is the most important, for not only is this scroll comparatively well preserved and so affords us many examples of exegesis Qumran style, but a key section of the scroll explains the principles of Qumranian exegesis, viz. the Teacher of Righteousness. A famous passage reads: "God told Habakkuk to write down the things that were to come upon the latter age, but He did not inform him when that moment would come to fulfillment. As to the phrase, "that he who runs may read," this refers to the teacher who expounds the Law aright, for God has made him the one who runs with all the deeper implications of the words of His servants the prophets" (commentary on Hab 2:1–2). Other pesharim include 1QpMic (1Q14), 1QpZeph (1Q15), 1QpPs (1Q16), 3QpIsa (3Q4), 4QpIsa^{a-e} (4Q161–165), 4QpHos^{a,b} (4Q166–167), 4QpMic (4Q168), 4QpNah (4Q169), 4QpZeph (4Q170), 4QpPs^{a,b} (4Q171, 173), and 4QpUnid[entified Texts] (4Q172). 4QTanh is treated below.

Normally Qumran texts are cited, using arabic numerals, by column and line number, e.g., 1QS 9:3–6 means *Serek* ("Rule") from Qumran, Cave 1, column 9, lines 3 to 6. But in the case of most of the pesharim, because of their fragmentary condition, they are cited as follows: 4QpNah 3–4 i 6, which means fragments 3 and 4 (arabic numerals), column 1 (lower case roman numerals), line 6 (arabic numerals).

Bibliography: W. H. Brownlee, *The Midrash Pesher of Habakkuk* (SBLMS 24; Missoula: Scholars, 1979); M. Burrows, ed., *The Dead Sea Scrolls of St. Mark's Monastery* (2 vols.; New Haven: American Schools of Oriental Research, 1950) vol. 1 [*The Isaiah Manuscript and the Habakkuk Commentary*], plates LV–LXI [photographs of 1QpHab]; D. Dimant, "Qumran Sectarian Literature," *JWSTP*, 505–14; A. Dupont-Sommer, *EWQ*, 258–78; T. H. Gaster, *DSSET*, 299–349; M. P. Horgan, "The Bible Explained (Prophecies)," *EJMI*, 250–53; idem, *Pesharim: Qumran Interpretations of Biblical Books* (CBQMS 8; Washington: Catholic Biblical Association, 1979); J. Murphy-O'Connor, "The Judean Desert," *EJMI*, 134–35; J. C. Trever, *Scrolls from Qumran Cave I* (Jerusalem: The Albright Institute of Archaeological Research and The Shrine of the Book, 1972) 149–63 [black and white photograph on left hand side, color photograph on right].

12. 1QS (*Serek hayyahad* [*Rule of the Community* or *Manual of Discipline*]). The *Manual of Discipline* is among the most significant finds at Qumran. This scroll lays down the requirements for admission into the community. The would-be adherent is repeatedly told that he must no longer "walk in the stubbornness of his heart." Topics that are touched on include the two natures of human beings, social relations in the community, rules of holiness, duties, regulations concerning malicious speech and other sins, and rules concerning community leaders. There are two appendices to 1QS (1QSa, 1QSb). There are also several fragments of the text in Cave 4 (4QS). 6QBen may also be related.

Bibliography: W. H. Brownlee, *The Dead Sea Manual of Discipline: Translation and Notes* (BASORSup 10–12; New Haven: American Schools of Oriental Research, 1951); M. Burrows, ed., *The Dead Sea Scrolls of St. Mark's Monastery* (2 vols.; New Haven: American Schools of Oriental Research, 1950) vol. 2, fasc. 2 [*Plates and Transcription of the Manual of Discipline*], plates I–X [photographs of 1QS]; D. Dimant, "Qumran Sectarian Literature," *JWSTP*, 497–503, 517–18, 524; A. Dupont-Sommer, *EWQ*, 68–113; J. A. Fitzmyer, *DSS*, 130–31; T. H. Gaster, *DSSET*, 44–65, 101–7; J. Murphy-O'Connor, "The Judean Desert," *EJMI*, 128–29; L. H. Schiffman, *The Eschatological Community of the Dead Sea Scrolls: A Study of the Rule of the Congregation* (SBLMS 38; Atlanta: Scholars, 1989); J. C. Trever, *Scrolls from Qumran Cave I* (Jerusalem: The Albright Institute of Archaeological Research and The Shrine of the Book, 1972) 125–47 [black and white photograph on left hand side, color photograph on right]; P. Wernberg-Møller, *The Manual of Discipline* (STDJ 1; Leiden: Brill, 1957).

13. 1QTLevi ar (Aramaic *Testament of Levi* = 1Q21). This fragment may be part of *T. Levi* 8:11. It is closely related to CTLevi ar ("C" refers to Cairo Genizah). See 4QTJos ar below.

14. 2QapDavid (*Apocryphon of David* = 2Q22). The *Apocryphon of David* is an apocryphal story about David, and is perhaps part of a collection of apocryphal psalms. See 4QapPs.

15. 2QapMoses (*Apocryphon of Moses* = 2Q21). An apocryphal writing about Moses.

16. 2QapProph (an apocryphal prophetic text = 2Q23).

17. 2QEnGiants (*Enoch's Book of Giants* = 2Q26). This text is part of the *Book of Giants*, a document that is extant as part of *1 Enoch* (see chaps. 6–11, 106–7). See also 6QEnGiants; 4QEnGiants[a–f]. Other parts of *1 Enoch* are found in various caves (cf. 4QEn[a–g]).

Bibliography: J. T. Milik, *BE*.

18. 3QHym (a hymn of praise = 3Q6).

19. 3QTJud? (possibly a fragment of the *Testament of Judah* = 3Q7). See 4QTJos ar below.

Bibliography: J. T. Milik, "Ecrits préesséniens de Qumrân: D'Hénoch à Amram," in M. Delcor, ed., *Qumrân: Sa piété, sa théologie et son milieu* (BETL 46; Gembloux: Duculot, 1978) 91–106, esp. 98–99.

20. 3QTreasure (*Copper Scroll* = 3Q15). The *Copper Scroll* provides the directions to several hidden treasures of gold and silver. It has been debated whether or not the scroll tells of real wealth.

Bibliography: D. Dimant, "Qumran Sectarian Literature," *JWSTP*, 531; A. Dupont-Sommer, *EWQ*, 379–93; T. H. Gaster, *DSSET*, 529–36; J. Murphy-O'Connor, "The Judean Desert," *EJMI*, 135.

21. 4QAgesCreat (*Ages of Creation* = 4Q180–181). *Ages of Creation* attempts to categorize world history into specific epochs of time (hence T. H. Gaster's title of this work "Epochs of Times"). From Adam to Noah and from Noah to Abraham are reckoned as ten generations apiece (cf. Matt 1:17 where "fourteen" generations are noted). The work then goes on to discuss the significance of the sin of the fallen angels (Gen 6:1–4). The fragmentary text concludes with an account of various events in the life of Abraham.

Bibliography: D. Dimant, "The 'Pesher on the Periods' (4Q180) and 4Q181," *IOS* 9 (1979) 77–102; T. H. Gaster, *DSSET*, 522–27.

22. 4QAmram[b–e] (*Testament* [or *Visions*] of Amram). A few fragments of a lost *Testament of Amram* have been found in Cave 4. In this Testament, Amram, grandson of Levi, warns his family on the day of his death of the coming prince of wickedness called Belial or Melkiresha. He exhorts his descendants (undoubtedly to be understood as the men of Qumran) to keep themselves pure and to ally themselves to the King of Light who is probably called Melchizedek (the last part of the text is lost).

Bibliography: J. A. Fitzmyer, *ESBNT*, 101–4; T. H. Gaster, *DSSET*, 512–16; J. T. Milik, "4Q Visions de 'Amram et une citation d'Origène," *RB* 79 (1972) 77–97, esp. 78–92.

23. 4QapLam[a,b] (*Lamentations Apocryphon* = 4Q179, 501). Gaster has entitled 4Q179 "Lament for Zion." It describes the destruction of Jerusalem and the lamentations of its inhabitants. It is not based upon canonical Lamentations. 4Q501 is another lamentations text.

Bibliography: T. H. Gaster, *DSSET,* 228–30, 265–66.

24. 4QapPs (two apocryphal Psalms = 4Q380, 381). The first psalm (4Q380) consists of seven fragments written on leather. The first fragment speaks of Jerusalem as God's chosen city. The seventh fragment speaks of God's wisdom in creation. The second psalm (4Q381) consists of some 104 fragments. The first fragment is in praise of God the Creator and Sustainer of the land. In fragment 15 there is a call for God's help, a call which closely parallels Ps 89:14, 7. Fragment 24 calls for victory over enemies. Fragment 31 refers to the "prayer of the king of Judah." According to line 8 of fragment 33, this is none other than the "Prayer of Manasseh, king of Judah, when the king of Assyria imprisoned him." The penitent king admits to his sins. Is this apocryphal psalm related to the apocryphal Prayer of Manasseh? Eileen Schuller does not think so. She suspects that only later was the psalm associated with Manasseh.

Bibliography: E. M. Schuller, *Non-Canonical Psalms from Qumran* (HSS 28; Atlanta: Scholars, 1986).

25. 4QCatena[a,b] (= 4Q177, 182). Gaster has entitled 4Q177 the "Rout of Belial." The work consists of a series of predictions based upon the interpretation of various prophetic texts (e.g., Hos 5:8; Isa 37:30; 32:7; 22:13).

Bibliography: T. H. Gaster, *DSSET,* 424–28, 457–62.

26. 4QPsAp[a–c] (apocryphal Psalms). Cave 4 has yielded a few apocryphal Psalms.

Bibliography: J. Starcky, "Psaumes apocryphes de la grotte 4 de Qumrân (4QPs[f] VII–X)," *RB* 73 (1966) 353–71.

27. 4QD[a,b,e] ([related to] *Damascus Document* = 4Q226, 266, 270). The Testaments of Melchizedek and Melkiresha describe the righteous Melchizedek and the wicked prince of darkness Melkiresha. It is related to 4QBer[a,b], a text that contains blessings and references to Melchizedek and Melkiresha.

Bibliography: J. T. Milik, "Milkî-sedeq et Milkî-resaʿ," *JJS* 23 (1972) 134–36.

28. 4QFlor (*Florilegium* or 4QEschMidr [*Eschatological Midrashim*] = 4Q174). This document consists of several brief commentaries on various biblical passages (2 Sam 7:10–14; Exod 15:17–18; Amos 9:11; Ps 1:1; Isa 8:11; Ps 2:1; Dan 12:10; 11:32; Deut 33:8–11, 19–21). The theme is escha-

tological. The eschatological interpretation of 2 Samuel 7 is significant for NT studies (cf. Luke 1:32–33; Rom 1:4).

Bibliography: G. J. Brooke, *Exegesis at Qumran: 4QFlorilegium in its Jewish Context* (JSOTSup 29; Sheffield, JSOT, 1985); D. Dimant, "Qumran Sectarian Literature," *JWSTP*, 518–21; A. Dupont-Sommer, *EWQ*, 311–14; T. H. Gaster, *DSSET*, 446–48, 474–75.

29. 4QGen–4QDan, possibly including fragments of Tobit and Susanna. Cave 4 has yield numerous fragments of biblical books, including fragments of the LXX of the Pentateuch as well.

Bibliography: F. M. Cross, "A New Qumran Biblical Fragment Related to the Original Hebrew Underlying the Septuagint," *BASOR* 132 (1953) 15–26 [on 4QSam^a]; J. E. Sanderson, *An Exodus Scroll from Qumran: 4QpaleoExod^m and the Samaritan Tradition* (HSS 30; Atlanta: Scholars, 1986); L. A. Sinclair, "A Qumran Biblical Fragment: Hosea 4QXII^d (Hosea 1:7–2:5)," *BASOR* 239 (1980) 61–65; P. W. Skehan, "Exodus in the Samaritan Recension from Qumran," *JBL* 74 (1955) 182–87 [on 4QpaleoExod^m]; idem, "A Fragment of the 'Song of Moses' (Deut 32) from Qumran," *BASOR* 136 (1954) 12–15 [on 4QDeut^q]; idem, "A Psalm Manuscript from Qumran (4QPs^b)," *CBQ* 26 (1964) 313–22; E. C. Ulrich, "4QSam^c: A Fragmentary Manuscript of 2 Samuel 14–15 from the Scribe of *Serek Hayyahad* (1QS)," *BASOR* 235 (1979) 1–25; idem, *The Qumran Text of Samuel and Josephus* (HSM 19; Missoula: Scholars, 1978) [on 4QSam^a]; J. de Waard, *A Comparative Study of the Old Testament Text in the Dead Sea Scrolls and in the New Testament* (Leiden: Brill, 1965).

30. 4QMess ar (Aramaic *Messianic Text*). Fitzmyer notes that this text is misnamed, for it is not messianic. Rather, it speaks of the elect of God.

Bibliography: J. A. Fitzmyer, *ESBNT*, 127–60; J. T. Milik, *BE*, 56.

31. 4QMMT (*Miqsat Ma'aseh Torah* = 4Q394–399). This document, at one time called 4QMishnah, appears to be an irenic letter, in six fragments (of four or five copies), from the Qumran community (the Teacher of Righteousness?), or at least those who would eventually form the community, to the high priest of Jerusalem. The letter may represent a period just prior to the final split between the Qumran community and the temple establishment. In one of the fragments there is a threefold reference to Scripture: "We have [written] to you [sing.], so that you might understand the book of Moses, and [the words of the pr]ophets, and Davi[d]" (my trans; cf. Luke 24:44). The irenic tone is in evidence here as well.

Bibliography: E. Qimron and J. Strugnell, "An Unpublished Halakhic Letter from Qumran," *IMJ* 4 (1985) 9–12.

32. 4QOrd^{a,b,c} (*Ordinances* = 4Q159, 513, 514). Some halakic rules and regulations. Apparently 4QOrd^a is critical of the requirement to pay the half-shekel temple tax annually: "as for the half-[shekel, the offering to the Lord] which they gave, each man as a ransom for his soul: only one

[time] shall he give it all his days" (2:6–8; cf. Exod 30:13–16; Matt 17:24–27).

Bibliography: J. M. Allegro, "An Unpublished Fragment of Essene Halakah (4Q Ordinances)," *JSS* 6 (1961) 71–73 [on 4QOrd[a]]; T. H. Gaster, *DSSET*, 92–93, 113–14 [on 4QOrd[a]].

33. **4QPBless** (*Patriarchal Blessings*). Because the text comments on Gen 49:10, it was at one time known as 4QpGen 49. The text is clearly messianic: "Until the Messiah of righteousness comes, the Branch of David; for to him and to his seed has been given the covenant of the kingship of his people for everlasting" (1:3–4). Note the allusion to 2 Samuel 7.

Bibliography: A. Dupont-Sommer, *EWQ*, 314–15; T. H. Gaster, *DSSET*, 443, 469–70.

34. **4QPrNab**. The *Prayer of Nabonidus* closely resembles the story of Nebuchadnezzar in Daniel 4. It tells of the king's pride, his fall, and his eventual restoration. Some scholars think that the account in Daniel is based upon an actual illness that Nabonidus, the last king of the neo-Babylonian empire (555–539 B.C.E.), had suffered and that the Danielic version has retold the story. This is possible, but some caution is required, for the name of the king in 4QPrNab is actually "Nabunai."

Bibliography: F. M. Cross, "Fragments of the Prayer of Nabonidus," *IEJ* 34 (1984) 260–64; A. Dupont-Sommer, *EWQ*, 322–23; T. H. Gaster, *DSSET*, 537; G. W. E. Nickelsburg, "Stories of Biblical and Early Post-Biblical Times," *JWSTP*, 35–37.

35. **4QpsDan ar[a,b,c]** (pseudo-Daniel = 4Q246), related to *Prayer of Nabonidus*. 4QpsDan ar[a] (formerly 4QpsDan A = 4Q243) contains some lines that are of significance for NT interpretation: "[But your son] shall be great upon the earth, [O King! All (men) shall] make peace, and all shall serve [him. He shall be called the son of] the [G]reat [God], and by his name shall he be named [1:6–9]. . . . He shall be hailed (as) the Son of God, and they shall call him Son of the Most High. As comets (flash) to the sight, so shall be their kingdom. (For some) year[s] they shall rule upon the earth and shall trample upon people, city upon ci[t]y [*vacat*] until there arise the people of God, and everyone rests from the sword [2:1–4]" (Fitzmyer, 393).

Bibliography: J. A. Fitzmyer, "The Contribution of Qumran Aramaic to the Study of the New Testament," *NTS* 20 (1974) 382–407, esp. 391–94.

36. **4QPsJosh[a,b]** (*Psalms of Joshua* = 4Q378, 379). Judging from what little is extant, the psalms seem to revolve around the theme of military victory over the powers of evil. A portion of this apocryphal work is quoted in 4QTestim (see below).

Bibliography: D. Dimant, "Qumran Sectarian Literature," *JWSTP*, 518; C. Newsom, "The 'Psalms of Joshua' from Qumran Cave 4," *JJS* 39 (1988) 56–73.

37. pap4QRitMar (*Ritual of Marriage Papyrus* = 5Q502). It has been assumed that the papyrus is some sort of marriage ritual, but J. M. Baumgarten has recently called this interpretation into question.

Bibliography: J. M. Baumgarten, "4Q502, Marriage or Golden Age Ritual?" *JJS* 34 (1983) 125–35.

38. pap4QRitPur (*Ritual of Purification* = 4Q512).

39. 4QSam^a. 4QSam^a should be noted because, in the words of Frank Cross, "4QSam^a preserves lost bits of the text of Samuel" (p. 26).

Bibliography: F. M. Cross, "New Directions in Dead Sea Scroll Research: Original Biblical Text Reconstructed from Newly Found Fragments," *BibRev* 1 (1985) 26–35.

40. 4QŠirŠabb^{a-h} (*Rule of the Eternal Song of the Sabbath*). This text describes the heavenly throne room and an angelic liturgy. See also 11QŠirŠabb and MasŠirŠabb.

Bibliography: D. Dimant, "Qumran Sectarian Literature," *JWSTP*, 524–25; T. H. Gaster, *DSSET*, 289–95; C. Newsom, *Songs of the Sabbath Sacrifice: A Critical Edition* (HSS 27; Atlanta: Scholars, 1985).

41. 4QTanh (*Tanhumim* = 4Q176). 4QTanh consists of various biblical quotations (Ps 79:2–3; Isa 40:1–5; 41:8–9; 49:7, 13–17; 43:1–2, 4–6; 51:22–23; 52:1–3; 54:4–10 [then pesher]; 52:1–2; Zech 13:9). Fragments 19–21 are from *Jubilees.*

Bibliography: T. H. Gaster, *DSSET*, 337; M. Kister, "New Identified Fragments of the Book of Jubilees: Jub. 23:21–23, 30–31," *RevQ* 12 (1985–87) 529–36.

42. 4QTestim (*Testimonia* = 4Q175). 4QTestimonies is made up of a series of quotations looking forward to the appearance of the prophet of Deut 18:18 and the "star of Jacob" and "scepter of Israel" of Num 24:17. It is not certain if a Davidic Messiah is in view, or some sort of prophetic, even priestly, deliverer is in view. The conflation of Deut 5:28–29 and 18:18–19 parallels the Samaritan Pentateuch.

Bibliography: J. M. Allegro, "Further Messianic References," *JBL* 75 (1956) 182–87; A. Dupont-Sommer, *EWQ*, 315–17; T. H. Gaster, *DSSET*, 444–46, 470–74.

43. 4QtgLev (*Targum of Leviticus* 16:12–15, 18–21 = 4Q156).

44. 4QtgJob (*Targum of Job* 3:5–9; 4:16–5:4 = 4Q157).

45. 4QTJos ar (Aramaic *Testament of Joseph*). A few of the *Testaments of the Twelve Patriarchs* are paralleled at Qumran, both in Aramaic (1QTLevi ar; 4QTJos ar; 4QTJud ar; 4QTLevi ar^{a,b,c}; cf. CTLevi ar) and in Hebrew (3QTJud?; 4QTJud?; 4QTNaph). Although clearly related to the

genre of the *Testaments of the Twelve Patriarchs*, it is not clear that these Hebrew and Aramaic fragments lie behind the Greek Testaments.

Bibliography: A. Dupont-Sommer, *EWQ*, 301–5; J. T. Milik, "Ecrits préesséniens de Qumrân: D'Hénoch à Amram," in M. Delcor, ed., *Qumrân: Sa Piété, sa théologie et son milieu* (BETL 46; Gembloux: Duculot; Louvain: Leuven University, 1978) 91–106, esp. 101–3.

46. 4QTQahat (*Testament of Qahat*). The *Testament of Kohat* (*Qahat*) is related to, or perhaps part of, the *Testament of Amram* (see 4QAmram above), for Kohat is the son of Levi, father of Amram.

Bibliography: J. T. Milik, "4Q Visions de 'Amram et une citation d'Origène," *RB* 79 (1972) 77–97, esp. 97.

47. 4QVisSam (*Vision of Samuel* = 4Q160). This brief, fragmentary text retells the story of Samuel's dream (1 Sam 3:14–17). The young Samuel tells the dream to Eli and goes on to describe what appears to be an apocalyptic vision.

48. 4QWiles (*Wiles of the Harlot* = 4Q184). Cave 4 has yielded a sapiential work that describes the "wiles of a wicked woman." The main danger of the harlot, according to this writing, is that she will steer men away from Torah.

Bibliography: J. M. Allegro, "The Wiles of the Wicked Woman: A Sapiential Work from Qumran's Fourth Cave," *PEQ* 96 (1964) 53–55; T. H. Gaster, *DSSET*, 497–503.

49. 5QapMal (*Apocryphon of Malachi* = 5Q10). The *Apocryphon of Malachi* is apparently based on Mal 1:13–14 in which those who offer blemished sacrifices are cursed.

Bibliography: J. Carmignac, "Vestiges d'un pesher de Malachie," *RevQ* 4 (1963–64) 97–100.

50. 5QCurses (= 5Q14). A liturgical text containing curses.

51. 5QRègle (*Rule* = 5Q13). 5QRègle is similar to 1QS and CD.

52. 6QAllegory (*Allegory of the Vine* = 6Q11). This Hebrew text may contain an allegory of the vine, a metaphor in the OT that is often used of Israel (cf. Ps 80:8; Jer 2:21; Ezek 17:7–8; Isa 5:1–7 ["vineyard"]; Jer 12:10).

53. 6QApoc ar (= 6Q14). Cave 6 has yielded an Aramaic apocalypse.

54. 6QapSam/Kgs (= 6Q9). Cave 6 has yielded a fragment of a Samuel-Kings Apocryphon in which the history of these OT books is retold.

55. 6QD (*Damascus Document* = 6Q15). See CD under Cairo Genizah below.

56. 6QPriestProph (= 6Q13). This Hebrew (*Priestly Prophecy*) text may be a priestly prophecy and may be related to Ezra-Nehemiah.

57. 6QProph *(Prophecy Text* = 6Q12). Cave 6 has yielded a Hebrew prophetic text that may be a pseudepigraphon.

58. 8QHym (a hymnic passage = 8Q5).

59. 11QBer *(Berakot)*. A benediction.

60. 11QHalakah. This text is related to 11QTemple[a] 20–21; cf. 11QTemple[b].

61. 11QHym[a,b]. Two hymns.

Bibliography: J. P. M. van der Ploeg, "Les manuscrits de la grotte 11 de Qumrân," *RevQ* 12 (1985) 3–15.

62. 11QMelch *(Melchizedek Text)*. This is a text treating the heavenly prince Melchizedek, a figure of great importance to the men of Qumran. The text is based on the Jubilee passage of Lev 25:13 and so describes the "Last Jubilee" (the title that T. H. Gaster gives it). Parts of Isa 61:1–3 and 52:7 are cited several times. Of interest is to note that the men of Qumran understood *šlm* of Isa 52:7 in a double sense, as *šālôm* ("peace") for themselves, but as *šillûm* ("retribution") for the wicked.

Bibliography: T. H. Gaster, *DSSET*, 433–36, 465–69; M. de Jonge and A. S. van der Woude, "11QMelchizedek and the New Testament," *NTS* 12 (1966) 301–26; P. J. Kobelski, *Melchizedek and Melchiresaʿ* (CBQMS 10; Washington: Catholic Biblical Association, 1981); M. P. Miller, "The Function of Isa. 61,1–2 in Melchizedek," *JBL* 88 (1969) 467–69.

63. 11QPs[a] *(Psalms Scroll)*. The *Psalms Scroll* contains portions of some thirty canonical Psalms, Psalms 151A, 151B, 154, 155, Sir 51:13–20, 30, and 2 Sam 23:7.

Bibliography: J. A. Sanders, *The Psalms Scroll of Qumran Cave 11 (11QPs^a)* (DJD 4; Oxford: Clarendon, 1965); idem, "The Qumran Psalms Scroll [11QPs[a]] Reviewed," in M. Black and W. A. Smalley, eds., *On Language, Culture, and Religion* (E. A. Nida Festschrift; The Hague: Mouton, 1974) 79–99.

64. 11QTemple[a] *(Temple Scroll)*. The *Temple Scroll* is the largest single scroll from Qumran, measuring some 28 feet in length (67 cols. of text) in "Herodian" script. This script dates the scroll to sometime between 30 B.C.E. and 70 C.E. It is believed that the original work was composed in the time of John Hyrcanus (134–105 B.C.E.). The scroll contains various laws, with the first section concerned with the temple, and the second section based on Deuteronomy 12–26. Unlike Deuteronomy, the *Temple Scroll* gives the laws in the first person, directly by God. Of interest is to note that some of the laws are given slightly different readings or emphases in order to underscore the distinctive beliefs of the men of Qumran. Columns 20–21 parallel 11QHalakah. 4QTemple[a] may be related. 11QTemple[b] is a second, fragmentary copy of the *Temple Scroll*. There are at least three dozen fragments.

Bibliography: G. J. Brooke, *Temple Scroll Studies* (JSPSup 7; Sheffield: JSOT, 1989); P. R. Callaway, "The Temple Scroll and the Canonization of the Jewish Law,"

RevQ 13 (Mémorial Jean Carmignac, 1988) 239–50; D. Dimant, "Qumran Sectarian Literature," *JWSTP*, 526–30; J. A. Fitzmyer, *DSS*, 144–48; M. Hengel and J. H. Charlesworth, "The Polemical Character of 'On Kingship' in the Temple Scroll: An Attempt at Dating 11QTemple," *JJS* 37 (1986) 28–38; J. Maier, *The Temple Scroll: An Introduction, Translation & Commentary* (JSOTSup 34; Sheffield: JSOT, 1985); J. Murphy-O'Connor, "The Judean Desert," *EJMI*, 136–37; H. Stegemann, "The Origins of the Temple Scroll," in J. A. Emerton, ed., *Congress Volume, Jerusalem 1986* (VTSup 40; Leiden: Brill, 1988) 235–56; Y. Yadin, *The Temple Scroll* (3 vols.; Jerusalem: Israel Exploration Society, 1983).

65. 11QtgJob *(Targum to Job)*. The *Targum to Job* (fragments of Job 17:14–42:11), along with 4QtgLev and 4QtgJob, proves the existence of written targums at the time of the emergence of Christianity. Certain features found in the major targums, such as the use of the periphrastic memra ("word"), do not occur in the Qumran targums.

Bibliography: S. A. Kaufman, "The Job Targum from Qumran," *JAOS* 93 (1973) 317–27; M. Sokoloff, *The Targum to Job from Qumran Cave XI* (Ramat-Gan: Bar-Ilan University, 1974); J. P. M. van der Ploeg and A. S. van der Woude, *Le Targum de Job de la grotte XI de Qumrân* (Leiden: Brill, 1971).

SUMMARIES OF MASADA DOCUMENTS

1. *Scripture*. Fragments of Genesis, Leviticus, Deuteronomy, Ezekiel, Psalms, and Sirach have been found at Masada. The sigla are MasGen, MasLev, etc. The largest fragments are MasPs (Ps 81:3–85:10) and MasSir (Sir 39:27–44:17).

2. *Apocryphal texts*. Fragments of *Jubilees* (MasJub) and ŠirŠabb (MasŠirŠabb) have been found. See 4QŠirŠabb above.

Bibliography: C. Newsom, *Songs of the Sabbath Sacrifice: A Critical Edition* (HSS 27; Atlanta: Scholars, 1985) 167–84; L. H. Feldman, "Masada: A Critique of Recent Scholarship," in J. Neusner, ed., *Christianity, Judaism and Other Greco-Roman Cults* (Leiden: Brill, 1975) 218–48; J. Strugnell, "Notes and Queries on 'The Ben Sira Scroll from Masada,' " *W. F. Albright Volume* (Eretz-Israel 9; Jerusalem: Israel Exploration Society, 1969) 109–19; Y. Yadin, *The Ben Sira Scroll from Masada: With Introduction, Emendations and Commentary* (Jerusalem: Israel Exploration Society, 1965).

SUMMARIES OF MURABBA'AT DOCUMENTS

1. *Scripture*. Several fragments of Scripture have been found: Genesis, Exodus, Numbers, Deuteronomy, Isaiah, a phylactery with verses from Exodus and Deuteronomy, and fragments of most of the Minor Prophets: Joel, Amos, Obadiah, Jonah, Micah, Nahum, Habakkuk, Zephaniah, Haggai, and Zechariah. The sigla are MurGen (= Mur 1), MurExod (= Mur 1), MurNum (= Mur 1), MurDeut (= Mur 2), MurIsa (= Mur 3), MurXII (= Mur 88 [the Minor Prophets]), etc.

2. *Non-Literary Documents and Letters.* Several contracts, writs of divorce, marriage contracts, deeds, letters (materials are in Aramaic, Hebrew, and Greek). Of special interest are letters from Simon ben Kosiba, (apparent messianic) leader of Israel's second revolt against Rome (132–135 C.E.): Mur 43MurEpBarC^a ("Letter of Shim'on ben Kosibah to Yeshua' ben Galgula' ") and Mur 44MurEpBar^b ("Letter of Shim'on ben Kosibah to Yeshua' ben Galgula' ").

Bibliography: P. Benoit, J. T. Milik, and R. de Vaux, *Les grottes de Murabba'at* (DJD 2; Oxford: Clarendon, 1961).

SUMMARIES OF NAHAL HEVER DOCUMENTS

1. *Scripture.* Several fragments of Scripture have been found: Genesis, Numbers, Psalms, and the Greek Minor Prophets Scroll (8HevXIIgr): Jonah, Micah, Nahum, Habakkuk, Zephaniah, Zechariah. The sigla are 5/6HevNum (= Num 20:7–8), 5/6HevPs (= Ps 15:1–5; 16:1; 7:14–31:22), and 8HevXIIgr.

2. *Non-Literary Documents.* Several letters and contracts have been found. Most important are the letters of Simon ben Kosiba (5/6HevEp 1–15).

Bibliography: Y. Yadin, *Bar-Kokhba: The Rediscovery of the Legendary Hero of the Second Jewish Revolt against Rome* (London: Weidenfeld and Nicolson, 1971) 124–253; idem, "Expedition D—The Cave of Letters," *IEJ* 12 (1962) 227–57.

SUMMARIES OF NAHAL ŞE'ELIM DOCUMENTS

Two phylactery fragments: 34ŞePhyl (= Exod 13:2–10, 11–16); an epistle: pap34Şe gr; and eight Greek fragments: pap34Şe gr 1–8.

Bibliography: Y. Aharoni, "Expedition B," *IEJ* 11 (1961) 11–24; B. Lifshitz, "The Greek Documents from Nahal Seelim and Nahal Mishmar," *IEJ* 11 (1961) 53–62.

SUMMARIES OF NAHAL MISHMAR DOCUMENTS

A papyrus with list of Greek names: papMiš gr.

Bibliography: P. Bar Adon, "Expedition C," *IEJ* 11 (1961) 25–35; B. Lifshitz, "The Greek Documents from Nahal Seelim and Nahal Mishmar," *IEJ* 11 (1961) 53–62.

SUMMARIES OF KHIRBET MIRD DOCUMENTS

Three Christian documents have been discovered: papMird A, Mird Acts cpa (Acts 10:28–29, 32–41), and MirdAmul cpa (magical amulet). Several Arabic papyri have been discovered: papMird 1–100 arab.

Bibliography: C. Perrot, "Un fragment christo-palestinien découvert à Khirbet Mird (Actes des Apôtres, X, 28–29; 32–41)," *RB* 70 (1963) 506–55.

SUMMARIES OF CAIRO GENIZAH DOCUMENTS

These documents were not found in the vicinity of the Dead Sea; they are medieval copies of some of these texts. In the genizah (a place where old sacred books were retired) of an old synagogue in Cairo three relevant items were found in 1896 or 1897: portions of Sirach (CSir), an Aramaic portion of the *Testament of Levi* (CTLevi ar), and the *Damascus Document* (CD). The latter was published in 1910 under the title, "Fragments of a Zadokite Work" (see R. H. Charles, *APOT*, 2.785–834).

Bibliography: P. R. Davies, *The Damascus Covenant: An Interpretation of the "Damascus Document"* (JSOTSup 25; Sheffield: JSOT, 1983); D. Dimant, "Qumran Sectarian Literature," *JWSTP*, 490–97; J. A. Fitzmyer, *DSS*, 132–36; J. C. Greenfield and M. E. Stone, "Remarks on the Aramaic Testament of Levi from the Genizah," *RB* 86 (1979) 214–30; M. L. Klein, *Genizah Manuscripts of the Palestinian Targum to the Pentateuch* (2 vols.; Cincinnati: HUC, 1986); J. Murphy-O'Connor, "The Judean Desert," *EJMI*, 126–28; S. Schecter and C. Taylor, *The Wisdom of Ben Sira: Portions of the Book Ecclesiasticus from Hebrew Manuscripts in the Cairo Genizah Collection Presented to the University of Cambridge by the Editors* (Cambridge: Cambridge University, 1899); S. Zeitlin, *The Zadokite Fragments: Facsimile of the Manuscripts in the Cairo Genizah Collection in the Possession of the University Library, Cambridge, England* (JQRMS 1; Philadelphia: Dropsie College, 1952).

DISCOVERIES IN THE JUDAEAN DESERT (DJD): J. M. Allegro, with A. A. Anderson, *Qumran Cave 4,I (4Q158–4Q186)* (DJD 5; Oxford: Clarendon, 1968); M. Baillet, *Qumran Grotte 4,III (4Q482–4Q520)* (DJD 7; Oxford: Clarendon, 1982); M. Baillet, J. T. Milik, and R. de Vaux, *Les 'Petites Grottes' de Qumrân: Exploration de la falaise, Les grottes 2Q, 3Q, 5Q, 6Q, 7Q à 10Q, Le rouleau de cuivre* (DJD 3; Oxford: Clarendon, 1962); D. Barthélemy and J. T. Milik, *Qumran Cave I* (DJD 1; Oxford: Clarendon, 1955); P. Benoit, J. T. Milik, and R. de Vaux, *Les grottes de Murabba'at* (DJD 2; Oxford: Clarendon, 1961); J. A. Sanders, *The Psalms Scroll of Qumran Cave 11 (11QPs^a)* (DJD 4; Oxford: Clarendon, 1965); E. Tov, with R. A. Kraft, *The Greek Minor Prophets Scroll from Nahal Hever (8HevXIIgr)* (DJD 8; The Seiyal Collection I; Oxford: Clarendon, 1990); R. de Vaux and J. T. Milik, *Qumran Grotte 4, II: I. Archéologie; II. Tefillin, mezuzot et targums (4Q128–4Q157)* (DJD 6; Oxford: Clarendon, 1977).

TRANSLATIONS OF THE DEAD SEA SCROLLS: M. Burrows, *The Dead Sea Scrolls* (New York: Viking, 1955); idem, *More Light on the Dead Sea Scrolls: New Scrolls and New Interpretations with Translations of Important Recent Discoveries* (New York: Viking, 1958); A. Dupont-Sommer, *EWQ*; T. H. Gaster, *DSSET*; M. A. Knibb, *The Qumran Community* (Cambridge and New York: Cambridge University, 1987); E. F. Sutcliffe, *The Monks of Qumran* (Westminster: Newman, 1960); G. Vermes, *The Dead Sea Scrolls in English* (London: Penguin; New York: Viking; 3d ed., 1987).

OTHER MAJOR WORKS: J. A. Fitzmyer and D. J. Harrington, *A Manual of Palestinian Aramaic Texts (Second Century B.C.–Second Century A.D.)* (BibOr 34; Rome: Pontifical Biblical Institute, 1978); K. G. Kuhn et al., *Konkordanz zu den Qumrantexten* (Göttingen: Vandenhoeck & Ruprecht, 1960) [augmented in *RevQ* 4 (1963–64) 163–234]; E. Lohse, *Die Texte aus Qumran: Hebräisch und deutsch, mit masoretischer Punktion, Übersetzung, Einführung und Anmerkungen* (2d ed.; Munich:

Kösel; Darmstadt: Wissenschaftliche Buchgesellschaft, 1971); E. Qimron, *The Hebrew of the Dead Sea Scrolls* (HSS 29; Atlanta: Scholars, 1986); E. L. Sukenik, *The Dead Sea Scrolls of the Hebrew University* (ed. N. Avigad and Y. Yadin; Jerusalem: Hebrew University and Magnes, 1955).

THEMES

In the introductory paragraphs above the point was made that the Dead Sea Scrolls provide valuable background information for NT study. In the paragraphs below a few of the major parallels between the Scrolls and John the Baptist and Jesus will be considered.

John the Baptist and Qumran. The discovery of the Qumran scrolls has raised again the question of John's possible relationship with the Essenes. There are at least six important parallels between the Baptist and Qumran: (1) Both John and Qumran appealed to Isaiah 40:3 ("The voice of one crying the wilderness, 'Prepare the way of the Lord' ") for their rationale for retreating to the wilderness (cf. 1QS 8:12–16; 9:19–20; Matt 3:1–3; Mark 1:2–4; Luke 3:2–6; John 1:23). John's upbringing in the wilderness (cf. Luke 1:80) allows for the possibility of his association with the wilderness community (cf. Josephus *J.W.* 2.8.2 §120: "The Essenes . . . adopt the children of others at a tender age in order to instruct them"). Essenes and Christians may have called their respective faiths "the Way" (1QS 9:17–18; Luke 20:21; Acts 9:2; 16:17; 18:26; cf. John 14:6) because of Isa 40:3. (2) Both John and Qumran called for repentance and practiced baptism (cf. 1QS 5:7–15; Pliny the Elder *Natural History* 5.17.4; Matt 3:5; Mark 1:4–5; Luke 3:7; John 1:25). (3) Both John and Qumran anticipated the imminent appearance of the kingdom of God (1QS 8:13–14; Matt 3:2; Mark 1:7). (4) John and Qumran employ similarly the words "water, spirit, and fire" (cf. 1QS 4:11–21; Matt 3:11–12; Mark 1:8; Luke 3:16; John 1:26; Isa 5:24). (5) John's strange diet may reflect the strict *kashruth* observed by the Essenes (cf. Josephus *J.W.* 2.8.8 §143 ["he cannot share the food of others . . . he eats grass"]; 2.8.10 §152; CD 6:17; Matt 3:4 ["locusts and wild honey"]; 11:18 ["John came neither eating nor drinking"]; Mark 1:6; Luke 1:15). (6) John's harsh criticism of the religious leaders (Matt 3:7–9: "You brood of vipers . . .") coheres with harsh epithets frequently found in the writings of Qumran (1QpHab 2:1–2 ["Man of Lies"]; 8:8 ["Wicked Priest"]; 10:9 ["Preacher of Lies"]; 1QS 9:16 ["men of the Pit"]; 9:17 ["men of perversity"]; 1QM 1:1 ["sons of darkness"]; 15:2–3 ["host of Belial"]).

The possibility that John was at one time an Essene is important, since Jesus in all likelihood had himself been a disciple or an associate of John. The writings of Qumran, therefore, in all probability are vital for understanding the ministry of John and perhaps aspects of the ministry of Jesus.

Bibliography: O. Betz, "Was John the Baptist an Essene?" *BibRev* 6/6 (1990) 18–25; W. H. Brownlee, "John the Baptist in the New Light of Ancient Scrolls," *Int* 9 (1955) 71–90; repr. in K. Stendahl, ed., *The Scrolls and the New Testament* (London: SCM, 1958) 33–53, 252–56; S. L. Davies, "John the Baptist and Essene Kashruth," *NTS* 29 (1983) 569–71; A. S. Geyser, "The Youth of John the Baptist," *NovT* 1 (1956) 70–75; S. Mason, *Josephus and the New Testament* (Peabody, Hendrickson Publishers, 1992); J. A. T. Robinson, "The Baptism of John and the Qumran Community," *HTR* 50 (1957) 175–91; repr. in Robinson, *Twelve New Testament Studies* (SBT 1/34; London: SCM, 1962) 11–27.

Jesus and Qumran. There are five suggestive similarities between the teachings and ministry of Jesus and those of Qumran. (1) Jesus was critical of an avaricious and oppressive temple establishment (Mark 12:38–13:2). So were the members of Qumran (1QpHab 8:11–12; 9:4–5; 10:1). (2) Both Jesus and Qumran apparently opposed the annual half-shekel temple tax (Matt 17:24–27; 4QOrd[a] 2:6–8), which, much to the consternation of some rabbis, the priests themselves did not pay (*m. Šeqal.* 1:4). Jesus may also have questioned the temple establishment's role in assisting Rome in the collection of imperial taxes (Mark 12:13–17; Luke 23:2). (3) Both Jesus and Qumran interpreted Gen 1:27 in such a way as to forbid divorce and remarriage (Matt 19:4; Mark 10:6; CD 4:20–5:2). (4) Both Jesus and Qumran spoke in terms of spiritual offerings, as opposed to literal animal offerings (Matt 9:13; 12:7 [cf. Hos 6:6]; Mark 12:28–34; 4QFlor 1:6–7; cf. Philo *Quod Omnis Probus Liber sit* 12 §75; Josephus *Ant.* 18.1.5 §19). Compare also Paul's statement in Rom 12:1: "present your bodies as a living sacrifice, holy and acceptable to God, which is your spiritual worship." (5) Both Jesus and Qumran thought of God's people as constituting a "spiritual temple" (Matt 12:6; Mark 14:58; John 2:19–21). Jesus' teaching probably underlies Paul's description of Christians as the "temple of the Holy Spirit" (2 Cor 6:16; cf. 1 Pet 2:4–5).

Bibliography: L. Gaston, *No Stone on Another: Studies in the Significance of the Fall of Jerusalem in the Synoptic Gospels* (NovTSup 23; Leiden: Brill, 1970) 127–28, 164; W. S. LaSor, *The Dead Sea Scrolls and the New Testament* (Grand Rapids: Eerdmans, 1972) 206–46; E. P. Sanders, *Jesus and Judaism* (Philadelphia: Fortress, 1985) 84.

GENERAL BIBLIOGRAPHY: M. Black, *The Scrolls and Christian Origins: Studies in the Jewish Background of the New Testament* (BJS 48; Chico: Scholars, 1983); idem, ed., *The Scrolls and Christianity* (London: SPCK, 1969); G. J. Brooke, "The Biblical Texts in the Qumran Commentaries: Scribal Errors or Exegetical Variants?" in C. A. Evans and W. F. Stinespring, eds., *Early Jewish and Christian Exegesis* (W. H. Brownlee Festschrift; Homage 10; Atlanta: Scholars, 1987) 85–100; idem, *Exegesis at Qumran: 4QFlorilegium in its Jewish Context* (JSOTSup 29; Sheffield, JSOT, 1985); W. H. Brownlee, "The Background of Biblical Interpretation at Qumran," in M. Delcor, ed., *Qumran: Sa piété, sa théologie et son milieu* (BETL 46; Paris: Duculot; Leuven: University of Louvain, 1978) 183–93; idem, *The Meaning of the Qumran Scrolls for the Bible with Special Attention to the Book of Isaiah* (New York: Oxford University, 1964); F. F. Bruce, *Biblical Exegesis in the Qumran Texts* (Grand Rapids: Eerdmans, 1959); J. H. Charlesworth, ed., *Graphic Concordance to the Dead Sea*

Scrolls (Louisville: Westminster / John Knox, 1992); F. M. Cross, Jr., *The Ancient Library of Qumran and Modern Biblical Studies* (rev. ed.; Garden City: Doubleday, 1961; repr. Grand Rapids: Baker, 1980); M. Fishbane, "Use, Authority and Interpretation of Mikra at Qumran," *Mikra*, 339–77; C. A. Evans, "Opposition to the Temple: Jesus and the Dead Sea Scrolls," in J. H. Charlesworth, ed., *Jesus and the Dead Sea Scrolls* (ABRL; New York: Doubleday, 1992) 235–53; J. A. Fitzmyer, "The Dead Sea Scrolls," *HBD*, 915–17; D. Flusser, *Judaism and the Origins of Christianity* (Jerusalem: Magnes, 1988) 3–225; W. S. LaSor, *The Dead Sea Scrolls and the New Testament* (Grand Rapids: Eerdmans, 1972); S. Mason, *Josephus and the New Testament* (Peabody, Hendrickson Publishers, 1992); J. Murphy-O'Connor and J. H. Charlesworth, eds., *Paul and the Dead Sea Scrolls* (New York: Crossroad, 1990); L. Rost, *Judaism Outside the Hebrew Canon: An Introduction to the Documents* (Nashville: Abingdon, 1976) 155–90; J. A. Sanders, "Palestinian Manuscripts 1947–1967," *JBL* 86 (1967) 431–44; idem, "Palestinian Manuscripts 1947–1972," *JJS* 24 (1973) 74–83.

CHAPTER FOUR

VERSIONS OF THE OLD TESTAMENT

HEBREW	GREEK
Masoretic Text	Septuagint
Samaritan Pentateuch	Recensions
Dead Sea Scrolls	SYRIAC
LATIN	Peshitta
Old Latin	
Vulgate	

Study of the versions of the OT is essential not only for determining the most primitive reading of the text, but also for determining the range of possible readings available to the NT authors. The versions themselves often yield valuable clues as to how a given passage of Scripture was understood.

The versions treated in this chapter represent several languages: Hebrew, Greek, Latin, and Syriac. Most of these languages are represented by more than one recension. (Because of their special features the Aramaic versions, known as the targums, are treated in a separate chapter; see chap. 6.) This field of study is therefore very complex. The purpose of this chapter, in keeping with the overall purpose of the present book, is to provide the reader with a basic overview. Those interested in pursuing matters further are directed to the major scholarly works, mostly in English, which are cited in the respective bibliographies.

SUMMARIES

Hebrew. When scholars speak of versions of the OT, they usually have in mind the Septuagint or the Vulgate, but not the Hebrew. In view of the plethora of Hebrew manuscripts that have been uncovered this century (e.g., the Cairo Genizah Fragments and the Dead Sea Scrolls) and the increasing evidence of the pluralism of the biblical text in the first century, it is probably better to regard all of the extant materials as versions. The Hebrew may have been the original language in which most of the OT was written, but it is extant today in at least three distinct Hebrew traditions: the Masoretic Text (MT), the Samaritan Pentateuch (SP), and thousands of fragments from Qumran and the Cairo Genizah. It is clear that no one of these extant traditions represents the exact original form. Therefore, it is appropriate to speak of all of these traditions, including the MT, as versions of the OT.

Masoretic Text. The official version of the OT for Judaism and Christianity since the early Middle Ages is the MT. (Of course, only for Christians is the Hebrew Bible the "OT"; for Jews it is the Bible, Mikra, or Tanak.) This version is called the MT because the scribes who preserved, edited, and pointed (i.e., added vowel signs, accents, and punctuation of a sort) it were called the Masoretes. Their notes are called the Masora. (Masora/Masoretic can be spelled with one *s* or with two, depending on which of two etymologies one thinks relates to the word.) The Western Masoretes are from Palestine, the Eastern Masoretes from Babylon. The Masoretic tradition probably originated in the late first or early second century. The Masora provides an interesting and complex array of sigla, whereby the scribes (or sopherim) noted their alterations of or reservations about this passage or that. Best known is *ketib/qere* ("written"/ "spoken"). In these cases, reluctant to change the written text, the scribes wrote in the margin what should be read aloud. The Masora *marginalis* is the material written in the four margins of the page. The Masora *finalis* represents an alphabetical compilation at the end of the OT. The Masora *parva* ("small Masora") is found in the side margins, while the Masora *magna* ("large Masora") is found at the top and bottom margins. The oldest MT manuscripts date from the late ninth century C.E. (e.g., Codex Cairensis [C] on the Prophets). No complete manuscript is earlier than the tenth century (e.g., the Aleppo Codex). Fragments from the Cairo Genizah date from the sixth (possibly fifth) to the eighth centuries.

The principal text is that edited by R. Kittel, *Biblia Hebraica* (with P. Kahle; Stuttgart: Württembergische Bibelanstalt, 1968), and the more recent edition by K. Elliger and W. Rudolph, *Biblia Hebraica Stuttgartensia* (Stuttgart: Deutsche Bibelgesellschaft, 1983). A smaller and less expensive edition has been produced by N. H. Snaith, *Tora, Nebi'im, Ketubim* (London: British and Foreign Bible Society, 1958). The standard concordance is G. Lisowsky, *Konkordanz zum hebräischen Alten Testament* (2d ed.; Stuttgart: Württembergische Bibelanstalt, 1958). A series of volumes devoted to the textual variants is being prepared by D. Barthélemy, ed., *Critique textuelle de l'Ancien Testament* (OBO 50; Fribourg: Editions Universitaires; Göttingen: Vandenhoeck & Ruprecht, 1982–). Two volumes have appeared: vol. 1 (OBO 50/1; 1982), which covers Joshua, Judges, Ruth, Samuel, Kings, Chronicles, Ezra, Nehemiah, and Esther; vol. 2 (OBO 50/2; 1986), which covers Isaiah, Jeremiah, and Lamentations. One more volume is anticipated for the Minor Prophets, and two additional volumes will treat the Pentateuch and the poetic books. For a discussion of the materials and principles see D. Barthélemy, ed., *Preliminary and Interim Report on the Hebrew Old Testament Project* (5 vols.; New York: United Bible Societies, 1973–80). The best ETs are the RSV, NRSV, and NASB.

Samaritan Pentateuch. As a distinct recension the Samaritan Pentateuch (SP) probably owes its origin to the schism in the second century B.C.E. There are 150 manuscripts of the SP, many nothing more than fragments, and most in Hebrew, though some Aramaic and Arabic are found. What makes the SP interesting is that in approximately 1,900 places it agrees with the LXX over against the MT. In some places it agrees with the NT over against both the LXX and the MT (e.g., Acts 7:4, 32). There are some fragments of the Pentateuch at Qumran reflecting a form of the text on which the SP was apparently based (cf. 4QpaleoExod^{m14}; 4Q158^{15}; 4Q364; 4QNum^b; 4QDeut^{n19}; 4Q175). The rabbis may have known of the SP: "Said Rabbi Eleazar ben R. Simeon, 'I stated to Samaritan scribes, "You have forged your own Torah, and it has done you no good" ' " (*y. Soṭa* 7.3).

S. Noja has argued that the SP was translated into Greek as the *Samareiticon,* a version which Origen often cited. Fragments of the *Samareiticon* survive in a fourth-century manuscript. Could this explain the agreements with the book of Acts, whose author likely did not know Hebrew? E. Tov disagrees, saying the evidence points only to a version of the LXX edited by the Samaritans. But others disagree with Tov.

The Samaritans awaited a Taheb, a sort of redeemer modeled after the prophet-like-Moses of Deut 18:15–19. It is perhaps because of this emphasis that Deut 18:18–22 has been inserted into Exod 20:22. The command to build an altar at Mount Gerizim is added to Exod 20:17, and the reading "Gerizim" in place of "Ebal" appears in Deut 27:4. Origen, Eusebius of Caesarea, Epiphanius, and Cyril of Jerusalem knew of the SP. Jerome used it in preparing his Latin translation of the Pentateuch.

The text of the SP has been edited by A. F. von Gall, *Der hebräische Pentateuch der Samaritaner* (5 vols.; Giessen: Töpelmann, 1914–18; repr. Berlin: Töpelmann, 1963–66). There is no ET.

Dead Sea Scrolls. The discovery of the Dead Sea Scrolls, both those of Qumran and those of Murabba'at and Masada, witnesses to the Hebrew text dating from the turn of the era. Probably best known is the Great Isaiah Scroll (1QIsa^a). Other than this scroll, the fragmentary texts of the pesharim (from caves 1 and 4), and a few other fragments, the bulk of the biblical materials have not been published. For a summary of the materials see J. A. Fitzmyer (bib. below) and chap. 3. For an assessment of the implications of the Dead Sea Scrolls for the biblical text see F. M. Cross and S. Talmon (bib. below).

Bibliography: R. T. Anderson, "Samaritan Pentateuch: General Account," in A. D. Crown, ed., *The Samaritans* (Tübingen: Mohr [Siebeck], 1989) 390–96; F. M. Cross and S. Talmon, eds., *Qumran and the History of the Biblical Text* (Cambridge: Harvard University, 1975); F. E. Deist, *Towards the Text of the Old Testament* (Pretoria: DR Church, 1978); A. Dotan, "Masorah," *EncJud* 16.1401–82; J. A. Fitzmyer, *The Dead Sea Scrolls: Major Publications and Tools for Study* (SBLRBS 20, rev. ed.; Atlanta: Scholars, 1990); M. Gertner, "The Masorah and the Levites," *VT* 10 (1960) 241–84; M. J. Mulder, "The Transmission of the Biblical Text," *Mikra*, 87–135; S. Noja, "The Samareitikon," in Crown, ed., *The Samaritans*, 408–12; J. D. Purvis, *The Samaritan Pentateuch and the Origin of the Samaritan Sect* (HSM 2; Cambridge: Harvard University, 1968); S. Talmon, "Old Testament Text," in P. R. Ackroyd and C. F. Evans, eds., *Cambridge History of the Bible* 1 (Cambridge: Cambridge University, 1970) 159–99; idem, "The Samaritan Pentateuch," *JJS* 2 (1951) 144–50; E. Tov, "Pap. Giessen 13, 19, 22, 26: A Revision of the LXX?" *RB* 78 (1971) 355–83; idem, "Proto-Samaritan Texts and the Samaritan Pentateuch," in Crown, ed., *The Samaritans*, 397–407; idem, "Une inscription Grecque d'origine Samaritaine trouvée à Thessalonique," *RB* 81 (1974) 394–99; B. Waltke, "The Samaritan Pentateuch and the Text of the Old Testament," in J. B. Payne, ed., *New Perspectives on the Old Testament* (Dallas: Word, 1970) 212–39; G. E. Weil, *Initiation à la Massorah* (Leiden: Brill, 1964).

Septuagint. The Septuagint (from the Latin *septuaginta*, "seventy") is the Greek translation of the OT (including the Apocrypha) and is abbreviated as LXX, the roman numeral for seventy. The name comes from the legend found in the pseudepigraphal *Letter of Aristeas* (see chap. 2), in which it is claimed that King Ptolemy II Philadelphus (285–247 B.C.E.) commissioned for the royal library seventy-two Palestinian scribes to translate the Hebrew Pentateuch into Greek. In isolation on the island of Pharos the scribes finished the task in seventy-two days. The story is recounted by Josephus (cf. *Ant.* 12.2.1 §11–12.2.15 §118). Philo himself accepted the story and regarded the translation as inspired, given, as it were, by divine dictation (cf. *Life of Moses* 2.7 §37), a view that came to be held by many of the early Fathers of the Christian church.

For several reasons the legendary account of Aristeas cannot be accepted. Although the date of the LXX, at least as it concerns the Pentateuch, may be as ancient as *Aristeas* purports, the reason for the translation was to make the Bible more readily accessible to the Greek-speaking Jews of Alexandria. The remaining portions of the Bible were translated in succeeding generations, perhaps not being completed until the first century C.E. Evidently several translators were involved in this long process, for the style varies from one book to another.

The LXX is an important pre-MT witness. Some of its readings that differ from the MT agree with readings found in the Dead Sea Scrolls. Some of its differing readings appear in the NT, whose authors follow the

LXX in more than one-half of their quotations of the OT. The diversity of the first-century Greek OT text has been documented by the discovery and publication of 8HevXIIgr, a fragmentary Greek scroll of the Minor Prophets (see Tov in bib.). This text differs from the LXX at several points, and agrees with at least three of the recensions (Aquila, Symmachus, and Theodotion) at several points.

The principal text of the LXX is A. Rahlfs, *Septuaginta* (2 vols.; Stuttgart: Württembergische Bibelanstalt, 1935). A multi-volume critical edition has been edited by A. Rahlfs, J. Ziegler et al., *Septuaginta: Vetus Testamentum Graecum* (Göttingen: Vandenhoeck & Ruprecht, 1931–). This work is not yet finished. The standard concordance is E. Hatch and H. A. Redpath, *A Concordance to the Septuagint and the Other Greek Versions of the OT* (2 vols.; Oxford: Clarendon, 1897; repr. Grand Rapids: Baker Book House, 1983). There is an old ET of the LXX by L. C. L. Brenton, *The Septuagint with Apocrypha: Greek and English* (London: Bagster, 1851; repr. Peabody: Hendrickson, 1986).

Bibliography: S. P. Brock, C. T. Fritsch, and S. Jellicoe, *A Classified Bibliography of the Septuagint* (ALGHJ 6; Leiden: Brill, 1973); F. C. Conybeare and St. G. Stock, *Grammar of Septuagint Greek* (Boston: Ginn, 1905; repr. Peabody: Hendrickson, 1989); P. Churgin, "The Targum and the Septuagint," *AJSL* 50 (1933) 41–65; D. Hill, *Greek Words and Hebrew Meanings* (SNTSMS 5; Cambridge: Cambridge University, 1967); S. Jellicoe, *The Septuagint and Modern Study* (Oxford: Oxford University, 1968); idem, *Studies in the Septuagint: Origins, Recensions and Interpretations* (New York: Ktav, 1974); R. W. Klein, *Textual Criticism of the Old Testament: The Septuagint after Qumran* (Philadelphia: Fortress, 1974); A. J. Saldarini, "Septuagint," *HBD*, 925; I. L. Seeligman, *The Septuagint Version of Isaiah: A Discussion of Its Problems* (Leiden: Brill, 1948); A. Sperber, "NT and the Septuagint," *JBL* 59 (1940) 193–293; H. B. Swete, *An Introduction to the Old Testament in Greek* (2d ed. rev. by R. R. Ottley; Cambridge: Cambridge University, 1914; repr. Peabody: Hendrickson, 1989); H. St. J. Thackeray, *A Grammar of the Old Testament in Greek according to the Septuagint* (Cambridge: Cambridge University, 1909; repr. 1970); E. Tov, *A Classified Bibliography of Lexical and Grammatical Studies on the Language of the Septuagint* (rev. ed.; Jerusalem: Academon, 1982); idem, *The Greek Minor Prophets Scroll from Nahal Hever (8HevXIIgr)* (DJD 8; Oxford: Clarendon, 1990); idem, "The Septuagint," *Mikra*, 161–88; idem and R. A. Kraft, "Septuagint," *IDBSup* (1976) 807–15; P. Walters, *The Text of the Septuagint: Its Corruptions and Their Emendations* (ed. D. W. Gooding; Cambridge: Cambridge University, 1973).

Greek Recensions. For various reasons, several recensions of the LXX were produced in the second and third centuries C.E. The oldest was by Aquila, who may have been a disciple of Rabbi Aqiba and who may be the Onqelos associated with the Pentateuch targum of that name (cf. *b. Git.* 56b; *b. Meg.* 3a). Aquila's Greek recension, which is really a new, woodenly literal translation of the Hebrew text, was published ca. 130 C.E. His recension survives in quotations, Hexaplaric fragments, and on a few sixth-century palimpsests. Symmachus produced a recension ca. 170 C.E. that represented a much more stylish Greek than that of Aquila.

According to Eusebius and Jerome, Symmachus was a Jewish Christian, but according to Epiphanius he was a Samaritan who had converted to Judaism. His work survives in a few Hexapla fragments. Following the Hebrew text Theodotion revised the LXX (or at least a Greek text that was very similar) sometime toward the end of the second century. Only fragments of Theodotion's translation are extant (principally in quotations). Scholars are beginning to think that what had passed as Theodotion's version of Daniel, which had all but displaced the LXX version, may not be Theodotionic after all.

There are three other recensions, all later, that we know of. Best known is Origen's Hexapla. His six parallel columns contained: (1) the Hebrew text, (2) the Hebrew text transliterated with Greek letters, (3) Aquila, (4) Symmachus, (5) the LXX (with readings distinctly Origen's), and (6) Theodotion. Origen also produced the Tetrapla, which contained only the Greek versions. For the most part all that remains of this great work are fragments. However, there are a few manuscripts that preserve Origen's version of the LXX. There is also a Syriac translation of it known as the Syro-Hexapla. The best source for the fragments of these recensions is F. Field, *Origenis Hexapla* (2 vols.; Hildesheim: Georg Olms, 1964). Finally, according to Jerome there were two other recensions, those by Lucian and Hesychius. Of the latter we know nothing. Of the former we know that he had been a presbyter from Antioch (d. 312). His recension survives in the quotations of Chrysostom and Theodoret of Cyrrhus and in several miniscules.

Bibliography: D. Barthélemy, *Les Devanciers d'Aquila* (VTSup 10; Leiden: Brill, 1962); D. W. Gooding, *Recensions of the Septuagint Pentateuch* (London: Tyndale, 1955); K. G. O'Connell, "Greek Versions," *IDBSup* (1976) 377–81; B. M. Metzger, "Lucian and the Lucianic Recension of the Greek Bible," *NTS* 8 (1962) 189–203; J. Reider and N. Turner, *An Index to Aquila* (VTSup 12; Leiden: Brill, 1966); E. Tov, "The Septuagint," *Mikra*, 181–87.

Old Latin. The Old Latin (OL) survives in fragmentary manuscripts, liturgical books, and quotations of early Latin Fathers (e.g., Tertullian, Cyprian, Ambrose). A few books survive in complete form as part of the Vulgate (Baruch, Epistle of Jeremiah, Wisdom, Sirach, 1 and 2 Maccabees). Jerome did not edit these books because he regarded them as uninspired (principally because they were not extant in Hebrew or Aramaic, and because they were not as ancient as the other books). The OL represents various translations of the LXX. The value of the OL is that it witnesses to the text of the LXX before the influences of the Greek recensions. It also includes the NT.

A multi-volume critical edition of the OL has been undertaken by B. Fischer and others, *Vetus Latina: Die Reste der altlateinischen Bibel, nach Petrus Sabatier neu gesammelt und herausgegeben von der Erzabtei Beuron* (Freiburg: Herder, 1949–). The work is not yet complete. Each volume appears a fascicle at a time over a period of years. Some of the volumes released include Genesis by Fischer (vol. 2, 1951–54), Ephesians by H. J. Frede (vol. 24/1, 1962–64), Philippians and Colossians by Frede (vol. 24/2, 1966–71), and the Catholic Epistles by W. Thiele (vol. 26/1, 1956–69). For an example see W. Thiele, *Vetus Latina* 11/1: *Sapientia Salomonis* (4 fascicles; Freiburg: Herder, 1977–80).

Vulgate. In 382 Pope Damascus I commissioned Jerome to prepare a reliable Latin translation of the Bible. Despite Augustine's protests, Jerome based the OT translation on the Hebrew, having for years studied Hebrew in Bethlehem. (See Jerome's letter to Pope Damascus [*Epistles* 18, ca. 381], where he defends the priority of the Hebrew over the Greek.) This work became the official Bible of the church, and eventually became known as the "Vulgate" (meaning "common"). It was not, however, until the ninth century that Jerome's version finally displaced the popular OL. The reluctance of many of the church's theologians to depart from the OL was because, unlike the Vulgate, it was dependent upon the LXX, regarded by many (e.g., Augustine) as divinely inspired. The major value of the Vulgate is that it represents an early witness to the Hebrew text.

The principal edition of the Vulgate is by R. Weber, ed., *Biblia Sacra iuxta Vulgatam Versionem* (3d ed., 2 vols.; Stuttgart: Deutsche Bibel-gesellschaft, 1985). There are various ETs available. An old classic is the Douay-Rheims, so called because it combines the Douay ET of the OT (1609) with the Rheims ET of the NT (1582): *The Holy Bible Translated from the Latin Vulgate* (New York: P. J. Kennedy & Sons, 1914). A multi-volume critical edition has also been produced by the Benedictine Order, *Biblia Sacra iuxta Latinam Vulgatam Versionem* (16 vols.; Rome: Typis Polyglottis Vaticanis, 1926–81). For a concordance see B. Fischer, ed., *Novae Concordantiae Bibliorum Sacrorum iuxta Vulgatam Versionem critice editam quas digessit* (5 vols.; Stuttgart: Frommann-Halzboog, 1977).

Bibliography: J. Barr, "St. Jerome and the Sounds of Hebrew," *JSS* 12 (1967) 1–36; idem, "St. Jerome's Appreciation of Hebrew," *BJRL* 49 (1966–67) 281–302; B. Kedar, "The Latin Translations," *Mikra*, 299–338; H. F. D. Sparks, "Jerome as Biblical Scholar," in P. R. Ackroyd and C. F. Evans, eds., *Cambridge History of the Bible* 1 (Cambridge: Cambridge University, 1970) 510–41; W. Schwarz, *Principles and Problems of Biblical Translation* (Cambridge: Cambridge University, 1955) 25–37.

The Peshitta. The Syriac version of the Bible came to be called the Peshitta (or Peshitto), which means "simple" (compare the Aramaic word *pešîtā*, "plain [meaning]"). One of the oldest manuscripts is MS Add. 14,425 of the British Museum (containing the Pentateuch, minus Leviticus), which is dated 464 C.E. The origin of the Peshitta is obscure. Scholars are now aware of this version's close relationship to the targums. In one case the targum (i.e., Proverbs Targum) may actually depend on the Peshitta. In all other cases, however, the relationship appears to be the reverse: the Peshitta relies on the targum. My own work on Isaiah 6 suggests that the Peshitta is dependent on both the Isaiah Targum and the LXX. Several Syriac words reflect distinctive targumic readings (esp. "forgive" in v. 10), on the one hand, and even syntax and words from the LXX (e.g., *gyr*, "for" in v. 10), on the other. Similar examples could be offered from other portions of Syriac Isaiah.

The principal edition of the Peshitta is A. M. Ceriani, *Translatio Syra Pescitto Veteris Testamenti ex Codex Ambrosiano II* (Milan: Impensis Bibliothecae Ambrosianae, 1876–83). A critical edition has been sponsored by the Peshitta Institute of Leiden on behalf of the International Organization for the Study of the Old Testament. The text has been divided into four major parts, with two or more fascicles making up each part: Genesis and Exodus (1/1a; 1977); Leviticus–Joshua (1/2, 2/1b; 1990); Judges and Samuel (2/2; 1978); Kings (2/4; 1976); Isaiah (3/1; 1987); Jeremiah (3/2; forthcoming); Ezekiel (3/3; 1985); the Minor Prophets, Daniel, and Bel and Dragon (3/4; 1980); the Psalms (2/3; 1980); Proverbs, Wisdom, Ecclesiastes, and Song of Songs (2/5; 1979); *Apocalypse of Baruch* and 4 Esdras (4/3; 1973); *Odes*, Prayer of Manasseh, apocryphal psalms, *Psalms of Solomon*, Tobit, and 3 Esdras (4/6; 1972). For an example see S. P. Brock, *Isaiah* (Vetus Testamentum Syriace 3/1; Leiden: Brill, 1987). Several fascicles are still in preparation. An ET of the Syriac Bible (based on Codex Ambrosianus) has been produced by G. Lamsa, *The Holy Bible from Ancient Manuscripts* (Nashville: Holman Bible Publishers, 1957). The standard lexicon is R. Payne Smith, *A Compendius Syriac Dictionary* (Oxford: Clarendon, 1903; repr. 1976).

Bibliography: W. Baars, *New Syro-Hexaplaric Texts: Edited, Commented upon and Compared with the Septuagint* (Leiden: Brill, 1968); P. A. H. de Boer and W. Baars, *The Old Testament in Syriac according to the Peshitta Version* (Leiden: Brill, 1972); F. C. Burkitt, *Early Eastern Christianity* (New York: Dutton, 1904) [argues that the Peshitta derives from the first century C.E.]; P. B. Dirksen, "The Old Testament Peshitta," *Mikra*, 255–97; C. A. Evans, *To See and Not Perceive: Isaiah 6.9–10 in Early Jewish and Christian Interpretation* (JSOTSup 64; Sheffield: JSOT, 1989) 77–80, 195; J. H. Hospers, "The Present-Day State of Research on the Pesitta (since 1948)," in T. P. van Baaren et al., eds., *Verbum* (H. W. Obbink Festschrift; STR-T 6; Utrecht: Kemink, 1964) 148–56; idem, "Some Remarks with regard to the Text and Language of the Old Testament Peshitta," in W. C. Delsman et al., eds., *Von Kanaan bis Kerala* (J. P. M. van der Ploeg Festschrift; Neukirchen-Vluyn: Neukirchener Verlag, 1982) 443–55; S. Isenberg, "Jewish-Palestinian Origins of the Peshitta," *JBL* 90 (1971) 69–81; G. A. Kiraz, *A Computer-Generated Concordance to the Syriac New Testament* (6 vols.; Leiden; New York: Brill, forthcoming); J. P. M. van der Ploeg, "The Peshitta of the Old Testament," in J. Vellian, ed., *The Malabar Church* (OCA 186; Rome: Pont Institutum Orientalium Studiorum, 1970) 23–32.

THEMES

Textual Criticism. Several of the above versions appear to be represented by the numerous quotations of the OT in the writings of the NT.

In some cases one particular version serves the NT writer's purposes better than the others. The second example below will illustrate this point. Sometimes the versions are also helpful in determining the antiquity, if not original form, of a given reading. The first and third examples not only illustrate how the versions contribute to OT textual criticism, they also help clear up problems involving the NT itself.

Deuteronomy 32:43. In Rom 15:10 Paul quotes part of Deut 32:43 ("Rejoice, O Gentiles, with his people") according to the LXX and not the MT. Similarly, in Heb 1:6 the author cites another line from Deuteronomy's Song of Moses (cf. Deut 32:1–43) and applies it to Jesus: "Let all the angels of God worship him." The quotation is again taken from the LXX (perhaps from the parallel *Odes* 2:43 or LXX Ps 96:7 ["Worship him, all his angels"], rather than Deut 32:43). Again, however, the MT has no Hebrew equivalent, nor do the Pentateuch targums. Are the clauses in LXX Deut 32:43 later scribal glosses? Have the NT writers followed a Greek tradition that has no basis in the Hebrew original? Probably not. 4QDeuteronomy[a] provides a Hebrew reading that comes very close to what the LXX translator may have been looking at: "Rejoice, O heavens, with him; and worship him, sons of God. Let all the sons of God praise him. Rejoice, O Gentiles, with his people. . . ." The presence in the Hebrew of "sons of God," instead of "angels," presents no difficulty, since the LXX sometimes translates "gods" (*'elōhîm*) as "angels" (cf. Pss 8:5; 96[97]:7) and "sons of the gods" (*benê 'elōhîm*) as "angels" (cf. Job 38:7). It is likely that 4QDeut[a] provides the original reading, which the MT in this instance has omitted through a scribal error.

Isaiah 6:9–10. According to Mark 4:11–12 Jesus tells parables "in order that" (*hina*) those who see will not perceive and those who hear will not understand, "lest they repent and be forgiven" (cf. Isa 6:9–10). Jesus has alluded to a version of Isaiah that approximates what we now find in the Isaiah Targum (see esp. "forgive" in v. 10). Seemingly he stated that the purpose of his parables was to keep "outsiders" in the dark. This seems to be the basic idea of the Isaiah Targum as well. There the prophet is to speak to those "people who hear but do not listen, and see but do not understand." The prophet is to "Make dull their heart and make heavy their ears." In other words, according to the Targum, the prophet is to harden only those who do not listen (i.e., the "outsiders"). This differs from the way it reads in the MT, in which the prophet is to harden the whole people. The Marcan passage has struck interpreters, ancient and modern, as very strange. Matthew, one of the first interpreters of this passage, paraphrased the text this way: "I speak parables to them, because [*hoti*] seeing they do not see and hearing they do not understand. And the prophecy of Isaiah is fulfilled which says, 'You will indeed hear but not understand . . . for the heart of this people has become fat . . .' " (Matt 13:13–15). Matthew has changed Mark's *hina* to *hoti*, from "in order that" to "because," and so has changed the idea of purpose to that of cause. He then reinforces his alteration by citing the LXX version of Isa 6:9–10 verbatim. For his part Luke abbreviates the Marcan passage (cf. Luke 8:10), omitting the offensive "lest they repent" clause. At the conclusion of Acts he will cite verbatim the full text of LXX Isa 6:9–10 (cf. Acts 28:26–27). John also quotes Isa 6:10, though in a completely different context: "He has blinded their eyes and hardened their heart . . . lest they should . . . turn for me to heal them" (John 12:40). Earlier John may have paraphrased Isa 6:9 in John 9:39: "I came into this world, in order that [*hina*] those who do not see should see, and those who see should become blind." Interpreters are undecided as to which OT version the Fourth Evangelist has followed. Some think that he has produced a free translation of the Hebrew. Thus, what we have in the four Gospels in this one instance are two (the Aramaic and the Greek) and possibly three (the Hebrew) OT versions represented in their respective quotations of a single OT passage.

Isaiah 6:13. Because the final clause of Isa 6:13 ("a holy seed is its stump") is missing in the LXX, some scholars have viewed its presence in the MT as a later scribal gloss. (Aquila and Symmachus retain it, while Origen and Theodotion mark it off with asterisks.) The fact that this clause is present in the Targum and Vulgate does not prove authenticity, only antiquity. But its presence in 1QIsaᵃ argues strongly for its antiquity, if not its authenticity. It seems better to view the absence of the clause in the LXX as due to scribal homoioteleuton, that is, an error of jumping from one place in the text to another that follows the same word or a word with a similar ending. In this case, the Greek scribe apparently jumped (parablepsis) from the *autēs* of 6:13b to 7:1, thus omitting the line containing *autēs* at the end of 6:13c.

Bibliography: W. F. Albright, "New Light on Early Recensions of the Hebrew Bible," *BASOR* 140 (1955) 32–33 [on 4QDeutᵃ]; J. A. Emerton, "The Translation and Interpretation of Isaiah vi. 13," in J. A. Emerton and S. C. Reif, eds., *Interpreting the Bible* (E. I. J. Rosenthal Festschrift; UCOP 32; Cambridge: Cambridge University, 1982) 85–118; C. A. Evans, *To See and Not Perceive: Isaiah 6.9–10 in Early Jewish and Christian Interpretation* (JSOTSup 64; Sheffield: JSOT, 1989); P. W. Skehan, "A Fragment of the 'Song of Moses' (Deut 32) from Qumran," *BASOR* 136 (1954) 12–15.

GENERAL BIBLIOGRAPHY: K. and B. Aland, *Der Text des Neuen Testaments* (Stuttgart: Deutsche Bibelgesellschaft, 1981); ET: *The Text of the New Testament* (Leiden: Brill; rev. ed.; Grand Rapids: Eerdmans, 1989); F. G. Kenyon, *The Text of the Greek Bible* (London: Gerald Duckworth, 1950); B. J. Roberts, *The Old Testament Text and Versions: The Hebrew Text in Transmission and the History of the Ancient Versions* (Cardiff: University of Wales, 1951); A. Sundberg, *The Old Testament of the Early Church* (HTS 20; Cambridge: Harvard University, 1964); J. Weingreen, *Introduction to the Critical Study of the Text of the Hebrew Bible* (Oxford: Clarendon, 1982); E. Würthwein, *Der Text des Alten Testaments* (4th ed.; Stuttgart: Württembergische Bibelanstalt, 1973); ET: *The Text of the Old Testament* (Grand Rapids: Eerdmans, 1979).

CHAPTER FIVE

PHILO AND JOSEPHUS

PHILO

*1. De Opificio Mundi (On the Creation
  of the World)
  Legum Allegoriae (Allegories of
  the Law)
2. De Cherubim (On the Cherubim)
  De Sacrificiis Abelis et Caini (On
  the Sacrifices of Abel and Cain)
  Quod Deterius Potiori insidiari solet
  (The Worse Attacks the Better)
  De Posteritate Caini (On the
  Posterity of Cain)
  De Gigantibus (On the Giants)
3. Quod Deus immutabilis sit (On
  the Unchangeableness of God)
  De Agricultura (On Agriculture)
  De Plantatione (On Planting)
  De Ebrietate (On Drunkenness)
  De Sobrietate (On Sobriety)
4. De Confusione Linguarum (On the
  Confusion of the Languages)
  De Migratione Abrahami (On the
  Migration of Abraham)
  Quis Rerum Divinarum Heres
  (Who Is the Heir?)
  De Congressu quaerendae
  Eruditionis gratia (On the
  Preliminary Studies)
5. De Fuga et Inventione (On Flight
  and Finding)
  De Mutatione Nominum (On the
  Change of Names)

  De Somniis (On Dreams)
6. De Abrahamo (On Abraham)
  De Iosepho (On Joseph)
  De Vita Mosis (On the Life of Moses)
7. De Decalogo (On the Decalogue)
  De Specialibus Legibus I–III (On the
  Special Laws, Books I–III)
8. De Specialibus Legibus IV (On the
  Special Laws, Book IV)
  De Virtutibus (On the Virtues)
  De Praemiis et Poenis (On Rewards
  and Punishments)
9. Quod Omnis Probus Liber sit (That
  Every Good Man Is Free)
  De Vita Contemplativa (On the
  Contemplative Life)
  De Aeternitate Mundi (On the
  Eternity of the World)
  In Flaccum (To Flaccus)
  Apologia pro Iudaeis (Hypothetica)
  De Providentia (On Providence)
10. De Legatione ad Gaium (On the
  Embassy to Gaius)
11. Quaestiones et Solutiones in Genesin
  (Questions and Answers on
  Genesis)
12. Quaestiones et Solutiones in Exodum
  (Questions and Answers on
  Exodus)

*Indicates vol. number in LCL.

JOSEPHUS

Vita (Life) [vol. 1*]
Contra Apionem (Against Apion)
[vol. 1]
Bellum Judaicum (Jewish War)
[vols. 2–3]
Antiquitates Judaicae (Jewish
Antiquities) [vols. 4–9]

Versions
Hegesippus (Latin)
Slavonic Josephus (Old Russian)
Yosippon (Hebrew)

PHILO

Philo (Judaeus) of Alexandria (ca. 20 B.C.E.–50 C.E.) was a prolific writer. Although he was Jewish, his language was Greek, the principal language of his city. What did he write? Most of his writings are extant, but scholars dispute whether they represent exegesis, philosophy, apologetics, or even psychology. Philo's writings probably reflect all of these interests, but his chief purpose, in my judgment, is to show that Judaism, particularly as seen in the scriptures of Judaism, constitutes a superior world view. His allegorical "exegesis" should be understood in this light. Philo was interested not in what actually happened, but in how the biblical story could speak to thinking persons of the Greco-Roman world. Philo carried out this purpose by interpreting the biblical stories (mostly those of the Pentateuch) in terms of Neo-Platonism (i.e., the view that what the physical senses perceive on earth below is but an imperfect reflection of the true and perfect reality of heaven above). Philo's approach resembles that of Stoic philosophers who allegorized Homer's epics. Similarly, Philo read allegorical meanings into the biblical narratives. For example, Cain is to be understood as "foolish opinion," which is to be replaced by Abel, to be understood as "good conviction" (On the Sacrifices of Abel and Cain 2 §5). Or again, when Abram was commanded to depart from his home country, the patriarch was actually commanded to escape the prison-house of his physical body and turn his thoughts God-ward (On the Migration of Abraham 1–2 §1–12).

Of special interest to the present book is the question of the relationship of Philo's exegesis to the targumic traditions of the synagogue and to the midrashic traditions of the rabbinic academies. Some studies have attempted to relate Philo's legal interpretations (i.e., halakah) to those of the rabbis. Erwin R. Goodenough (The Jurisprudence of the Jewish Courts of Egypt [New Haven: Yale University, 1929; repr. Amsterdam: Philo, 1968]) and Isaak Heinemann (Philons griechische und jüdische Bildung [Breslau: M. & H. Marcus, 1932; repr. Hildesheim: Olms, 1962]) have concluded that Philo's halakic interpretation is distinctive to Alexandria. Edmund Stein (*Philo und Midrasch* [BZAW 57; Giessen: Töpelmann, 1931]) and Samuel Belkin (*Philo and the Oral Law* [Cambridge: Harvard University, 1940]) disagree, thinking that it is in basic continuity with Palestinian halakah. For a recent assessment see the studies by Richard D. Hecht ("The Exegetical Contexts of Philo's Interpretation of Circumcision," in F. E. Greenspahn et al., eds., *Nourished with Peace: Studies in Hellenistic Judaism in Memory of Samuel Sandmel* [Homage 9; Chico: Scholars, 1984] 51–79; idem, "Preliminary Issues in the Analysis of Philo's *De Specialibus Legibus*," *Studia Philonica* 5 [1979] 1–56). Comparing haggadic traditions, Samuel Sandmel (*Philo's Place in Judaism: A Study of Conceptions of Abraham in Jewish Literature* [New York: Ktav, 1971]) concluded that Philo and early Palestinian rabbis have very different interpretive intentions. This may be so, but the similarities call for explanation (as seen in the works of Borgen and Meeks in the following paragraph).

Philo's allegorical interpretation of Scripture has shed some light on the NT. Peder Borgen (*Bread from Heaven: An Exegetical Study of the Concept of Manna in the Gospel of John and the Writings of Philo* [NovTSup 10; Leiden: Brill, 1965; repr. 1981]) has shown that the use of the manna tradition in John 6 coheres at many points with Philonic and early rabbinic interpretation. Two years later Wayne Meeks (*The Prophet-King: Moses Traditions and the Johannine Christology* [NovTSup 14; Leiden: Brill, 1967]) found additional points of coherence between John and Philo (and other early Jewish materials) in their respective interpretations of Moses (for further comparisons between John and Philo see Gen. Bib.). Hebrews has been another NT writing that has often been compared to Philonic principles of interpretation (see L. K. K. Dey, *The Intermediary World and Patterns of Perfection in Philo and Hebrews* (SBLDS 25; Missoula: Scholars, 1975); S. G. Sowers, *The Hermeneutics of Philo and Hebrews: A Comparison of the Interpretation of the Old Testament in Philo Judaeus and the Epistle to the Hebrews* [BST 1; Zürich: EVZ; Richmond: John Knox, 1965]; R. Williamson, *Philo and the Epistle to the Hebrews* [ALGHJ 4; Leiden: Brill, 1970]). This NT writer's comparisons between the earthly priesthood and the heavenly, the earthly tabernacle and the heavenly, and the earthly sacrifice and the eternal are very much in step with the Neo-Platonic approach taken by Philo. Paul's Sarah/Hagar allegory in Galatians 4 probably represents another example of this kind of thinking.

The standard critical edition of Philo's works is by L. Cohn and P. Wendland, *Philonis Alexandrini opera quae supersunt* (7 vols.; Berlin: G. Reimer, 1896–1930; repr. 1962). Volume 7, parts 1 and 2 (published by de Gruyter, 1926–30) constitute an index compiled by H. Leisegang. The Loeb Classical Library offers an edition containing the Cohn-Wendland Greek text and an ET: F. H. Colson and G. H. Whitaker, *Philo* (10 vols.; Cambridge: Harvard University, 1927–62 [with J. W. Earp for vol. 10; this volume contains a Scripture index]; see abbreviations in vol. 1, pp. xxiii–xxiv); R. Marcus, *Philo Supplement I: Questions and Answers on Genesis* (Cambridge: Harvard University, 1953); idem, *Philo Supplement II: Questions and Answers on Exodus* (Cambridge: Harvard University, 1953). See also *The Works of Philo* (trans. C. D. Yonge; London: H. G. Bohn, 1854; repr. Peabody: Hendrickson, forthcoming). There are two concordances available: G. Mayer, *Index Philoneus* (Berlin and New York: de Gruyter, 1974), and P. Borgen and R. Skarsten, *Complete KWIC-Concordance of Philo's Writings* (Trondheim: Bergen, 1973) [machine readable]. The last volume of *Biblia Patristica* indexes quotations of Scripture in Philo: A. Benoit et al., *Biblia Patristica: Supplément, Philon d'Alexandrie* (vol. 5; Paris: Editions du CNRS, 1982).

At one time it was thought that Philo was the author of *Biblical Antiquities* (or *Liber Antiquitatum Biblicarum*). This pseudepigraphal work often circulated along with the Latin translations of Philo's authentic writings. A century ago scholars abandoned the traditional view that Philo had written this work. They did so for two reasons: (1) The interpretive approach taken by the author of *Biblical Antiquities* is not allegorical. (2) *Biblical Antiquities* was probably written in Hebrew before later being translated into Greek and then eventually into Latin. Most scholars today believe that whereas Philo may have known a little Hebrew, he never would have been able to compose in that language. Greek was Philo's language. For further discussion of *Biblical Antiquities* see chapter 2.

PHILO AND THE NEW TESTAMENT

The Logos. According to the well-known words of John 1, "in the beginning was the Word, and the Word was with God, and the Word was God . . . and through him (the Word) all things came into being" (vv. 1, 3). Interpreters have frequently appealed to Philo's use of Word (or Logos) for aid in understanding the background against which the Johannine Prologue should be understood. According to these opening verses the Word is from the beginning, in God's presence, is in some sense to be identified with God, and is the agent of creation. Philo assigns similar qualities to the Word: "[God] created the world through the Word" (*On Flight and Finding* 18 §95); "let him press to take his place under God's First-Born, the Word, who holds eldership among the angels, their ruler as it were. And many names are his, for he is called, 'the Beginning,' 'Name of God,' 'Word,' and 'Man after His Image' " (*On the Confusion of the Languages* 28 §146); "Nothing mortal can be made in the likeness of the most High One and Father of the universe but (only) in that of the second God, who is his Word" (*Questions and Answers on Genesis* 2.62 [on Gen 9:6]); "[Scripture] gives the title of 'God' to His chief Word" (*On*

Dreams 2.39 §230). These ideas are not only relevant to the Johannine Logos, but significantly contribute to the background of other christological confessions in the NT. One thinks of Col 1:15–16 ("He is the image of the invisible God, the first-born of all creation, because in him all things were created") and Heb 1:3 ("[The Son] reflects the glory of God and bears the very stamp of his nature, upholding the universe by his word of power").

Philo's Logos may also be related to the targumic Memra (Aramaic for "Word"). Philo had asserted that God's Logos, also called "the Beginning," was the agent through whom the world was created. Similarly, *Targum Neofiti* (see chap. 6) paraphrases Gen 1:1: "From the beginning with wisdom the Word of the Lord perfected the heavens and the earth" (cf. also *Tg. Neof.* Gen 1:26–27: "And the Lord said: 'Let us create man . . .' and the Word of the Lord created man in his own image"). Recall that the Johannine Logos is introduced in a manner that clearly echoes Genesis 1: "In the beginning was the Word." It is possible, therefore, that the Logos was suggested to Philo by its usage in the synagogue (where the targums took shape) as much as by its usage in Stoic and Neo-Platonic circles.

Bibliography: A. W. Argyle, "Philo and the Fourth Gospel," *ExpTim* 63 (1951) 385–86; P. Borgen, "Observations on the Targumic Character of the Prologue of John," *NTS* 16 (1970) 288–95; idem, "Philo of Alexandria," *JWSTP*, 273–74; D. A. Hagner, "The Vision of God in Philo and John: A Comparative Study," *JETS* 14 (1971) 81–93; L. Hurtado, *One God, One Lord: Early Christian Devotion and Ancient Jewish Monotheism* (Philadelphia: Fortress, 1988); R. Middleton, "Logos and Shekinah in the Fourth Gospel," *JQR* 29 (1933) 101–33; T. H. Tobin, "The Prologue of John and Hellenistic Jewish Speculation," *CBQ* 52 (1990) 252–69; R. McL. Wilson, "Philo and the Fourth Gospel," *ExpTim* 65 (1953) 47–49.

The Perfect Man. Paul's Adam-Christ typology is similar to and may even reflect Philo's interesting interpretation of the two creation accounts. According to Philo, the Adams of the two creation accounts must be distinguished (*On the Confusion of the Languages* 14 §§62–63; *Questions and Answers on Genesis* 1.4 [on Gen 2:7]). The Adam of the first creation account was "created in the image of God" (Gen 1:26–27). This Adam did not fall, but remained perfect. He is the "heavenly man." But the Adam of the second creation account was "formed from the dust of the earth" (Gen 2:7). Because he was sensual, his need for physical gratification clouded his reason and he fell when tempted: "Yet though he should have kept that image undefiled . . . when the opposites were set before him to choose or avoid, good and evil, honorable and base, true and false, he was quick to choose the false, the base, and the evil . . . with the natural consequence that he exchanged mortality [*thnēton*] for immortality [*athanatos*], forfeited his blessedness and happiness, and found an easy passage to a life of toil and misery" (*On the Virtues* 37 §205). Those who aspire "to be called a son of God" must follow the example of the man created in God's image (*eikon*) (*On the Confusion of the Languages* 28 §146).

This interpretation may have assisted Paul in working out his Adam-Christ typology. The first Adam was weak and fell prey to temptation, the second Adam, Christ, was perfect and did not succumb to temptation. In 1 Corinthians 15 the apostle quotes from Gen 2:7, "The first man, Adam became a living soul. The last Adam [i.e., Christ] became a life-giving spirit" (1 Cor 15:45). Two verses later he adds, "The first man [i.e., Adam] is from the earth, earthy [alluding to Gen 2:7]; the second man [i.e., Christ] is from heaven" (1 Cor 15:47). Two verses later Paul's typology draws still closer to Philo's allegory: "Just as we have borne the image of the earthy, we shall also bear the image [*eikōn*] of the heavenly" (1 Cor 15:49). Paul's typology may be assuming a distinction between the Adams of the two creation accounts that approximates Philo's exegesis. That is, the first Adam (i.e., the one formed of the dust of the earth) sinned, but Jesus Christ, the second Adam (i.e., the one modeled after the one created in the image of God, the one who is from heaven) was obedient and becomes himself a model for those who wish to aspire to heavenly virtue, or, as Philo puts it, to aspire to becoming a "son of God" (cf. Rom 8:14, 19, 29 ["predestined to be conformed to the image of his Son"]). Finally, Paul's reference to the resurrection hope may echo Philo's exegesis: "Flesh and blood cannot inherit the kingdom of God, nor does the perishable inherit the imperishability. . . . For this perishable nature must put on the imperishable, and this mortal nature [*thnēton*] must put on immortality [*athanasia*]" (1 Cor 15:50, 53). Philo's distinction between the two Adams is not precisely the same as Paul's, but his language does illuminate the context in which Paul's discussion may be better understood.

Shadow and Substance. In keeping with Neo-Platonic language (cf. Plato *Republic* §514a–518b) Philo speaks of the contrast between "shadow" and "substance": "Monstrous it is that shadow [*skia*] should be preferred to substance [*sōma*] or a copy to originals . . . and it behooves the man, whose aim it is to be rather to seem, to dissociate himself from the former [i.e., the shadow] and hold fast to the latter [i.e., the substance]" (*On the Migration of Abraham* 2 §12). One is reminded of the polemic directed against Colossian errorists: "Let no one judge you in eating and in drinking or with regard to a festival or a new moon or a sabbath, which is a shadow [*skia*] of things to come, while the substance [*sōma*] is of Christ" (Col 2:16–17). Those who are concerned with eating and drinking are those who do not "hold fast" to Christ (Col. 2:19). The dichotomy between earthly shadow and heavenly substance may explain Luke's editing of the account of Jesus' baptism: "the Holy Spirit descended upon him in bodily form [*sōmatikōs*], like a dove" (Luke 3:22; cf. Mark 1:10). By inserting the word *sōmatikōs* the third evangelist may have wished to interpret the dove symbol in language that the educated readers of his time would have understood.

Bibliography: H. Chadwick, "St. Paul and Philo of Alexandria," *BJRL* 48 (1966) 286–307; H. Conzelmann, *1 Corinthians* (Hermeneia; Philadelphia: Fortress, 1975) 286; J. D. G. Dunn, "I Corinthians 15:45—last Adam, life-giving spirit," in B. Lindars and S. Smalley, eds., *Christ and the Spirit in the New Testament* (C. F. D. Moule Festschrift; Cambridge: Cambridge University, 1973) 127–41; E. Käsemann, *Commentary on Romans* (Grand Rapids: Eerdmans, 1980) 144–47; P. T. O'Brien, *Colossians, Philemon* (WBC 44; Dallas: Word, 1982) 139–40; A. J. M. Wedderburn, "Philo"s 'Heavenly Man'," *NovT* 15 (1973) 301–26; R. Williamson, "Philo and New Testament Christology," in E. A. Livingstone, ed., *Studia Biblica 1978* (vol. 3; Sheffield: JSOT, 1980) 439–45; N. T. Wright, "Adam in Pauline Christology," *SBLSP* 22 (1983) 359–89.

GENERAL BIBLIOGRAPHY: Y. Amir, "Authority and Interpretation of Scripture in the Writings of Philo," *Mikra*, 421–53; H. W. Attridge, "Jewish Historiography," *EJMI*, 322–24; P. Borgen, "Philo of Alexandria," *JWSTP*, 233–82; idem, "Quaestiones et Solutiones: Some Observations on the Form of Philo's Exegesis," *Studia Philonica* 4 (1976–77) 1–15; F. M. Colson, "Philo's Quotations from the Old Testament," *JTS* 41 (1940) 237–51; L. H. Feldman, *Scholarship on Philo and Josephus (1937–1962)* (Yeshiva Studies in Judaica 1; New York: Yeshiva University, 1963); H. L. Goodhart and E. R. Goodenough, "A General Bibliography of Philo Judaeus," in Goodenough, *The Politics of Philo Judaeus* (New Haven: Yale University, 1938) 130–321; E. R. Goodenough, *An Introduction to Philo Judaeus* (2d ed.; Oxford: Blackwell, 1962); E. Hilgert, "Bibliographia Philoniana 1935–1975," *ANRW* 2.21.1 (1984) 47–97; idem, "A Bibliography of Philo Studies, 1963–1970," *Studia Philonica* 1 (1972) 57–71, with updates in 2 (1973) 51–54; 3 (1974–75) 117–25; 4 (1976–77) 79–85; 5 (1978) 113–20; 6 (1979–80) 197–200; W. L. Knox, "A Note on Philo's Use of the Old Testament," *JTS* 41 (1940) 30–34; B. L. Mack, "Wisdom Literature," *EJMI*, 387–95; S. Sandmel, *Philo of Alexandria* (Oxford and New York: Oxford University, 1979); idem, "Philo's Environment and Philo's Exegesis," *JBR* 22 (1954) 248–53; E. M. Smallwood, *Philonis Alexandrini Legatio ad Gaium* (Leiden: Brill, 1961; 2d ed., 1970).

JOSEPHUS

The writings of Josephus provide us with invaluable information touching history, politics, religious ideas, Jewish sects, and biblical interpretation. Born in the year of Gaius Caligula's accession (37/38 C.E.), young Josephus ben Matthias studied Jewish law, contemplated which sect he would join (Pharisees, Sadducees, or Essenes), and visited the Roman capital. When the first war with Rome broke out, Josephus assumed command of part (or of all) of Galilee. Besieged at Jotapata for forty-seven days, he surrendered to the Romans and prophesied that Vespasian, the commander of the Roman forces in Israel, would someday become the Roman emperor. When his prophecy came to pass in 69 C.E., Josephus was released from prison and was made part of Titus' advisory council. Shortly after the war ended in 70, Josephus went to Rome where he was granted Roman citizenship. He took the name "Flavius" from the family name of Vespasian and Titus. In the late 70s he wrote the *Jewish War* (seven books). (An earlier version of this work, written in Aramaic, was sent to Jews of Mesopotamia to discourage them from revolt.) In the mid-90s he completed the *Jewish Antiquities* (twenty books). Shortly after 100 C.E. he published his *Life* (an appendix to *Antiquities*) and *Against Apion* (two books). (From *Ant.* 20.12.1 §267 one may infer that much of the *Life* had been written by 93–94 C.E., although it would not be published for another seven years or so.) Josephus died in the early years of the second century. All of his writings, with the exception of the aforementioned earlier draft of *Jewish War*, were originally published in Greek. Greek was not Josephus' mother-tongue, but he had studied it and could with some difficulty write and speak it. In composing his books he had assistance with the Greek (*Ag. Ap.* 1.9 §50).

There are several topics treated in the writings of Josephus that are especially relevant to NT study. His description of the religious/political sects (i.e., Pharisees, Sadducees, Essenes, and the "Fourth Philosophy") is of great importance (cf. *Life* 2 §§10–12; *J.W.* 2.8.2–14 §§119–166; *Ant.* 18.1.2–6 §§11–23). His description of the Samaritan-Jewish hostility (*J.W.* 2.12.3 §§232–244; *Ant.* 18.2.2 §30; 20.6.1–3 §§118–136) aids us in understanding what the NT presupposes (Matt 10:5; Luke 9:52; 10:30–39; John 4:9; 8:48). His portrait of Pontius Pilate as insensitive and brutal is illuminating (*Ant.* 18.3.1–3 §§55–62; *J.W.* 2.9.2–4 §§169–177; cf. Philo *Embassy to Gaius* 38 §§299–305) and coheres with the NT (Luke 13:1–2; Acts 4:27). His portrait of the high priesthood indicates corruption, avarice, collaboration with Rome, and on occasion violence (*Ant.* 20.8.8 §181; 20.9.2 §§206–207), details which certainly cohere with the portrait in the Gospels and Acts (Mark 14:1, 43, 53–65; 15:1–15, 31–32; Acts 4:1–3; 5:17–18; 7:1; 8:1; 9:1–2; 23:2; 24:1). Jesus' critical stance toward the ruling priests is thus clarified (Mark 11:15–17, 27–33; 12:1–12, 38–40, 41–44). His personal prophecies (*J.W.* 3.8.3 §§351–352; 6.2.1 §109; 6.4.5 §250; 6.5.4 §311) and the prophecies of others (*J.W.* 6.5.3 §§301–309) that he records regarding the destruction of Jerusalem and the temple are instructive in making comparison with Jesus' similar prophecies (Mark 13:1–2; Luke 19:41–44; 23:27–31). His description of would-be kings and prophets, his retelling of the biblical narratives, and his references to John the Baptist and Jesus will be considered in the section below.

There are two critical editions of the writings, one by S. A. Naber, *Flavii Josephi Opera Omnia* (6 vols.; Leipzig: Teubner, 1888–96), and another by B. Niese, *Flavii Josephi Opera* (7 vols.; Berlin: Weidmann, 1885–95). The Loeb Classical Library presents the Greek text and ET in ten volumes by H. St. J. Thackeray, R. Marcus, A. Wikgren, and L. H. Feldman, *Josephus* (10 vols.; Cambridge: Harvard University, 1926–65). The standard concordance is that produced by K. H. Rengstorf, ed., *A*

Complete Concordance to Flavius Josephus (4 vols.; Leiden: Brill, 1973–83). A helpful subject concordance has been prepared by Cleon L. Rogers, Jr., *The Topical Josephus* (Grand Rapids: Zondervan, 1992).

Bibliography: M. Black, "The Account of the Essenes in Hippolytus and Josephus," in W. D. Davies and D. Daube, eds., *The Background of the New Testament and Its Eschatology* (C. H. Dodd Festschrift; Cambridge: Cambridge University, 1956) 172–75; J. Blenkinsopp, "Prophecy and Priesthood in Josephus," *JJS* 25 (1974) 239–62; I. Hahn, "Josephus und die Eschatologie von Qumran," in H. Baardtke, ed., *Qumran-Probleme* (Berlin: Akademie, 1963) 167–91 [thinks that the prophecies of *Ant.* 6.13.9 §312 and *J.W.* 3.8.3 §352 are of Essene origin]; J. Neusner, "Josephus's Pharisees," in C. J. Bleeker et al., eds., *Ex orbe religionum: Studia Geo Widengren oblata* (vol. 1; Studies in the History of Religions 21; Leiden: Brill, 1972) 224–44; M. Smith, "The Description of the Essenes in Josephus and the Philosophoumena," *HUCA* 29 (1958) 273–313.

JOSEPHUS AND THE NEW TESTAMENT

Brigands and Prophets of Salvation. Josephus' descriptions of the ambitions and activities of those who hoped to lead Israel to freedom and renewal help us understand better how the authorities responded to Jesus and possibly how Jesus understood his mission. Several claimed kingship following the death of Herod: Judas of Gamala (*Ant.* 18.1.1 §4; *J.W.* 2.17.8 §§433–434; cf. Acts 5:37), Judas of Sepphoris (*Ant.* 17.10.5 §§271–272; *J.W.* 2.4.1 §56), Simon of Perea (*Ant.* 17.10.6 §§273–276; *J.W.* 2.4.2 §§57–59), Athronges the shepherd of Judea (*Ant.* 17.10.7 §§278–284; *J.W.* 2.4.3 §§60–65). Others had royal ambitions during the war with Rome: Menahem (*J.W.* 2.17.8–10 §§433–448), John of Gischala (*J.W.* 4.7.1 §§389–394), and Simon bar Gioras (*J.W.* 4.9.4 §510; 7.1.2 §29). There were also prophets who proclaimed deliverance: Theudas (*Ant.* 20.5.1 §§97–98; cf. Acts 5:36), who claimed that at his command the Jordan River would be parted, the Egyptian Jew (*Ant.* 20.8.6 §§169–170; cf. Acts 21:38), at whose command the walls of Jerusalem would collapse, Jonathan the refugee (*J.W.* 7.11.1 §§437–438; *Life* 76 §§424–425), who promised the people signs in the wilderness, and others (*Ant.* 20.8.10 §188). Although Josephus regularly calls the would-be kings "brigands" *(lēstai)* and the prophets "false prophets" *(pseudoprophētai)* and "impostors" *(goētēs)*, it is probable that most of these people were sincere messianic claimants and visionaries who had hopes of delivering Israel. The Roman response in almost every case was swift and ruthless. The prophets' habit of promising signs in the wilderness, many of which are reminiscent of the events of the Exodus and Conquest under Moses and Joshua, are particularly illuminating for Jesus research. On NT warnings regarding the dangers of "false christs" and "false prophets" see Matt 24:11, 24; Mark 13:5, 22. For fuller details see Appendix 6.

Bibliography: D. Hill, "Jesus and Josephus' 'Messianic Prophets'," in E. Best and R. McL. Wilson, eds., *Text and Interpretation: Studies Presented to Matthew Black* (Cambridge and New York: Cambridge University, 1979) 143–54; R. A. Horsley and J. S. Hanson, *Bandits, Prophets, and Messiahs: Popular Movements at the Time of Jesus* (San Francisco: Harper & Row, 1985); J. Reiling, "The Use of ψευδοπροφήτης in the Septuagint, Philo and Josephus," *NovT* 13 (1971) 147–56.

Josephus and Miracles. In two studies Otto Betz has discussed Josephus' understanding of miracles and magic. He studies Josephus' descriptions of various persons who claimed to have miraculous powers (*J.W.* 2.13.4 §259; 2.13.5 §262; *Ant.* 20.5.1 §97; 20.8.6 §170), observing that the first-century historian does not distinguish between miracle and magic as sharply as do the rabbis (cf. *Ant.* 14.2.1 §§22–24 [on Onias the Righteous]). Betz concludes that Josephus' understanding of miracle (e.g., Exod 7:1–13) has been influenced by his knowledge of miracle-workers of his time. Josephus frequently calls miracle-workers, particularly those who promised Israel deliverance, "imposters" *(goētes).* The word *goēs* occurs in 2 Tim 3:13: "evil men and impostors [*goētai*] will go from bad to worse, deceiving and being deceived." According to Philo: "If anyone cloaking himself under the name and guise of a prophet and claiming to be possessed by inspiration lead us on to the worship of the gods recognized in the different cities, we ought not to listen to him and be deceived by the name of a prophet. For such a one is no prophet, but an impostor [*goēs*], since his oracles and pronouncements are falsehoods invented by himself" (*Special Laws* 1.58 §315). For several examples of positive accounts of miracle-workers see Appendix 5.

Bibliography: O. Betz, "Jesu Heiliger Krieg," *NovT* 2 (1957) 116–37; idem, "Das Problem des Wunders bei Flavius Josephus im Vergleich zum Wunderproblem bei den Rabbinen und im Johannesevangelium," in O. Betz, K. Haacker, and M. Hengel, eds., *Josephus-Studien: Untersuchungen zu Josephus, dem antiken Judentum und dem Neuen Testament* (O. Cullmann Festschrift; Göttingen: Vandenhoeck & Ruprecht, 1974) 23–44.

Josephus and the Rewritten Bible. Josephus' motives and techniques of retelling biblical history shed light on synoptic relationships. In his study of *Jewish Antiquities,* Harold Attridge has concluded that Josephus redefined Jewish history and tradition so that they would become "relevant, comprehensible and attractive in a new environment" (1976, p. 181). Gospel interpreters have for years assumed that this is what the evangelists did when they edited their sources and composed their respective accounts. As a case in point, F. G. Downing has compared Josephus' rewriting of the Joshua-Judges narratives in *Jewish Antiquities* to Luke. He observes five basic ways in which Josephus rewrites the biblical narrative. (1) Josephus omits material to avoid discrepancies in multiple accounts, to avoid repetition, to avoid interruptions in the flow of the story, to avoid miraculous and magical details, to excise inappropriate theology, and to excise apologetically awkward material. (2) Josephus adds material to promote harmony and continuity in the narrative, to advance his view of divine providence and prophetic fulfillment, to emphasize the piety of major biblical characters, to promote Jewish apologetic, and to clarify and stimulate interest in the biblical story. (3) Josephus rearranges materials to promote harmony and continuity in the biblical narrative. (4) Josephus assembles and compiles his materials so as to unify the narrative around specific themes and verbal similarities. (5) Finally, Josephus conflates parallel accounts to promote harmony and continuity. When parallel accounts differ greatly, however, he often abandons conflation and opts, instead, to write a fresh account. Downing concludes that Luke's rewriting of Mark corresponds almost exactly to Josephus' rewriting.

Bibliography: H. W. Attridge, *The Interpretation of Biblical History in the Antiquitates Judaicae of Flavius Josephus* (HDR 7; Missoula: Scholars, 1976); idem, "Jewish Historiography," *EJMI*, 324–28; N. G. Cohen, "Josephus and Scripture: Is Josephus' Treatment of the Scriptural Narrative Similar Throughout the Antiquities I–XI?" *JQR* 54 (1963–64) 311–32; D. Daube, "Typology in Josephus," *JJS* 31 (1980) 18–36; F. G. Downing, "Redaction Criticism: Josephus' Antiquities and the Synoptic Gospels," *JSNT* 8 (1980) 46–65; 9 (1980) 29–48; L. H. Feldman, "Use, Authority and Exegesis of Mikra in the Writings of Josephus," *Mikra*, 455–518; T. W. S. Franxman, *Genesis and the "Jewish Antiquities" of Flavius Josephus* (BibOr 35; Rome: Pontifical Biblical Institute, 1979); S. Sowers, "On the Reinterpretation of Biblical History in Hellenistic Judaism," in F. Christ, ed., *Oikonomia, Heilsgeschichte als Thema der Theologie* (O. Cullmann Festschrift; Hamburg and Bergstadt: Evangelische Verlag, 1967) 18–25.

References to John the Baptist and Jesus. In three passages Josephus refers to John the Baptist and Jesus. The authenticity of the passage concerned with John is not disputed:

> But to some of the Jews the destruction of Herod's army seemed to be divine vengeance, and certainly a just vengeance, for his treatment of John, surnamed the Baptist. For Herod had put him to death, though he was a good man and had exhorted the Jews to lead righteous lives, to practise justice towards their fellows and piety towards God, and so doing to join in baptism. In his view this was a necessary preliminary if baptism was to be acceptable to God. They must not employ it to gain pardon for whatever sins they committed, but as a consecration of the body implying that the soul was already thoroughly cleansed by right behaviour. When others too joined the crowds about him, because they were aroused to the highest degree by his sermons, Herod became alarmed. Eloquence that had so great an effect on mankind might lead to some form of sedition, for it looked as if they would be guided by John in everything that they did. Herod decided therefore that it would be much better to strike first and be rid of him before his work led to an uprising, than to wait for an upheaval, get involved in a difficult situation and see his mistake. Though John, because of Herod's suspicions, was brought in chains to Machaerus, the stronghold that we

have previously mentioned, and there put to death, yet the verdict of the Jews was that the destruction visited upon Herod's army was a vindication of John, since God saw fit to inflict such a blow on Herod. (*Ant.* 18.5.2 §§116–119 [LCL])

Some think that this account is at variance with the Synoptics' account (cf. Mark 6:17–29) where it is said that Herod imprisoned John for condemning the marriage to Herodias. While it is true that in the above passage Josephus underscores Herod's political motives and fears for eliminating John, later he does disapprove of the union: "Herodias, taking it into her head to flout the way of our fathers, married Herod, her husband's brother by the same father, who was tetrarch of Galilee; to do this she parted from a living husband" (*Ant.* 18.5.4 §136).

On Jesus (not disputed). "And so he [Ananus the high priest] convened the judges of the Sanhedrin and brought before them a man called James, the brother of Jesus who was called the Christ, and certain others. He accused them of having transgressed the law and delivered them up to be stoned" (*Ant.* 20.9.1 §§200–203 [LCL]).

On Jesus (disputed).

> About this time there lived Jesus, a wise man, if indeed one ought to call him a man. For he was one who wrought surprising feats and was a teacher of such people as accept the truth gladly. He won over many Jews and many of the Greeks. He was the Messiah. When Pilate, upon hearing him accused by men of the highest standing amongst us, had condemned him to be crucified, those who had in the first place come to love him did not give up their affection for him. On the third day he appeared to them restored to life, for the prophets of God had prophesied these and countless other marvellous things about him. And the tribe of Christians, so called after him, has still to this day not disappeared (*Ant.* 18.3.3 §§63–64 [LCL]).

This passage is repeated, with a couple of very slight differences, in Eusebius (*Eccl. Hist.* 1.11.7–8; *Defense of the Gospel* 3.5.105).

Very few scholars have argued that this passage is wholly authentic. Those who have include F. C. Burkitt, "Josephus and Christ," *TTij* 47 (1913) 135–44; F. Dornseiff, "Zum Testimonium Flavium," *ZNW* 46 (1955) 245–50; and J. Salvador, "E Autêntico o 'Testimonium Flavianum'?," *RCB* 2 (1978) 137–51. Ernst Bammel ("Zum Testimonium Flavianum," in O. Betz et al., eds., *Josephus-Studien* [Göttingen: Vandenhoeck & Ruprecht, 1974] 9–22) and Albert A. Bell, Jr. ("Josephus the Satirist? A Clue to the Original form of the Testimonium Flavianum," *JQR* 68 [1976] 16–22) have argued that the passage is essentially authentic, but was originally intended to be understood in terms of satire. Solomon Zeitlin ("The Christ Passage in Josephus," *JQR* 18 [1927–28] 231–55) argued that the passage as a whole is nothing more than an interpolation. Most argue, however, that Josephus did refer to Jesus but that Christians have tampered with the text: Z. Baras, "Testimonium Flavium: The State of Recent Scholarship," in M. Baras and Z. Baras, eds., *Society and Religion in the Second Temple Period* (Jerusalem: Masada, 1977) 303–13, 378–85; S. G. F. Brandon, "The Testimonium Flavium," *History Today* 19 (1969) 438; A. M. Dubarle, "Le témoignage de Josèphe sur Jésus d'après des publications récentes," *RB* 94 (1977) 38–58; L. H. Feldman, "The *Testimonium Flavium*: The State of the Question," in R. F. Berkey and S. A. Edwards, eds., *Christological Perspectives* (H. K. McArthur Festschrift; New York: Pilgrim, 1982) 179–99, 288–93; John P. Meier, "Jesus in Josephus: A Modest Proposal," *CBQ* 52 (1990) 72–103; P. Winter, "Josephus on Jesus," *Journal of Historical Studies* 1 (1967–68) 289–302. This is likely the correct position. Although some Christian writers knew of the passage (such as Eusebius, ca. 324), none of the early Fathers thought that Josephus regarded Jesus as the Messiah (see Origen [ca. 280], *Against Celsus* 1.47; idem, *Commentary on Matthew* 13.55). This could hardly have been the case if there had been no passage at all or that the pro-Christian version that is now extant was original. The best explanation is that Josephus did refer to Jesus, but not in such positive, almost confessional terms. Moreover, as Louis Feldman and others have shown, the passage for the most part betrays the writing style of Josephus. Only in one or two places do words or phrases occur that are uncharacteristic of his style. This leads Feldman to conclude that "our text represents what Josephus substantially wrote, but that some alterations have been made by a Christian interpolator" (LCL 9, p. 49, n. *b*).

How, then, did the passage originally read? Joseph Klausner (pp. 55–56) thought that the passage originally read something like this:

> Now, there was about this time Jesus, a wise man; for he was a doer of wonderful works, a teacher of such men as receive the truth with pleasure. He drew over to him both many of the Jews and many of the Gentiles. And when Pilate, at the suggestion of the principal men among us, had condemned him to the cross, those that loved him at the first ceased not so [to do]; and the race of Christians, so named from him, are not extinct even now.

Robert Eisler thought that the passage originally had a critical and cynical slant. He argued (pp. 61–62) that the original text read like this:

> Now about this time arose (an occasion for new disturbances) a certain Jesus, a wizard of a man, if indeed he may be called a man (who was the most monstrous of all men, whom his disciples call a son of God, as having done wonders such as no man hath every yet done). . . . He was in fact a teacher of astonishing tricks to such men as accept the abnormal with delight.
>
> And he seduced many Jews and many also of the Greek nation, and (was regarded by them as) the Messiah.

And when, on the indictment of the principal men among us, Pilate had sentenced him to the cross, still those who before had admired him did not cease (to rave). For it seemed to them that having been dead for three days, he had appeared to them alive again, as the divinely-inspired prophets had foretold—these and ten thousand other wonderful things—concerning him. And even now the race of those who are called "Messianists" after him is not extinct.

Klausner's more or less neutral reconstruction, however, enjoys the support of the Arabic version found in Agapius' *Book of the Title*, as translated by S. Pines (p. 16):

Similarly Josephus the Hebrew. For he says in the treatises that he has written on the governance [?] of the Jews: "At this time there was a wise man who was called Jesus. And his conduct was good, and [he] was known to be virtuous. And many people from among the Jews and the other nations became his disciples. Pilate condemned him to be crucified and to die. And those who had become his disciples did not abandon his discipleship. They reported that he had appeared to them three days after his crucifixion and that he was alive; accordingly he was perhaps the Messiah concerning whom the prophets have recounted wonders."

Bibliography: R. Eisler, *The Messiah Jesus and John the Baptist* (London: Methuen; New York: Dial, 1931) 36–62; J. Klausner, *Jesus of Nazareth* (New York: Macmillan, 1925); S. Pines, *An Arabic Version of the Testimonium Flavianum and its Implications* (Jerusalem: Israel Academy of Sciences and Humanities, 1971).

VERSIONS OF JOSEPHUS' WRITINGS

Some of Josephus' writings have been translated, edited, and abridged in a variety of languages and forms. The three principal versions will be briefly considered.

Hegesippus (Latin Josephus). By the sixth century the writings of Josephus had been translated into Latin. In the fourth century a loose Latin paraphrase of the *Jewish War* appeared under the name of a certain Hegesippus. The name is probably not genuine. The significance of the readings found only in Hegesippus is disputed. Some think that they may witness authentic Josephan traditions. Most suspect that they represent nothing more than later embellishments and legends. Solomon Zeitlin has argued that Hegesippus made use of the Yosippon. His argument, however, rests on the unlikely prior conclusion that the Yosippon is quite old (see discussion of the Yosippon below).

Bibliography: A. A. Bell, Jr., "Classical and Christian Traditions in the Work of Pseudo-Hegesippus," *Indiana Social Studies Quarterly* 33 (1980) 60–64 [discusses the relationship of Hegesippus and Yosippon]; F. Blatt, *The Latin Josephus. I, Introduction and Text. The Antiquities, Books I–IV* (Acta Jutlandica 30.1; Aarhus and Copenhagen: Munksgaard, 1958); K. Boysen, *Flavii Josephi opera ex versione latina antiqua. Pars VI. De Judaeorum vetustate sive contra Apionem* (CSEL 37; Vindobonae: F. Tempsky, 1898; repr. New York: Johnson, 1964); V. Ussani, *Hegesippi qui dicitur historiae libri V* (CSEL 66; Vienna and Leipzig; Hölder-Pichler-Tempsky, 1932) [critical text of Hegesippus]; S. Zeitlin, "Josippon," *JQR* 53 (1962–63) 277–97.

Slavonic Josephus (Old Russian). The Slavonic (or Old Russian) version of Josephus' *Jewish War* contains numerous passages not found in the Greek version. Many of these passages relate to John the Baptist or Jesus. It is thought that the Slavonic version may be a translation of a different, perhaps unedited, version of the Greek, or perhaps it may be a translation of the earlier Aramaic version of the Jewish War. Scholars are divided over every question pertaining to the origin, authenticity, and historical value of the Slavonic "additions." Here are a few of the most relevant texts:

> His works, that is to say, were godly, and he wrought wonder-deeds amazing and full of power. Therefore it is not possible for me to call him a man. But again, looking at the existence he shared with all, I would not call him an angel. [follows 2.9.3, between §§174 and 175]

> Some said of him, that our first Lawgiver has risen from the dead and shows forth many cures and arts. [follows 2.9.3, between §§174 and 175]

> But when they saw his power, that he accomplished everything that he would by word, they urged him that he should enter the city and cut down the Roman soldiers and Pilate and rule over us. But that one scorned it. [follows 2.9.3, between §§174 and 175]

> [The temple curtain] had, you should know, been suddenly rent from top to the ground. . . . [follows 5.5.4 §214]

> And over these [gates] with inscriptions hung a fourth tablet with inscription in these [Greek, Roman, and Jewish] characters, to the effect: Jesus has not reigned as king; he has been crucified by the Jews because he proclaimed the destruction of the city and the laying waste of the Temple. [inserted in 5.5.2 §195]

> Some indeed by this understood Herod, but others the crucified wonder-doer Jesus, others say again Vespasian. [inserted at 6.5.4, replacing §313]

A. J. Berendts concluded that they are genuine. Robert Dunkerley agrees that they probably do go back to Josephus, but they are not necessarily historically accurate. J. Frey argued that they were early interpolations. J. M. Creed and J. W. Jack agree, arguing that the additions are late, spurious, and completely worthless. H. St. J. Thackeray translated into English the principal passages.

Bibliography: A. J. Berendts, *Die Zeugnisse vom Christentum im slavischen "De bello judaico" des Josephus* (TU 29 [= n.s. 14]; Leipzig: Hinrichs, 1906); J. M. Creed, "The Slavonic Version of Josephus' History of the Jewish War," *HTR* 25 (1932) 277–319; R. Dunkerley, "The Riddles of Josephus," *HibJ* 53 (1954–55) 127–34;

R. Eisler, *The Messiah Jesus and John the Baptist* (London: Methuen; New York: Dial, 1931) 113–69; J. Frey, *Der slavische Josephusbericht über die urchristliche Geschichte nebst seinen Parallelen* (Dorpat: Mattiesen, 1908); J. W. Jack, *The Historic Christ* (London: Clarke, 1933); G. R. S. Mead, *The Gnostic John the Baptizer* (London: Watkins, 1924) 97–119; A. Rubinstein, "Observations on the Old Russian Version of Josephus' Wars," *JJS* 2 (1957) 329–48; H. St. J. Thackeray, "The Principal Additional Passages in the Slavonic Version," in Thackeray, *Josephus III: The Jewish War Books IV–VII* (LCL 210 [vol. 3]; Cambridge: Harvard University, 1928) 635–58 [ET]; S. Zeitlin, *Josephus on Jesus: With Particular Reference to Slavonic Josephus and the Hebrew Josippon* (Philadelphia: Dropsie College, 1931) 52–60; idem, "The Slavonic Josephus and its Relation to Yosippon and Hegesippus," *JQR* 20 (1929–30) 1–50.

Yosippon (Hebrew Josephus). In the Middle Ages a Hebrew translation based on the *Jewish War, Antiquities, Against Apion,* and even the Latin Hegesippus appeared under the name of Yosippon (or Josippon), which is the Hebraizing form of the Greek name Josephus. Many rabbis of the Middle Ages believed that the Yosippon was the work of Josephus. The Constantinople version of the Yosippon claims that Josephus was the author: "Behold, this book I, Joseph ben Gorion the Priest, wrote for Israel" (i.e., in Hebrew, as opposed to Greek, which was for the Romans). The name "ben Gorion" probably arose from confusing Josephus with a general named "Joseph ben Gorion." (Josephus, it should be remembered, had also been a general.) One of the manuscripts of the Yosippon claims that the work was written in 953 C.E. From this it is inferred that the Yosippon was composed in the tenth century. Solomon Zeitlin disagrees, claiming that the work is late third or early fourth century, though edited in later centuries. He claims that the author made use of the Babylonian Talmud, the Greek Apocrypha, and classical Greek authors. Few scholars follow Zeitlin, however. Since the Yosippon has made use of many sources, including the Talmud, the later date is more likely. Louis Feldman, moreover, has concluded that Hegesippus was the Yosippon's main source (Gen. Bib., 1984, p. 68). Therefore, in all probability the work is quite late (probably ninth or tenth century).

Did the original Yosippon mention Jesus? All of the early manuscripts give evidence of the work of the censors, both Jewish and Christian. Christian censors required offensive materials to be deleted, but often Jewish converts to Christianity would add confessional elements that later Jewish censors would delete. The net result is that Yosippon's witness to Jesus, if there every was any, is mutilated. Robert Eisler thinks that the Yosippon did mention Jesus. Comparing three manuscripts, he has reconstructed what he thinks the original contained (p. 111):

> in those days there were wars and quarrels in Judaea between the Pharisees and the "robbers of our nation" who strayed after Jesus, son of Joseph. And there went out some of those robbers and wandered in the wilderness where this is no way, and made unto themselves signs and miracles through their sorceries. And there came some of the sons of the city of Edom, robbers

(too), and they (all) went into the hiding-places of Edom and seduced many (saying): "in the days (of . . .) Jesus came to . . . (us). . . . Arrived has the angel (messenger) of God foretold by the prophets throughout the ages, and he has said . . . but they listened not to him, but sought how they might kill him.

In support of his reconstruction he notes that the *Toledot Yeshu* (see chap. 7) apparently depends upon the earlier anti–Christian versions of the Yosippon. The opening paragraphs of this curious book may support Eisler's reconstruction.

The Yosippon has been translated into Arabic, Ethiopic, Latin, and Old Slavonic. There are various Hebrew editions available (see Flusser). There is also an old and unreliable ET: Peter Morvvyng, *A Compendious and Most Marveilous History of the Latter Tymes of the Jewes Commune-Weale* (1558; republished some twelve times, from 1561 to 1662). The title page of this work adds: "in Hebrew by Joseph ben Gorion, a nobleman of the same countrey, who saw the most things himselfe, and was the author and doer of a great part of the same" (Reiner, "Yosippon," 132, n. 12).

Bibliography: R. Eisler, *The Messiah Jesus and John the Baptist* (London: Methuen; New York: Dial, 1931) 93–112; D. Flusser, "Josippon," *EncJud* 10.296–98; A. A. Neuman, "A Note on John the Baptist and Jesus in Josippon," *HUCA* 23 (1950–51) 137–49; idem, "Josippon and the Apocrypha," *JQR* 43 (1952–53) 1–26; J. Reiner, "The English Yosippon," *JQR* 58 (1967–68) 126–42; idem, "The Original Hebrew Yosippon in the Chronicle of Jerahmeel," *JQR* 60 (1969–70) 128–46; S. Zeitlin, "Josippon," *JQR* 53 (1962–63) 277–97.

GENERAL BIBLIOGRAPHY: H. W. Attridge, "Josephus and His Works," *JWSTP,* 185–232; D. A. Barish, "The Autobiography of Josephus and the Hypothesis of a Second Edition of his Antiquities," *HTR* 71 (1978) 61–75; O. Betz et al., eds., *Josephus-Studien: Untersuchungen zu Josephus, dem antiken Judentum und dem Neuen Testament* (O. Michel Festschrift; Göttingen: Vandenhoeck & Ruprecht, 1974); P. Bilde, *Flavius Josephus between Jerusalem and Rome: His Life, His Works, and Their Importance* (JSPSup 2; Sheffield: JSOT, 1988); S. J. D. Cohen, *Josephus in Galilee and Rome: His Vita and Development as a Historian* (Studies in the Classical Tradition 8; Leiden: Brill, 1979); L. H. Feldman, *Josephus and Modern Scholarship (1937–1980)* (Berlin and New York: de Gruyter, 1984) [bib. on Slavonic Josephus, pp. 48–56; on Yosippon, pp. 57–74]; L. H. Feldman and G. Hata, eds., *Josephus, the Bible, and History* (Detroit: Wayne State University, 1987); *Josephus, Judaism, and Christianity* (Detroit: Wayne State University, 1987); G. Hata, "Is the Greek Version of Josephus' Jewish War a Translation or a Rewriting of the First Version?" *JQR* 66 (1975) 89–108; S. Mason, *Josephus and the New Testament* (Peabody, Hendrickson Publishers, 1992); T. Rajak, *Josephus: The Historian and His Society* (London: Duckworth; Philadelphia: Fortress, 1983); H. Schreckenberg, *Bibliographie zu Flavius Josephus* (ALGHJ 1; Leiden: Brill, 1968); idem, *Bibliographie zu Flavius Josephus: Supplementband mit Gesamtregister* (ALGHJ 14; Leiden: Brill, 1979); R. J. H. Shutt, *Studies in Josephus* (London: SPCK, 1961); H. St. J. Thackeray, *Josephus, the Man and the Historian* (New York: Jewish Institute of Religion, 1929; repr. New York: Ktav, 1967) [regarded by Attridge as the best general introduction available]; G. Sterling, *Historiography and Self-Definition: Josephos, Luke–Acts and Apologetic Historiography* (Leiden; New York: Brill, 1992).

CHAPTER SIX

THE TARGUMS

Produced over generations in the homiletical and liturgical setting of the synagogue, the targums constitute an Aramaic translation/paraphrase/interpretation of the Hebrew Bible. The word "targum," from the Aramaic word *trgm*, "to translate," basically means a paraphrase or interpretive translation. The Aramaic translator was called the meturgeman. Targums to all of the books of the OT, with the exceptions of Ezra-Nehemiah and Daniel (large portions of which were already in Aramaic), are extant in manuscripts which date, for the most part, from the Middle Ages. Until recent years New Testament interpreters have made little use of them, primarily because it was assumed that they originated too late to be relevant. However, Paul Kahle's discovery and publication of the Cairo Genizah fragments and the discovery of targum fragments among the Dead Sea Scrolls have led several scholars to reconsider this assumption.

Martin McNamara, in addition to others, has argued that there existed in NT times, and probably even earlier, a Palestinian targum, which, he thinks, "is now found in its entirety in Codex Neofiti, and in part in the texts of Pseudo-Jonathan, the Fragment Targum and in fragments from the Cairo Geniza" (*Targum and Testament*, 12). Joseph Fitzmyer, in reviews of McNamara's work (see *TS* 29 [1968] 321–26) and of Matthew Black's work on the Aramaic tradition underlying the Gospels (see *CBQ* 30 [1968] 417–28) thinks that it is more appropriate to speak of Palestinian targums. Moreover, he is skeptical of the relevance of the targums for NT research, for he is not persuaded of their great antiquity by the arguments presented thus far. He thinks that appeals to parallels with the NT lead to circular reasoning: A parallel with the NT suggests antiquity of targum, therefore targum is relevant for NT comparison. McNamara has said by way of reply that parallels also occur in other datable traditions (such as early Fathers, early Jewish art, Qumran, early OT Pseudepigrapha, early translations of the OT, and early Jewish liturgy). From such comparative work he concludes, and I think rightly, that the targums do preserve some tradition that dates to, and possibly before, the time of the NT. Bruce Chilton's approach, by which he searches for "dictional" and "thematic coherence" between Jesus' sayings and readings distinctive of the Isaiah Targum, has sharpened comparative analysis, with positive results (see discussion of the *Isaiah Targum* below).

The standard Aramaic edition is Alexander Sperber, *The Bible in Aramaic Based on Old Manuscripts and Printed Texts* (4 vols.; Leiden: Brill, 1959–68). Other Aramaic editions will be noted below. A *Comprehensive Aramaic Lexicon* (Baltimore: Johns Hopkins University) is being prepared under the direction of Delbert R. Hillers, Stephen A. Kaufman, and Joseph A. Fitzmyer. Publisher Michael Glazier (Liturgical Press) is currently preparing an ET of all extant targums. The project director is Martin McNamara. The volumes that have appeared to date are listed in the relevant sections below.

Bibliography: M. Black, *An Aramaic Approach to the Gospels and Acts* (3d ed.; Oxford: Clarendon, 1967) 35–49; R. Le Déaut, *The Message of the New Testament and the Aramaic Bible (Targum)* (Subsidia Biblica 5; Rome: Pontifical Biblical Institute, 1982); D. W. Gooding, "On the Use of the LXX for Dating Midrashic Elements in the Targums," *JTS* 25 (1974) 1–11; M. McNamara, *The New Testament and the Palestinian Targum to the Pentateuch* (AnBib 27A; Rome: Pontifical Biblical Institute, 1978); idem, *Targum and Testament: Aramaic Paraphrases of the Hebrew Bible: A Light on the New Testament* (Shannon: Irish University; Grand Rapids: Eerdmans, 1972); S. Schulz, "Die Bedeutung der neuen Targumforschung für die synoptische Tradition," in M. Hengel et al., eds., *Abraham unser Vater* (O. Michel

Festschrift; Leiden: Brill, 1973) 425–36; P. Wernberg-Møller, "An Inquiry into the Validity of the Text-critical Argument for an Early Dating of the Recently Discovered Palestinian Targum," *VT* 12 (1962) 312–31; A. D. York, "The Dating of Targumic Literature," *JSJ* 5 (1974) 49–62.

SUMMARIES

Targums to the Pentateuch. Most of the targums are to the Pentateuch. The extant manuscripts and the traditions underlying them range in date from NT times to well into the Middle Ages. Four of these targums are complete (*Onqelos, Pseudo-Jonathan, Neofiti,* and the *Samaritan Targum*), one represents a selection of texts *(Fragment Targum),* and others are extant only as fragments (Cairo Genizah Fragments and 4QtgLeviticus).

Targum Onqelos. Targum Onqelos is regarded as the official targum to the Pentateuch. It is the most literal of the targums to the Pentateuch, but it is not without some noteworthy interpretive elements, including mishnaic material (e.g., see Gen 6:1–6; 49:1–27; Num 24; Deut 32–33). Some scholars think that a "proto-Onqelos" may have originated in Palestine prior to the defeat of Simon ben Kosiba (or bar Kokhba), with the final redaction taking shape sometime in the third century and probably with Babylonian influence. This conclusion may receive a measure of support from rabbinic tradition. According to the Babylonian Talmud (cf. *b. Giṭ.* 56b; *b. Meg.* 3a) the author was Onqelos the Proselyte, a disciple of Rabbi Eliezer ben Hyrcanus (and possibly Aqiba). However, this Onqelos, who is referred to as Aqylos in the Palestinian Talmud (*y. Meg.* 1.9) may actually be the translator of the Greek recension of the LXX, which goes by the name of Aquila. In any case, the possibility of a Pentateuch targum existing as early as the first century has to be taken seriously in view of the discovery among the Qumran writings of targums to Job and Leviticus.

The SBL abbreviation for *Targum Onqelos* is *Tg. Onq.* The biblical book, with chapter and verse, is cited in the conventional manner: *Tg. Onq.* Lev 3:2.

Text: A. Sperber, *The Bible in Aramaic Based on Old Manuscripts and Printed Texts. Vol. I: The Pentateuch according to Targum Onkelos* (Leiden: Brill, 1959). *Translation:* M. Aberbach and B. Grossfeld, *Targum Onkelos to Genesis* (Hoboken: Ktav, 1982) [Aramaic and ET]; I. Drazin, *Targum Onkelos to Deuteronomy* (Hoboken: Ktav, 1982) [Aramaic and ET]; idem, *Targum Onkelos to Exodus* (New York: Ktav, 1990) [Aramaic and ET]; J. W. Etheridge, *The Targum of Onkelos and Jonathan ben Uzziel on the Pentateuch with the Fragments of the Jerusalem Targum* (2 vols.; London: Green, Longman, and Roberts, 1862–65; repr. as one vol. New York: Ktav, 1968) [unreliable in places]; B. Grossfeld, *The Targum Onqelos* (ArBib 6–9; Wilmington: Glazier, 1988). *Critical Studies:* J. W. Bowker, "Haggadah in the Targum Onqelos," *JSS* 12 (1967) 51–65; E. Brederek, *Konkordanz zum Targum Onkelos* (BZAW 9; Giessen: Töpelmann, 1906); M. H. Goshen-Gottstein, "The Language of Targum

Onqelos and the Model of Literary Diaglossia in Aramaic," *JNES* 37 (1978) 169–79; G. Vermes, "Haggadah in the Onkelos Targum," *JSS* 8 (1963) 159–69.

Targum Pseudo-Jonathan. *Pseudo-Jonathan* (also called *Targum Yerushalmi I*) was at one time called *Targum Jonathan*, perhaps because of the confusion caused by the abbreviation "T.Y." inscribed on one of the major manuscripts. "T.Y." was an abbreviation for *Targum Yerushalmi* (i.e., Jerusalem) but was probably taken as an abbreviation for *Targum Yehonathan* (i.e., Jonathan). It came to be called "Pseudo-Jonathan" so as not to be confused with *Targum Jonathan* to the Prophets. *Pseudo-Jonathan* contains a diversity of traditions. Some of it is early (e.g., Gen 37:36); some of it is late (Gen 21:21, where the names of Mohammed's wife and daughter appear). Some is Palestinian; some is European. Scholars are divided over the questions of this targum's origin and relation to the other targums. Martin McNamara and others have pointed out that some of its distinctive readings offer remarkable parallels to the NT. Its paraphrase of Lev 22:28 reads: "My people, children of Israel, as our Father is merciful in heaven, so shall you be merciful on earth." This reading is quite close to a saying of Jesus found in Q (Matt 5:48; Luke 6:36). Its midrashic paraphrase of the story of Jannes and Jambres (Exod 7:11–12) parallels 2 Tim 3:8.

The SBL abbreviation is *Tg. Ps.-J.*, e.g., *Tg. Ps.-J.* Num 11:8.

Text: E. G. Clark, *Targum Pseudo-Jonathan of the Pentateuch: Text and Concordance* (Hoboken: Ktav, 1984). *Translation:* J. Bowker, *The Targums and Rabbinic Literature* (Cambridge: Cambridge University, 1969) 95–297 [ET of most of Genesis, with comparative notes]; J. W. Etheridge, *The Targum of Onkelos and Jonathan ben Uzziel on the Pentateuch with the Fragments of the Jerusalem Targum* (2 vols.; London: Green, Longman, and Roberts, 1862–65; repr. as one vol. New York: Ktav, 1968) [unreliable in places]; M. Maher, *Targum Pseudo-Jonathan: Genesis* (ArBib 1b; Wilmington: Glazier, 1992.

Fragment Targum. The *Fragment Targum* (also called *Targum Yerushalmi II*) is aptly named, for it is made up of a selection of texts and targumic paraphrases (about 30% of the Pentateuch). There are five manuscripts extant. Since they cover approximately the same passages, it is assumed that they derive from a common ancestor. Again scholars are divided as to its origin, purpose, and relation to the other targums. It is valuable because it contains some unique readings, some of which appear to be quite early.

The SBL abbreviation is *Frg. Tg.*, e.g., *Frg. Tg.* Num 11:26.

Text: M. Ginsburger, *Das Fragmententhargum* (Berlin: Calvary, 1899; repr. Jerusalem: Makor, 1969) [MS Paris]; *Text and Translation:* M. L. Klein, *The Fragment-Targums of the Pentateuch* (2 vols.; AnBib 76; Rome: Pontifical Biblical Institute, 1980) [MS Vatican]; *Critical Study:* M. C. Doubles, "Indications of Antiquity in the Orthography and Morphology of the Fragment Targum," in

M. Black and G. Fohrer, eds., *In Memoriam Paul Kahle* (BZAW 103; Berlin: Töpelmann, 1968) 79–89.

Targum Neofiti. Alejandro Díez Macho's discovery of *Targum Neofiti* (or *Neophyti*) was a sensation for targum scholars. Some scholars think that it may have originated in the second century C.E. or even earlier. It is sometimes called *Neofiti 1* because it is manuscript 1 of the Neofiti collection of the Vatican Library.

The SBL abbreviation is *Tg. Neof.*, e.g., *Tg. Neof.* Gen 1:1.

Text and Translation: A. Díez Macho, *Neophyti 1* (6 vols.; Madrid and Barcelona: Consejo Superior de Investigaciones Científicas, 1968–79); M. McNamara, *Targum Neofiti 1: Genesis* (ArBib 1a; Wilmington: Glazier, 1992). *Critical Studies:* B. J. Bamberger, "Halakic Elements in the Neofiti Targum: A Preliminary Statement," *JQR* 66 (1975) 27–38; A. Díez Macho, "The Recently Discovered Palestinian Targum: Its Antiquity and Relationship with the other Targums," *Congress Volume, Oxford 1957* (VTSup 7; Leiden: Brill, 1960) 222–45; S. Lund and J. Foster, *Variant Versions of Targumic Traditions within Codex Neofiti 1* (SBLAS 2; Missoula: Scholars, 1977).

Cairo Genizah Fragments. In 1930 Paul Kahle published the fragments of six manuscripts found in the genizah of an ancient synagogue. (A "genizah" [from Aramaic *genaz*, "to set aside" or "hide"] is a closet where sacred books that have been set aside or withdrawn from service are placed in storage.) Some believe that these fragments apparently represent the Palestinian targum. Alejandro Díez Macho eventually published four additional fragments of a seventh manuscript. Kahle dated the oldest fragments to 600–800 C.E. Other than the targumic materials found at Qumran, these fragments are some six or seven centuries older than the other extant targum manuscripts. Their discovery cast targum studies into a new light. (Note: It is estimated that there may be as many as 200,000 fragments from the Cairo Genizah. Most of these fragments are of biblical manuscripts, the Mishna, the Tosepta, or the Talmud.) The contents of the targum manuscripts are as follows:

MS A: Exod 21:1; 22:27

MS B: Gen 4:4–16

MS C: Gen 31:38–54; 32:13–30; 34:9–25; 35:7–15

MS D: Gen 7:17; 8:8; 37:20–34; 38:16–26; 43:7; 44:23; 48:11–20; Exod 5:20; 6:10; 7:10–22; 9:21–33; Deut 5:19–26; 26:18; 27:11; 28:15–18, 27–29

MS E: Gen 37:15–44; 40:5–18; 40:43–53

MS F: Exod 19:1–20, 23; Lev 22:26; 23:44; Num 28:16–31

MS G: Exodus 15 and 20

There is no SBL abbreviation for the Cairo Genizah fragments. I would recommend using "CG" for Cairo Genizah, followed by letter designating appropriate MS, e.g., CG A Exod 21:1, CG B Gen 4:4, CG C Gen 31:38, and so forth.

Text and Critical Studies: A. Díez Macho, "Nuevos fragmentos del Targum Palestinense," *Sefarad* 15 (1955) 31–39; Paul Kahle, *Masoreten des Westens II: Das palästinische Pentateuch-Targum* (Stuttgart: Kohlhammer, 1930; repr. Hildesheim: Olms, 1967); idem, *The Cairo Geniza* (London: Oxford University, 1947; 2d ed., Oxford: Blackwell, 1959).

4QtgLev. 4QtgLev (= 4Q156) is a fragment of a targum to Leviticus found in Cave 4 of the caves near Qumran. All that is extant is Lev 16:12–15, 18–21. This fragment proves that written targums to the Pentateuch existed as early as the first century C.E.

Text: R. de Vaux and J. T. Milik, *Qumrân Grotte 4,II: I. Archéologie; II. Tefillin, mezuzot et targums (4Q128–4Q157)* (DJD 6; Oxford: Clarendon, 1977) 86–89, 92–93.

Samaritan Targum. The *Samaritan Targum* survives in eight extant manuscripts, only one of which is complete. Of these manuscripts the oldest one dates to the twelfth century. Unlike the Jewish targums, the *Samaritan Targum* represents an attempt to translate word for word (though some paraphrase is present). Portions of the *Samaritan Targum* are quoted in other Samaritan writings, such as *Memar Marqah* (see chap. 11). The *Samaritan Targum*, of course, translates only the Pentateuch (see also discussion of the Samaritan Pentateuch in chap. 4).

The SBL abbreviation is *Sam. Tg.*, e.g., *Sam. Tg.* Gen 2:7.

Text: A. Brüll, *Das Samaritanische Targum zum Pentateuch* (5 vols.; Frankfurt am Main: Wilhelm Erras, 1873–76; repr. as one vol., Hildesheim and New York: Olms, 1971); J. W. Nutt, *Fragments of a Samaritan Targum* (London: Trübner, 1874; repr. Hildesheim and New York: Olms, 1980); A. Tal, *The Samaritan Targum of the Pentateuch: A Critical Edition* (3 vols.; Tel Aviv: Tel Aviv University, 1980–83). *Critical Study:* A. Tal, "The Samaritan Targum of the Pentateuch," *Mikra,* 189–216.

Targum of the Prophets. It is conventional to refer to "Targum Jonathan to the Prophets," a convention that probably originated with the tradition that the *Targum of the Prophets* was composed by Jonathan ben Uzziel (*b. Meg.* 3a). Some scholars (e.g., Smolar and Aberbach) have argued that the targum was produced by the school of Aqiba, but this hypothesis is problematic. Bruce Chilton has argued that the targum reflects layers of tradition, so that it is better to speak of editions and meturgemanim, rather than sources and one principal meturgeman (or school). He also thinks that it is better to view the respective targums to the various prophets as more or less distinctive works. In other words, there really is not a unified "Jonathan Targum" with its own distinctive features, as in the case of *Onqelos* over against *Neofiti.* Samson Levey's survey of the appearance of "Messiah" seems to bear this out, for the appearance and function of the messianic idea varies, at times greatly (compare Ezekiel with Isaiah, for example), from one prophet to the next.

The *Targums of the Prophets* are abbreviated thus: *Tg.* Isa 5:1–7, *Tg.* Jer 23:1, and so forth.

Text: P. de Lagarde, *Prophetae Chaldaice* (Leipzig: Teubner, 1872; repr. Osnabrück: Zeller, 1967); A. Sperber, *The Bible in Aramaic Based on Old Manuscripts and Printed Texts. Vol. II: The Former Prophets according to Targum Jonathan* (Leiden: Brill, 1959); *Vol. III: The Latter Prophets according to Targum Jonathan* (Leiden: Brill, 1962) [for fragments of Palestinian targum to the prophets see Sperber, 3.23–25 (Isa 10:32–33), 3.462–65 (Hab 3:1–5:11), 3.479–80 (Zech 2:14–15)]. *Critical Studies:* P. Churgin, *Targum Jonathan to the Prophets* (Yale Oriental Series 14; New Haven: Yale University, 1927; repr. New York: Ktav, 1983); S. H. Levey, "The Date of Targum Jonathan to the Prophets," *VT* 21 (1971) 186–96; L. Smolar and M. Aberbach, *Studies in Targum Jonathan to the Prophets* (New York: Ktav, 1983).

The Former Prophets. The *Targum to the Former Prophets* (Joshua, Judges, 1–2 Samuel, and 1–2 Kings) contains traditions ranging from the second (and possibly earlier) to the seventh century. In many places the biblical narrative has been edited to reflect rabbinic law. One of the more interesting passages is 1 Sam 2:1–10, where Hannah's song of praise is transformed into an apocalypse. Israel's enemies will be routed, the wicked will be consigned to Gehenna, and the kingdom of the Messiah will be magnified (cf. 2:10). It is interesting to recall that Mary's Magnificat (Luke 1:46–55), which speaks of the overthrow of the mighty and the exaltation of the humble, was modeled after Hannah's song.

Bibliography: D. J. Harrington and A. J. Saldarini, *Targum Jonathan of the Former Prophets* (ArBib 10; Wilmington: Glazier, 1987); D. J. Harrington, "The Prophecy of Deborah: Interpretive Homiletics in Targum Jonathan of Judges 5," *CBQ* 48 (1986) 432–42; idem, "The Apocalypse of Hannah: Targum Jonathan of 1 Samuel 2:1–10," in D. M. Golomb, ed., *"Working With No Data": Semitic and Egyptian Studies* (T. O. Lambdin Festschrift; Winona Lake: Eisenbrauns, 1987) 147–52; A. J. Saldarini, " 'Is Saul Also Among the Scribes?': Scribes and Prophets in Targum Jonathan," in B. Braude, ed., *Essays on Aggadah and Judaica* (W. G. Braude Festschrift; New York: Ktav, forthcoming).

The Latter Prophets. As briefly mentioned above, the targums to the Latter Prophets (Isaiah, Jeremiah, Ezekiel, and the Twelve Minor Prophets) bear individual characteristics. They will be considered briefly.

Isaiah Targum. Bruce Chilton has concluded that the *Isaiah Targum* contains early traditions (i.e., first and second centuries C.E.), though the process of interpretation and redaction continued into the Islamic period. This targum has proven to be valuable for NT study, particularly in Jesus research (see examples below). Chilton notes special interest in the Messiah (an idea largely shaped in the period between the two wars with Rome) and the regathering of the Jewish exiles. Isaiah 53 (or 52:13–53:12 to be precise) is interpreted messianically. But the Messiah is not a suffering Servant; he is a glorious and conquering hero. For example, whereas the Hebrew of 53:9 reads, "they made [the Servant's] grave with the wicked," the *Targum* reads, "[the Servant] will hand over the wicked to Gehenna." This Messiah will build the Sanctuary (53:5) and God will establish his kingdom (53:10).

Bibliography: B. D. Chilton, *The Isaiah Targum* (ArBib 11; Wilmington: Glazier, 1987) [ET, with bibliography]; idem, *The Glory of Israel: The Theology and Provenience of the Isaiah Targum* (JSOTSup 23; Sheffield: JSOT, 1983) [valuable critical study of the *Isaiah Targum*]; S. R. Driver and A. Neubauer, *The Fifty-Third Chapter of Isaiah according to the Jewish Interpreters* (2 vols.; Oxford: J. Parker, 1876–77; repr. New York: Ktav, 1969); J. F. Stenning, *The Targum of Isaiah* (Oxford: Clarendon, 1949) [Aramaic text and ET]; J. B. van Zijl, *A Concordance to the Targum of Isaiah* (SBLAS 3; Missoula: Scholars, 1979); idem, "Errata in Sperber's Edition of Targum Isaiah," *ASTI* 4 (1965) 189–91; 7 (1968–69) 132–34.

Jeremiah Targum. Robert Hayward has concluded that the evidence suggests that the *Jeremiah Targum* originated in the first century, perhaps even earlier (see 2:23–25, where the references to pagan idolatry might reflect the struggle with Antiochus IV and his successors). Of interest for Jesus research, Hayward concludes that the *Targum's* criticism of the high priesthood probably reflects first-century abuses. For example, see *Tg. Jer.* 8:10 ("robbers of money, both scribe and priest"). This emphasis could clarify and perhaps even corroborate the Synoptic portrait of Jesus' action in the temple (Mark 11:15–17).

Bibliography: R. Hayward, *The Targum of Jeremiah* (ArBib 12; Wilmington: Glazier, 1987) [ET, with bibliography].

Ezekiel Targum. Samson Levey thinks that much of the tradition of the *Ezekiel Targum* derives from the late first century, perhaps reflecting the editorial hand of Yohanan ben Zakkai, who replaced messianic expectation and speculation with Merkabah mysticism. The fact that the word "messiah" never occurs in the *Ezekiel Targum*, though messianic ideas are present, coheres with Levey's views. In other matters, especially those pertaining to halakah, the *Targum* reflects the thinking of Rabbi Aqiba.

Bibliography: S. H. Levey, *The Targum of Ezekiel* (ArBib 13; Wilmington: Glazier, 1987) [ET, with bibliography].

Minor Prophets Targum. The *Minor Prophets Targum* originated in Palestine and was subsequently edited in Babylon. Although some traditions in all likelihood are pre-70 C.E., as coherence at points with 1QpHab would suggest (see Brownlee), most of the interpretive tradition took shape after the Roman destruction of Jerusalem. The *Minor Prophets Targum* offers several points of theological interest. In at least two places the Memra seems to take on the role of personality (cf. Amos 4:11; Hab 1:12). This could bear on the question of the relation of the Johannine Logos to the targumic Memra. There is also anticipation of resurrection in the Messianic Age (cf. Hos 6:2; 14:8; Zech 3:7) and hope for a new world (Mic 7:14; Hab 3:2).

Bibliography: W. H. Brownlee, "The Habakkuk Midrash and the Targum of Jonathan," *JJS* 7 (1956) 169–86; K. J. Cathcart and R. P. Gordon, *The Targum of the*

Minor Prophets (ArBib 14; Wilmington: Glazier, 1989) [ET, with bibliography]; R. P. Gordon, "The Targum to the Minor Prophets and the Dead Sea Texts: Textual and Exegetical Notes," *RevQ* 8 (1974) 425–29; E. Levine, *The Aramaic Version of Jonah* (New York: Sepher-Hermon, 1975) [Aramaic and ET]; N. Wieder, "The Habakkuk Scroll and the Targum," *JJS* 4 (1953) 14–18.

Targums to the Writings. There is no official version of the targums to the Writings (Psalms, Proverbs, Job, Song of Songs, Ruth, Lamentations, Qohelet, Esther, and 1–2 Chronicles). There are no traditions of authors or relationship, as in the case of the Pentateuch or the Prophets, and so it is probably best to treat them as relatively independent works. Furthermore, these targums played no official role in the synagogue, though the Five Megillot (Ruth, Qohelet, Song of Songs, Lamentations, Esther) functioned in holiday liturgy.

Bibliography: B. Grossfeld, ed., *The Targum to the Five Megilloth* (New York: Hermon, 1973); P. de Lagarde, *Hagiographa Chaldaice* (Leipzig: Teubner, 1873; repr. Osnabrück: Zeller, 1967) [Aramaic text]; E. Levine, *The Targum to the Five Megillot: Ruth, Ecclesiastes, Canticles, Lamentations, Esther* (Jerusalem: Makor, 1977) [Aramaic and ET]; A. Sperber, *The Bible in Aramaic: Volume IVA: The Hagiographa* (5 vols.; Leiden: Brill, 1968) [Aramaic text of only Chronicles, Ruth, Song of Songs, Lamentations, Qohelet, and Esther].

Psalms. The *Psalms Targum*, like most of the other targums to the Writings, contains traditions spanning centuries. Much appears to date from the Roman period. (The western Roman Empire is mentioned in 108:10.) Indeed, the earliest traditions likely derive from the first century C.E., and perhaps even earlier. One interesting reading may have something to do with the function of Ps 118:22 at the conclusion of the parable of the Wicked Vineyard Tenants (Mark 12:1–12). Whereas the Hebrew reads, "the stone which the builders rejected," the Aramaic reads, "the child [or son] which the builders rejected" thus linking the quotation more obviously to the rejected son of the parable proper. This passage will be discussed further in chapter 12 below. Some eight passages are interpreted overtly as messianic (see discussion below).

Bibliography: W. Bacher, "Das Targum zu den Psalmen," *MGWJ* 21 (1872) 408–16, 462–73; J. Shunary, "Avoidance of Anthropomorphism in the Targum of Psalms," *Textus* 5 (1966) 133–44; G. L. Techen, *Das Targum zu den Psalmen* (2 vols.; Wismar: n.p., 1896–1907).

Proverbs. The *Proverbs Targum* presents scholars with a very curious feature: It appears that this targum is based directly on the Syriac version of the OT (i.e., the Peshitta), rather than on the Hebrew Bible. Matthew Black (*Aramaic Approach*, 25 [see bib. above]) thinks that this is improbable, since it is hard to believe that in producing a targum the Synagogue would depend on a Christian version of the Bible. But most scholars are persuaded that the evidence cannot be explained in any other way. If this is correct, the targum cannot be older than the mid-second century, when the Peshitta first emerged. Another oddity about this targum is the absence of midrashic expansions. There are modifications, but not to the degree one finds in the other targums.

Bibliography: J. F. Healey, "The Targum of Proverbs," in C. Mangan, J. F. Healey, and P. S. Knobel, *The Targums of Job, Proverbs, Qohelet* (ArBib 15; Wilmington: Glazier, 1991) [ET, with bibliography].

Job. Céline Mangan has concluded that the *Job Targum* probably represents an edited compilation of various targums of Job, extending from the first century into the eighth and ninth centuries. The likelihood that some traditions derived from the first century is supported by three facts: (1) Two copies of a Job targum have been discovered at Qumran (11QtgJob = Job 17:14–42:11; 4QtgJob [4Q157] = Job 3:5–9; 4:16–5:4). (2) The Babylonian Talmud relates a story of a Job targum found near the temple mount and shown to Hillel the Elder (ca. 50 C.E.; cf. *b. Šabb.* 115a). (3) There are several significant points of dictional coherence between the *Job Targum* and first-century materials such as the NT and some of the Pseudepigrapha (some of these are discussed below).

Bibliography: J. A. Fitzmyer, "Some Observations on the Targum of Job from Qumran Cave 11," *CBQ* 36 (1974) 503–24; C. Mangan, "Some Observations on the Dating of Targum Job," in K. J. Cathcart and J. F. Healey, eds., *Back to the Sources: Biblical and Near Eastern Studies in Honour of Dermot Ryan* (Dublin: Glendale, 1989) 67–78; idem, "The Targum of Job," in C. Mangan, J. F. Healey, and P. S. Knobel, *The Targums of Job, Proverbs, Qohelet* (ArBib 15; Wilmington: Glazier, 1991) [ET, with bibliography]; M. Sokoloff, *The Targum to Job from Qumran Cave XI* (Ramat-Gan: Bar-Ilan University, 1974) [Aramaic and ET]; R. de Vaux and J. T. Milik, *Qumrân Grotte 4,II: I. Archéologie; II. Tefillin, mezuzot et targums (4Q128–4Q157)* (DJD 6; Oxford: Clarendon, 1977) 90 [Aramaic].

Song of Songs. The *Song of Songs Targum* interprets the biblical book as an allegory of the relationship of God with Israel and with Israel's history. Although there is little in the Song of Songs that carries with it a messianic implication, the targum introduces messianic ideas in half a dozen passages (see tabulation below). The traditional association of Song of Songs with King Solomon, son of David, probably accounts for this.

Bibliography: L. J. Liebreich, "The Benedictory Formula in the Targum to the Song of Songs," *HUCA* 18 (1944) 177–97; R. J. Loewe, "Apologetic Motifs in the Targum to the Song of Songs," in A. Altmann, ed., *Biblical Motifs* (Lown Institute Studies and Texts 3; Cambridge: Harvard University, 1966) 159–96; idem, "The Sources of the Targum to the Song of Songs," in D. Sinor et al., eds., *Proceedings of the Twenty-Seventh International Congress of Orientalists, at Ann Arbor, Michigan, 1967* (Wiesbaden: Harrassowitz, 1971) 104–5; R. H. Melamed, "The Targum to Canticles According to Six Yemen Mss.," *JQR* 10 (1919–20) 377–410; 11 (1920–21) 1–20; 12 (1921–22) 57–117.

Ruth. Hebrew Ruth was used liturgically during the Feast of Weeks, but the Aramaic version was not. The *Ruth Targum* has much in common with the other Megillot targums. Palestinian in origin, the targum contains some pre-70 C.E. halakic traditions. The haggadic elements are more diverse, but they too point to an early, Palestinian origin. The *Ruth Targum* twice introduces the Messiah (after the ten famines in 1:1, and as one of the six blessings in 3:15).

Bibliography: E. Levine, *The Aramaic Version of Ruth* (AnBib 58; Rome: Pontifical Biblical Institute, 1973) [Aramaic and ET].

Lamentations. Much of the tradition of the *Lamentations Targum* probably derives from the period following the destruction of the second temple, though some of it could be earlier. There is later tradition in which a measure of polemic with Christianity may be in evidence (though I think Levine reads into some passages nuances that are not there). In its earliest form the targum was Palestinian, though it has been influenced in later years by the eastern Aramaic of the Babylonian Talmud. The hope that God would send the Messiah becomes part of the prophet's plea in behalf of vanquished Judah (2:22). When Israel's sins are expiated, deliverance will come at the hands of the King Messiah and Elijah the high priest (4:22).

Bibliography: E. Levine, *The Aramaic Version of Lamentations* (New York: Sepher-Hermon, 1976) [Aramaic and ET].

Qohelet. The *Qohelet* (or *Ecclesiastes*) *Targum* probably emerged in the late Roman period (see 10:6, where "Edom" probably refers to Rome), though it may contain traditions from earlier periods. The targum explicitly identifies King Solomon as the Preacher. Through the Holy Spirit the famous king predicts the division of the Israelite kingdom and the destruction of the temple. The entire book is cast as a prophecy: Whereas the Hebrew reads, "The words of the Preacher, the son of David," the targum reads, "The words of the prophecy which the Preacher, that is, Solomon the son of David . . . prophesied" (1:1; cf. 1:4; 3:11; 4:15; 9:7). This interpretation coheres with the haggadic tradition that Solomon was a prophet (cf. *Sipre Deut.* §1 [on 1:1]; *Tg.* 1 Kgs 5:13; *m. 'Ed.* 5:3 ["it {Qohelet} defiles the hands {because it is inspired}"]; *t. Yad.* 2.14 ["it was said by the Holy Spirit"]). The targum introduces the Messiah in two passages (1:11; 7:24). The *Qohelet Targum* seems closer in language to *Pseudo-Jonathan* than to either *Onqelos* or *Neofiti.*

Bibliography: P. S. Knobel, "The Targum of Qohelet," in C. Mangan, J. F. Healey, and P. S. Knobel, *The Targums of Job, Proverbs, Qohelet* (ArBib 15; Wilmington: Glazier, 1991) [ET, with bibliography]; E. Levine, *The Aramaic Version of Qohelet* (New York: Sepher-Hermon, 1978) [Aramaic and ET].

Esther. There are two targums to Esther: *Targum Rishon* (or *Esther Targum I*) and *Targum Sheni* (or *Esther Targum II*). *Targum Rishon* (ca. 500 C.E.) is written in western (i.e., Palestinian) Aramaic. (Grossfeld assigns it to lower Galilee.) Its translation is fairly literal. *Targum Sheni* (ca. 650 C.E.), also written in western Aramaic, extensively embellishes the story. The targums are so different that Grossfeld believes that "they are two independent compositions" (*First Targum*, v). The messianic idea is introduced by *Sheni* as part of a historical scheme made up of ten kingdoms (1:1). The ninth kingdom is that of the Messiah (and the tenth is that of God).

Bibliography: B. Grossfeld, *Concordance of the First Targum to the Book of Esther* (SBLAS 5; Missoula: Scholars, 1984); idem, *The First Targum to Esther* (New York: Sepher-Hermon, 1983) [Aramaic and ET]; idem, *The Two Targums of Esther* (ArBib 18; Wilmington: Glazier, 1992) [ET, with bibliography].

Chronicles. The *Chronicles Targum* offers a literal rendering, with occasional midrashic expansion (e.g., 1 Chr 1:20–21; 4:18; 7:21; 11:11–12; 12:32; 2 Chr 2:6; 3:1; 23:11). The meturgeman made use of the Palestinian targums to the Pentateuch (e.g., Gen 10:20 and 1 Chr 1:21; Gen 36:39 and 1 Chr 1:43) and was familiar with the Prophets targums. Vocabulary (including Greek and Latin loan words), place names, and style suggest a Palestinian provenance for the *Chronicles Targum*. In only one place does the meturgeman show any interest in the Messiah theme. Seizing upon the name Anani (1 Chr 3:24), which approximates "clouds of," an association is made with Dan 7:13: "Behold, with the clouds of [*'ānānê*] heaven came one like a son of man." This association leads the meturgeman to understand "Anani" as the actual name of the Messiah: ". . . and Anani, who is the King Messiah who is destined to be revealed."

Bibliography: R. Le Déaut and J. Robert, *Targum des Chroniques* (2 vols.; AnBib 51; Rome: Pontifical Biblical Institute, 1971) [vol. 1: introduction and French translation; vol. 2: Aramaic text and glossary]; M. Rosenberg and K. Kohler, "Das Targum zur Chronik," *JZWL* 8 (1870) 72–80, 135–63, 263–78.

THEMES

Messianic emphases in the Targums. "Messiah" occurs in the following targumic passages (as identified by Samson Levey; *Neofiti* not taken into account):

Gen 3:15 *(Ps.-J., Frg.)*	Ezek 37:21–28
Gen 35:21 *(Ps.-J.)*	Hos 2:2
Gen 49:1 *(Ps.-J., Frg.)*	Hos 3:3–5
Gen 49:10–12 *(Onq., Ps.-J., Frg.)*	Hos 14:5–8
Exod 12:42 *(Frg.)*	Mic 4:8
Exod 17:16 *(Ps.-J.)*	Mic 5:1–3
Exod 40:9–11 *(Ps.-J.)*	Hab 3:17–18
Num 11:26 *(Frg.)*	Zech 3:8
Num 23:21 *(Ps.-J.)*	Zech 4:7
Num 24:7 *(Frg.)*	Zech 6:12–13
Num 24:17–24 *(Onq., Ps.-J., Frg.)*	Zech 10:4
Deut 25:19 *(Ps.-J.)*	Ps 18:28–32 [ET 27–31]

Deut 30:4–9 *(Ps.-J.)*	Ps 21:1–8
1 Sam 2:7–10	Ps 45:7–18
1 Sam 2:35	Ps 61:7–9 [ET 6–8]
2 Sam 22:28–32	Ps 72:1–20
2 Sam 23:1–5	Ps 80:15–18 [ET 14–17]
1 Kgs 5:13	Ps 89:51–52
Isa 4:1–6	Ps 132:10–18
Isa 9:5–6	Song 1:8
Isa 10:24–27	Song 1:17
Isa 11:1–16	Song 4:5
Isa 14:29–30	Song 7:4
Isa 16:1–5	Song 7:12–14
Isa 28:5–6	Song 8:1–4
Isa 42:1–9	Ruth 1:1
Isa 43:10	Ruth 3:15
Isa 52:13–53:12	Lam 2:22
Jer 23:1–8	Lam 4:22
Jer 30:8–11	Qoh 1:11
Jer 30:21	Qoh 7:24
Jer 33:12–26	Esth (II) 1:1
Ezek 17:22–24	1 Chr 3:24
Ezek 34:20–31	

Bibliography: S. H. Levey, *The Messiah: An Aramaic Interpretation* (MHUC 2; Cincinnati: Hebrew Union College-Jewish Institute of Religion, 1974).

The Targums and the Teaching of Jesus. Through analysis of dictional, thematic, and stylistic coherence, Bruce Chilton has shown how Jesus' statements and language at points reflect targumic tradition. Comparative study can lead to a better understanding of the saying in question and, in some cases, to firmer grounds for regarding a given saying as authentic. Chilton and others find dictional coherence in the following examples:

(1) According to Mark 4:12, Jesus paraphrased Isa 6:9–10 to explain in part why some did not comprehend or respond supportively to his teaching: ". . . in order that seeing they should see and not perceive, and hearing they should hear and not understand, lest they should turn [i.e., repent] and it be forgiven them." Only the *Isaiah Targum* reads "forgive"; the Hebrew (MT and 1QIsa[a]) and the LXX read "heal." (The Peshitta also reads "forgive," either because it has followed the targum or because it has been influenced by the version found in Mark.) I might add that not only is there dictional coherence, there may be thematic coherence as well. According to the targum, the prophet is to speak the word of obduracy to those *who* do not hear and do not see. In other words, the word of obduracy is directed only to the obdurate. In the Marcan context Jesus' word is directed to "outsiders." This application approximates the idea of the targum. Jesus' quotation, therefore, appears to have been influenced by an Aramaic reading heard in the synagogue of his day (see Chilton, *Galilean Rabbi*, 90–98; Evans, "Isaiah 6:9–10," 417).

(2) According to Matt 26:52, Jesus rebuked Peter for his rash act of striking the high priest's servant: "All who take a sword on the sword will be destroyed" (only in Matthew). Chilton suspects (*Galilean Rabbi*, 98–101) that Jesus has alluded to the Aramaic version of Isa 50:11: "Behold, all you kindling a fire, *grasping a sword*, go, fall in the fire you kindled and *on the sword* you grasped. This is yours from my word: you shall return to your *destruction*" (with the distinctive elements of the targum emphasized). The Greek words of Jesus' saying ("take a sword," "on the sword," "destroyed") cohere with the distinctive elements of the targum.

(3) When Jesus warns his followers to beware of being cast into "Gehenna" (Mark 9:47), he quotes part of Isa 66:24: "where 'their worm does not die and the fire is not quenched' " (Mark 9:48). The Hebrew version of Isaiah says nothing about Gehenna, but the targum does: "for their *breaths* will not die and their fire shall not be quenched, and *the wicked* shall be *judged in Gehenna*" (with the distinctive elements of the targum emphasized). Again, Jesus' use of this verse from Isaiah may very well reveal a familiarity with the Aramaic tradition that is now preserved in the *Isaiah Targum* (see Chilton, *Galilean Rabbi*, 101–7). Moreover, Jesus' warning that the one who hates his brother is liable to be cast into the "Gehenna of fire" (Matt 5:22; 18:9) may also echo targumic diction: "a fire *of Gehenna* not fanned will consume him" (*Tg.* Job 20:26, with the distinctive element emphasized; cf. *Tg. Neof.* Gen 15:17).

(4) In a tradition that enjoys multiple attestation Jesus avers: "With the measure you measure shall it be measured to you" (Q: Matt 7:2=Luke 6:38; cf. Mark 4:24). Jesus' expression appears to echo the diction of the Aramaic tradition: "With *the* measure *with which you were measuring they will measure to you*" (*Tg.* Isa 27:8, with the distinctive elements of the targum emphasized). Jesus' saying follows neither the obscure Hebrew reading ("measure by measure") nor the LXX. Although similar sayings are found in the rabbinic writings (*b. Šabb.* 127b; *b. Meg.* 28a; *b. Roš Haš.* 16b), the language of the targum provides the closest parallel (see Chilton, *Galilean Rabbi*, 123–25).

(5) Jesus' metaphorical saying about new wine bursting old wineskins (Mark 2:22 par.) coheres with Job 32:19: "My heart is like wine that has no vent; like new wineskins, it is ready to burst." The *Job Targum* parallels it even more closely: "My belly is like *new* wine" (*Tg.* Job 32:19, with the distinctive element of the targum emphasized).

(6) In Luke 16:9 Jesus tells his disciples to "make friends of the mammon of injustice [*or* dishonesty]." Although the Aramaic word *māmônā'* occurs in the talmuds, especially the Palestinian version, the expression "mammon of injustice/dishonesty" coheres with the targumic description of bribery as "mammon of falsehood/deceit" (cf. *Tg.* 1 Sam 12:3; *Tg.* Hos 5:11; *Tg.* Isa 5:23; 33:15; *Tg.* Job 27:8). The targumic expression, especially since it often has to do with political corruption or

economic oppression, appears to offer a closer parallel than the Qumranic expressions "wealth of violence" (1QS 10:19) or "wealth of evil" (CD 6:15). Not only are the respective concerns different, Qumran used the word *hôn*, not *māmônā'*. The appearance of *māmônā'* in 11QtgJob 11:8 (at MT Job 27:17) proves, moreover, that the word was utilized in the targumic tradition in the first century (see Chilton, *Galilean Rabbi*, 117–23).

There are also instances of thematic coherence between targumic traditions and Jesus' teaching. Two examples may be considered:

(1) Jesus bases his parable of the Wicked Vineyard Tenants (Mark 12:1–11) upon Isaiah's Song of the Vineyard (Isa 5:1–7). When the parable is finished, the chief priests perceive that he has told the parable against them (Mark 12:12). Although Jesus has clearly drawn upon Isaiah's song for the imagery of his parable, it is not clear that he has drawn upon its message. According to the Hebrew and Greek versions of Isaiah, the people of Judah as a whole are guilty of fruitlessness, and it is they who are in danger of judgment. But according to Jesus' parable it is the religious leaders, not the people, who are guilty and in danger of judgment. From the *Isaiah Targum* we are able to explain this apparent discrepancy. According to it God did not build a *tower* (as in the MT and LXX), but his *sanctuary* in the midst of his people. He did not provide a *wine vat* (as in the MT and LXX), but his *altar to atone for their sins*. But despite these benefits the people did not produce *good deeds* (instead of the MT's "grapes"); they produced *evil deeds*. Therefore God will remove his *Shekinah* and will break down their *sanctuaries* (i.e., temple and synagogues). The *Isaiah Targum* has narrowed the focus from the people of Judah to the temple establishment. It is therefore quite probable that Jesus' usage of Isa 5:1–7, which was directed against the temple establishment, presupposed the interpretation that is now reflected in the *Isaiah Targum* (see Chilton, *Galilean Rabbi*, 111–14). See chapter 12 for further discussion of this passage.

(2) One of the most obvious characteristics of Jesus' public ministry is his proclamation of the in-breaking kingdom of God (cf. Mark 1:15; 9:1; 14:25; Luke 11:20). Chilton has observed an important point of coherence with the *Isaiah Targum* that may clarify Jesus' proclamation. He finds that at many points the targum inserts hopeful expressions of the revelation of the kingdom. Where the MT reads, "because the Lord of hosts reigns on Mount Zion" (Isa 24:23), the targum reads: "because the kingdom of the Lord of hosts will be revealed on Mount Zion" (cf. the MT and targum at 31:4; 40:9; 52:7). What the meturgeman hoped would soon be revealed, Jesus declared imminent and in some sense present in his ministry (see Chilton, *Galilean Rabbi*, 58–63; idem, *Glory of Israel*, 77–81).

Finally, two examples of stylistic coherence between targumic traditions and Jesus' teaching may be considered:

(1) One of the distinctive stylistic characteristics of Jesus' speech was his practice of prefacing certain solemn statements with the word "amen" (probably the Aramaic form; from *'āman*, "to be certain" or "sure"): "Amen, I say to you, all sins will be forgiven the sons of men" (Mark 3:28; cf. 8:12; 9:1 passim). Its rarity in Judaica led some scholars to suppose that Jesus' usage was unique. The closest parallel that Gustaf Dalman could find was *hemānûtā'* (which is from the *'āman* stem) in two places in the Babylonian Talmud (*b. Ned.* 49b [of Judah ben Ilai, ca. 150 C.E.]; *b. Sanh.* 38b; see Dalman, *Words of Jesus*, 226–29). However, Chilton thinks that Jesus' practice may reflect a similar practice in the targums, where "amen" sometimes prefaced "a sentence as a solemn asseveration" (Chilton, *Galilean Rabbi*, 202). Two helpful examples are found in the *Isaiah Targum*: "They will . . . *give thanks, saying, 'Amen, God is with you'* " (*Tg.* Isa 45:14); and, "*Amen, you are God*" (*Tg.* Isa 45:15, with the distinctive elements of the targum emphasized). (*Tg.* Isa 37:18 is less helpful, since *'āman* is present in the Hebrew text as well.) Jesus' style of speaking evidently was not unique, but reflected a convention which his contemporaries would have heard in the synagogue.

(2) Some twenty-one times Jesus speaks of "your/our Father in heaven" (Mark 11:25; Matt 5:45; 6:1, 9; 18:10 passim). This expression does not occur in the OT or the OT Apocrypha. But "Father in heaven" qualified by a personal pronoun does occur in the targums (*Ps.-J.* Exod 1:19; *Frg. Tg.* Gen 21:33; *Frg. Tg.* [MS M] Exod 17:11; *Frg. Tg.* Num 21:9; *Ps.-J.* Deut 28:32 passim). Since it occurs elsewhere in early Judaica (e.g., *m. 'Abot* 5:20; *Mek.* on Exod 20:6 [*Bahodeš* §6.143]), one cannot claim that its derivation is distinctly targumic. However, since its function seems often to be liturgical, the provenance of the synagogue, in which the targumic tradition grew, does suggest itself. Perhaps here again Jesus' style of speaking (and praying) may be clarified by comparison with the targums (see McNamara, *Targum and Testament*, 115–19).

Bibliography: B. D. Chilton, *A Galilean Rabbi and His Bible: Jesus' Use of the Interpreted Scripture of His Time* (GNS 8; Wilmington: Glazier, 1984); idem, *The Glory of Israel: The Theology and Provenience of the Isaiah Targum* (JSOTSup 23; Sheffield: JSOT, 1982); G. Dalman, *The Words of Jesus* (Edinburgh: T. & T. Clark, 1902); C. A. Evans, "The Text of Isaiah 6:9–10," *ZNW* 94 (1982) 415–18; M. McNamara, *Targum and Testament: Aramaic Paraphrases of the Hebrew Bible: A Light on the New Testament* (Shannon: Irish University; Grand Rapids: Eerdmans, 1972).

GENERAL BIBLIOGRAPHY: P. S. Alexander, "Jewish Aramaic Translations of Hebrew Scriptures," *Mikra*, 217–53; J. Bowker, *The Targums and Rabbinic Literature: An Introduction to Jewish Interpretation of Scripture* (Cambridge: Cambridge University, 1969); R. Le Déaut, "The Current State of Targumic Studies," *BTB* 4 (1974) 3–32; idem, "Targumic Literature and New Testament Interpretation," *BTB* 4 (1974) 243–89; J. T. Forestell, *Targumic Traditions and the New Testament* (SBLAS 4; Chico: Scholars, 1979); P. Grelot, *What Are the Targums?* (Old Testament Studies 7; Wilmington: Glazier, 1992); B. Grossfeld, *A Bibliography of Targum Literature* (2 vols.; Bibliographica Judaica 3 and 8; Cincinnati: Hebrew Union College; New York: Ktav, 1972–77) [see the review and supplement by W. Baars, *VT* 25 (1975) 124–28]; idem, "Bible: Translations, Aramaic (Targumim)," *EncJud* 4.841–51; M. Jastrow, *A Dictionary of the Targumim, the Talmud Babli and Yerushalmi, and the Midrashic Literature* (2 vols.; London and New York: Putnam, 1886–94; repr. New York: Pardes, 1950); E. Levine, *The Aramaic Version of the Bible: Contents and Context* (BZAW 174; Berlin and New York: de Gruyter, 1988); M. McNamara, "Targumic Studies," *CBQ* 28 (1966) 1–19; idem, "Targums," *IDBSup* (1976) 856–61; P. Nickels, *Targum and New Testament: A Bibliography together with a New Testament Index* (Rome: Pontifical Biblical Institute, 1967); J. L. Teicher, "A Sixth-Century Fragment of the Palestinian Targum," *VT* 1 (1951) 125–29; A. P. Wikgren, "The Targums and the New Testament," *JR* 24 (1944) 89–95.

CHAPTER SEVEN

RABBINIC LITERATURE

Mishna
Tosepta
Jerusalem Talmud
Babylonian Talmud
Minor Tractates of the Talmud
  'Abot de Rabbi Nathan
  Kalla Rabbati
  Soperim
  Semaḥot
  Kalla
  Derek Ereṣ Rabba
  Derek Ereṣ Zuṭa
  Pereq ha-Šalom
  Gerim
  Kutim
  'Abadim
  Seper Torah
  Tepillin
  Zizith
  Mezuzah
Mekilta
Sipra Leviticus
Sipre Numbers
Sipre Deuteronomy
Seder 'Olam Rabbah
Megillat Ta'anit
Midraš Rabbah
  Genesis Rabbah
  Exodus Rabbah
  Leviticus Rabbah
  Numbers Rabbah
  Deuteronomy Rabbah
  Lamentations Rabbah

Ruth Rabbah
Ecclesiastes Rabbah
Esther Rabbah
Song of Songs Rabbah
Seder Elijah Rabbah
Pesiqta de Rab Kahana
Pesiqta Rabbati
Midraš Tanhuma
Midraš Tehillin
Pirqe de Rabbi Eliezer
Seder 'Olam Zuṭa
Chronicle of Jerahmeel
Later Midrashim
  Midraš 'Aggadah
  'Aggadat Berešit
  Midraš Megillot Zuṭa
  Berešit Rabbati
  Midraš Šemuel
  Midraš Mišle
  Midraš Yob
  Midraš Šir haŠir
  Midraš Haggadol
  Yalqut Šimeoni
  'Aggadat Esther
Medieval Commentators
  Saadya ben Joseph
  Solomon ben Isaac
  Abraham Ibn Ezra
  Joseph Kimhi
  Moses Maimonides
  David Kimhi
  Moses Kimhi
  Moses Nahmanides

As John Townsend has pointed out, rabbinic writings that are used to aid in the interpretation of early Christianity fall into three categories: Targum, Talmud, and Midrash (*Midraš*). The first category is treated in another chapter; the latter two are considered in this chapter. The writings that fall into the category of Talmud are the first four listed above: Mishna, Tosepta, the Jerusalem (or Palestinian) Talmud, and the Babylonian Talmud, along with its several minor tractates. Of these only a few will be discussed. The remaining writings, from *Mekilta* to *'Aggadat Esther*, fall into the category of Midrash.

These rabbinic writings also fall into two broad periods of time: tannaic (or tannaitic) and amoraic. The tannaic period extends roughly from 50 B.C.E. to 200 C.E., that is, from the establishment of the early academies, Bet Shammai ("House of Shammai") and Bet Hillel ("House of Hillel"), to the compiling and editing of the Mishna under Rabbi Judah ha-Nasi ("the Prince" or "Patriarch"; 135–217 C.E.) in the first decade or so of the third century C.E. The teachers or sages of this period are called the Tannaim ("teachers," from the Aramaic word *tenā'*, which literally means "to repeat"). Midway through this period, probably following Yavne (or Jamnia; late first century C.E.), ordained sages were given the title "Rabbi," which literally means "my master." Informal use of "rabbi," of course, was earlier, as seen in the NT Gospels. Babylonian scholars were called "Rab." The achievement of the tannaic period was the production of the Mishna (Mishnah). Tannaic sayings found in later writings outside of Mishna are called *baraitot* (an Aramaic word which literally means "standing outside"; sing. *baraita*). The amoraic period is from 220 C.E. to 500 C.E. Rabbis of this period are called the Amoraim ("expounders" or "spokesmen," from the Aramaic word *'amar*, which literally means "to say"). The achievement of the amoraic period was the production of the two Talmuds and several of the Midrashim.

There are two later rabbinic periods. The first is the saboraic (500–650 C.E.). The rabbis of this period are called Saboraim ("reasoners," from Aramaic, *sebar*, "to reason"). The Saboraim edited the Babylonian Talmud. The second period is the geonic (650–1050 C.E.). The major Babylonian rabbis of this period are called the Geonim ("excellent," from Hebrew, *gā'ôn*, "majesty," "pride"). "Gaon" was a title of honor reserved for the chief rabbis, e.g., Saadya Gaon (see below).

PRINCIPAL TANNAIM OF THE MISHNAIC PERIOD*

First Generation (80–120 C.E.)	Second Generation (120–140 C.E.)	Third Generation (140–165 C.E.)
Eleazar ben Arak	Aqiba (ben Joseph)	Abba Saul
Eleazar ben Azaria	Elai	Eleazar ben Shammua
Eliezer (ben Hyrcanus)	Eleazar ben Judah	Eliezer ben Jacob II
Eliezer ben Jacob I	Ishmael (ben Elisha)	Judah ben Elai

Gamaliel (II), the Patriarch	Judah ben Baba	Meir
Joshua (ben Hananiah)	Yohanan ben Nuri	Nehemiah
Judah ben Bathyra	Yose the Galilean	Sim(e)on ben Gamaliel II
Yohanan ben Zakkai	Sim(e)on ben Azzai	Sim(e)on (ben Yohai)
Yose the Priest	Tarfon	Yose (ben Halafta)

Fourth Generation (165–200 C.E.)	Fifth Generation (200–220 C.E.)	Post-Tannaic (220–240 C.E.)
Eleazar ben Sim(e)on (ben Yohai)	Gamaliel III	Joshua ben Levi
Judah the Patriarch (or "Rabbi")	Sim(e)on ben Judah (the Patriarch)	Yannai
Nathan the Babylonian		
Sim(e)on ben Eleazar		
Yose ben Judah (ben Elai)		

*(Adapted from A. Goldberg, "Mishnah," *LS*, 236–38; H. Danby, *Mishnah*, 799–800. Goldberg's "first generation" is Danby's "second," and so forth. Note: The names that begin with "J" are sometimes spelled with "Y," e.g., Yoshua, instead of Joshua, Yehudah, instead of Judah, etc.)

The exegesis of the rabbis is called midrash. This word comes from the Hebrew verb *dāraš* ("to search"). Midrash, therefore, literally means a "search" or the activity of "searching" (cf. John 5:39: "You search the scriptures"; cf. 7:52). In the context of the rabbinic writings, the word means interpretation of Scripture. Midrash is often broken down into two categories: Halakic midrash and haggadic midrash (see below). Rabbinic interpretation is in large measure founded on the assumption that Scripture contains potentially unlimited meaning. One rabbi explained it this way: " 'Is not my word like a hammer that breaks the rock in pieces?' [Jer 23:29]. As the hammer causes numerous sparks to flash forth, so is a verse of Scripture capable of many interpretations" (*b. Sanh.* 34a). According to Ben Bag Bag, a student of Hillel: "Turn it [Scripture] and turn it again, for everything is in it; and contemplate it and grow grey and old over it and stir not from it, for thou canst have no better rule than it" (*m. 'Abot* 5:22). A single exegesis is called a midrash (pl. *midrašim*). Commentaries on Scripture are called Midrashim, although the Mishna, the Tosepta, and the two Talmuds are themselves filled with midrash.

The word *midrash*, as well as its Greek equivalent *ereunan* ("to search"), was associated with biblical interpretation in the first century. This is shown by the Qumran materials: "This is the study [*midraš*] of the Law" (1QS 8:15); "The interpretation [*midraš*] of 'Blessed is the man . . .' [cf. Ps 1:1]" (4QFlor 1:14). Indeed, Qumran's leader, the Teacher of Righteousness, is called the "searcher of the Law" (CD 6:7). Philo, the Greek-speaking Jew of Alexandria, urges his readers to join him in searching (*ereunan*) Scripture (*The Worse Attacks the Better* 17 §57; 39 §141; *On the Cherubim* 5 §14). John 5:39, cited above, also uses the Greek equivalent *ereunan*.

According to early rabbinic tradition Hillel the Elder articulated seven rules (or *middot*) by which Scripture was to be interpreted. Evidently they were practiced in the first century, for all of these rules are found in the NT. They are as follows (cf. *t. Sanh.* 7.11; *'Abot R. Nat.* A §37):

(1) *Qal wa-homer* (lit. "light and heavy"). According to this rule, what is true or applicable in a "light" (or less important) instance is surely true or applicable in a "heavy" (or more important) instance. This rule is at work when Jesus assures his disciples (cf. Matt 6:26; Luke 12:24) that because God cares for the birds (light), they can be sure that he cares for them (heavy). See also John 10:31–38; 2 Cor 3:6–11; Heb 9:13–14.

(2) *Gezera shawa* (lit. "an equivalent regulation"). According to this rule one passage may be explained by another, if similar words or phrases are present. Comparing himself to David, who on one occasion violated the law in eating consecrated bread (1 Sam 21:6), Jesus justified his apparent violation of the Sabbath (Mark 2:23–28). See also Rom 4:3–7; Heb 7:1–28; Jas 2:21–24.

(3) *Binyan 'ab mikkatub 'ehad* (lit. "constructing a father [i.e., principal rule] from one [passage]"). Since God is not the God of the dead, but of the living, the revelation at the burning bush, "I am the God of Abraham" (Exod 3:14–15), implies that Abraham is to be resurrected. From this one text and its inference one may further infer, as Jesus did (Mark 12:26), the truth of the general resurrection. See also Jas 5:16–18.

(4) *Binyan 'ab mishshene ketubim* (lit. "constructing a father [i.e., principal rule] from two writings [or passages]"). From the commands to unmuzzle the ox (Deut 25:4) and share sacrifices with the priests (Deut 18:1–8) it is inferred that those who preach are entitled to support (Matt 10:10; Luke 10:7; 1 Cor 9:9, 13; 1 Tim 5:18). See also Rom 4:1–25; Jas 2:22–26.

(5) *Kelal uperat uperat ukelal* (lit. "General and particular, and particular and general"). When Jesus replies that the greatest commandment (the "general") is to love the Lord with all one's heart (Deut 6:4–5) and to love one's neighbor as one's self (Lev 19:18), he has summed up all of the "particular" commandments (Mark 12:28–34). See also Rom 13:9–10.

(6) *Kayotze bo mi–maqom 'aher* (lit. "To which something [is] similar in another place [or passage]"). If the Son of Man (or Messiah) is to sit on one of the thrones set up before the Ancient of Days (Dan 7:9, which is how Rabbi Aqiba interprets Daniel's plural reference to "thrones," cf. *b. Hag.* 14a; *b. Sanh.* 38b), and if Messiah is to sit at God's right hand (Ps 110:1), it may be inferred that when the Son of Man comes with the clouds (Dan 7:13–14), he will be seated at the right hand of God and will judge his enemies. This is evidently what Jesus implied in his reply to Caiaphas (Mark 14:62; see further discussion below). See also Gal 3:8–16; Heb 4:7–9; 8:7–13.

(7) *Dabar halamed me'inyano* (lit. "word of instruction from the context"). This rule is exemplified in Jesus' teaching against divorce (Matt

19:4–8). Although it is true that Moses allowed divorce (Deut 24:1–3), it is also true that God never intended the marriage union to be broken, as implied in Gen 1:27 and 2:24. See also Rom 4:10–11; Heb 11:1–13, 35–40.

Tradition holds that these rules were expanded to thirteen by Ishmael, a rabbi of the second century (cf. *Bar. R. Ishmael* §1 in Prologue to *Sipra*). Rabbi Eliezer ben Yose the Galilean is credited with expanding the rules of midrash, particularly as they relate to the interpretation of narrative. He is evidently the author of the tractate, *Thirty-Two Rules for Interpreting the Torah*, often called the *Baraita of Thirty-Two Rules* (cf. the beginning of *Midr. Mishnat R. Eliezer* and the beginning of *Midr. Haggadol* to Genesis). Many of these rules are atomistic (e.g., finding significance in the numerical value of the letters themselves) and have little or nothing to do with the literary or historical context of the scriptural passage under consideration. Most of these thirty-two rules, rules which made it possible to enjoy the "savory dishes of wisdom" (*m. 'Abot* 3:19), were applied to homiletical midrash, not legal.

The distinction between homiletical midrash and legal interpretation also requires explanation. Legal midrash is halakic, from the word *hālak* ("to walk"), i.e., how one should walk or conduct himself or herself in life. A legal opinion is called a *halakah* (pl. *halakot*). Homiletical interpretation is haggadic, from the word *nāgad* ("to draw"), i.e., how one narrates a story or explains a problem in the text. A homiletical interpretation is called a *haggadah* (pl. *haggadot*; note that sometimes it is spelled *'Aggadah*). Best known is the *Passover Haggadah* (cf. *b. Pesaḥ.* 115b, 116b). Haggadic midrash was much more imaginative in its attempts to fill in the gaps in Scripture and to explain away apparent discrepancies, difficulties, and unanswered questions. Legal rulings were not to be derived from haggadic interpretation (cf. *y. Pe'a* 2.6).

The following summaries are chronological in their respective categories to the best of our knowledge. Rabbinic literature is notoriously difficult to date. Part of the problem is that a given work, which may have been edited in the Middle Ages, may contain a great deal of tannaic tradition. What then is being dated? If the sayings are genuine, the work could be considered tannaic. If the sayings are not, or at least have been heavily edited, or inaccurately transmitted, then the work should be considered amoraic (or later). There is also the problem of pseudonymity. Sayings may be credited to a famous Tanna (such as Aqiba or Ishmael), but in reality they derive from a much later Amora.

SUMMARIES OF TALMUDIC LITERATURE

The word *mishna(h)* (lit. "repetition") comes from the Hebrew verb *šānāh*, "to repeat." It later came to connote learning by repetition, perhaps under the influence of the Aramaic word *tenā'*, which has this meaning. The Mishna was edited and published under the direction of Rabbi Judah ha-Nasi, ca. 200–220 C.E. Rabbi Aqiba and his pupils were the most influential contributors to this corpus, especially at Usha (ca. 150 C.E.), following the defeat of Bar Kokhba (Simon ben Kosibah). Representing a large portion of tannaic oral tradition, the themes of Mishna are organized into six major divisions (i.e., *sedarim*, "orders"), each containing several tractates *(massektot)*, whose names are either Hebrew or Aramaic:

MISHNA

1. Zera'im ("seeds")	2. Mo'ed ("set [feasts]")	3. Našim ("women")
Berakot ("benedictions")	Šabbat ("sabbath")	Yebamot ("sisters-in-law")
Pe'a ("corner [for gleaning]")	'Erubin ("mixtures")	Ketubot ("marriage deeds")
Demai ("doubtful [produce]")	Pesaḥim ("Passovers")	Nedarim ("vows")
Kil'ayim ("diverse kinds")	Šeqalim ("shekels")	Nazir ("the nazirite vow")
Šebi'it ("seventh [year]")	Yoma ("the day [of atonement]")	Soṭa ("the suspected adultress")
Terumot ("heave-offerings")	Sukka ("tabernacle")	Giṭṭin ("bills of divorce")
Ma'aserot ("tithes")	Yom Ṭob/Beṣa ("good day"/"egg")	Qiddušin ("betrothals")
Ma'aser Šeni ("second tithe")	Roš Haššana ("New Year")	
Ḥalla ("dough-offering")	Ta'anit ("fast day")	
'Orla ("uncut [young trees]")	Megilla ("the Scroll [of Esther]")	
Bikkurim ("first-fruits")	Mo'ed Qaṭan ("lesser set [feasts]")	
	Ḥagiga ("the festal offering")	

4. Neziqin ("damages")	5. Qodašin ("sacred things")	6. Ṭoharot ("cleannesses")
Baba Qamma ("first gate")	Zebaḥim ("sacrifices")	Kelim ("vessels")
Baba Meṣi'a ("middle gate")	Menaḥot ("meal offerings")	Oholot ("tents")
Baba Batra ("last gate")	Ḥullin ("non-holy things")	Nega'im ("plagues")
Sanhedrin ("the Council")	Bekorot ("firstlings")	Para ("cow")
Makkot ("stripes")	'Arakin ("vows of valuation")	Ṭohorot ("cleannesses")
Šebu'ot ("oaths")	Temura ("exchange")	Miqwa'ot ("ritual baths")
'Eduyyot ("testimonies")	Keritot ("uprootings")	Niddah ("the menstruant")
'Aboda Zara ("idolatry")	Me'ila ("sacrilege")	Makširin ("defilers")
(Pirqe) 'Abot ("the fathers")	Tamid ("always")	Zabim ("those with flux")
Horayot ("instructions")	Middot ("measurements")	Ṭebul Yom ("immersed that day")
	Qinnim ("birds' nests")	Yadayim ("hands")
		'Uqṣin ("stalks")

Mishna represents a codification of the oral tradition of the tannaic sages and rabbis. As the table of contents above shows, these materials have been arranged according to topic. For example, the order *Neziqin* contains tractates concerned with civil and criminal law. (*Pirqe 'Abot*, it should be noted, is not really a mishnaic tractate, but a collection of the sayings of tannaic sages and rabbis that is more akin to wisdom literature than the halakic materials one encounters in the Mishna.) The "gate" tractates, once originally combined, primarily treat civil law. *Baba Qamma* deals with personal injury. *Baba Meṣi'a* deals with lost property, questions of guardianship, usury, and the hire of laborers. *Baba Batra* deals with problems relating to the ownership of real estate and other immovable property. *Sanhedrin* deals primarily with criminal law, especially as it pertains to capital punishment, while *Makkot,* originally part of *Sanhedrin,* deals with the question of punishment for false witnesses. Below are sample passages from *Sanhedrin* (6:4; 7:5) that could have some relevance for NT interpretation:

> "All that have been stoned must be hanged." So Rabbi Eliezer [late first, early second century C.E.]. But the Sages [first century C.E.] say: "None is hanged save the blasphemer and idolator." "A man is hanged with his face to the people and a woman with her face towards the gallows." So Rabbi Eliezer. But the Sages say: "A man is hanged but a woman is not hanged." Rabbi Eliezer said to them: "Did not Simeon ben Shetah [first century B.C.E.] hang women in Askelon?" They answered: "He hanged eighty women, whereas two ought not to be judged in the one day." How did they hang a man? They put a beam into the ground and a piece of wood jutted from it. The two hands [of the body] were brought together and [in this fashion] it was hanged. Rabbi Yose [early second century C.E.] says: "The beam was made to lean against a wall and one hanged the corpse thereon as butchers do. And they let it down at once: if it remained there overnight a negative command is thereby transgressed, for it is written, 'His body shall not remain all night upon the tree, but you shall surely bury him the same day; for he that is hanged is a curse of God' [Deut 21:23]; as if to say: 'Why was this one hanged? Because he blessed [euphemism for cursed] the Name, and the Name of Heaven was found profaned.' "

> "The blasphemer" [Lev 24:10–23] is not culpable unless he pronounces the Name itself. Rabbi Joshua ben Karha [second century C.E.] says: "On every day [of the trial] they examined the witnesses with a substituted name, [such as] 'May Yose strike Yose.' When sentence was to be given they did not declare him guilty of death [on the grounds of the evidence given] with the substituted name, but they sent out all the people and asked the chief among the witnesses and said to him, 'Say expressly what you heard,' and he says it; and the judges stand up on their feet and tear their garments, and they may not mend them again. And the second witness says, 'I also heard the like,' and the third says, 'I also heard the like.' "

These passages may clarify certain features of Jesus' trial before Caiaphas the high priest and the Sanhedrin (Mark 14:53–65). Caiaphas asked Jesus if he was the Messiah, the Son of the Blessed (v. 61). When Jesus affirmed the question and alluded to Ps 110:1 and Dan 7:13–14 (v. 62), Caiaphas tore his garments and accused Jesus of blasphemy (vv. 63–64). The Sanhedrin agreed that Jesus deserved death (v. 64). Some think that the mishnaic rules do not apply, at least not exactly, since Jesus did not pronounce the Divine Name, but employed a circumlocution ("You will see the Son of Man seated at the right hand of Power"). But it is possible that what we have in Mark is the public report of what Jesus said. This report would not have used the Divine Name. What Jesus may have said before Caiaphas and the Sanhedrin was, "You will see the Son of Man seated at the right hand of Yahweh." Jesus' claim to be seated at God's right hand and someday to come with clouds of heaven as the Son of Man would have been blasphemous in itself (see discussion below). Pronouncing the Divine Name would have allowed the Sanhedrin to sentence him to death. The use of Deut 21:23 could explain why Jesus was taken down from the cross the same day of his crucifixion (Mark 15:42–46). Note also the theological use of the verse in Paul (Gal 3:13; cf. 2 Cor 5:21).

Although most of this material arose after the destruction of the Jewish temple in 70 C.E., some of it does derive from the time of Jesus and his disciples. The criticisms leveled at Jesus for associating with "sinners" (Mark 2:15–17), failing to fast (Mark 2:18–20), gleaning on the Sabbath (Mark 2:23–27), healing on the Sabbath (Mark 3:1–6), and eating with unwashed hands (Mark 7:1–13) are all based on the oral tradition current in the early first century that was developed further, collected, edited, and eventually published as the Mishna.

Deserving of comment is Jacob Neusner's controversial view of the Mishna as an ahistorical, even anti–historical philosophy, which is neither interested in eschatology or messianology and which as such represents the essence of Judaism (*Judaism: The Evidence of the Mishnah* [Chicago: University of Chicago, 1981]; cf. idem, *Messiah in Context: Israel's History and Destiny in Formative Judaism* [Philadelphia: Fortress, 1984]; idem, *Judaism as Philosophy: The Method and Message of the Mishnah* [Columbia: University of South Carolina, 1991]). E. P. Sanders (*Jewish Law from Jesus to the Mishnah* [London: SCM; Philadelphia: Trinity Press International, 1990] 309–31) has pointed out that this assessment founders on the question of genre. Mishna is a compendium of law; it is not a philosophy of history, nor an apocalypse. Since its concern is primarily legal (i.e., how to obey the commandments of Torah), one should expect to find in it little historical narrative and little eschatology. Neusner's assessment also is vulnerable for assuming that what is not in the Mishna was therefore of no interest to the rabbis. Sanders rightly comments that this is a false use of the argument from silence. (See the related discussion below on Messiah in rabbinic literature.)

References to Mishna are usually cited with an *m.* followed by the name of the tractate, its chapter (or *pereq*) and its paragraph (or *mishnah*). For example, the two passages from *Sanhedrin* cited above would appear as *m. Sanh.* 6:4; 7:5. For the SBL's recommended abbreviations of mishnaic tractates see *SBL Membership Directory and Handbook 1991* (Decatur: SBL, 1991) 199–200.

Text and Commentary: P. Blackman, *Mishnayoth* (6 vols.; 2d ed.; New York: Judaica, 1990); J. Rabbinowitz, *Mishnah Megillah* (Oxford: Oxford University, 1931). *Translations:* H. Danby, *The Mishnah* (Oxford: Clarendon, 1933); J. Neusner, *The Mishnah: A New Translation* (New Haven and London: Yale University, 1988). *Critical Studies:* A. Goldberg, "The Mishna—A Study Book of Halakha," *LS*, 211–62; J. Neusner, *The Modern Study of the Mishna* (Leiden: Brill, 1973); idem, *Judaism: The Evidence of the Mishnah* (Chicago and London: University of Chicago, 1981).

PRINCIPAL AMORAIM OF THE TALMUDIC PERIOD

First Generation (220–250 C.E.)	Second Generation (250–290 C.E.)	Third Generation (290–320 C.E.)
Hanina ben Hama	Eleazar ben Pedat	Abbahu
Joshua ben Levi	Hamnuna	Hisda
Oshaya Rabbah	Huna	Joseph ben Hiyya
Rab (Abba ben Aibu)	Judah ben Ezekiel	Rabbah ben Huna
Samuel	Simeon ben Lakish	Rabbah ben Nahmani
Yannai	Yohanan	Zeira

Fourth Generation (320–350 C.E.)	Fifth Generation (350–375 C.E.)	Sixth Generation (375–425 C.E.)
Abbaye	Huna ben Joshua	Ameimar
Haggai	Mana ben Jonah	Mar Zutra
Jeremiah	Pappa	Rab Ashi
Jonah	Tanhuma ben Abba	Rabina
Raba ben Joseph	Yose ben Abin	
Yose	Zevid	

Seventh Generation (425–460 C.E.)	Eighth Generation (460–500 C.E.)
Geviha of Bet-Katil	Ahai ben Huna
Mar ben Rab Ashi	Rabina II ben Huna
Yeimar	Yose

(adapted from *EncJud* 1.866)

Tosepta (Tosefta). Tosepta ("addition") was probably published about one generation after Mishna (220–230 C.E.), though some, such as Jacob Neusner, have argued for a later date (e.g., 300 C.E.). Tosepta contains mostly tannaic traditions, but adds the next two generations of rabbis. It is thus an admixture of tannaic and early amoraic materials. The major contributor of the new material is Rabbi Judah ha-Nasi, the compiler of Mishna. The editor of Tosepta was Rabbi Judah's pupil Rabbi Hiya the Elder. Tosepta complements, explains, expands upon, identifies anonymous sayings, and at times explicitly comments on the Mishna. (One could say that its relationship to Mishna is somewhat analogous to Matthew's and Luke's respective relationships to Mark.) As a result, it is more than twice the length of the Mishna. In a very real sense it is the forerunner of Talmud itself.

Tosepta follows the same format and structure as the Mishna and has the same basic contents. There are some differences, however. In the first order, *Zera'im*, a few of the tractates are in different positions. The fourth order, *Neziqin*, does not contain *Pirqe 'Abot*. The fifth order, *Qodašin*, lacks the tractates *Tamid, Middot,* and *Qinnim.* The sixth order, *Toharot,* arranges *Kelim* differently. In both *Qodašin* and *Toharot* some tractates are in different positions.

There is material in Tosepta that may shed light on the NT. Supplementing and commenting on the last part of *m. Menaḥ.* 13:10, the Tosepta has this to say about activities of the last two generations of the ruling priests (*t. Menaḥ.* 13.18–22; cf. *t. Zebaḥ.* 11.16–17; *b. Pesaḥ.* 57a):

> At first [the lower-ranking priests] brought the hides of Holy Things to the room of *bet happarvah* and divided them in the evening to each household which had served on that day. But the powerful men of the [ruling] priesthood would come and take them by force. [Then] they ordained that they should divide [them] on Fridays to each and every watch [of lower-ranking priests]. But still violent men of the [ruling] priesthood came and took [them] away by force. [Therefore,] the owners went and dedicated them to Heaven.

> Abba Saul [ca. 140 C.E.] says, "Beams of sycamore were in Jericho. And strong-fisted men would come and take them by force. The owners went and dedicated them to Heaven." [The Sages said,] "The owners dedicated to Heaven only beams of sycamore alone." Concerning these and people like them and people who do deeds like their deeds Abba Saul ben Batnit [ca. 80 C.E.] and Yose ben Yohanan of Jerusalem [ca. 10 C.E.] say, "Woe is me because of the House of Boethus. Woe is me because of their clubs. Woe is me because of the house of Qadros. Woe is me because of their pen. Woe is me because of the House of Hanin. Woe is me because of their whispering. Woe is me because of the House of Ishmael ben Phiabi. For they are High Priests, and their sons [are] treasurers, and their sons-in-law [are] supervisors, and their servants come and beat us with clubs." Yohanan ben Torta [ca. 120 C.E.] said, "On what account was Shiloh [cf. Jer 7:12] destroyed? Because of the disgraceful disposition of the Holy Things which were there. As to Jerusalem's first [temple], on what account was it destroyed? Because of idolatry and licentiousness and bloodshed which was in it. But [as to] the latter [temple] we know that they devoted themselves to Torah and were meticulous about tithes. On what account did they go into exile? Because they love money and hate one another."

These passages describe the last two generations of the ruling priests of Jerusalem. In the "woes" of Abba Saul ben Batnit and Yose ben Yohanan of Jerusalem we find criticism leveled at three of the four principal ruling families during the period of the Herodian temple. "Boethus" was the lower-ranking priest whose son Simon Herod the Great made high priest (22–5 B.C.E.) in return for the hand of his daughter (cf. Josephus *Ant.* 15.9.3 §320). "Qadros" is probably "Simon Cantheras," another son of Boethus (*Ant.* 19.6.2 §297; 19.6.4 §313), who served less than one year as high priest (41 C.E.). The House of Boethus is remembered for its clubs and for its pen, by which they wrote their oppressive and unfair decrees. "Hanin" is the Annas of the NT (Luke 3:2; John 18:13, 14; Acts 4:6), who served as high priest (6–15 C.E.) and whose five sons, a grandson, and son-in-law Caiaphas at various times served as high priest (*Ant.* 18.2.1 §26; 20.9.1 §198, where he is called Ananus). Ben Batnit and ben Yohanan lament their "whispering," by which they probably mean their conspiracies. Tosepta does not tell us specifically why "Phiabi" and his son Ishmael (*Ant.* 18.2.2 §34) were a cause for lamentation. The Talmud (*b. Pesaḥ.* 57a) tells us it was "because of their fists." In reference to all of these priestly families, the woes are summed up: "they are High Priests, and their sons [are] treasurers, and their sons-in-law [are] supervisors, and their servants come and beat us with clubs."

Tosepta also explains why the Herodian temple was destroyed. Because of greed, avarice, and nepotism, the second temple, like the sanctuary at Shiloh and the first temple of Jerusalem, was destroyed. The "powerful men of the [ruling] priesthood" stole the tithes that rightfully belonged to the lower-ranking priests. With the profits they were able to cover the temple with gold (part of *t. Menaḥ.* 13.19 omitted in the quotation). If any one opposed them, they had their servants beat them with clubs.

The tradition is apparently very ancient. The "woes" originated with Yose ben Yohanan of Jerusalem, a sage from the turn of the era, and probably reached the form we now have them in Abba Saul ben Batnit. Yohanan ben Torta adds later moralizing commentary. His statement that it was because of hatred and the love of money is quite significant. The tradition enjoys a measure of confirmation from Josephus. He specifically mentions another Ishmael, part of the Phiabi family, who served as high priest (59–61 C.E.), whose servants beat the lower-ranking priests and stole their tithes (*Ant.* 20.8.8 §§179–181; 20.9.2 §207).

These passages may clarify several aspects of Jesus' relationship to the temple establishment and why he was arrested. First, it could help us understand Jesus' criticism of the economic policies of the temple establishment. This is seen in Jesus' statement that the sons of the king are free from the obligation to pay the annual half-shekel temple tax (Matt 17:24–27). It is clearly seen in his Vineyard parable (Mark 12:1–12), in which the priestly aristocracy is threatened with the loss of their position. Jesus' warning of the scribes who "devour widows' houses" (Mark 12:38–40), his lament (not praise!) over the poor widow's offering (Mark 12:41–44), and his prediction of the destruction of the "wonderful buildings" (Mark 13:1–2) should be understood as criticisms of the economic policies and practices of the first-century ruling priesthood.

Second, Jesus' action in the temple (Mark 11:15–17) is now clarified. His action was no protest against "external" religion or against the sacrificial system itself. He protested against the profit-motivated policies of Caiaphas the high priest and his aristocratic supporters. By alluding to Jeremiah 7 Jesus implied that his contemporaries were guilty of some of the same practices of the priests of Jeremiah's time. Some scholars have doubted the authenticity of the saying in Mark 11:17, because Jeremiah's reference to "robbers" implies violence, taking by force, not thievery or swindling. But according to Josephus and the Tosepta's version of *Menaḥot*, violence perpetrated by the first-century ruling priesthood *was* a problem. Of course, Jesus did not imply that people were being mugged in the temple precincts, any more than they were in the days of Jeremiah. But the ruling priesthood was avaricious and at times violent, just as in the days of Jeremiah. Calling them robbers would not have been unintelligible. Jesus' action would have been understood as a prophetic condemnation of temple polity. Since the high priest is directly responsible for temple polity, this action would have been keenly felt by Caiaphas.

Third, details of Jesus' arrest cohere with Tosepta's picture. Judas, bribed by the ruling priests (Mark 14:10–11), assisted Caiaphas in his conspiracy to take Jesus by stealth. Thus far, he has lived up to Tosepta's picture of the family that "whispers." While alone in Gethsemane, Jesus was approached by "a crowd with swords and clubs, from the ruling priests and the scribes and elders" (Mark 14:32, 43). Again we are reminded of Tosepta's *Menaḥot*. In the minor scuffle that ensued the "slave of the high priest" is struck (v. 47). It is interesting that the only person of the arresting party to be mentioned is the servant of the *high priest*. His presence and violent involvement suggest that Caiaphas had taken a personal interest in seeing Jesus arrested.

Finally, Caiaphas' interest in the case is further documented by his personal appearance at Jesus' hearing before the Sanhedrin (Mark 14:53–65). Indeed, the proceedings apparently took place in his home (v. 54). When Jesus was charged with blasphemy and condemned to death he was slapped and spat upon (v. 65). Thus we find at several points coherence between the Gospels' portrayal of Jesus' criticisms of the ruling priesthood and the traditions and reminiscences preserved in one of the Tosepta tractates.

References to Tosepta, as in the case of Mishna, are usually cited with a *t.* followed by the name of the tractate, its chapter, and its paragraph (or halakah), e.g., *t. Soṭa* 9.15. In his translation Jacob Neusner has very helpfully outlined the logical flow of the topics and arguments. The abbreviations of Tosepta's tractates are the same as those of Mishna.

Text and Commentary: S. Lieberman, *Tosefot Rishonim* (4 vols.; Jerusalem: Bamberger & Wahrmann, 1936–39) [Hebrew]; *Translation:* J. Neusner, ed., *The Tosefta: Translated from the Hebrew* (6 vols.; New York: Ktav, 1977–86). *Critical Studies:* A. Goldberg, with M. Krupp, "The Tosefta—Companion to the Mishna," *LS*, 283–302; H. L. Strack and G. Stemberger, *Einleitung in Talmud und Midrasch* (7th ed.; Munich: Beck, 1982) 150–62; S. Zeitlin, "The Tosefta," *JQR* 47 (1956–57) 382–99.

Jerusalem Talmud. The Hebrew name of the Jerusalem Talmud is *Talmud Yerushalmi.* In English it is usually referred to as the Jerusalem or Palestinian Talmud. "Jerusalem" is a misnomer, since this version of the Talmud took shape in Galilee. In his new translation Jacob Neusner calls it the Talmud of the Land of Israel, which actually reflects the earliest name given to it. The word *talmud* means "learning" or "study," from *lāmad* "to learn" or "study." (A disciple is a *talmid,* i.e., a "learner." These are the same words, only in Greek, used in the NT.) The Talmud is made up of Mishna (and Tosepta) plus interpretive expansions called Gemara (from the Hebrew word *gāmar,* "to complete"). The Palestinian Talmud was completed ca. 400–425 C.E. The first published edition made its appearance in 1522 (Venice). Not every tractate of Mishna is commented upon. Thirty-nine of the sixty-three tractates have gemara. Most of them are the tractates of the first three orders. Not all of the gemara is commentary on the given *mishnah;* some of it is related discussion; some of this discussion derives from the tannaic period (i.e., *baraitot*). The best known MS is in the University Library of Leiden. In the seventies E. S. Rosenthal discovered that the Escorial MS (Spain) contains the Jerusalem Talmud. Jacob Neusner is currently completing an English translation; to date most of the thirty-five volumes have appeared. Another English translation, including pointed text, is being prepared by A. Ehrman.

When citing a passage from the Jerusalem Talmud it is customary to use a *y.* (for *Yerushalmi*) followed by tractate name and chapter and paragraph, e.g., *y. Ta'an.* 4.5. Since these are the names of the mishnaic tractates they are abbreviated the same way as the Mishna tractates.

Texts: Talmud Yerushalmi (New York: Shulsinger, 1948); *Talmud Yerushalmi* (4 vols.; Jerusalem: Kedem, 1971); A. Ehrman, ed., *The Talmud with English Translation and Commentary* (Jerusalem: El-'Am, 1965–). *Translation:* J. Neusner, *The Talmud of the Land of Israel* (35 vols.; Chicago and London: University of Chicago, 1982–). *Critical Studies:* A. Goldberg, with M. Krupp, "The Palestinian Talmud," *LS,* 303–22; S. Liebermann, "A Tragedy or a Comedy?" *JAOS* 104 (1984) 315–19 [offers an important critique of Neusner's translation]; H. L. Strack and G. Stemburger, *Introduction to the Talmud and Midrash* (trans. M. Bockmuehl; Edinburgh: T. & T. Clark, 1990).

Babylonian Talmud. Like the shorter Palestinian Talmud, the Babylonian Talmud (or Talmud Babli) combines Mishna (and some Tosepta—less than in the case of the Palestinian Talmud) with gemara. There is gemara on thirty-six of the mishnaic tractates, most from the second, third, fourth, and fifth orders. The Babylonian Talmud was probably completed ca. 500–550 C.E. Unlike its Palestinian counterpart, the Babylonian Talmud underwent a later editing which has left it smoother and much more polished. During this later editing some of the sayings of the Saboraim were added. The Babylonian Talmud is longer than the Palestinian, primarily because the former contains much more haggadic material than the latter (though ironically, much of this haggadic material is Palestinian in origin). Whereas the Babylonian Talmud is about one-third haggadah, the Palestinian is one-sixth. The first published edition appeared in 1484 (Soncino, near Milan). The oldest complete MS is in Munich.

The Mishna used by the Babylonian Talmud is not identical to that used in the Palestinian Talmud. The Babylonian Mishna is the official version of Mishna. But scholars think that the Palestinian Talmud is closer to the original edition of Mishna produced by Rabbi Judah ha-Nasi. When citing a passage from the Babylonian Talmud it is customary to use a *b.* (for *Babli*) followed by tractate name and folio, front side ("a") or backside ("b"), e.g., *b. B. Bat.* 14a. Since these are the names of the mishnaic tractates they are abbreviated the same way as the Mishna tractates.

Text: *Talmud Babli* (Vilna: Romm, 1886); I. Epstein, ed., *Hebrew-English Edition of the Babylonian Talmud* (London: Soncino, 1960–). *Translation:* I. Epstein, *The Babylonian Talmud* (35 vols.; London: Soncino, 1935–48); J. Neusner is preparing a new American translation. *Critical Studies:* A. Goldberg, with M. Krupp, "The Babylonian Talmud," *LS*, 323–66; J. Neusner, *The Formation of the Babylonian Talmud* (Leiden: Brill, 1970); H. L. Strack and G. Stemberger, *Introduction to the Talmud and Midrash* (trans. M. Bockmuehl; Edinburgh: T. & T. Clark, 1990).

The "Minor" Tractates. Gathered at the end of the Babylonian Talmud are fifteen tractates largely comprising tannaic traditions, though in many cases edited and augmented well into the amoraic period and even later. They are as follows:

MINOR TRACTATES

'Abot de Rabbi Nathan ("The Fathers according to Rabbi Nathan")

Kalla Rabbati ("The Long [Version of] Kalla")

Soperim ("Scribes")

Ṣemaḥot ("Rejoicings")

Kalla ("A Bride")

Derek Ereṣ Rabba ("The Major Way of the Land")

Derek Ereṣ Zuṭa ("The Minor Way of the Land")

Pereq ha-Šalom ("The Chapter of Peace")

Gerim ("Proselytes")

Kutim ("Cutheans [i.e., Samaritans]")

'Abadim ("Slaves")

Seper Torah ("The Book of Torah")

Tepillin ("Phylacteries")

Zizit ("Fringes")

Mezuzah ("Doorpost")

For NT interpretation perhaps the most important is *'Abot de Rabbi Nathan* (late third century C.E.). This work is an expansion of *Pirqe 'Abot* ("Chapters of the Fathers"; see discussion of Mishna above) and is preserved in two versions (A and B). It is not clear why this tractate is associated with the name of Rabbi Nathan. Perhaps he was the editor.

Pereq §4 of version A contains several items of interest. The chapter opens with a discussion of Hos 6:6: "I desire mercy and not sacrifice, and the knowledge of God rather than burnt offerings," a passage that Jesus had appealed to in halakic disputes (Matt 9:13; 12:7). A sage infers from the passage that "the study of Torah is more beloved by God than burnt offerings." After a few paragraphs concerning the temple service, the discussion returns to Hos 6:6. Taken up now is the story of Yohanan ben Zakkai and the destruction of the Herodian temple:

> "Woe unto us!" Rabbi Joshua cried, "that this, the place where the iniquities of Israel were atoned for, is laid waste!"

> "My son," Rabbi Yohanan said to him, "be not grieved; we have another atonement as effective as this. And what is? It is acts of loving-kindness, as it is said, 'For I desire mercy and not sacrifice' [Hos 6:6]."

In the next paragraph the story is told of ben Zakkai's opposition to the rebellion, the plot against his life, and his escape to the Romans via concealment in a coffin carried outside of the walls of Jerusalem. When he later heard that the temple had been destroyed, he tore his clothes and wept. The final paragraph of pereq §4 begins with a quotation of Zech 11:1, where "Lebanon" is understood as an allusion to the temple, and an interpretation: "This refers to the High Priests who were in the Temple, who took their keys in their hands and threw them up to the sky, saying to the Holy One, blessed be He: 'Master of the Universe, here are your keys which you gave us, for we have not been trustworthy custodians to do the King's work and to eat of the King's table.' " The interpretation of Hos 6:6 and the recognition of improper stewardship of the temple service align with Jesus' earlier criticisms.

The minor tractates are usually cited by name, followed by chapter and paragraph, e.g., Ṣemaḥot 2.1, or simply the chapter, §2. In the case of 'Abot de Rabbi Nathan it is necessary to indicate which version is being cited, e.g., 'Abot de Rabbi Nathan B §9. The SBL has recommended abbreviations for a few of these tractates: 'Abot R. Nat., Kalla R., Sop., Ṣem., Der. Er. Rab., Der. Er. Zuṭ.

Text and Translations of Minor Tractates: A. Cohen, The Minor Tractates of the Talmud (2 vols.; London: Soncino, 1965); J. Goldin, The Fathers According to Rabbi Nathan (YJ 10; New Haven: Yale University, 1955) [version A, including H. Danby's translation of Pirqe 'Abot]; A. J. Saldarini, The Fathers According to Rabbi Nathan (Leiden: Brill, 1975) [translation and commentary on version B]. Critical Study: M. B. Lerner, "The External Tractates," LS, 367–409.

SUMMARIES OF TANNAIC MIDRASHIC LITERATURE

Mekilta. The Mekilta (Aramaic for "measure" or "form") is a collection of tannaic commentary related to portions of Exodus. The best known and most fully preserved version is the *Mekilta of Rabbi Ishmael* (ca. 60–140 C.E.), possibly named after this great Tanna because a large portion of the material derives from him. Compiled sometime in the mid to late fourth century C.E. and published in 1515 (Constantinople) this work is divided into nine tractates named after key words (Hebrew or Aramaic) from the text of Exodus:

Pisha (Aramaic for "the Passover")	Exod 12:1—13:16
Bešallah ("when he had let go")	Exod 13:17—14:26–31
Širata (Aramaic for "the Song")	Exod 15:1–21
Vayassaʾ ("and he led")	Exod 15:22—17:7
ʾAmalek ("Amalek")	Exod 17:8—18:27
Bahodeš ("in the [third] month")	Exod 19:1—20:23
Neziqin (Aramaic for "damages")	Exod 21:1—22:23
Kaspa (Aramaic for "the money")	Exod 22:24—23:19
Šabbata (Aramaic for "the Sabbath")	Exod 31:12—35:3

There is also a *Mekilta de Rabbi Simeon ben Yohai* (compiled ca. 400–450 C.E.), which is extant as fragments contained in *Midraš Haggadol* ("the Great Midrash"), a thirteenth-century compilation of midrash on the Pentateuch.

Let us consider the opening midrash in *Širata* 1.1–10 on Exod 15:1: "Then Moses sang." The midrash begins with a word study, after a fashion, on *ʾāz* ("then"). It is observed that *ʾāz* is used in contexts referring to the past ("Then men began to call upon the name of the Lord" [Gen 4:26], etc.) and to the future ("Then shall the eyes of the blind be opened" [Isa 35:5], etc.). The implication of this observation is that *ʾāz* in Exod 15:1 may be referring to the future, and not only to the past. The midrash makes a second observation concerning the verb. Although Exod 15:1 reads *yāšîr*, which as a consecutive and in context should probably be read as a preterite ("he sang"), it is also the form of the future tense. Therefore, with the futuristic possibilities of *ʾāz* in mind, Exod 15:1 can be read: "Then Moses *will* sing." If Moses, who died centuries ago, will someday sing again, then, in the words of the midrashist, "we find that we can derive the resurrection of the dead from the Torah."

This interesting piece of midrashic exegesis closely resembles the approach Jesus took in answering the Sadducees' question about levirate marriage, which "Moses wrote for us" (cf. Deut 25:5; Gen 38:8), and the resurrection (cf. Mark 12:18–27). The Sadducees did not believe in the resurrection. References to Isa 26:19 or Dan 12:2 would have been pointless, since they only accepted the Books of Moses, the Torah, as authoritative (cf. Josephus *Ant.* 18.1.4 §16). Therefore, if they are to be answered in a manner that they would find compelling, it must be from Torah, as *Mekilta*'s exegesis had been. Jesus argued that since God, centuries after the Patriarchs had died, identified himself to Moses as "the God of Abraham, and the God of Isaac, and the God of Jacob" (Exod 3:6), the implication is that these persons will live again, or why would God, the living God (cf. Num 14:28), identify himself with the dead? By appealing explicitly to Exodus 3, one of the passages of Torah most treasured by Jewish interpreters, and implicitly to texts such as Num 14:28 which speak of God as living, Jesus has answered the Sadducees on their own ground. He has, as has the midrashist of the *Mekilta*, derived the resurrection from the Torah.

Mekilta is sometimes cited in this manner: "*Mekilta* on Exod 12:2." Sometimes it is cited by tractate, chapter, and the line number(s) according to Lauterbach's edition, e.g., "*Mekilta, Pisha* 2.1–4." For the sake of clarity I recommend combining both: "*Mekilta* on Exod 12:2 (*Pisha* 2.1–4)." The SBL abbreviation for *Mekilta* is *Mek*. There are no recommended abbreviations for the tractates (except *Nez.* for *Neziqin*).

Critical Text: H. S. Horovitz and A. Rabin, *Mechilta d'Rabbi Ismael* (Frankfurt am Main: J. Kauffmann, 1928–31; repr. Jerusalem: Bamberger & Wahrmann, 1960). *Texts and Translations:* J. Z. Lauterbach, *Mekilta De-Rabbi Ishmael* (3 vols.; Philadelphia: JPS, 1933–35; repr. 1976) [Hebrew text with ET]; Y. N. Epstein and E. Z. Melamed, *Mekilta De-Rabbi Shimeon Ben Yohai* (Jerusalem: Mekize Nirdamim, 1955; repr. Jerusalem: Hillel, 1980) [Hebrew, no ET available; based on fragments from the Cairo Genizah].

Sipra (Sifra) (on Leviticus). *Sipra* (Aramaic, "the book"), or *Torat Kohanin* ("The Law of Priests"), is a compendium of tannaic halakot devoted to the interpretation of Leviticus. It originated in the late second and early third centuries, possibly under the leadership of the school of Aqiba, and was completed sometime around 400 C.E. The first published edition appeared in 1552 (Constantinople). Portions of Mishna and Tosepta appear in *Sipra*. Jacob Neusner has observed that *Sipra* and Mishna "cover the same ground, sharing something like 90–95 percent of the same themes and ideas, not to mention laws" (*Sifra*, 1.32). Neusner believes that *Sipra* is an integrated, unified document (contrary to James Kugel, *Early Biblical Interpretation* [Philadelphia: Westminster, 1986], who tends to view *Sipra* and other Midrashim as haphazard collections of unrelated midrashic traditions).

Sipra is made up of some 277 "chapters" and "explanations" extended over thirteen thematic sections (e.g., *Nega'im* ["plagues," i.e., leprosy], *Zabim* ["those with flux"], *'Aharê Mot* ["after death"], *Qedošim* ["holy things"]). A prologue entitled *Baraita de Rabbi Ishmael* ("Rabbi's Ishmael's [teachings that] stand outside [of Mishna]") prefaces the work and explains the Rabbi's famous thirteen rules *(middot)* of exegesis.

Sipra is usually cited by referring to the passage in Leviticus, e.g., "*Sipra* on Lev 2:14–16," though including reference to section and chapter *(pereq)* or explanation *(parashah)* would be more helpful, e.g., "*Sipra* on Lev 2:14–16 (*Dibura Denedabah* §13)." This manner of citation is analogous to that recommended for citing *Mekilta*. Since the letter *p* is aspirated, the work is often spelled *Sifra*, but in citations it is often spelled *Sipra*. The same holds for *Sipre on Numbers* and *on Deuteronomy*. Unlike *Sipre on Numbers* and *on Deuteronomy*, the name *Sipra* can stand alone; everyone knows that it refers to Leviticus ("*the* Book").

Text: L. Finkelstein, *Sifra or Torat Kohanim according to Codex Assemani LXVI* (New York: JTSA, 1956) [facsimile]; idem, *Text of Sifra according to Vatican Manuscript Assemani 66* (New York: JTSA, 1983). *Translation:* J. Neusner, with G. G. Porton, *Sifra: An Analytical Translation* (BJS 138–40; 3 vols.; Atlanta: Scholars, 1988). *Critical Study:* Ibid., 1.1–53.

Sipre on Numbers. *Sipre* (Hebrew, "book") *on* (or to) *Numbers* was compiled ca. 350–400 C.E. and published in 1545 (Venice). It is associated with the school of Rabbi Ishmael. Like *Sipra*, it is made up of tannaic traditions. There is also a *Sipre Zuṭa* ("Minor Book") on Numbers.

Sipre on Numbers is divided into 161 sections or *pisqaot* (from Aramaic meaning "[biblical] verses" or "sections"; sing. *pisqa* [lit. "cut"]). Each pisqa begins with a passage from Numbers, e.g., pisqa §1 treats Num 5:1–4, pisqaot §2–6 treat Num 5:5–10, pisqaot §7–21 treat Num 5:11–10. Exegetical discussion then ensues, often prompted by leading questions.

Sipre on Numbers is normally cited by reference to the pisqa, with the biblical passage in parentheses, e.g., "*Sipre Num.* §12 (on Num 5:15–22)."

Text: H. S. Horovitz, *Sipre 'al Bemidbar we-Sipre Zuṭa* (Jerusalem: Wahrmann, 1966) [Hebrew]; S. Lieberman, *Sipre Zuṭa* (New York: JTSA, 1968) [Hebrew]. *Translation:* P. P. Levertoff, *Midrash Sifre on Numbers* (London: SPCK, 1926) [not complete]; J. Neusner, *Sifre to Numbers* (3 vols.; Atlanta: Scholars, 1986 [vols. 1–2 = BJS 118–19; vol. 3 by W. S. Green forthcoming]); K. G. Winter, *Der tannaitische Midrasch Sifre zu Numeri* (Rabbinische Texte, 2d ser.; Tannaitische Midraschim 3; Stuttgart: Kohlhammer, 1959) [GT].

Sipre on Deuteronomy. *Sipre on Deuteronomy* was completed ca. 350–400 C.E. It is traditionally associated with the school of Rabbi Aqiba. Like *Sipra* and like *Sipre on Numbers*, with which there is a close relationship, *Sipre on Deuteronomy* is made up of tannaic traditions and may have been compiled shortly after *Sipre on Numbers*. It has been pointed out that *Sipre Deuteronomy* resembles *Mekilta de Rabbi Simeon ben Yohai*. There have been discovered Genizah fragments of a *Mekilta to Deuteronomy* (or *Midraš Tannaim on Deuteronomy*) from the school of Rabbi Ishmael.

Sipre on Deuteronomy is divided into 357 pisqaot and covers ten lessons, e.g., *Debarim* ("words," §1–25), *Wa-'etḥannan* ("and I besought," §§26–36), *'Eqeb* ("because," §§37–52), etc. The names for these lessons come from the verses that open the new sections. Thus, *Debarim* is taken from Deut 1:1 ("These are the *words* which Moses spoke to all Israel"), *Wa-'etḥannan* from Deut 3:23 ("*And I besought* the Lord"), and *'Eqeb* from Deut 7:12 ("And it was *because* you hearken to these ordinances"). These are the standard lections noted in most Hebrew Bibles.

As an example of how *Sipre Deuteronomy* can be of value for NT interpretation let us consider the latter part of pisqa §105 (on Deut 14:22, "Thou shalt surely tithe all the increase of thy seed," and 14:23, "and thou shalt eat before the Lord thy God"). The midrash concludes that the commandment to tithe applies not only to what is grown, but also to stored produce. Then comes an interesting and very old tannaic tradition (also found in *y. Pe'a* 2.16):

> The Sages said: "The (produce) stores of the children of Hanan [= Annas] were destroyed three years before the rest of the Land of Israel because they failed to set aside tithes from their produce, for they interpreted 'Thou shalt surely tithe . . . and thou shalt eat' as excluding the seller, and 'The increase of thy seed' as excluding the buyer."

The Sages are talking about the house of high priest Annas, the same priestly family discussed above in *t. Menaḥ.* 13. The reference to the destruction of their property three years before the destruction of the rest of the land of Israel (70 C.E.) is to some extent clarified by Josephus. He tells us that Ananias the high priest was caught and killed by the zealots (*J.W.* 2.16.9 §441) and that his house was burned (*J.W.* 2.17.6 §426). This was in 66 C.E. Later Josephus describes the Zealot-Idumean coalition that looted and murdered many of the aristocracy, including Ananus the son of Annas the high priest and the former high priest, Jesus the son of Gamalas the high priest (*J.W.* 4.5.2 §§314–317). This probably took place in late 67 or early 68 C.E. It is in reference to these murders and acts of looting committed against high priests that the comment of the Sages should be understood.

The failure of the high priests, at least those of the family of Annas, to tithe on the wealth that they accumulated from the temple offerings may shed light on one aspect of Jesus' parable of the Wicked Vineyard Tenants (Mark 12:1–12). In the parable, the vineyard tenants represent the ruling priests and the owner represents God. When the owner sends for "some of the fruit of the vineyard," the tenants refuse to give it. Their failure to pay what is owed will lead to their destruction. This is very similar to the point made in *Sipre Deuteronomy*. Through a clever interpretation of Deut 14:22–23 the family of Annas justified their failure to pay tithes on the profits of their trade in sacrificial commodities. For this reason they suffered the loss of their wealth three years before the Romans crushed the Jewish rebellion. This parable will be discussed at greater length in chapter 12 below.

Sipre on Deuteronomy is normally cited in the same manner as *Sipre on Numbers*, e.g., "*Sipre Deut.* §251 (on Deut 27:7)."

Text: L. Finkelstein, *Sipre Debarim* (New York: JTSA, 1969) [Hebrew]; D. Hoffmann, *Midrash Tannaim zum Deuteronomium* (Berlin: M. Poppelaver, 1908–

1909); *Translation:* R. Hammer, *Sifre: A Tannaic Commentary on the Book of Deuteronomy* (YJ 24; New Haven and London: Yale University, 1986).

Seder 'Olam Rabbah. *Seder 'Olam Rabbah* ("The Long Order of the World") is mentioned in the Talmud (*b. Šabb.* 88a). According to Rabbi Yohanan (a third-century amora) the work was produced by Rabbi Yose ben Halafta (a second-century tanna) (*b. Yebam.* 82b; *Nid.* 46b). The work is divided into three major parts, each consisting of ten chapters. Part one is concerned with biblical events from the creation to the crossing of the Jordan under the leadership of Joshua. Part two is concerned with the conquest of the promised land to the murder of Zechariah. Part three is concerned with the destruction of the temple by Nebuchadnezzar to the defeat of Simon ben Kosiba. This history is embellished with haggadic traditions and in places may depend on Demetrius the Chronographer (see chap. 2). The work has been translated into Latin (1577 and 1692). Part one has been translated into German (1903). There is no ET. See *Seder 'Olam Zuṭa* below. The SBL abbreviation is *S. 'Olam Rab.*

Text and Critical Study: B. Ratner, *Seder 'Olam Rabba (Die grosse Weltchronik)* (2 vols.; Vilna: Romm, 1894–97; repr. 1966). *Translation:* A. Marx, *Seder 'Olam* (Berlin: H. Itzkowski, 1903) [GT]. *Critical Study:* S. Gandz, "The Calendar of the Seder 'Olam," *JQR* 43 (1952–53) 177–92.

Megillat Ta'anit. *Megillat Ta'anit* ("Scroll of Fasts") is principally concerned with noting the days on which fasting was forbidden. It may have some value for chronological studies. Since the document is mentioned in the Mishna (cf. *m. Ta'an.* 2:8), it apparently originated, at least in part, in the second century. The SBL abbreviation is *Meg. Ta'an.*

Text: H. Lichtenstein, "Megillath Taanith," *HUCA* 8 (1931–32) 318–51. *Translation:* A. Edersheim, *The Life and Times of Jesus the Messiah* (2 vols.; 3d ed.; London: Longmans, 1886; repr. Peabody: Hendrickson) 2.698–700. *Critical Study:* S. Zeitlin, "Megillath Taanith as a Source," *JQR* 9 (1918–19) 71–102; 10 (1919–20) 49–80.

SUMMARIES OF AMORAIC MIDRASHIC LITERATURE

Midrash Rabbah. *Midrash Rabbah* ("The Long Midrash") consists of commentary on the five books of Moses (*Berešit [Genesis] Rabbah, Šemot [Exodus] Rabbah, Vayyiqra' [Leviticus] Rabbah, Bemidbar [Numbers] Rabbah,* and *Debarim [Deuteronomy] Rabbah*), and commentary on the five Megillot, or "Scrolls" (*Šir haŠir [Song of Songs] Rabbah, Ruth Rabbah, 'Ekah [Lamentations] Rabbah, Qohelet [Ecclesiastes] Rabbah,* and *Esther Rabbah*). The work as a whole ranges ca. 450–1100 C.E. with Genesis being the oldest (ca. 425–450), followed closely by Lamentations (ca. 450) and Leviticus (550). The Middle Age Midrashim include Song of Songs (ca. 600–650), Qohelet (ca. 650), and Ruth (ca. 750). The late Midrashim are Deuteronomy (ca. 900), Exodus (ca. 1000), and Numbers (ca. 1100).

Esther presents special problems. There are indications that the work is quite old, perhaps as early as 500 C.E., but there are portions that are quite late, such as material from the tenth-century Yosippon (e.g., Mordecai's dream in chap. 8). The younger elements, however, may represent late interpolations, in which case the original form of *Esther Rabbah* is much older.

Although much of the material is tannaic and amoraic, there is material from later authorities and there are numerous glosses (and late interpolations). Moreover, much of this material has been taken from other Midrashim and talmudic writings. Study of these Midrashim should bear this in mind.

These Midrashim are cited in two ways. All but *Song Rabbah, Lamentations Rabbah,* and *Qohelet Rabbah* are cited as follows: "*Gen. Rab.* 28.4 (on Gen 6:7)" or "*Lev. Rab.* 12.1 (on Lev 10:9)." Sometimes the Hebrew names of the books are used, e.g., "*Ber. Rab.* 28.4 (on 6:7)." In these examples the chapter and paragraph of the Midrash is cited, with the chapter and verse of the biblical book noted in parentheses. Song, Lamentations, and Qohelet are cited in this manner: "*Song Rab.* 5:15 §2" or "*Lam. Rab.* 1:9 §37." In these examples the chapter and verse of the biblical book is cited, followed by the paragraph number of the Midrash. These two systems of citation reflect the different ways the Midrashim of *Midrash Rabbah* have been compiled.

Text and Commentary: M. Mirkin, *Midrash Rabbah* (11 vols.; Tel Aviv: Yavneh, 1977) [Hebrew]. *Translation:* H. Freedman and M. Simon, eds., *Midrash Rabbah* (10 vols.; London: Soncino, 1983).

Seder Elijah Rabbah. According to an old rabbinic legend, *Seder Elijah* (or *Eliyyahu*) *Rabbah* ("The Major Work of Elijah"), also called *Tanna debe Elijah* ("The Lore of Elijah"), represents material revealed by Elijah the prophet to Rabbi Anan, a late third-century Amora (cf. *b. Ketub.* 106a). Although many modern scholars dismiss this legend out of hand, Meir Friedmann has accepted it. William Braude and Israel Kapstein think that there may be an element of truth behind the legend. They reason that since mystical experiences were not uncommon, it is entirely possible that Rabbi Anan had some sort of vision or experience which he assumed was given by the prophet Elijah, the patron of heavenly revelations. (On Jewish mysticism see G. Scholem, *Major Trends in Jewish Mysticism* [Jerusalem: Schocken, 1941]; idem, *Jewish Gnosticism, Merkabah Mysticism and Talmudic Tradition* [New York: JTSA, 1960].) Braude and Kapstein also point out that the work may derive from Rabbi Elijah and that through later confusion a legend grew up involving the prophet Elijah. Whatever the circumstances of the work's origin, on internal grounds there is no reason why the work could not have been compiled ca. 300 C.E. Other scholars, however, have argued that the work could be as late as 850 C.E. The first printed edition appeared in 1598 (Venice). It is referred to as *Teni Elijah* in *Gen. Rab.* 54.4 (on Gen 21:28) and simply as Elijah in *Num. Rab.* 4.20 (on Num 4:16).

Seder Elijah Rabbah accompanies a smaller work entitled *Seder Elijah Zuṭa* ("The Minor Work of Elijah"). One cites the chapter of *Seder Elijah Rabbah* or *Zuṭa* and in parentheses the page number of Friedmann's text (which are noted in the margins of the translation by Braude and Kapstein), e.g., "*Seder Elijah Rabbah* §17 (83)." There is no SBL abbreviation.

Text: M. Friedmann, *Seder Eliahu rabba und Seder Eliahu Zuta (Tanna d'be Eliahu); Pseudo-Seder Eliahu* (Jerusalem: Bamberger & Wahrmann, 1960; repr. Jerusalem: Wahrmann, 1969) [Friedmann's two earlier editions combined in one volume]. *Translation:* W. G. Braude and I. Kapstein, *Tanna Debe Eliyyahu: The Lore of the School of Elijah* (Philadelphia: JPS, 1981). *Critical Study:* M. Kadushin, *The Theology of Seder Eliahu* (New York: Bloch, 1932).

Pesiqta de Rab Kahana. *Pesiqta de Rab Kahana* ("Lessons of Rab Kahana") is a compilation of Rab Kahana's discourses or lessons for Sabbaths and holidays. It was compiled in Palestine ca. 500 C.E. The authorities, therefore, are tannaic and amoraic. Although several rabbis of the geonic period (650–1050 C.E.) refer to or cite *Pesiqta de Rab Kahana*, it was not published until 1832. The work consists of twenty-eight pisqas (i.e., pisqaot or pesiqta), with seven supplementary pisqas added later. Each pisqa begins with a citation of Scripture, which is then tied into the ensuing discussion concerned with a holiday.

It is customary to cite pisqa and paragraph, e.g., "*Pesiqta de Rab Kahana* 11.18." It is not necessary to cite the Scripture passage that heads the pisqa. The recommended SBL abbreviation is *Pesiq. Rab Kah.*

Text: M. Mandelbaum, *Pesikta de Rav Kahana* (2 vols.; New York: JTSA, 1962) [Hebrew/Aramaic and ET]. *Translation:* W. G. Braude and I. J. Kapstein, *Pesikta de-Rab Kahana: R. Kahana's Compilation of Discourses for Sabbaths and Festal Days* (Philadelphia: JPS, 1975) [contains several helpful indexes].

Pesiqta Rabbati. *Pesiqta Rabbati* ("The Long Lessons") was compiled in Palestine ca. 550–650 C.E. It is simply called "Pesiqta" in *b. Yebam.* 81b. Over one half of the homilies begin in the name of Rabbi Tanhuma, an Amora who flourished at the end of the fourth and the beginning of the fifth centuries. *Pesiqta Rabbati* bears a close relationship to *Pesiqta de Rab Kahana.* Ten pisqas of the former parallel pisqas in the latter. It is possible that it was called *Pesiqta Rabbati* in order to distinguish it from the shorter version of Rab Kahana. *Pesiqta Rabbati* is made up of 53 pisqas devoted to holidays, seasons, feasts, fasts, and special Sabbaths. The first printed edition appeared in 1654 (Prague).

It is customary to cite pisqa and paragraph, e.g., "*Pesiqta Rabbati* 5.2." It is not necessary to cite the Scripture passage that heads the pisqa. The recommended SBL abbreviation is *Pesiq. R.*

Text: M. Friedmann, *Pesikta Rabbati: Midrasch für den Fest-Cyclus und die ausgezeichneten Sabbathe* (Vienna: [self-published], 1880; repr. Tel Aviv: Esther, 1963). *Translation:* W. G. Braude, *Pesikta Rabbati: Discourses for Feasts, Fasts, and Special Sabbaths* (2 vols.; YJ 18; New Haven: Yale University, 1968) [contains several very helpful indexes].

Midraš Tanhuma. A commentary on the Pentateuch, *Midraš Tanhuma* ("The Exegesis of Rabbi Tanhuma") was compiled ca. 800 C.E., possibly in Italy. Solomon Buber, however, argued for a fourth-century date because all of the authorities cited in the work date from the fourth century or earlier. John Townsend believes that the Buber recension cannot be much earlier than the ninth century, since it quotes a chapter from Rabbi Ahai's Aramaic *Se'iltot* (ca. 750 C.E.). Since *Tanhuma* is otherwise a Hebrew document (with a sprinkling of Latin and Greek loan words—a fact that argues for an Italian provenance), it is more likely that *Tanhuma* borrowed from the *Se'iltot* than the reverse. Nevertheless, although the recension itself may be late, the traditions it contains are early and potentially of value for NT study. Whichever date is accepted, *Midraš Tanhuma* is the oldest commentary on the whole Pentateuch.

There are three recensions of *Midraš Tanhuma.* The first two, A and B, were known to the author of *Yalqut,* a thirteenth-century compilation of midrashic traditions. He called recension A *Tanhuma* and recension B *Yelammedenu* ("Let [our Master] teach us"). Recension A is the recension that Buber edited and published in 1885. Other than fragments (see bib.), recension B is lost. Recension C apparently drew upon the earlier recensions.

The structure of *Tanhuma* is based on a triennial lectionary cycle, though most printed editions structure it on the basis of the traditional one-year cycle of readings. Each lesson has a name, e.g., the first is *Berešit,* which comments on Gen 1:1–6:4; the second is *Noah,* which comments on Gen 6:9–11:7; the third is *Lek-Leka,* which comments on Gen 12:1–17:3; and so forth.

I suggest citing *Tanhuma* (Buber) as follows: "*Tanh.* (B) on Gen 18:2 (*Wayyera* §5)." See Townsend (p. xiii) for his recommendation. Beyond using *Midr.* as the abbreviation for *Midraš,* there is no SBL abbreviation for *Midraš Tanhuma.*

Text: S. Buber, *Midrash Tanchuma: Ein agadischer Commentar zum Pentateuch von Rabbi Tanchuma ben Rabbi Abba* (Vilna: Romm, 1885; repr. Jerusalem: Ortsel, 1963–64). Translation: J. T. Townsend, *Midrash Tanhuma,* vol. 1: *Genesis* (Hoboken: Ktav, 1989) [remaining volumes in preparation]. *Published Fragments of Yelammedenu:* A. Jellinek, *Bet ha-Midrasch* (6 vols.; Leipzig: C. W. Vollrath, 1853–77; repr. Jerusalem: Wahrmann, 1967) 6.79–105; A. Neubauer, "Le Midrasch Tanchuma et extraits du Yélammdénu et petits midraschim," *Revue des études juives* 13 (1886) 224–38; 14 (1887) 92–113; S. Grünhut, *Sefer Haliqqutim,* vols. 4–6 (Frankfurt am Main: J. Kauffmann, 1900–1903); L. Ginzberg, *Genizah Studies in Memory of Doctor Solomon Schecter,* vol. 1: *Midrash and Haggadah* (Texts and Studies of JTSA 7; New York: JTSA, 1928; repr. New York: P. Feldheim, 1969).

Midraš Tehillin. Midraš Tehillin ("Exegesis on the Psalms") or *Šoḥer Ṭob* (from Prov 11:27, "he that seeks good") was compiled ca. 750–800 C.E. Most of the authorities are Palestinian Tannaim and Amoraim. The earliest quoted authorities are Hillel and Shammai. No post-Talmudic authorities are quoted by name. In the midrashim on certain Psalms, nearly every verse is commented upon, in others only a few selected verses are treated.

This work is normally cited by Psalm and paragraph of exegesis, followed by the Psalm's chapter and verse in parentheses, e.g., "*Midr. Ps.* 18.36 (on Ps 18:51)" or "*Midr. Ps.* 18 §36 (on Ps 18:51)."

Text: S. Buber, *Midrasch Tehillim (Schocher Tob): Sammlung agadischer Abhandlungen über die 150 Psalmen* (Vilna: Romm, 1891; repr. Jerusalem, 1965/66) [Hebrew and Aramaic]. *Translation:* W. G. Braude, *The Midrash on Psalms* (2 vols.; YJ 13; New Haven: Yale University, 1959) [contains several helpful indexes].

Pirqe de Rabbi Eliezer. Pirqe de Rabbi Eliezer ("Chapters of Rabbi Eliezer") was compiled ca. 750–850 C.E. The work consists of 53 chapters devoted to various scriptural themes or personalities, e.g., *pereq* §3 treats the first day of creation, *pereq* §10 treats Jonah, *pereq* §24 treats Nimrod and the Tower of Babel, and so forth. Scholars suspect that this work may be an example of a rabbinic pseudepigraphon (see also *3 Enoch,* a pseudepigraphon credited to Rabbi Ishmael).

The work is usually cited in this manner: "*Pirqe de Rabbi Eliezer* §7." The SBL abbreviation is *Pirqe R. El.*

Text: M. Higger, "Pirqe Rabbi Eli'ezer," *Horeb* 8 (1944) 82–98; 9 (1946) 94–166; 10 (1948) 185–294. *Translation:* G. Friedlander, *Pirke de-Rabbi Eliezer* (1912; repr. New York: Sepher-Hermon, 1981).

Seder 'Olam Zuṭa. On the basis of a date given in the De Rossi MS many think that *Seder 'Olam Zuṭa* ("The Short Order of the World") was composed in 804 C.E. Others have contended that this date is a gloss and that the work was composed in the sixth century. It is made up of ten chapters. The first six cover the period from Adam to Jehoiachin. Chapters 7–10 cover the period from Jehoiachin to the collapse of the Sassanid dynasty ca. 640 C.E. For the biblical period the author made use of *Seder 'Olam Rabbah.* For the later period the author drew on chronological materials available in the Babylonian academies. There is no ET. The SBL abbreviation is *S. 'Olam Zuṭ.*

Text: M. Grossberg, *Seder 'Olam Zuta* (London: n.p., 1910); M. J. Weinstock, *Seder 'Olam Zuta ha-Shalem* (Jerusalem: Metivta Torat, 1957). *Critical Study:* A. D. Goode, "The Exilarchate in the Eastern Caliphate, 637–1258," *JQR* 31 (1940–41) 149–69.

Chronicle of Jerahmeel. Jerahmeel ben Solomon (ca. 1150) lived in southern Italy and produced a work called *Megillat Yerahme'el* ("The

Scroll of Jerahmeel") or *Seper ha-Yerahme'el* ("The Book of Jerahmeel"). The work is a compilation of Jewish legend and lore. In two places the author identifies himself: "I, Jerahmeel, have found in the Book of Strabo of Caphtor that Nimrod was the son of Shem . . ." (32:1); "And I, Jerahmeel, have discovered in the Book of Nicholas of Damascus . . ." (35:2). As is clear from these statements, Jerahmeel used many authors (e.g., in addition to Strabo and Nicholas, he drew upon Josephus, Philo, and various apocryphal works and midrashim, such as *Pirqe de Rabbi Eliezer*). Portions of the *Chronicle of Jerahmeel* were incorporated by Eleazar ben Asher ha-Levi (ca. 1325) in his work, *Seper ha-Zikronot* ("The Book of Records"). Moses Gaster believes that most of Jerahmeel's materials are no later than the seventh century. Many dispute this claim, however. The use of *Pirqe de Rabbi Eliezer* (Jerahmeel's first seven chapters are copied from this work), which dates from the eighth or ninth century, tells against Gaster's view.

Translation: M. Gaster, *The Chronicle of Jerahmeel; or, the Hebrew Bible Historiale* (Oxford: Oxford University, 1899; repr. New York: Ktav, 1971). *Critical Study:* J. Reiner, "The Original Hebrew Yosippon in the Chronicle of Jerahmeel," *JQR* 60 (1969–70) 128–46.

LATER MIDRASHIM

Midraš 'Aggadah (on the Pentateuch)—10th century
'Aggadat Berešit (on Genesis)—10th century
Midraš Megillot Zuṭa (on the Song of Songs)—10th century
Berešit Rabbati (on Genesis)—11th century
Midraš Šemuel (on Samuel)—11th century; GT available: A. Wünsche, *Aus Israels Lehrhallen*, vol. 5, part 1: *Der Midrasch Samuel* (Leipzig: E. Pfeiffer, 1910; repr. Hildesheim: Olms, 1967).
Midraš Mišle (on Proverbs)—11th century; ET: B. L. Visotzky, *The Midrash on Proverbs* (YJ 27; New Haven and London: Yale University, 1992); GT: A. Wünsche, *Bibliotheca Rabbinica*, vol. 5, part 3: *Der Midrasch Mischle* (Leipzig: O. Schulze, 1885; repr. Hildesheim: Olms, 1967).
Midraš Yob (on Job)—date unknown, only fragments extant
Midraš Šir haŠir (on the Song of Songs)—12th century
Midraš Haggadol (on the Pentateuch)—13th century
Yalqut Šimeoni (on Tanak)—13th century
'Aggadat Esther (on Esther)—14th century

MEDIAEVAL COMMENTATORS

Rabbi Saadya ben Joseph ("Saadya Gaon")—882–942
Rabbi Solomon ben Isaac ("Rashi")—1040–1105

Rabbi Abraham Ibn Ezra—1089–1164
Rabbi Joseph Kimhi—ca. 1105–1170 (father of David and Moses Kimhi)
Rabbi Moses ben Maimon/Maimonides ("Rambam")—1135–1204
Rabbi David Kimhi ("Radak")—ca. 1160–1235
Rabbi Moses Kimhi ("Ramak")—date unknown
Rabbi Moses ben Nahman/Nahmanides ("Ramban")—1194–1270

Special Themes

Messianic Ideas in the Rabbinic Literature. Messianic ideas are quite diverse in the rabbinic literature. There was fervent messianic expectation even after the two disastrous wars with Rome in 66–70 and 132–135 C.E. Some of it coheres at points with the messianic ideas in the NT. The following is a sample of the early traditions:

Yohanan ben Zakkai predicted the destruction of the temple (ca. 60 C.E.): "O Temple, why do you frighten us? We know that you will be destroyed" (*y. Soṭa* 6.3; *b. Yoma* 39b). According to another tradition, he hailed Vespasian, the general in command of the Roman forces that were trying to put down the first Jewish rebellion, as "Lord Emperor." When Vespasian objected (since he was not emperor), Yohanan prophesied: "If you are not the king, you will be eventually, because the Temple will only be destroyed by a king's hand" (*Lam. Rab.* 1:5 §31). Rabbi Zadok, Yohanan's disciple, also anticipated the temple's destruction (*b. Giṭ.* 56a). These traditions are not necessarily messianic, at least not explicitly, but there may have been a relationship between Messiah and the temple (viz., that he will build a new temple) in first-century thinking. In any case, these predictions have relevance for NT messianism.

Just before his death (ca. 80 C.E.) Yohanan also predicted the coming of Messiah: "Remove all vessels lest they be rendered unclean, and prepare a throne for Hezekiah, king of Judea, who is come" (*b. Ber.* 28b). Evidently the aged Sage felt that "Hezekiah," that is, Israel's Messiah, had arrived. Whether ben Zakkai had in mind a recently born infant or an adult is not clear. According to later tradition King Messiah, whose name is Menahem son of Hezekiah, was born on the day that the temple was destroyed (*y. Ber.* 2.4; cf. *b. Sanh.* 98b, 99a). Although it is possible that this tradition had something to do with Menahem the zealot and apparent messianic claimant who, as a "veritable king," entered Jerusalem in 66 C.E. (cf. Josephus *J.W.* 2.17.8–10 §§433–448), I do not think that it is too probable.

Aqiba was one of many rabbis who predicted the appearance of the Messiah (*b. Sanh.* 97b). Apparently shortly after the destruction of the temple he predicted that Messiah would come in forty years, by analogy of Israel's forty-year period of wandering in the wilderness (*Pesiq. R.* 1.7).

The forty-year expectation may have had something to do with the Jewish revolt in Judea, Egypt, and Cyrene in 114 or 115 C.E. According to Eusebius, the Jewish people rallied to one Lukuas, "their king" (*Eccl. Hist.* 4.2.1–4). Rabbis Eleazar ben Azariah, Yose the Galilean, Ishmael, Nathan, and Simeon ben Yohai predicted the approach of Messiah (*b. Sanh.* 99a, 97b; *Midr. Ps.* 90.17 [on Ps 90:15]; *Song Rab.* 8:9 §3). Calculations of the Messiah's appearance continued on into and through the Middle Ages (see A. H. Silver in bib.).

Aqiba also taught that the plural "thrones" of Dan 7:9 implied that Messiah would sit next to God, an interpretation that shocked his contemporaries Yose the Galilean and Eleazar ben Azariah (*b. Ḥag.* 14a; *b. Sanh.* 38b). Aqiba also proclaimed Simon ben Kosiba Messiah (*y. Ta'an.* 4.5; cf. *Lam. Rab.* 2:2 §4). Aqiba's identification of ben Kosiba had to do with a wordplay by which he was identified with the star of Num 24:17, a passage that was understood in a messianic sense in the first century, if not earlier (cf. Philo *On Rewards and Punishments* 16 §95; Josephus *J.W.* 6.5.4 §§312–313; cf. 3.8.9 §§400–402; Matt 2:2; 4QTest 9–13; CD 7:18–21; cf. *Tgs.* Num 24:17).

Finally, a late tannaic commentary should be noted: "With the footprints of the Messiah presumption shall increase and dearth reach its height; the vine shall yield its fruit but the vine shall be costly. . . . Galilee shall be laid waste and Gablan shall be made desolate. . . . The wisdom of the Scribes shall become insipid. . . . Children shall shame the elders, and the elders shall rise up before the children, 'for the son dishonors the father, the daughter rises up against her mother, the daughter-in-law against her mother-in-law; a man's enemies are the men of his own house' [Mic 7:6]" (*m. Soṭa* 9:15; cf. *Pesiq. Rab Kah.* §5.9; *Song Rab.* 2:13 §4).

The NT parallels these messianic traditions at four points. *First,* Jesus also predicted the destruction of the temple: "Do you see these great buildings? There will not be left here one stone upon another, that will not be thrown down" (Mark 13:2 par.). Jesus is later accused of threatening to destroy the temple: "We heard him say, 'I will destroy this temple that is made with hands, and in three days I will build another, not made with hands' " (Mark 14:58; cf. John 2:19: "Destroy this temple and in three days I will raise it up").

Second, the NT witnesses fervent messianic expectation. There are warnings to beware of false prophets and false christs who claim that the end is at hand (Matt 24:5, 11; Mark 13:5–6; Luke 21:8–9). Not all of those who made false predictions of the end were necessarily non-Christians. It is quite likely that Christians, too, predicted the end and the appearance of the glorified Christ (cf. 2 Thess 2:1–3).

Third, Aqiba's exegesis of Dan 7:9 coheres with Jesus' response to Caiaphas in Mark 14:64. Jesus says that he will be "seated at the right hand" and will be "coming on the clouds of heaven" (cf. Ps 110:1; Dan 7:13–14). Some commentators have wondered how Jesus could be both stationary (i.e., seated) and moving (i.e., coming on the clouds). Because of the apparent discrepancy, it has been suggested that two separate traditions have been combined. (The juxtaposition of Ps 110:1 and Dan 7:13–14 occurs several times in the rabbis; cf. *b. Sanh.* 96b–97a, 98a; *Num. Rab.* 13.14 [on Num 7:13]; *Midr. Ps.* 21.5 [on Ps 21:7]; 93.1 [on Ps 93:1].) What has been overlooked, however, is that the throne that is being alluded to is the divine chariot throne (Dan 7:9: "thrones were placed and one what was ancient of days took his seat . . . his throne was fiery flames, its *wheels* were burning fire"; cf. Ezek 1). Jesus can speak of sitting and coming because he will be seated next to God on his chariot throne and will, with him, come thundering from heaven in judgment. The saying in Mark 14:64 is, therefore, intelligible. Moreover, the idea is not without parallel. According to *1 Enoch* 51:3, the "Elect One shall sit on [God's] throne." According to Rev 3:12, the risen Christ says, "He who conquers, I will grant him to sit with me on my throne, as I myself conquered and sat down with my father on his throne." Caiaphas' outrage, "You have heard his blasphemy" (Mark 14:65) parallels the responses of Yose the Galilean and Eleazar ben Azariah: "Aqiba, how long will you profane the Divine Presence!"

Fourth, Mishna's reference to the "footprints of the Messiah" and the fulfillment of Mic 7:6 parallels NT Gospel tradition. Jesus also spoke of approaching times of trouble: "Brother will deliver up brother to death, and the father his child, and children will rise against parents and have them put to death; and you will be hated by all" (Mark 13:12–13). The allusion to Mic 7:6 is unmistakable. In Q (Matt 13:35–36; Luke 12:52–53) it is explicit. All of this social turmoil is in reference to Jesus as Israel's Messiah. The use of Mic 7:6 in *m. Soṭa* 9:15 clarifies the exegetical background against which these synoptic traditions should be studied.

Before ending this discussion a few comments on Jacob Neusner's understanding of Messiah in formative Judaism are in order. Neusner finds in the Mishna—what he calls the foundational document of Judaism—a "doctrine of history" (*Messiah*, 41) which has little interest in messianic ideas of salvation, indeed, little interest in history itself. Other than a minor passage in *Soṭa* 9:15 there is no mention of Messiah in the Mishna. From this he infers that "the fundamental issues addressed by mishnaic 'Judaism' are simply not messianic" (*Messiah*, 53). He underscores this point by observing that although Tosepta, the document so closely related to and dependent upon the Mishna, addresses itself to heresies and various kinds of sinners, the "Messiah in the sense of redeemer and savior plays no part whatsoever" (*Messiah*, 55). "These facts about the use and neglect of the Messiah myth point to a single conclusion. The philosophers of the Mishna chose to talk about other things.

Hence they were addressing people other than those eager to learn about the Messiah, about when he would come, and what he would do" (*Messiah,* 222).

Apparently Neusner finds this very revealing. But he is faced with a problem: If the foundational documents of Judaism show no interest in Messiah, why did "the Talmuds g[i]ve prominence to a concept ignored in the Mishnah" (*Messiah,* 229)? One might also ask, why did the Targums give prominence to messianic ideas? (For discussion of messianism in the Targums see chap. 6.) Neusner is not sure how to answer this question. He can only guess. He suspects that it was because an eschatological element is present in Scripture and that the desperate condition of the people of Israel "called into question the credibility of the ahistorical construction of the Mishnah" (*Messiah,* 229). Neusner's first guess is quite correct: Scripture is itself eschatological. Therefore, we should expect this fact to give rise to interest in things eschatological. His second guess, however, is not helpful, since it presupposes his skewed view of the genre of the Mishna (see discussion on Mishna above). Mishna is a compilation of laws; it is not an apocalypse. Therefore, one should not expect to find a significant eschatological component.

Furthermore, Neusner's interpretation of "formative" Judaism through the lens of Mishna creates another problem: He overlooks large chunks of Judaism. While formative Judaism was busy developing and assembling the legal traditions that would eventually comprise the Mishna, formative Judaism was also busy producing various testaments, apocalypses, and biblical histories that spoke of the meaning of history, of the end of the age, of the appearance of a Messiah, and of judgment. But these documents are of no interest to Neusner. During this same formative period of time Israel's Scripture underwent reinterpretation by the meturgamanim, who interjected eschatological and messianic ideas, such as the regathering of the twelve tribes, the rebuilding of Jerusalem, the rebuilding of the temple, the coming of Messiah, and judgment. But these documents also are of little interest to Neusner. Having narrowed his field to Mishna/Tosepta, the "foundational document," a document which contains little by way of eschatology, Neusner concludes that messianism was unimportant to formative Judaism. Only because of the eschatological elements of Scripture and popular dissatisfaction with Mishna's ahistorical view of reality, claims Neusner, did the later Amoraim give much greater prominence to messianism and eschatology.

On the contrary, I don't think that Mishna's ahistoricism had anything to do with the prominence that the Talmuds gave to messianism and eschatology. The difference between Mishna and the Talmuds is very simple. The former contains halakah almost exclusively, while the latter contain large amounts of haggadah. One-sixth of the Palestinian Talmud is haggadah, while one-third of the Babylonian Talmud is haggadah. It is within the haggadic traditions that we encounter the messianic components. The Talmuds do not represent a fundamental shift in thinking, a yielding to pressures to allow the eschatological Scripture to speak and to offer some sort of historical and eschatological comfort to a beleaguered and discouraged people. The Talmuds represent a widening of focus, a widening from an almost exclusive concern with law to an inclusive interest in everything Jewish—law, lore, eschatology, and all.

In short, Neusner has minimized the significance of the messianic idea in early Judaism. While it may be true that scholars have in the past created synthetic constructs of "the Messiah" that may not reflect ideas that anyone ever held—and Neusner's criticism at this point is on target—his conclusion that the messianic idea played an unimportant role in formative Judaism cannot be sustained. Ironically, he ends up guilty of the very thing that he has tried so hard to avoid: identifying a particular strand of Judaism as "normative." Neusner may speak of "formative" Judaism, but his odd interpretation of Mishna, together with his hypothesis of the "foundational" role that it played in the life of Israel in the first two to three centuries C.E., is very reminiscent of the way scholars earlier in this century spoke of a "normative Judaism." There is yet another irony in that the Messiah idea has not been studied "in context," as the title of his book claims. Until Neusner has taken into account the numerous apocryphal, pseudepigraphal, Qumranic, and early Christian writings, he has not treated Messiah in the context of early Judaism.

Bibliography: J. Klausner, *The Messianic Idea in Israel: From Its Beginning to the Completion of the Mishnah* (New York: Macmillan, 1955); J. Neusner, *Messiah in Context: Israel's History and Destiny in Formative Judaism* (Philadelphia: Fortress, 1984); G. Scholem, *The Messianic Idea in Judaism and Other Essays on Jewish Spirituality* (New York: Schocken, 1971) 1–36; A. H. Silver, *A History of Messianic Speculation in Israel* (New York: Macmillan, 1927; repr. Gloucester: Peter Smith, 1978).

References to Jesus. There are some references to Jesus in the writings of the rabbis. Because of the fear of persecution during the Middle Ages, scribes omitted or altered several explicit references to Jesus. In place of the name "Jesus" *(Yeshu)* or "Jesus the Nazarene" *(Yeshu ha-Noṣri)* were inserted various other names (e.g., "ben Stada" or "ben Pantera") and disparaging terms (e.g., "so-and-so"). Therefore, it is not always easy to determine which passages actually refer to Jesus and which do not. The following is a sampling of passages that have from time to time been identified as having to do with Jesus.

(1) *On Jesus' parents and birth.* "She who was the descendant of princes and governors [i.e., Mary], played the harlot with carpenters [i.e., Joseph]" (b. Sanh. 106a). "[The angel of death] said to his messenger, 'Go, bring me Miriam [Mary] the Women's hairdresser!' He went and brought

him Miriam" (*b. Ḥag.* 4b; "hairdresser" is *megaddelā'*, which probably refers to Mary Magdalene, who was sometimes confused with Mary the mother of Jesus).

(2) *On the life of Jesus.* Stories are told of Jesus' being rejected by various rabbis: "When King Janneus [104–78 B.C.E.] slew our Rabbis [ca. 87 B.C.E.], Rabbi Joshua [ben Perahiah] and Jesus fled to Alexandria of Egypt" where Jesus was later excommunicated and condemned for worshipping an idol (*b. Sanh.* 107b; *b. Soṭa* 47a; cf. *y. Ḥag.* 2.2; *y. Sanh.* 6.6). The association of Jesus with a flight to Egypt may have been suggested by Matt 2:13–15. The anachronism of the rabbinic tradition is obvious, but does not offer a serious difficulty to the identification of the character with Jesus of Nazareth.

(3) *On the ministry of Jesus.* We are told that "Jesus had five disciples: Matthai, Nakai, Nezer, Buni, and Todah" (*b. Sanh.* 107b). Although the first name does resemble one of the disciples' names (i.e., Matthew), and the last possibly that of another (Thaddeus), these names are only meant to serve the purpose of creating word-plays, as seen in the subsequent paragraph of *Sanhedrin*, that, casting aspersions against Jesus and his disciples, justify their deaths. Jesus' ministry of miracles was explained as sorcery: "Jesus the Nazarene practiced magic and led Israel astray" (*b. Sanh.* 107b; cf. *t. Šabb.* 11.15; *b. Sanh.* 43a; *b. Šabb.* 104b; *b. Soṭa* 47a). The charge of practicing magic parallels the accusation in the Gospels that Jesus cast out demons by the power of Satan (cf. Mark 3:22). Celsus held similar views (cf. Origen *Against Celsus* 1.6, 38, 71).

(4) *On the teaching of Jesus.* The rabbis expressed the hope that they will "not have a son or a disciple who burns his food in public [i.e., teaches heresy], like Jesus the Nazarene" (*b. Sanh.* 103a; *b. Ber.* 17a–b). "One of the disciples of Jesus . . . told me, 'Thus did Jesus the Nazarene teach me: "For of the hire of a harlot has she gathered them, and to the hire of a harlot shall they return" [cf. Deut 23:18]' " (*b. 'Abod. Zar.* 16b–17a; *t. Ḥul.* 2.24 [". . . Jesus ben Pantera . . ."]; cf. *Qoh. Rab.* 1:8 §3; *Yal. Šimeoni* on Mic 1 and Prov 5:8). "The disciples of Balaam the wicked shall inherit Gehenna and go down to the pit of destruction" (*m. 'Abot* 5:19). "He [a judge] said to them: 'I looked at the end of the book, in which it is written, "I am not come to take away the Law of Moses and I am not come to add to the Law of Moses" [cf. Matt 5:17], and it is written, "Where there is a son, a daughter does not inherit" [cf. Num 27:8].' She said to him: 'Let your light shine forth as a lamp' [cf. Matt 5:16]. Rabbi Gamaliel said to her: 'The ass came and kicked the lamp over' " (*b. Šabb.* 116b). From the same tradition we find a proverbial statement that probably sums up very well the rabbinic view of Jesus' teaching: "Since the day that you were exiled from your land [i.e., the destruction of Jerusalem in 70 C.E.] the Law of Moses has been abrogated, and the law of the *euangelion* has been given" (*b. Šabb.* 116a). In fact, by playing on the Greek word *euangelion,*

the rabbis sometimes referred to it as the *'āwen-gillāyôn* ("falsehood of the scroll") or the *'awôn-gillāyôn* ("perversion of the scroll"). Most offensive to the rabbis was Jesus' claim to be God and Son of Man (cf. Mark 14:61–62; John 19:7), who would ascend to heaven (cf. John 20:17). Rabbi Abbahu (late third, early fourth century) is reported to have said: "If a man says to you, 'I am God,' he is a liar; [or] 'I am the son of man,' in the end he will regret it'; [or] 'I will go up to heaven'—he that says it will not perform it" (*y. Ta'an.* 2.1). Again from Abbahu: "[God] says . . . ' "I am the first"—I have no father; "I am the last"—I have no son' " (*Exod. Rab.* 29.5 [on Exod 20:2]). Similarly Rabbi Aha (fourth century) declares: "There is One that is alone, and he has not a second; indeed, he has neither son nor brother—but: 'Hear O Israel, the Lord our God, the Lord is One' " (*Deut. Rab.* 2.33 [on Deut 6:4]). "There was a man, the son of a woman, who would rise up and seek to make himself God, and cause the entire world to err. . . . If he says that he is God, he lies; and in the future he will cause to err—that he departs and returns in the end. He says, but will not do. . . . Alas, who shall live of that people that listens to that man who makes himself God?" (*Yal. Šimeoni* on Num 23:7). Elsewhere we are told that Moses warns Israel not to expect "another Moses" who will "arise and bring another Law from heaven" (*Deut. Rab.* 8.6 [on Deut 30:11–12]). The rabbis predict that "the 'servant' [i.e., Jesus] will bow down to the [real] Messiah" (*b. Sanh.* 61b). Lying behind this statement is the Christian view of Jesus as the Lord's Servant.

(5) *On the crucifixion of Jesus.* "On the eve of Passover they hanged Jesus the Nazarene. And a herald went out before him for forty days, saying: 'He is going to be stoned, because he practiced sorcery and enticed and led Israel astray. Anyone who knows anything in his favor, let him come and plead in his behalf.' But, not having found anything in his favor, they hanged him on the eve of Passover" (*b. Sanh.* 43a; cf. *t. Sanh.* 10.11; *y. Sanh.* 7.12; *Tg. Esth I* 7:9). "They brought him to the Beth Din [i.e., "House of Judgment," perhaps the Sanhedrin] and stoned him . . . and they hanged him on the eve of Passover" (*b. Sanh.* 67a; *y. Sanh.* 7.16). Jesus' execution "on the eve of Passover" agrees with Johannine chronology (cf. John 18–19). "Balaam the lame was thirty-three years (old) when Phineas the brigand killed him" (*b. Sanh.* 106b). Although it is disputed, "Phineas the brigand" may refer to Pontius Pilate. If this is correct, then the thirty-three year old "Balaam" must be Jesus. "The robber was caught and they hanged him on the gallows, and all passersby say: 'It seems that the ruler is hanged.' Thus, it is said, 'He that is hanged is a reproach to God' [cf. Deut 21:23]" (*t. Sanh.* 9.7). Excluded from the "World to Come" (*m. Sanh.* 10:2), Jesus will be boiled in filth in Gehenna (*b. Giṭ.* 56b–57a).

(6) *On the resurrection of Jesus.* "He then went and raised Jesus by incantation" (*b. Giṭ.* 57a, MS M). "Woe to him who makes himself alive

by the name of God" (*b. Sanh.* 106a). Jesus' resurrection is probably viewed here as part of the general accusation that Jesus was a magician.

(7) *On healing in the name of Jesus.* "It once happened that [Eliezer] ben Dama, the son of Rabbi Ishmael's sister, was bitten by a snake; and Jacob [James? cf. Jas 5:14–15], a native of Kefar Sekaniah, came to him in the name of Jesus ben Pantera. But Rabbi Ishmael did not permit him." Ishmael goes on to say that it is better to die in peace than to be healed in the name of Jesus (*t. Ḥul.* 2.22–23; cf. *y. Šabb.* 14.4; *y. 'Abod. Zar.* 2.2; *b. 'Abod. Zar.* 27b; *Qoh. Rab.* 10:5 §1).

(8) *Seper Toledot Yeshu.* In the Middle Ages, perhaps as early as the eighth century, many of these traditions were compiled into a small book known as the *Seper Toledot Yeshu* ("The Book of the Generations of Jesus"). This title is taken from the opening words of Matt 1:1. Alternate titles are *Ma'aseh Talui* ("The Deeds of the Hanged One"), *Ma'aseh de'oto we-'et Beno* ("The Deeds of That One and His Son"), or *Ma'aseh Yeshu* ("The Deeds of Jesus"). The earliest references to this writing date from the ninth century. In places it is dependent upon the Yosippon (see chap. 5). For an edited version see M. Goldstein (*Jesus*, 148–54).

(9) *The Gospels.* The Gospels are sometimes alluded to: "The books of the evangelists and the books of the *minim* [heretics] they do not save from the fire. But they are allowed to burn" (*t. Šabb.* 13:5). The rabbis discuss whether or not it is required to cut out references to the Divine Name before the heretical books are burned.

Bibliography: G. H. Dalman, *Jesus Christ in the Talmud, Midrash, Zohar, and the Liturgy of the Synagogue* (with H. Laible; Cambridge: Deighton, Bell, 1893; repr. New York: Arno, 1973); M. Goldstein, *Jesus in the Jewish Tradition* (New York: Macmillan, 1950); R. T. Herford, *Christianity in Talmud and Midrash* (London: Williams and Norgate, 1903; repr. New York: Ktav, 1975); J. Z. Lauterbach, "Jesus in the Talmud," in Lauterbach, *Rabbinic Essays* (Cincinnati: Hebrew Union College, 1951) 473–570; J. Maier, *Jesus von Nazareth in der talmudischen Überlieferung* (Erträge der Forschung 82; Darmstadt: Wissenschaftliche Buchgesellschaft, 1978); D. Rokeah, "Ben Stada is Ben Pantera—Towards the Clarification of a Philological-Historical Problem," *Tarbiz* 39 (1969–70) 9–18 [Hebrew; doubts that Jesus should be identified with either ben Stada or ben Pantera]; H. J. Zimmels, "Jesus and 'Putting Up a Brick,' " *JQR* 43 (1952–53) 225–28.

The Halakah of Jesus. Did the teaching of Jesus influence rabbinic Judaism? In a recent investigation into this interesting question Phillip Sigal has concluded that Jesus probably did have an impact on rabbinic halakah. He believes that some of Jesus' views entered the tannaic stream of tradition, but either anonymously or under the names of other authorities. One of his most compelling examples is Jesus' teaching on the priority of the human being over the Sabbath:

> One sabbath he was going through the grainfields; and as they made their way his disciples began to pluck heads of grain. And the Pharisees said to

him, "Look, why are they doing what is not lawful on the sabbath?" And he said to them, "Have you not read what David did, when he was in need and was hungry, he and those who were with him: how he entered the house of God, when Abiathar was high priest, and ate the bread of the Presence, which it is not lawful for any but the priests to eat, and also gave it to those who were with him?" And he said to them, "The sabbath was made for man, not man for the sabbath; so the Son of man is lord even of the sabbath" (Mark 2:23–28 par.).

Sigal draws our attention to the parallel saying attributed to Rabbi Simon ben Menasya, who said: "Behold, it says: 'And you shall keep the sabbath, for it is holy unto you' [Exod 31:14]. This means: The sabbath is given to you but you are not surrendered to the sabbath" (Mek. on Exod 31:12–17 [Šabb. 1.25–28]; Lauterbach, 3.198). Sigal reasons that since this parallel is too close to be regarded as nothing more than a coincidence, and since Jesus, who antedates Simon ben Menasya by more than 200 years, is the first to have articulated this halakah, it is most likely that what is credited to Menasya originated with Jesus. Sigal suspects that in other areas, such as in his stricter views of personal piety and more lenient views of cultic requirements, Jesus influenced tannaic Judaism. As an example of the latter one thinks of Jesus' citation of Hos 6:6 (Matt 9:13; 12:7) and the parallel saying of Yohanan ben Zakkai ca. 75–80 C.E. ('Abot R. Nat. A §4; see discussion above).

Bibliography: S. T. Lachs, A Rabbinic Commentary on the New Testament: The Gospels of Matthew, Mark, and Luke (Hoboken: Ktav, 1987); E. P. Sanders, Jewish Law from Jesus to the Mishnah (London: SCM; Philadelphia: Trinity Press International, 1990) 19–23; P. Sigal, The Halakah of Jesus of Nazareth according to the Gospel of Matthew (Lanham and New York: University Press of America, 1986).

GENERAL BIBLIOGRAPHY: J. M. Davis, "Bibliography on the Story in Ancient Judaism," in J. Neusner, ed., New Perspectives on Ancient Judaism (Lanham: University Press of America, 1987); E. E. Ellis, "Biblical Interpretation in the New Testament Church," JWSTP, 699–709; B. Gerhardsson, Memory and Manuscript: Oral Tradition and Written Transmission in Rabbinic Judaism and Early Christianity (ASNU 22; Uppsala: Almqvist & Wiksells, 1961); L. Haas, "Bibliography on Midrash," in J. Neusner, ed., The Study of Ancient Judaism (2 vols.; New York: Ktav, 1972) 1.93–106; D. W. Halivni, Midrash, Mishnah, and Gemara: The Jewish Predilection for Justified Law (Cambridge: Harvard University, 1986); A. Hyman, Torah HaKetuba VeHaMessurah: A Reference Book of the Scriptural Passages Quoted in Talmudic, Midrashic and Early Rabbinic Literature (2d ed.; 3 vols.; Tel Aviv: Dvir, 1979); M. Jastrow, A Dictionary of the Targumim, the Talmud Babli and Yerushalmi, and the Midrashic Literature (2 vols.; London and New York: Putnam, 1886–94; repr. New York: Pardes, 1950); G. F. Moore, Judaism in the First Centuries of the Christian Era. The Age of the Tannaim (3 vols.; Cambridge: Harvard, 1927); R. C. Musaph-Andriesse, From Torah to Kabbalah (New York: Oxford University, 1982); J. Neusner, Midrash in Context: Exegesis in Formative Judaism (Philadelphia: Fortress, 1983); idem, The Study of Ancient Judaism (2 vols.; New York: Ktav, 1981); idem, What Is Midrash? (Philadelphia: Fortress, 1987); idem, The Workings of Midrash: Major Trends in Rabbinic Bible Interpretation (San Francisco: Harper &

Row, 1987); G. G. Porton, *Understanding Rabbinic Midrash* (Hoboken: Ktav, 1985); A. J. Saldarini, "Reconstructions of Rabbinic Judaism," *EJMI*, 437–77; E. P. Sanders, *Jewish Law from Jesus to the Mishnah* (London: SCM; Philadelphia: Trinity Press International, 1990); D. Sperber, *A Dictionary of Greek and Latin Terms in Rabbinic Literature* (Ramat-Gan: Bar-Ilan University, 1984); H. L. Strack and G. Stemberger, *Introduction to the Talmud and Misrash* (trans. M. Bockmuehl; Edinburgh: T. & T. Clark, 1991); J. T. Townsend, "Rabbinic Sources," in J. Neusner, ed., *The Study of Judaism* (New York: Ktav, 1972) 35–80; S. Zeitlin, "Hillel and the Hermeneutical Rules," *JQR* 54 (1963–64) 161–73.

CHAPTER EIGHT

THE NEW TESTAMENT APOCRYPHA AND PSEUDEPIGRAPHA

Agrapha
Abbaton, Angel of Death
Apostolic Histories of Pseudo-
  Abdias
Gospel of the Adversary of the
  Law and the Prophets
Acts of Andrew
Acts of Andrew and Matthias
Acts of Andrew and Paul
Epistle of the Apostles
Memoria of Apostles
Acts of Barnabas
Gospel of Barnabas
Book of the Resurrection of Christ
  by Bartholomew
Martyrdom of Bartholomew
Letters of Christ and Abgarus
Letter of Christ from Heaven
Pseudo-Clementines
Coptic Narratives of the Ministry
  and the Passion
Testamentum Domini ("Testament
  of the Lord")
Gospel of the Ebionites*
Gospel of the Egyptians*
Book of Elchasai
Gospel of Eve
Gospel of Gamaliel
Gospel of the Hebrews*
Arabic Gospel of the Infancy

Armenian Gospel of the Infancy
Latin Gospel of the Infancy
Acts of James (the Greater)
Ascent of James (the Greater)
Protevangelium of James*
Acts of John
Acts of John by Procurus
Apocryphal Gospel of John
Book of John
1 Revelation of John
2 Revelation of John
3 Revelation of John
Syriac History of John
John the Baptist
Narrative of Joseph in Arimathea
History of Joseph the Carpenter
Letter of Lentulus
Acts of Mark
Birth of Mary
Gospel of the Birth of Mary
Passing of Mary
Questions of Mary
Gospel of Pseudo-Matthew
Martyrdom of Matthew
Gospel and Traditions of Matthias
Gospel of the Nazoreans*
Gospel of Nicodemus
Acts of Paul
Greek Acts of Peter and Paul
Apocalypse of Paul

(continued on next page

Correspondence between Seneca and Paul	Letters of Pilate and Herod
	Letter of Pilate to Tiberius
Epistle of Paul to the Alexandrians	Letter of Tiberius to Pilate
Paul's Third Letter to the Corinthians	Report and Paradosis of Pilate
	The Avenging of the Savior
Epistle to the Laodiceans	Sibylline Oracles
Martyrdom of Paul	Revelation of Stephen
Vision of Paul	Acts of Thaddeus
Acts of Peter	Acts of Thomas
(Slavonic) Acts of Peter	Minor Acts of Thomas
Acts of Andrew and Peter	Apocalypse of Thomas
Apocalypse of Peter	Consumption of Thomas
Gospel of Peter*	Gospel of Thomas
Martyrdom of Peter	Infancy Gospel of Thomas*
Passions of Peter and Paul	Martyrdom of Thomas
Preaching of Peter	The Dialogue of Timothy and Aquila
Acts of Philip	
(Syriac) Acts of Philip	Epistle of Titus
Gospel of Philip	Gospel of the Twelve Apostles
Martyrdom of Philip	Apocalypse of the Virgin
Translation of Philip	Assumption of the Virgin
Acts of Pilate*	Coptic Lives of the Virgin
Death of Pilate	Acts of Xanthippe and Polyxena
Letter of Pilate to Claudius	Apocalypse of Zechariah

The title New Testament Apocrypha and Pseudepigrapha is a misnomer, since it implies that these are writings of the NT itself. In reality these are post-NT Christian apocryphal and pseudepigraphal writings, some of which date from the Middle Ages. Those writings marked with an asterisk (*) are discussed below in a section concerned with apocryphal gospels and the historical Jesus. Portions of this large corpus are translated in M. R. James and in E. Hennecke and W. Schneemelcher (see General Bibliography below).

STUDIES

Agrapha. Genuine sayings of Jesus? According to Eusebius (*Eccl. Hist.* 3.39.11), Papias "adduces other accounts, as though they came to him from unwritten [*agrapha*] tradition, and some strange parables and teachings of the Savior, and some other more mythical accounts." An example of a NT agraphon is Acts 20:35: "Always I have shown you that by so laboring one must help the weak, remembering the words of the Lord Jesus, that he said, 'It is more blessed to give than to receive.' " From Jeremias (pp. 49–87):

> On the same day he saw a man performing a work on the Sabbath. Then he said to him: "Man! If you know what you are doing, you are blessed. But if you do not know, you are cursed and a transgressor of the Law" (from Codex D, following Luke 6:5).

> He who is near me is near the fire; he who is far from me is far from the Kingdom (from Origen *Homilies on Jeremiah* 20.3; also found in Didymus, *Commentary on the Psalms* 88.8 and *Gos. Thom.* §82).

> No one can obtain the kingdom of heaven who has not passed through temptation (from Tertullian *On Baptism* 20).

> You have rejected the Living One who is before your eyes, and talk idly of the dead (from Augustine *Against the Enemy of the Law and the Prophets* 2.4.14).

> There will be dissensions and squabbles (Justin *Dialogue with Trypho* 35.3).

> The Kingdom is like a wise fisherman who cast his net into the sea; he drew it up from the sea full of small fish; among them he found a large (and) good fish; that wise fisherman threw all the small fish down into the sea; he chose the large fish without regret (*Gos. Thom.* §8).

> Ask for the great things, and God will add to you the little things (first quoted by Clement of Alexandria, *Stromateis* 1.24.158).

Hofius is less sanguine. He tentatively accepts two of the above and recommends the following two:

> And never be joyful, save when you look upon your brother in love (*Gos. Heb.* §5; cf. Jerome *Commentary On Ephesians* 5.4).

> [He that] stands far off [today] will tomorrow be [near you] (POxy 1224 §2).

Hofius believes that only nine agrapha are worth serious attention. Of these only four have a reasonable chance of being authentic (i.e., [1] the addition to Luke 6:5 in Codex D; [2] Origen *Homilies on Jeremiah* 20.3; Didymus *On the Psalms* 88.8; *Gos. Thom.* §82; [3] *Gos. Heb.* §5; cf. Jerome *Commentary on Ephesians* 5.4; [4] POxy 1224 §2). From this he concludes that the canonical Gospels preserve virtually all of the dominical tradition that the church of the second half of the first century had retained. He thinks therefore that assumptions that there was a vast amount of genuine material in circulation outside of the NT Gospels are unfounded.

Bibliography: J. D. Crossan, *Sayings Parallels: A Workbook for the Jesus Tradition* (Foundations and Facets: New Testament; Philadelphia: Fortress, 1986) [limited to "units which could or did exist in the tradition as isolated segments passed on in different contexts." Given this limitation, cites all instances of sayings in canonical and early extracanonical sources]; O. Hofius, "Unknown Sayings of Jesus," in P. Stuhlmacher, ed., *The Gospel and the Gospels* (Grand Rapids: Eerdmans, 1991) 336–60; J. Jeremias, *Unknown Sayings of Jesus* (London: SPCK, 1958); W. D. Stroker, *Extracanonical Sayings of Jesus* (SBLRBS 18; Atlanta: Scholars, 1989) [extremely valuable tool that provides texts (Coptic, Greek, and Latin), translations, and helpful indexes; excellent bibliography].

The Early Church's Awareness of Pseudepigraphy. The early church was aware of pseudepigraphy and did not approve of it. The Muratorian Canon rejects the "forged" letters of Paul to the Laodiceans and Alexandrians (§§63–67). Tertullian defrocked an elder for writing the *Acts of Paul* and possibly also *3 Corinthians* (*On Baptism* 17). Eusebius avers:

> Among the books which are not genuine must be reckoned the Acts of Paul, the work entitled the Shepherd, the Apocalypse of Peter, and in addition to them the letter called of Barnabas and the so-called Teachings of the Apostles. And in addition, as I said, the Revelation of John, if this view prevail. For as I said, some reject it, but others count it among the Recognized Books. Some have also counted the Gospel according to the Hebrews in which those of the Hebrews who have accepted Christ take a special pleasure. These would all belong to the disputed books, but we have nevertheless been obliged to make a list of them distinguishing between those writings which, according to the tradition of the Church are true, genuine, and recognized, and those which differ from them in that they are not canonical but disputed, yet nevertheless are known to most of the writers of the Church, in order that we might know them and the writings that are put forward by heretics under the name of the apostles containing gospels such as those of Peter, and Thomas, and Matthias, and some others besides, or Acts such as those of Andrew and John and the other apostles. To none of these has any who belonged to the succession of the orthodox ever thought it right to refer in his writings. Moreover, the type of phraseology differs from apostolic style, and the opinion and tendency of their contents are widely dissonant from true orthodoxy and clearly show that they are the forgeries of heretics. They ought, therefore, to be reckoned not even among spurious books but shunned as altogether wicked and impious (Eusebius *Eccl. Hist.* 3.25.4–7 [LCL 1.257–59]).

According to Eusebius, Serapion, bishop of Antioch, condemned the *Gospel of Peter:*

> Another book has been composed by him [Serapion (d. 211 C.E.) entitled,] *Concerning what is known as the Gospel of Peter,* which he has written refuting the false statements in it, because of certain [people] in the community of Rhossus, who on the ground of the said writing turned aside into heterodox teachings. It will not be unreasonable to quote a short passage from this work, in which he puts forward the view he held about the book, writing as follows: "For our part, brethren, we receive both Peter and the other apostles as Christ, but the writings which falsely [*pseudepig*-

rapha] bear their names we reject, as men of experience, knowing that such were not handed down to us" (Eusebius *Eccl. Hist.* 6.12.2–3 [LCL 2.41]).

To this a general word of condemnation of all "poisonous books" is added by the *Apostolic Constitutions,* itself a pseudepigraphon:

> We [i.e., the Apostles] have sent all things to you, that you may know what our opinion is; and that you may not receive those books which obtain in our name, but are written by the ungodly. For you are not to attend to the names of the apostles, but to the nature of the things, and their settled opinions. For we know that Simon and Cleobius, and their followers, have compiled poisonous books under the name of Christ and of his disciples, and carry them about in order to deceive you who love Christ, and us his servants (*Apostolic Constitutions* 6:16).

For a concise discussion of the criteria of canonicity in the early church see Lee McDonald. For studies concerned with the problem of pseudonymity see the studies by David Meade and Bruce Metzger.

Bibliography: L. M. McDonald, *The Formation of the Christian Biblical Canon* (Nashville: Abingdon, 1988); D. G. Meade, *Pseudonymity and Canon: An Investigation into the Relationship of Authorship and Authority in Jewish and Earliest Christian Tradition* (Grand Rapids: Eerdmans, 1986); B. M. Metzger, "Literary Forgeries and Canonical Pseudepigrapha," *JBL* 91 (1972) 3–24.

Apocryphal Gospels and the Historical Jesus. But what of the synoptic parallels in the apocryphal gospels? The writings marked with asterisks on pages 149–50 have in recent years found a place in the scholarly discussion of the historical Jesus. Could some of these parallels represent more primitive tradition? In recent studies John Dominic Crossan argued that some of the apocryphal gospels (e.g., *Gospel of Thomas,* Papyrus Egerton 2, *Secret Gospel of Mark,* and *Gospel of Peter*) have retained primitive, perhaps even pre-synoptic traditions. He argues, for example, that the *Gospel of Peter* offers evidence for a "Cross Gospel," which was the "single known source for the Passion and Resurrection narrative. It flowed into Mark, flowed along with him into Matthew and Luke, flowed along with the three synoptics into John, and finally flowed along with the intracanonical tradition into the pseudepigraphal *Gospel of Peter*" (*The Cross that Spoke,* 404).

For descriptions, parallels with NT Gospels, and principal bibliography see Appendix 3. For a more detailed discussion of a passage which may be significantly clarified by appeal to an apocryphal gospel see chapter 12.

Bibliography: P. Beskow, *Strange Tales about Jesus: A Survey of Unfamiliar Gospels* (Philadelphia: Fortress, 1983); R. Cameron, *The Other Gospels: Non-Canonical Gospel Texts* (Philadelphia: Westminster, 1982); J. D. Crossan, *The Cross that Spoke: The Origins of the Passion Narrative* (San Francisco: Harper & Row, 1988); idem, *Four Other Gospels: Shadows on the Contours of Canon* (Minneapolis: Winston, 1985); A. A. T. Ehrhardt, "Judaeo-Christians in Egypt, the Epistula Apostolorum and the Gospel to the Hebrews," *SE* 3 (1961) 360–82; J. Hills, *Tradition and Composition in the Epistula Apostolorum* (HDR 24; Minneapolis: Fortress, 1990); L. L. Kline, *The Sayings of Jesus in the Pseudo-Clementine Homilies* (SBLDS 14; Missoula: Scholars, 1975); H. Koester, "Apocryphal and Canonical Gospels," *HTR* 73 (1980) 105–30; J. P. Meier, *A Marginal Jew: Rethinking the Historical Jesus* (ABRL; New York: Doubleday, 1991) 112–66 [questions the independence and authenticity of the Jesus tradition in the noncanonical gospels]; M. Smith, *Clement of Alexandria and a Secret Gospel of Mark* (Cambridge: Harvard University, 1973); idem, *The Secret Gospel: The Discovery and Interpretation of the Secret Gospel according to Mark* (New York: Harper & Row, 1973) [a popular version of the former]; D. Wenham, ed., *The Jesus Tradition Outside the Gospels* (Gospel Perspectives 5; Sheffield: JSOT, 1985) [several essays examine Jesus tradition in Paul, James, 1 Peter, *Gospel of Thomas*, apostolic fathers, apocryphal gospels, early Jewish and classical authors; bibliography]; R. McL. Wilson, "The New Passion of Jesus in the Light of the New Testament," in E. E. Ellis and M. Wilcox, eds., *Neotestamentica et Semitica* (M. Black Festschrift; Edinburgh: T. & T. Clark, 1969) 264–72.

GENERAL BIBLIOGRAPHY: J. H. Charlesworth, *The New Testament Apocrypha and Pseudepigrapha: A Guide to Publications, with Excurses on Apocalypses* (with J. R. Mueller; ATLA Bibliography Series 17; London and Meteuchen: ATLA, 1987); E. Hennecke and W. Schneemelcher, eds., *New Testament Apocrypha* (2 vols.; Philadelphia: Westminster, 1974 [in the GT a 6th ed. of vol. 1 appeared in 1990; a 5th ed. of vol. 2 appeared in 1989]); M. R. James, *The Apocryphal New Testament* (Oxford: Clarendon, 1924); H. Koester, *Ancient Christian Gospels: Their History and Development* (Philadelphia: Trinity Press International, 1990); D. R. MacDonald, "Apocryphal New Testament," *HBD*, 38–39.

CHAPTER NINE

EARLY CHURCH FATHERS

APOSTOLIC FATHERS
1 Clement
2 Clement
Ignatius
Polycarp
Martyrdom of Polycarp
Didache
Barnabas
Shepherd of Hermas
Diognetus
Papias

EARLY APOLOGISTS, EXEGETES, AND
THEOLOGIANS
Aristides
Athenagoras
Clement of Alexandria
Irenaeus
Justin Martyr
Melito of Sardis
Origen
Quadratus
Tatian

Tertullian
Theophilus of Antioch

LATER MAJOR WRITERS
Ambrose
Athanasius
Augustine
Cassiodorus
John Chrysostom
Commodian
Cyril of Jerusalem
Cyprian
Epiphanius
Eusebius
Hippolytus
Jerome
Methodius

Only a select number of early apologists, exegetes, and theologians are listed in this chapter. Those that are listed are those who were early and interpret Scripture, both OT and NT, and preserve early traditions. The major contributions that these writers make to NT interpretation are enumerated in the following paragraphs. Most of the attention is given to the apostolic fathers.

SUMMARIES

Apostolic Fathers. The so-called apostolic fathers in reality is a collection of post-apostolic writings that were revered and, in some cases, rivalled the very writings that now make up the canon of the NT. This corpus represents a collection of early writings, mostly epistles, of late first- and early- to mid-second century church leaders. This collection contributes to NT studies in at least five important areas: (1) OT text types with which the early church was familiar; (2) dominical traditions parallel to and in some instances outside of the NT Gospels; (3) early interpretations of NT books and passages; (4) traditions relating to early church history; and (5) traditions regarding the authorship of NT books.

1 Clement. 1 Clement is a letter to the church at Corinth that was commissioned by a small group of presbyters of the church at Rome. Clement was one of these presbyters and may very well have been the leader of the group; hence his name's association with the letter. The letter, penned in either 95 or 96 C.E., urges the Corinthians to settle their disputes peaceably. The writer sometimes appeals to Paul's Corinthian correspondence (cf. 13:27; 35:8; 37:3). The SBL abbreviation is *1 Clem.*

Bibliography: L. W. Barnard, "St. Clement of Rome and the Persecution of Domitian," in Barnard, *Studies in the Apostolic Fathers and Their Background* (Oxford: Blackwell, 1966) 5–18; G. L. Cockerill, "Heb 1:1–14, 1 Clem 36:1–6 and the High Priest Title," *JBL* 97 (1978) 437–40; D. A. Hagner, *The Use of the Old and New Testaments in Clement of Rome* (NovTSup 34; Leiden: Brill, 1973); C. C. Tarelli, "Clement of Rome and the Fourth Gospel," *JTS* 48 (1947) 208–9; L. L. Welborn, "On the Date of First Clement," *BR* 29 (1984) 35–54; A. E. Wilhelm-Hooijbergh, "A Different View of Clemens Romanus," *HeyJ* 16 (1975) 266–88; F. W. Young, "The Relation of 1 Clement to the Epistle of James," *JBL* 67 (1948) 339–45.

2 Clement. From antiquity the writing that is called *2 Clement* was associated with *1 Clement.* However, its authorship, date, place of writing, and occasion are unknown. Moreover, it is not a letter, but a sermon based on Isa 54:1 (cf. *2 Clem.* 2:1). The SBL abbreviation is *2 Clem.*

Bibliography: K. P. Donfried, *The Setting of Second Clement in Early Christianity* (NovTSup 38; Leiden: Brill, 1974); idem, "The Theology of Second Clement," *HTR* 66 (1973) 487–501; C. C. Richardson, "An Anonymous Sermon, Commonly Called Clement's Second Letter," in Richardson, ed., *Early Christian Fathers* (Philadelphia: Westminster, 1953; repr. New York: Macmillan, 1970) 183–202; W. C. van Unnik, "The Interpretation of 2 Clement 15,5," *VC* 27 (1973) 29–34.

Ignatius. After his arrest in Syrian Antioch, Ignatius was sent to Rome, where he presumably was martyred. While on his journey he penned seven letters (six to churches [*Ephesians, Magnesians, Philadelphians, Romans, Smyrnaeans, Trallians*], one to Polycarp), though the authenticity of a few of them from time to time has been doubted. The matter has been complicated by the preservation of three recensions (short, middle, and long). Most scholars now accept the authenticity of all seven letters (see the discussion in William Schoedel's commentary). The letters are dated broadly to 100–118 C.E., though some narrow the span to 107–110. Ignatius wrote to encourage and promote harmony, especially in his home church of Antioch. The SBL abbreviation is Ign. *Eph.*, Ign. *Magn.*, etc.

Bibliography: L. W. Barnard, "The Background of St. Ignatius of Antioch," *VC* 17 (1963) 193–206; C. K. Barrett, "Jews and Judaizers in the Epistles of Ignatius," in R. Hamerton-Kelly and R. Scroggs, eds., *Jews, Greeks and Christians: Religious Cultures in Late Antiquity* (SJLA 21; Leiden: Brill, 1976) 220–44; R. Bultmann, "Ignatius and Paul," in Bultmann, *Existence and Faith: Shorter Writings of Rudolf Bultmann* (ed. S. M. Ogden; New York: Meridian, 1960) 267–77; P. J. Donahue, "Jewish Christianity in the Letters of Ignatius of Antioch," *VC* 32 (1978) 81–93; W. R. Schoedel, "Are the Letters of Ignatius of Antioch Authentic?" *RelSRev* 6 (1980) 196–201; idem, *Ignatius of Antioch* (Hermeneia; Philadelphia: Fortress, 1985); G. F. Snyder, "The Historical Jesus in the Letters of Ignatius of Antioch," *BR* 8 (1963) 3–12.

Polycarp to the Philippians. Polycarp's letter to the Philippians was apparently written shortly after the martyrdom of Ignatius, since Polycarp evidently assumes that the bishop is dead (1:1; 9:1) but has received no final word (13:2). In response to a written request (cf. 3:1), Polycarp offers encouragement and admonition to the Philippians. Percy Harrison's hypothesis that this writing is actually a conflation of two letters has not won acceptance. The SBL abbreviation is Pol. *Phil.*

Bibliography: L. W. Barnard, "The Problem of St. Polycarp's Epistle to the Philippians," in Barnard, *Studies in the Apostolic Fathers and Their Background* (Oxford: Blackwell, 1967) 31–40; P. N. Harrison, *Polycarp's Two Epistles to the Philippians* (Cambridge: Cambridge University, 1936); W. R. Schoedel, *Polycarp, Martyrdom of Polycarp, Papias* (Apostolic Fathers 5; Camden: Nelson, 1967); idem, "Polycarp's Witness to Ignatius of Antioch," *VC* 41 (1987) 1–10.

Martyrdom of Polycarp. This writing offers itself as an eyewitness account ("from the papers of Irenaeus"; 22:2) of the martyrdom of Polycarp (cf. 15:1; 18:1), bishop of the church of Smyrna. Polycarp, who was 86 years old at the time of his death (cf. 9:3), was martyred sometime after 160 C.E. The purpose of the writing seems to have been to set up Polycarp as an example of piety and faithfulness in the face of torture and death. The SBL abbreviation is *Mart. Pol.*

Bibliography: M. H. Shepherd, Jr., "The Martyrdom of Polycarp, as Told in the Letter of the Church of Smyrna to the Church of Philomelium," in C. C. Richardson, ed., *Early Christian Fathers* (Philadelphia: Westminster, 1953; repr. New York: Macmillan, 1970) 141–58; W. Telfer, "The Date of the Martyrdom of Polycarp," *JTS* 3 (1952) 79–83.

The Didache. The *Didache*, or *Teaching of the Twelve Apostles*, may have been written as early as 70–80 C.E. Its purpose is to underscore the "Two

Ways," that is, the way of life and the way of death (1:1–6:2), and to provide instruction in church order and practice (6:3–16:8). The SBL abbreviation is *Did.*

Bibliography: J. Draper, "The Jesus Tradition in the Didache," in D. Wenham, ed., *The Jesus Tradition Outside the Gospels* (Gospel Perspectives 5; Sheffield: JSOT, 1985) 269–87; R. Glover, "The Didache's Quotations and the Synoptic Gospels," *NTS* 5 (1958) 12–29; B. Layton, "The Source, Date and Transmission of Didache 1.3b–2.1," *HTR* 61 (1968) 343–83; F. E. Vokes, "The Didache and the Canon of the New Testament," *SE* 3 (1964) 427–36.

Barnabas. The *Epistle of Barnabas*, written either in the late first century or in the early second, is concerned with the question of how Christians are to interpret the Jewish scriptures. (In reality this writing is not a letter, and it was not penned by Barnabas.) The author's approach, like the Jewish interpreter Philo before him and the Christian interpreter Origen after him, was to allegorize the scriptures. The SBL abbreviation is *Barn.*

Bibliography: See L. W. Barnard, "The Epistle of Barnabas and the Tannaitic Catechism," *ATR* 41 (1959) 177–90; idem, "The Testimonium concerning the Stone in the New Testament and in the Epistle of Barnabas," *SE* 3 (1961) 306–13; R. A. Kraft, *Barnabas and the Didache* (Apostolic Fathers 3; New York: Nelson, 1965); idem, "Barnabas' Isaiah Text and the 'Testimony Book' Hypothesis," *JBL* 79 (1960) 336–50; idem, "An Unnoticed Papyrus Fragment of Barnabas," *VC* 21 (1967) 150–63.

Shepherd of Hermas. The *Shepherd of Hermas* is the longest writing of the apostolic fathers. It appears in three major sections: (five) *Visions*, (twelve) *Mandates*, and (ten) *Similitudes* (or *Parables*). The work, which was composed sometime in the first half of the second century, is a Christian apocalypse comparable to *1 Enoch*. It may have originally been two parts (*Visions* 1–4 and *Vision 5–Similitude* 10). The SBL abbreviations are *Herm. Vis., Herm. Man., Herm. Sim.*

Bibliography: D. E. Aune, "Herm. Man. 11.2: Christian False Prophets Who Say What People Wish to Hear," *JBL* 97 (1978) 103–4; L. W. Barnard, "Hermas and Judaism," *SP* 8 (1966) 3–9; idem, "The Shepherd of Hermas in Recent Study," *HeyJ* 9 (1968) 29–36; G. D. Kilpatrick, "A New Papyrus of the Shepherd of Hermas," *JTS* 48 (1947) 204–5; C. Osiek, *Rich and Poor in the Shepherd of Hermas: An Exegetical-Social Investigation* (CBQMS 15; Washington: Catholic Biblical Association, 1983); J. Reiling, *Hermas and Christian Prophecy: A Study of the Eleventh Mandate* (NovTSup 37; Leiden: Brill, 1973); O. J. F. Seitz, "Relationship of the Shepherd to the Epistle of James," *JBL* 63 (1944) 131–40.

Diognetus. The *Epistle to Diognetus* is in reality an apologetic tract in the form of an open letter. It is not written to Christians, but to non-Christians. As such, it is an invitation to embrace the Christian faith. The writing likely originated in the late second or early third century. The SBL abbreviation is *Diogn.*

Bibliography: P. Andriessen, "The Authorship of the Epistula ad Diognetum," *VC* 1 (1947) 129–36; E. R. Fairweather, "The So-called Letter to Diognetus," in C. C. Richardson, ed., *Early Christian Fathers* (Philadelphia: Westminster, 1953; repr. New York: Macmillan, 1970) 205–24; H. G. Meecham, *The Epistle to Diognetus: The Greek Text with Introduction, Translation and Notes* (Manchester: University of Manchester, 1949).

Papias. Some two dozen fragments of Papias' five-volume work, *Expositions of the Sayings of the Lord,* are preserved in Eusebius and other church theologians and historians. This early Father (ca. 70–160 C.E.) is well known for his statements regarding the transmission of the dominical tradition and the authorship of the Gospels.

Bibliography: R. Annand, "Papias and the Four Gospels," *SJT* 9 (1956) 46–62; J. F. Bligh, "The Prologue of Papias," *TS* 13 (1952) 234–40; D. D. Deeks, "Papias Revisited," *ExpTim* 88 (1977) 296–301, 324–29; R. M. Grant, "Papias and the Gospels," *ATR* 25 (1943) 218–22; R. G. Heard, "Papias' Quotations from the New Testament," *NTS* 1 (1954) 122–29; T. Mullins, "Papias on Mark's Gospel," *VC* 14 (1960) 216–24; idem, "Papias and Clement and Mark's Two Gospels," *VC* 30 (1976) 189–92; "Papias and the Oral Tradition," *VC* 21 (1967) 137–40.

Early Apologists, Exegetes, and Theologians. The writings of several other early apologists, exegetes, and theologians are worth examining in doing NT interpretation. Most of these writers quoted the OT and NT, often preserving older interpretations. Comparative study, therefore, can sometimes aid the interpreter in appreciating the full range of ancient interpretive traditions and may, in some instances, clarify a tradition that is only hinted at in the NT. One such example is treated in chapter 12 below. These writers will be treated quite briefly.

Among the earliest apologists are Aristides (ca. 145), Athenagoras (ca. 170–180), Justin Martyr (d. 165), Melito of Sardis (d. ca. 190), Tatian (d. 180?), and Theophilus of Antioch (ca. 180–185). Justin is famous for his *Apologia* ("Apology" or "Defense") and his *Dialogus cum Tryphone* ("Dialogue with Trypho the Jew"), while Tatian is best known for the *Diatessaron* ("Fourfold book"), a work in which he wove together the four NT Gospels into a unified narrative. (He sometimes made use of a fifth—the *Gospel according to the Hebrews.*) This work remained popular in the Eastern church, displacing the canonical Gospels for nearly three centuries. Melito's best known surviving work is his *Homily on the Passover.* Clement of Alexandria (ca. 150–215) is well known for his *Protreptikos pros Hellenas* ("Exhortation to the Greeks"), the *Paedagogus* ("Pedagogue" or "Tutor"), and the *Stromata* (or *Stromateis,* "Miscellanies"). All of his works are replete with quotations of and allusions to the OT and NT. One of the most influential early Christian apologists and exegetes was Origen of Alexandria (ca. 185–254). He is best known for his allegorical interpretation of Scripture, as seen in his numerous commentaries (e.g., Matthew, John, Romans, Psalms), his *Hexapla* (a work containing the Hebrew, LXX, and the recensions in parallel columns), and his polemical work *Contra Celsum* ("Against Celsus"). Other early apologists and theologians include Irenaeus (ca. 140–202) and Tertullian (ca. 160–220). The former is best known for his *Adversus Haereses* ("Against Heresies"), while the latter authored *Adversus Marcionem* ("Against Marcion"), *Apologia* ("Apology" or "Defense"), and various tracts on Christian doctrines. Hippolytus (ca. 170–235) was an early heresiologist who authored *Refutation of All Heresies.* Cyprian (d. 258) authored the *Testimonies to Quirinus.*

Later Major Writers. Other Fathers whose writings are worth consulting include Ambrose, Athanasius, Augustine, Cassiodorus, John Chrysostom, Commodian, Cyril of Jerusalem, Epiphanius, Eusebius, Jerome, and Methodius. The writings of Eusebius (ca. 260–339) and Jerome (ca. 342–420) should be mentioned briefly. The former is well known for his *Historia Ecclesia* (or "Ecclesiastical History"), which contains many early and valuable traditions (such as the fragments of Papias), and for his *Praeparatio Evangelica* ("Preparation of the Gospel") and *Demonstratio Evangelica* ("Defense of the Gospel"), which are extant only in fragments. Eusebius also authored a commentary and several homilies on the Psalms. Jerome is probably best known for his Latin translation of the Bible (ca. 390) that became known as the Vulgate. This late fourth-century translation is based on the Hebrew for the OT and as such is an early witness to the text of the OT. (Outside of Qumran, no extant Hebrew manuscript is earlier than the ninth century C.E.) Several of Jerome's letters and commentaries are extant. These also contain significant exegetical traditions (Jewish as well as Christian), some of which derive from early times.

In citing the Fathers it is customary to follow the volume and column numbers of J. Migne's *Patrologia graeca* and *Patrologia latina.* (Some journals require that Migne be followed.) The SBL abbreviations are *PG* and *PL,* respectively.

GENERAL BIBLIOGRAPHY: B. Altaner, *Patrology* (Edinburgh and London: Nelson, 1960; New York: Herder and Herder, 1961); L. W. Barnard, *Studies in the Apostolic Fathers and Their Background* (Oxford: Blackwell, 1966); A. Benoit et al., *Biblia Patristica: Index des citations et allusions bibliques dans la Littérature Patristique* (5 vols.; Paris: Editions du CNRS, 1975–82) [vol. 5 indexes the writings of Philo of Alexandria]; L. Berkowitz and K. A. Squitier, *The Thesaurus Linguae Graecae Canon of Greek Authors and Works* (2d ed.; New York and Oxford: Oxford University, 1986); R. E. Brown, *The Churches the Apostles Left Behind* (Mahwah: Paulist, 1984); C. A. Evans, "Isaiah 6:9–10 in Rabbinic and Patristic Writings," *VC* 36 (1982) 275–81; idem, "Jerome's Translation of Isaiah 6:9–10," *VC* 38 (1984) 202–4; F. Field, *Origenis Hexapla* (2 vols.; Hildesheim: Olms, 1964) [a compilation of the fragments of Origen's *Hexapla*]; R. Glover, "Patristic Quotations and Gospel Sources," *NTS* 31 (1985) 234–51; E. J. Goodspeed, *Index Patristicus* (Naperville: Allenson, 1907; repr. 1960) [Greek concordance]; R. M. Grant, *After the New Testament* (Philadelphia: Fortress, 1967); idem, ed., *The Apostolic Fathers: A New Translation and*

Commentary (6 vols.; New York: Nelson, 1964–68); N. G. L. Hammond and H. H. Scullard, eds., *The Oxford Classical Dictionary* (2d ed.; Oxford: Clarendon, 1970); H. J. de Jonge, "On the Origin of the Term 'Apostolic Fathers'," *JTS* 29 (1978) 503–5; H. Koester, *Synoptische Überlieferung bei den apostolischen Vätern* (TU 65; Berlin: Akademie, 1957); K. Lake, *Apostolic Fathers* (2 vols.; LCL; Cambridge: Harvard, 1912–13) [Greek text and ET]; G. W. H. Lampe, ed., *A Patristic Greek Lexicon* (Oxford: Clarendon, 1961–68); J. B. Lightfoot, *The Apostolic Fathers* (2d ed.; 5 vols.; Macmillan, 1889, 1890; repr. Peabody: Hendrickson, 1989); J. B. Lightfoot and J. R. Harmer, *The Apostolic Fathers* (ed. M. W. Holmes; Grand Rapids: Baker, 1989) [ET, with bibliographies and current introduction]; L. M. McDonald, *The Formation of the Christian Biblical Canon* (Nashville: Abingdon, 1988) [provides quotations of all the pertinent primary literature]; J. Quasten, *Patrology* (4 vols.; Utrecht: Spectrum, 1950; repr. Westminster: Newman, 1983); W. R. Schoedel, "The Apostolic Fathers," in E. J. Epp and G. W. MacRae, eds., *The New Testament and Its Modern Interpreters* (Atlanta: Scholars, 1989) [excellent bibliography].

CHAPTER TEN

GNOSTIC WRITINGS

(continued on next page)

Until the twentieth century, Gnosticism was believed to have been a Christian heresy that emerged in the late first and early second centuries. It was assumed, for example, that the Johannine writings and the Pastorals were composed in part to counter a gnosticizing tendency in certain circles which tended to deemphasize the incarnation and the need of repentance and faith. Rather than a Jesus who came as Israel's Messiah, physically suffered, and rose bodily from the grave, Gnostics taught that Jesus only "appeared" to be physical (the basic tenet of docetism), or perhaps only temporarily inhabited a physical body (adoptionism), and that, instead, it was very important to possess knowledge *(gnōsis)* about the cosmos and how to defeat the evil spiritual powers. Because of the emphasis placed on knowledge, these people were called Gnostics (i.e., "knowers" [of ultimate truths]). Just as the apostles John and Paul combatted this heresy, so the heirs (such as Justin Martyr, Epiphanius, Irenaeus, and Hippolytus) of the apostolic gospel combatted it. This was the impression left us by the Fathers of the church.

In the twentieth century scholars came to doubt this portrait as idealistic and inaccurate. Most now believe that the picture was much more complicated. There may very well be more to Gnosticism than just an aberration within the early church. Its roots are probably diverse, geographically, culturally, and religiously, with some of these roots reaching back to the first century C.E. and even further. Moreover, the assumption about how certain NT writings actually relate to Gnosticism is not nearly as simple as the Fathers would have us believe. For example, if John was written to combat early Gnosticism, why did the Gnostics of the second century find this Gospel so attractive? See the convenient collection of the fragments of gnostic exegesis of this book in Elaine Pagels, *The Johannine Gospel in Gnostic Exegesis* (New York: Abingdon, 1973). One might raise the same question with respect to Paul; see Pagels, *The Gnostic Paul* (Philadelphia: Fortress, 1975). Moreover, since the publication of Walter Bauer's *Orthodoxy and Heresy in Earliest Christianity* (Philadelphia: Fortress, 1971), scholars have come to recognize that making sharp distinctions between "orthodoxy" and "heresy" in the first two or three centuries of Christianity tends to be anachronistic and misleading in that it obscures the theological pluralism of this period.

Perhaps the most hotly debated question is whether or not gnostic mythology played a significant role in the formation of NT Christology. This issue is addressed in the studies below.

The most important collection of Gnostic writings are the Nag Hammadi Codices (NHC). Thirteen codices, containing fifty-two tractates, were discovered in upper Egypt in 1945. Six of these tractates are duplicates. Six others were already extant. The remaining forty represented wholly new finds. A complete ET was prepared and published in 1977 under the direction of James M. Robinson (cf. J. M. Robinson, *The Nag Hammadi Library* [San Francisco: Harper & Row, 1977; 3d ed., 1988]). Robinson also supervised the publication of the facsimile edition, which is listed below. The principal critical editions are also cited.

COPTIC GNOSTIC LIBRARY:
THE FACSIMILE EDITION OF THE NAG HAMMADI CODICES*

Codex I	(1977)
Codex II	(1974)
Codex III	(1976)
Codex IV	(1975)
Codex V	(1975)
Codex VI	(1972)
Codex VII	(1972)
Codex VIII	(1976)
Codices IX and X	(1977)
Codices XI, XII, XIII	(1973)
Cartonage	(1979)

* (ed. J. M. Robinson et al. [Leiden: Brill])

COPTIC GNOSTIC LIBRARY: TEXT, TRANSLATION, AND COMMENTARY

NHC I: H. W. Attridge, ed., *Nag Hammadi Codex I (The Jung Codex)* (NHS 22–23; Leiden: Brill, 1985)

J.-E. Ménard, *L'Evangile de vérité* (NHS 2; Leiden: Brill, 1972)

NHC II: S. Giversen, *Apocryphon Johannis: The Coptic Text of the Apocryphon Johannis in the Nag Hammadi Codex II* (ATDan 5; Leiden: Brill, 1963)

A. Guillaumont et al., *The Gospel according to Thomas: Coptic Text, Established and Translated* (2d ed.; Leiden: Brill, 1976)

J.-E. Ménard, *L'Evangile selon Thomas* (NHS 5; Leiden: Brill, 1975)

F. Wisse, ed., *Nag Hammadi Codices II, 2 and IV, 1: The Apocryphon of John, Long Recension* (NHS 32; Leiden: Brill, forthcoming)

B. Layton, ed., *Nag Hammadi Codices II, 2–7, together with XIII, 2*, Brit. Lib. Or. 4926 (1) and P. Oxy. 1, 654, 655* (NHS 20–21; Leiden: Brill, 1989)

M. Scopello, *L'exégèse de l'âme: Nag Hammadi Codex II, 6* (NHS 25; Leiden: Brill, 1985)

NHC III: F. Wisse, ed., *Nag Hammadi Codex III, 1 and Papyrus Berolinensis 8502, 2: The Apocryphon of John, Short Recension* (NHS 33; Leiden: Brill, forthcoming)

A. Böhlig and F. Wisse, with P. Labib, eds., *Nag Hammadi Codices III, 2 and IV, 2: The Gospel of the Egyptians (The Holy Book of the Great Invisible Spirit)* (NHS 4; Leiden: Brill, 1975)

D. M. Parrott, ed., *Nag Hammadi Codices III, 3–4 and V, 1 with Papyrus Berolinensis 8502, 3 and Oxyrhynchus Papyrus 1081: Eugnostos and the Sophia of Jesus Christ* (NHS 27; Leiden: Brill, 1991)

C. Schmidt, V. MacDermot, and R. McL. Wilson, *Pistis Sophia* (NHS 9; Leiden: Brill, 1978)

S. Emmel, ed., *Nag Hammadi Codex III, 5: The Dialogue of the Savior* (NHS 26; Leiden: Brill, 1984)

NHC IV: F. Wisse, ed., *Nag Hamadi Codices II, 2 and IV, 1: The Apocryphon of John, Long Recension* (NHS 32; Leiden: Brill, forthcoming)

NHC V: D. M. Parrott, ed., *Nag Hammadi Codices V, 2–5 and VI with Papyrus Berolinensis 8502, 1 and 4* (NHS 11; Leiden: Brill, 1979)

NHC VI: D. M. Parrott, ed., *Nag Hammadi Codices V, 2–5 and VI with Papyrus Berolinensis 8502, 1 and 4* (NHS 11; Leiden: Brill, 1979)

NHC VII: F. Wisse, ed., *Nag Hammadi Codex VII* (NHS 30; Leiden: Brill, forthcoming)

NHC VIII: J. Sieber, ed., *Nag Hammadi Codex VIII* (NHS 31; Leiden: Brill, 1991)

NHC IX: B. A. Pearson, ed., *Nag Hammadi Codices IX and X* (NHS 15; Leiden: Brill, 1981)

NHC X: B. A. Pearson, ed., *Nag Hammadi Codices IX and X* (NHS 15; Leiden: Brill, 1981)

NHC XI: C. W. Hedrick, ed., *Nag Hammadi Codices XI, XII and XIII* (NHS 28; Leiden: Brill, 1990)

NHC XII: C. W. Hedrick, ed., *Nag Hammadi Codices XI, XII and XIII* (NHS 28; Leiden: Brill, 1990)

NHC XIII: C. W. Hedrick, ed., *Nag Hammadi Codices XI, XII and XIII* (NHS 28; Leiden: Brill, 1990)

B. Layton, ed., *Nag Hammadi Codices II, 2–7, together with XIII, 2*, Brit. Lib. Or. 4926 (1) and P. Oxy. 1, 654, 655* (NHS 20–21; Leiden: Brill, 1989)

J.-E. Ménard, *L'évangile de vérité* (NHS 2; Leiden: Brill, 1972)

STUDIES

Gospel of Thomas and the Jesus Tradition. So far as the NT is concerned the most important tractate of the Nag Hammadi library is the *Gospel of Thomas* (not to be confused with the various pseudepigraphal infancy gospels of Thomas). Parts of Thomas had already been known from the Oxyrhynchus Papyri. But the discovery of what appears to be a version of the entire *Gospel of Thomas*, comprising some 114 sayings or logia, has answered at least one vital question relating to the origins of the Synoptic Gospels. One of the major objections raised against the Two Document Hypothesis (i.e., that Matthew and Luke made use of two "documents"—Mark and "Q") is that there was no evidence that a gospel devoid of a narrative framework, but rather consisting only of sayings, ever existed or would have been desirable. With the discovery of the *Gospel of Thomas* that objection has been met. Although not in itself a version of Q, the *Gospel of Thomas* is certainly an example of the Q genre (to a lesser extent so is the *Dialogue of the Savior*). *Thomas* may also make a second important contribution to synoptic studies. Of all the gnostic writings, the *Gospel of Thomas* may be the only one that contains authentic sayings of Jesus not already found in the NT Gospels (for examples see chap. 8). It may also contain more primitive forms of sayings than are found in the NT Gospels, though this is debatable. In any case, *Thomas* has added a new dimension to comparative study of the origin of the gospel tradition.

Bibliography: J. B. Bauer, "The Synoptic Tradition in the Gospel of Thomas," *SE* 3 (1961) 314–17; C. A. Evans, "Jesus in Gnostic Literature," *Bib* 62 (1981) 406–12; J. A. Fitzmyer, "The Oxyrhynchus logoi of Jesus and the Coptic Gospel according to Thomas," in Fitzmyer, *ESBNT,* 355–433; J. M. Robinson, "LOGOI SOPHON: On the *Gattung* of Q," in Robinson and H. Koester, *Trajectories through Early Christianity* (Philadelphia: Fortress, 1971) 71–113; T. Säve-Söderbergh, "Gnostic and Canonical Gospel Tradition," in U. Bianchi, ed., *Le Origini dello Gnosticismo* (1966 Messina Colloquium; Leiden: Brill, 1967) 552–59.

Pre-Christian Gnosticism (?) and New Testament Christology. The major issue that scholars have debated is whether or not Gnosticism, in its earliest forms, contributed to NT theology, particularly Christology, in any significant way. Specifically, attention has focused on the question of whether or not there existed a myth of a descending and ascending redeemer and whether or not if such a myth existed, it existed early enough to have influenced NT Christology. A few scholars answer these questions in the affirmative. Most, it would appear, have grave reservations. Edwin Yamauchi has reviewed all of the proposed evidence and finds little that suggests that Gnosticism existed prior to Christian origins. Charles Talbert finds no reason to believe that Christianity derived its Christology of a descending/ascending heavenly savior from anything other than its Jewish roots. I think that his position is essentially correct. Moreover, the recent assertions of Gesine Robinson and Jack Sanders that the Prologue of the Fourth Gospel has more in common with the mythology of a gnostic work like the *Trimorphic Protennoia* than it has with anything else are wholly unjustified. Pheme Perkins is much closer to the truth when she concludes that the gnostic writings of Nag Hammadi "developed their picture of the Savior from traditions quite different from those which underlie NT christological assertions" (p. 606). Martin Hengel adds: "In reality there is no gnostic redeemer myth in the sources which can be demonstrated chronologically to be pre-Christian" (p. 33). The basic problem with the views of Robinson and Sanders is that those gnostic writings that bear the closest affinities with John contain allusions to, and sometimes explicit quotations of, the writings of the NT. A. D. Nock was right when he commented: "Certainly it is an unsound proceeding to take Manichaean and other texts [viz. Mandaean and Coptic gnostic texts], full of echoes of the New Testament, and reconstruct from them something supposedly lying back of the New Testament" (2.958).

Bibliography: C. K. Barrett, "The Theological Vocabulary of the Fourth Gospel and of the Gospel of Truth," in W. Klassen and G. F. Snyder, eds., *Current Issues in New Testament Interpretation* (O. Piper Festschrift; New York: Harper & Row, 1962) 210–23; C. A. Evans, "On the Prologue of John and the *Trimorphic Protennoia*," NTS 27 (1981) 395–401; C. W. Hedrick and R. Hodgson, Jr., eds., *Nag Hammadi, Gnosticism, and Early Christianity* (Peabody: Hendrickson, 1986); M. Hengel, *Son of God* (Philadelphia: Fortress, 1976); A. D. Nock, *Essays on Religion and the Ancient World* (2 vols.; Cambridge: Harvard University, 1972); P. Perkins, "Gnostic Christologies and the New Testament," CBQ 43 (1981) 590–606; G. Robinson, "The Trimorphic Protennoia and the Prologue of the Fourth Gospel," in J. E. Goehring et al., eds., *Gnosticism & the Early Christian World* (J. M. Robinson Festschrift; Sonoma: Polebridge, 1990) 37–50; J. T. Sanders, "Nag Hammadi, Odes of Solomon, and NT Christological Hymns," in Goehring et al., eds., *Gnosticism & the Early Christian World*, 51–66; C. H. Talbert, "The Myth of the Descending-Ascending Redeemer in Mediterranean Antiquity," NTS 22 (1976) 418–40; E. M. Yamauchi, *Pre-Christian Gnosticism: A Survey of the Proposed Evidences* (Grand Rapids: Eerdmans, 1973; 2d ed.; Grand Rapids: Baker, 1983) 163–69, 243–45.

MANDAEAN MATERIALS

There are also various gnostic writings produced by the Mandaeans, a small sect that survives in southern Iraq. Their primary works from antiquity (i.e., from the sixth to eighth centuries) consist of the *Book of John*, which extolls John the Baptist as a Mandaean and Jesus as a false Messiah, and the *Ginza*, which treats the origin and nature of the cosmos. Scholars who think that these materials may contain traditions that pre-date NT Christology have attempted to find traces of Mandaean ideas in earlier writings, such as the *Odes of Solomon* or the *Acts of Thomas*. The best known attempt to explain the origins of NT Christology along such lines was that by Rudolf Bultmann in his commentary on John. Although some scholars, such as Kurt Rudolph and James Robinson, still think that Mandaeanism and other forms of Gnosticism help explain the origins of NT Christology, most are doubtful.

Bibliography: R. Bultmann, *The Gospel of John* (trans. G. R. Beasley-Murray; Philadelphia: Westminster, 1971) [1st German ed., 1941]; E. S. Drower, *The Canonical Prayer-Book of the Mandaeans* (Leiden: Brill, 1959); M. Lidzbarski, *Ginza: Das grosse Buch der Mandäer* (Göttingen: Vandenhoeck & Ruprecht; Leipzig: Hinrichs, 1925; repr. 1978); idem, *Das Johannesbuch der Mandäer* (2 vols.; Giessen: Töpelmann, 1905–15; repr. Berlin: Töpelmann, 1966); idem, *Mandäische Liturgien* (Göttingen: Vandenhoeck & Ruprecht, 1920; repr. Hildesheim: Olms, 1962) [parts of this work have been translated by G. R. S. Mead, *The Gnostic John the Baptizer* (London: Watkins, 1924)]; K. Rudolph, *Mandaeism* (Leiden: Brill, 1978); E. M. Yamauchi, *Mandaic Incantation Texts* (AOS 49; New Haven: Yale University, 1967); idem, *Pre-Christian Gnosticism: A Survey of the Proposed Evidences* (Grand Rapids: Eerdmans, 1973) 117–42; idem, "The Present Status of Mandaean Studies," *JNES* 25 (1966) 88–96.

GENERAL BIBLIOGRAPHY: A. Atiya et al., eds., *Coptic Encyclopedia* (8 vols.; New York/Toronto/Oxford: Macmillan/Collier/Maxwell, 1991); W. E. Crum, ed., *A Coptic Dictionary* (Oxford: Clarendon, 1939) [the standard Coptic lexicon]; E. S. Drower and R. Macuch, *A Mandaic Dictionary* (Oxford: Clarendon, 1963); C. A. Evans, "Current Issues in Coptic Gnosticism for New Testament Study," *Studia Biblica et Theologica* 9/2 (1979) 95–129; J. M. Robinson, "Gnosticism and the New Testament," in B. Aland, ed., *Gnosis* (H. Jonas Festschrift; Göttingen: Vandenhoeck & Ruprecht, 1978) 125–43; K. Rudolph, *Gnosis* (San Francisco: Harper & Row, 1980); D. M. Scholer, *Nag Hammadi Bibliography, 1948–1969* (NHS 1; Leiden: Brill, 1971) [updated annually in *NovT*]; R. McL. Wilson, *Gnosis and the New Testament* (Philadelphia: Fortress, 1968).

CHAPTER ELEVEN

OTHER WRITINGS

GRECO-ROMAN AUTHORS	CORPUS HERMETICUM
Tacitus	SAMARITAN WRITINGS
Suetonius	Memar Marqah
Pliny the Younger	The Chronicles
Celsus	The Liturgy
Thallus the Samaritan	
Mara bar Serapion	MAGICAL PAPYRI
Plutarch	
Lucian of Samosata	

This chapter will only briefly touch on some of the miscellaneous writings that have some bearing on NT study. Some of these writings may contain parallels to ideas in the NT. All contribute to our understanding of the diverse and pluralistic context in which the NT emerged.

GRECO-ROMAN AUTHORS

The importance of the first six Greco-Roman authors listed in this section lies in the fact that they refer to Jesus and/or early Christianity. Their comments give us some idea, as limited as it is, as to how those outside of the church viewed Christianity in its earliest stages. The last two writers, Plutarch and Lucian, are included because some think that their writings are helpful for understanding various theological, philosophical, and ethical ideas in the NT.

Tacitus. In his *Annals* (15.44) Tacitus (110–120 C.E.) states:

This name [i.e., "Christian"] originates from "Christus" who was sentenced to death by the procurator, Pontius Pilate, during the reign of Tiberius. This detestable superstition, which had been suppressed for a while, spread anew not only in Judea where the evil had started, but also in Rome, where everything that is horrid and wicked in the world gathers and finds numerous followers.

Tacitus' knowledge is at best thirdhand. It would be interesting to know precisely what he means by saying that Christianity "had been suppressed for a while." Could he be referring to the active opposition and persecution of the Jewish religious authorities, as described in Acts and alluded to in places in Paul's letters?

Suetonius. In his *Life of Emperor Claudius* (25.4) Suetonius (110–120 C.E.) states that "Claudius expelled the Jews from Rome who, instigated by Chrestus, never ceased to cause unrest." By "Jews" Suetonius means Christians, though Christianity, at that time still in its infancy, was probably predominantly Jewish, even toward the beginning of the second century C.E. "Chrestus" is an error, probably from confusing the word *chrestus* (sometimes used as a personal name, especially for slaves) with the Jewish title *christus*, a title with which a Roman might not be familiar.

Pliny the Younger. In his tenth epistle (*Epistles* 10.96 [to Emperor Trajan]) Pliny the Younger (110 C.E.) seeks Trajan's advice in dealing with Christians. His description of Christian beliefs and practices is interesting:

They [the Christians] assured me that the sum total of their guilt or their error consisted in the fact that they regularly assembled on a certain day before daybreak. They recited a hymn antiphonally to Christ as (their) God and bound themselves with an oath not to commit any crime, but to abstain from theft, robbery, adultery, breach of faith, and embezzlement of property entrusted to them. After this it was their custom to separate, and then to come together again to partake of a meal, but an ordinary and innocent one.

Celsus. According to Origen, Celsus claimed that Jesus performed his miracles by the power of magic (*Against Celsus* 1.6), a power that he had acquired while living in Egypt (1.38). When he returned to Palestine he dazzled people and called himself God (1.38). The charges of Celsus are similar to those found in the rabbinic writings.

Thallus the Samaritan Chronicler. In reference to the darkness at the time of Jesus' crucifixion (see Mark 15:33), Julius Africanus (d. after 240 C.E.) reports (according to frg. 18 of Africanus' five-volume *Chronography*, preserved in Georgius Syncellus, *Chronology*) that "this darkness Thallus, in the third book of his *History*, calls, as appears to me without reason, an eclipse of the sun."

Mara bar Serapion. In a letter to his son (perhaps late first century), Mara bar Serapion asks: "For what advantage did . . . the Jews [gain] by the death of their wise king, because from that same time their kingdom was taken away?"

Bibliography: F. F. Bruce, *Jesus and Christian Origins Outside the New Testament* (Grand Rapids: Eerdmans, 1974); H. Chadwick, *Origen: Contra Celsum* (Cambridge: University, 1953; repr. 1965) [on Celsus]; H. Conzelmann, *History of Primitive Christianity* (Nashville: Abingdon, 1973) 163–78 [on Tacitus, Suetonius, Pliny the Younger]; W. Cureton, *Spicilegium Syriacum* (London: Rivington, 1855) 73 [on Mara bar Serapion]; A. Roberts and J. Donaldson, eds., *The Ante-Nicene Fathers* (10 vols.; Grand Rapids: Eerdmans, 1951) 6.136 [on Thallus].

Plutarch. Plutarch of Chaeronea (ca. 49–119 C.E.) was associated with the sanctuary of Apollo at Delphi and in his later years served as a priest of Apollo. Plutarch's principal works are *Moralia* and *Lives.* Both of these writings are Greek and have been translated by F. C. Babbitt et al., and published in the Loeb Classical Library (15 vols.; Cambridge: Harvard University, 1957–69). Hans Dieter Betz and members of the Corpus Hellenisticum Novi Testamenti have prepared critical editions that investigate Plutarch's theological and ethical themes, subject by subject, as found in the *Moralia.*

Bibliography: H. D. Betz, ed., *Plutarch's Ethical Writings and Early Christian Literature* (SCHNT 4; Leiden: Brill, 1978); idem, ed., *Plutarch's Theological Writings and Early Christian Literature* (SCHNT 3; Leiden: Brill, 1975).

Lucian of Samosata. Lucian, who called himself a Syrian, was born sometime before 125 C.E. at Samosata in Commagene. He died sometime after 180. His Greek writings, with ET, are found in the Loeb Classical Library by A. M. Harmon et al. (8 vols.; Cambridge: Harvard University, 1953–67). For a study that considers the significance of Lucian's writings for the NT see Hans Dieter Betz.

Bibliography: H. D. Betz, *Lukian von Samosata und das Neue Testament: religionsgeschichtliche und paränetische Parallelen* (TU 76; Berlin: Akademie, 1961).

CORPUS HERMETICUM

Corpus Hermeticum (CH), named after the mythical Hermes Trismegistus (lit. the "Thrice-Greatest Hermes"), is an interesting collection of Greek theosophical writings. The Hermetica are eclectic, lacking a coherent philosophy. In some ways they resemble the *Sibylline Oracles* (see chap. 2). Parts of the collection are monotheistic, but others are polytheistic (esp. *Asclepius*). There is interest in God, the human race, and the cosmos. With regard to its literary form, the Hermetica are arranged as didactic conversations, with six figures portrayed as teachers and/or pupils: (1) Hermes Trismegistus, (2) Hermes' son Tat (or Thot), (3) Asclepius, (4) Agathos Daimon (lit. "Good Demon"), also known as the Egyptian god Kneph, (5) Hammon, and (6) Poimandres (lit. "Shepherd of

Men"), whose name is also associated with the whole collection. Even the great Hermes, normally himself the master-teacher, is instructed by Nous (lit. "Mind").

Following G. R. S. Mead, *Thrice-Greatest Hermes: Studies in Hellenistic Theosophy and Gnosis* (3 vols.; London: John M. Watkins, 1949), who provides text and commentary, the sources of Corpus Hermeticum may be outlined as follows:

1. Corpus Hermeticum Graecum, which includes Poimandres and Asclepius (18 tractates in all, with Tractate I on Poimandres, Tractate II on Asclepius)

2. Latin Asclepius, also known as the "Perfect Sermon" (41 chapters)

3. Excerpts by John Stobaeus, a pagan writer from the late fifth or early sixth century (27 excerpts in all)

4. References, allusions, and fragments in the church fathers (some 25 fragments from Justin Martyr, Clement of Alexandria, Tertullian, Cyprian, Arnobius, Lactantius, Augustine, and Cyril of Alexandria)

5. References, allusions, and fragments in the Philosophers (from Zosimus, Fulgentius, Iamblichus, and Julian the Emperor-Philosopher)

Various writers of antiquity exhibit dependence upon or close parallels to hermetic ideas (e.g., Philo of Alexandria, the Naassenes [early Jewish and Christian mystics], Zosimus, Plutarch, various gnostic sects).

Bibliography: For parallels with the NT see J. Büchli, *Der Poimandres: Ein paganisiertes Evangelium* (WUNT 2.27; Tübingen: Mohr [Siebeck], 1987); W. C. Grese, *Corpus Hermeticum XIII and Early Christian Literature* (SCHNT 5; Leiden: Brill, 1979); and K.-W. Tröger, *Mysterianglaube und Gnosis in Corpus Hermeticum XIII* (TU 110; Berlin: Akademie, 1971). For texts see R. Reitzenstein, *Poimandres: Studien zur griechisch-ägyptischen und frühchristlichen Literatur* (Leipzig: Teubner, 1904) [provides Greek text of CH I, XIII, XVI–XVIII]. For Greek text and French translation and commentary see A. D. Nock and A.-J. Festugière, *Hermès Trismégiste: Corpus Hermeticum* (4 vols.; Paris: Les belles lettres, 1946–54; repr. 1981). For Greek and Latin text, ET, commentary, and introduction see W. Scott, *Hermetica* (4 vols.; Oxford: Clarendon, 1924–36). For general discussion see A.-J. Festugière, *L'hermétisme* (Lund: Gleerup, 1948); G. van Moorsel, *The Mysteries of Hermes Trismegistus* (Utrecht: Kemink, 1955); and B. A. Pearson, "Jewish Sources in Gnostic Literature," *JWSTP,* 474–75.

Corpus Hermeticum and the Johannine Writings. C. H. Dodd (*The Interpretation of the Fourth Gospel* [Cambridge: Cambridge University, 1953] 34–35, 50–51) offers several parallels. Here are those that appear to be the most promising:

Corpus Hermeticum
"I am that light . . . your God" (1.6)

"This one remains in darkness
   deceived" (1.19)
"They ascend to the Father" (1.26)
"Holy God the Father" (1.31)
"I shall enlighten my brothers who are
   in ignorance" (1.32)
"I believe and I bear witness" (1.32)

"I advance unto life and light" (1.32)
"none can be saved before
   regeneration" (13.1)
"The true seed is good" (13.2)
"the begetting by God" (13.6)
"cleanse yourself" (13.7)

"knowledge of God came to us" (13.8)

"no longer no punishment of darkness
   came upon you" (13.9)
"a child of that One" (13.14)
"I rejoice in the joy of my mind" (13.18)

"The Powers which are in me . . .
   complete your will" (13.19)
"The mind shepherds . . ." (13.19)

Johannine Writings
"I am the light of the world" (John 8:12)
"God is light" (1 John 1:5)
"in order that every one who believes in
   me should not remain in darkness"
   (John 12:46)
"I ascend to my Father" (John 20:17)
"Holy Father" (John 17:11)
"the true light which enlightens every
   man" (John 1:9)
"he came for a witness . . . that all should
   believe through him" (John 1:7)
"he will have the light of life" (John 8:12)
"except one be born again, he cannot see
   the kingdom of God" (John 3:4)
"His seed abides forever" (1 John 3:9)
"they were begotten of God" (John 1:13)
"He cleanses every one bearing fruit"
   (John 15:2)
"that they should know you, the only
   true God" (John 17:3)
"lest darkness overcome you" (John
   12:35; cf. John 1:5)
"We have one Father, God" (John 8:41)
"in order that my joy might be in you"
   (John 15:11)
"in order that I should do the will of
   the One who sent me" (John 4:34)
"I am the Good Shepherd" (John 10:11)

SAMARITAN WRITINGS

In addition to the Samaritan Pentateuch (see chap. 4) and the *Samaritan Targum* (see chap. 6) there are several writings that contain various biblical traditions and legends. These writings fall into three broad categories: midrash, chronicles, and liturgy. The origin of the Samaritan sect is disputed. The Samaritans themselves claim that they are the descendants of the ten northern tribes that were exiled by the Assyrian Empire in the eighth century B.C.E. Jewish Scripture and tradition, however, tell a different story. According to them, the Samaritans are at best part Jewish, having intermarried with people from Cuthea, one of the regions of the old Assyrian Empire. For this reason they are called "Cutheans" or Kutim. (One of the minor tractates of the Babylonian Talmud treats Jewish laws pertaining to the Kutim.) Scholars today are inclined to think that the Samaritans, as a distinct movement separated from Judah, emerged in the second century, especially after the destruction of their temple at Gerizim.

Samaritans awaited a *Taheb* (lit. "returning one"), who is expected to be a descendant of either Jacob, Seth, Phineas, Moses, or Noah. His name is unknown. He will be like Moses (cf. Deut 18:18). Repentance must precede his coming. He will come from the east, to Mount Gerizim. He will bring the staff of Aaron, manna, and the holy tabernacle. He is not a priest; he is a prophet and king. He will reign over the whole world.

The Dosithean sect was founded by Dosithius, a man who may have been the leader of a Samaritan group, though who this person was and what his teachings were is disputed. He may have applied Deut 18:15–19 to himself. After his death an aretalogy (i.e., a legendary account of one's virtues and accomplishments) developed. His following awaited his return, perhaps as the *Taheb*. The sect died out (or was assimilated into mainstream Samaritan culture) by the fourteenth century.

Bibliography: J. Bowman, *Samaritan Documents Relating to Their History, Religion and Life* (Pittsburgh: Pickwick, 1977); J. M. Cohen, *A Samaritan Chronicle: A Source-critical Analysis of the Life and Times of the Great Samaritan Reformer, Baba Rabbah* (SPB 30; Leiden: Brill, 1981); A. D. Crown, *A Bibliography of the Samaritans* (ATLA Bibliography Series 10; Metuchen: ATLA and Scarecrow, 1984); F. Dexinger, *Der Taheb: Ein "messianischer" Heilsbringer der Samaritaner* (Salzburg: Müller, 1986); idem, "Samaritan Eschatology," in A. D. Crown, ed., *The Samaritans* (Tübingen: Mohr [Siebeck], 1989) 266–92, esp. 272–76; M. Gaster, *The Samaritans: Their History, Doctrines and Literature* (London: British Academy, 1925); S. J. Isser, *The Dositheans: A Samaritan Sect in Late Antiquity* (SJLA 17; Leiden: Brill, 1976); J. Macdonald, *The Theology of the Samaritans* (London: SCM, 1964); L. A. Mayer, *Bibliography of the Samaritans* (ed. D. Broadriff; Leiden: Brill, 1964); J. D. Purvis, *The Samaritan Pentateuch and the Origin of the Samaritan Sect* (HSM 2; Cambridge: Harvard University, 1968); A. Tal, "Samaritan Literature," in Crown, ed., *The Samaritans*, 413–67.

Memar Marqah. The *Memar Marqah* (or *Marqe*) are the "sayings of Marqah." This work, which has also been called *Seper Peli'ata* ("Book of Wonders")—which has more to do with book 1 than with the rest of the work—dates roughly to the second, third, and fourth centuries. Outside of the Samaritan Pentateuch and the *Samaritan Targum*, it is the most important of the Samaritan writings. It comprises six books, written in Hebrew and Aramaic. The themes of these books are as follows:

Book 1: Moses and the burning bush, Moses and Pharaoh, the Exodus (parallels Exod 3–14)

Book 2: how God defeated the Egyptians, commentary on Exodus 15

Book 3: on priests, elders, princes, judges, teachers, and leaders of Israel

Book 4: theology (how God deals with humanity, humanity's duty to God), commentary on Exodus 32, the promise that the *Taheb* will arise (4:12)

Book 5: on Moses' death, ascension, and glorification

Book 6: on creation, wisdom, Word of God, alphabet

The following excerpts could have some relevance for NT interpretation (the page numbers refer to vol. 2 of John Macdonald's book):

"To Mount Gerizim, the House of God, which I have desired, I shall go before I die" (5:2; p. 198).

"The great prophet Moses ascended Mount Nebo with great majesty, crowned with light. All the hosts of the heavenly angels gathered to meet him" (5:3; p. 202).

"The Glory drew near to him and embraced him, while all the hosts of the hidden regions and of the revealed ones came to do honour to Moses the man" (5:3; p. 203).

"He ascended from human status to that of the angels" (5:3; p. 206 [recalling Moses receiving the Ten Commandments]).

"The great prophet Moses went up Mount Nebo to see six hundred thousand [Israelites below] and all the angels [above] waiting to meet him. When he reached the top of the mountain, the cloud came down and lifted him up from the sight of all the congregation of Israel" (5:4; p. 208; cf. Acts 1:9).

Several of these excerpts are reminiscent of Moses and Samaritan traditions in the book of Acts, and especially in the Fourth Gospel. For further discussion see W. A. Meeks, *The Prophet-King: Moses Traditions and the Johannine Christology* (NovTSup 14; Leiden: Brill, 1967).

Bibliography: A. Broadie, *A Samaritan Philosophy: A Study of the Hellenistic Cultural Ethos of the Memar Marqah* (SPB 31; Leiden: Brill, 1981); S. Lowy, *The Principles of Samaritan Bible Exegesis* (SPB 28; Leiden: Brill, 1977); J. Macdonald, *Memar Marqah. The Teaching of Marqah* (2 vols.; BZAW 84; Berlin: Töpelmann, 1963) [vol. 1 provides text; vol. 2 provides ET].

The Samaritan Chronicles. A few of the *Samaritan Chronicles* may date to the early centuries of the church and so are worth mentioning briefly. Moses Gaster thinks that the Aramaic Chronicle I *(Asatir)*, which relates the teachings of Moses, derives from the third century. Other scholars disagree. Z. Ben-Hayyim thinks that the work derives from the tenth century. It is not clear why Gaster calls it the "Book of the Secrets of Moses," for nowhere in Samaritan literature is it ever called this. Chronicle II *(Seper he-Yamim)*, which may have been a "Book of Joshua," is written entirely in Hebrew and may derive from the third century C.E. Among other things, it retells the story of Samuel and David, with the focus on the ark of the covenant. According to the Samaritan version, Samuel the prophet-priest is evil, like Eli and his sons. Saul and Jesse fight the northern tribes because they (the tribes) have remained loyal to Mount Gerizim. Saul and Jesse, under Samuel's influence, worship at Shiloh. But the Samaritan chronicler likes David, because he opposed

Saul. In fact, David used to send offerings to Mount Gerizim. Unfortunately, the Judahites persuaded David to build a temple in Jerusalem, an act which angered the Samaritans. However, because of the displeasure of the Samaritan high priest Jair the son of Jehonathan, David stopped building and said, "My son Solomon shall build the house for the Ark, for I have shed much blood" (Macdonald, 135). Nathan's oracle (2 Sam 7) is omitted, but David's sins (e.g., the affair with Bathsheba) are emphasized. Chronicle IV *(Sepher Yehoshua)* is an embellished retelling of the story of Joshua and subsequent Samaritan history. The compiler claims that his Arabic chronicle is a translation from the Hebrew, but John Bowman doubts this. Contents: Chapters 1–25 concern Joshua son of Nun, paralleling the biblical book of Joshua. Chapters 26–37 tell of war of war between Joshua and Shaubak, king of Persia. Chapters 38–44 tell of Joshua's death and burial. Chapters 45–50 continue the story right on through the intertestamental period. Chapter 46 recounts the exploits of Alexander the Great. Chapter 47 tells of the reign of the Roman Emperor Hadrian. Chapters 48–50 tell of various Samaritan high priests during Roman persecution. Some of this material may be early. Some of it was available in Hebrew, but some is known only from Arabic sources.

Bibliography: Z. Ben-Hayyim, "The Book of Asatir," *Tarbiz* 14 (1944) 104–25, 174–90; 15 (1945) 71–87; J. Bowman, *Samaritan Documents Relating to Their History, Religion and Life* (Pittsburgh: Pickwick, 1977); J. M. Cohen, *A Samaritan Chronicle: A Source-critical Analysis of the Life and Times of the Great Samaritan Reformer, Baba Rabbah* (SPB 30; Leiden: Brill, 1981) [Cohen discusses the non-biblical portions of Chronicle II]; M. Gaster, *The Asatir, the Book of the Secrets of Moses* (The Oriental Translation Fund 26; London: Royal Asiatic Society, 1927); J. Macdonald, *The Samaritan Chronicle No. II (or: Sepher Ha-Yamim) From Joshua to Nebuchadnezzar* (BZAW 107; Berlin: de Gruyter, 1969) [provides ET of the biblical portions of the Chronicle]; P. Stenhouse, "Samaritan Chronicles," in A. D. Crown, ed., *The Samaritans* (Tübingen: Mohr [Siebeck], 1989) 218–65.

Samaritan Liturgy. Two items from the Samaritan liturgy, both dating from the fourth century, should be mentioned. The first is the *Defter.* The name is from a Greek loan word (*diphthera,* meaning "skin" or "parchment"). The *Defter* represents the oldest collection of Samaritan prayers and poems for weekly religious services and for holidays. This collection remained in use until the fourteenth century. The second item is the *Durran,* which receives its name from the Arabic (*bit durran,* meaning a "string of pearls"). The *Durran* is made up of the poems of 'Amram Dare, which, like the *Defter,* played an important role in the Samaritan liturgy.

Bibliography: J. Bowman, *Samaritan Documents Relating to Their History, Religion and Life* (Pittsburgh: Pickwick, 1977).

MAGICAL PAPYRI

The Greek Magical Papyri, mostly dating from the NT period and later, contain a variety of formulas, oaths, and religious concepts. Some of these interesting traditions may be of some use in NT research. This corpus of material is usually abbreviated PGM (*Papyri graeca magicae*).

Bibliography: For Greek texts see K. Preisendanz et al., *Papyri Graecae Magicae: Die Griechischen Zauberpapyri* (2d ed.; 2 vols.; Stuttgart: Teubner, 1973–74); and F. L. Griffith and H. Thompson, *The Leyden Papyrus: An Egyptian Magical Book* (3 vols.; London: Grevel, 1904; repr. New York: Dover, 1974) [also contains translation and commentary]. For introduction and ET of the papyri see H. D. Betz, ed., *The Greek Magical Papyri in Translation, including the Demotic Spells* (Chicago and London: University of Chicago, 1986) [comparison with the NT is made]. For bibliography see E. G. Turner, *Greek Papyri, an Introduction* (2d ed.; Oxford: Oxford University, 1980). For additional sources see C. Bonner, *Studies in Magical Amulets Chiefly Graeco-Egyptian* (Ann Arbor: University of Michigan, 1950); O. Kern, ed., *Orphicorum Fragmenta* (2d ed.; Dublin and Zürich: Weidmann, 1972); E. A. Wallis Budge, *Amulets and Talismans* (New York: Dover, 1978).

CHAPTER TWELVE

EXAMPLES OF NEW TESTAMENT EXEGESIS

This final chapter offers a few examples to illustrate the value of the various literatures surveyed for NT interpretation. The examples are taken from the Gospels and the Epistles. These examples do not represent attempts to deal with all of the questions that the interpreter is expected normally to address. The point here will be simply to show how the noncanonical writings at times significantly contribute to the exegetical task.

THE NAZARETH SERMON

When Jesus preached in the synagogue of Nazareth he touched off an outburst that nearly resulted in his being cast down a cliff, possibly as a prelude to stoning (Luke 4:16–30). Commentators have often wondered what it was that so angered the audience. The suggestion that it was the realization that Jesus was Joseph's son (v. 22) and therefore, as the son of a humble carpenter, he had no right to make great claims for himself is probably not the reason. The audience's recognition that it was indeed Jesus who stood before them should be interpreted as a joyful and expectant discovery. The proverb that Jesus quotes in the next verse and the interpretation that he gives it confirm this. The real turning point in the sermon comes when Jesus cites the examples of Elijah and Elisha and by doing so suggests that the blessings and benefits of his messianic ministry will be shared with Israel's traditional enemies.

The reason for the audience's angry reaction has been clarified through the discovery and publication of 11QMelchizedek. In this Dead Sea Scroll portions of Isa 61:1–2, the very passage with which Jesus began his Nazareth sermon (cf. Luke 4:18–19), are cited and linked with Isa 52:7, in order to expound upon the meaning of Lev 25:13, a passage understood to promise the coming of an eschatological era of jubilee. In understanding Isa 61:1–2 in an eschatological sense the author of 11QMelchizedek agrees with Jesus, who had proclaimed to his audience: "Today this scripture has been fulfilled in your hearing" (Luke 4:21). But in emphasizing the judgmental nature of the passage the author of 11QMelchizedek moves in a completely different direction. The very line that Jesus had omitted from his quotation, "and the day of vengeance of our God" (cf. Isa 61:2), seems to hold the key to Qumran's understanding, not only of the jubilee of Lev 25:13, but even of the "good news" passage, Isa 52:7. The Hebrew text, which consists of consonants, not vowels, has been revocalized, so that it not only promises "peace" (šālôm) to the faithful, but "retribution" (šillûm) to Qumran's enemies.

If Qumran's understanding of Isa 61:1–2 approximated the understanding of the audience of the Nazareth synagogue, we are able to appreciate much better the dynamics at work. When Jesus quoted Isa 61:1–2 and announced that it was fulfilled, he and his audience would have drawn two opposing conclusions. For Jesus the eschatological jubilee meant forgiveness and mercy for all, but for his kinsmen and long-time friends it meant blessings for them and judgment for their enemies. Jesus' omission of the line, "and the day of vengeance of our God," might have initially slipped by unnoticed. But when he illustrated his understanding of the prophetic passage by appealing to the examples of mercy Elijah and Elisha showed Israel's enemies, his audience clearly understood his position and they did not like it. They viewed Jesus' interpretation as a betrayal of their messianic hopes.

Bibliography: M. P. Miller, "The Function of Isa. 61, 1–2 in Melchizedek," *JBL* 88 (1969) 467–69; J. A. Sanders, "From Isaiah 61 to Luke 4," in J. Neusner, ed., *Christianity, Judaism and Other Greco-Roman Cults* (M. Smith Festschrift; Leiden: Brill, 1975) 75–106.

THE PARABLE OF THE TALENTS

Can the apocryphal gospels (cf. chap. 8 and Appendix 3) shed light on the NT Gospels? Sometimes. Consider the parable of the Talents (Matt 25:14–30; roughly paralleled by Luke 19:11–27). Commentators have usually assumed that Jesus intended his hearers to understand that the heroes of the parable are the servants who doubled their master's money. These servants are models for Jesus' followers: "All of this constitutes an appeal to good works as demonstrating the reality of professed discipleship" (Gundry, 505). The servant who hid his master's money, and did not even lend to bankers for interest, is understood to be a poor model: "Thus the parable closes on a threatening note concerning the punishment Jesus will mete out to disciples who falsify their profession by failing to do good works" (Gundry, 510).

The traditional interpretation runs into problems when we are mindful of the biblical principles and economical realities by which the majority of Palestinians in Jesus' day lived. The first problem has to do with the master. He expects exorbitant profits, he is a "hard" man, he reaps the fields of others, gathers the grain that others have threshed, and has no difficulty with usury (Matt 25:24–27). Moreover, he is merciless (Matt 25:30). At the very least this is a hardnosed businessman who does not observe the law's express prohibition against the practice of usury (cf. Exod 22:25; Ps 15:5). But it is more probable that the picture is worse. This man may be an oppressive gouger and a thief. In any case, it is hard to imagine how an agrarian audience, for the most part peasants, could have heard this parable and understood the master in a favorable sense. (This observation has been made recently by Richard Rohrbaugh.)

The second problem has to do with the actions of the servants. The first two double their master's money. In the minds of first-century peasants such margins of profit were not fair, but could take place only through high interest rates, excessive returns from tenant farmers, taxation, or outright theft. However these profits were obtained, the peasants knew that it would be at their expense. (For a recent study that treats this subject see Douglas Oakman.) The third servant neither cheated anyone, nor made a profit at anyone's expense. He kept his master's money safe and returned it to him. Although guiltless in the eyes of the peasants, this servant is "worthless" in the eyes of his master and is punished.

For these reasons one may well wonder if the parable as we now have it in the canonical Gospels has been misunderstood. Eusebius wondered this also. Commenting on the Matthean version of the parable he discusses the different perspective of the *Gospel of the Nazoreans* (*Gos. Naz.* §18; cf. Eusebius *Theophania* 22 [on Matt 25:14–15]):

> But since the Gospel in Hebrew characters which has come into our hands enters the threat not against the man who had hid [the talent], but against him who had lived dissolutely—for he [the master] had three servants: one who squandered his master's substance with harlots and flute-girls, one who multiplied the gain, and one who hid the talent; and accordingly one was accepted (with joy), another merely rebuked, and another cast into prison—I wonder whether in Matthew the threat which is uttered after the word against the man who did nothing may refer not to him, but by epanalepsis to the first who had feasted and drunk with the drunken.

The parable of the *Gospel of the Nazoreans* seems to be a combination of the parable of the Talents (Matt 25:14–30) and the parable of the Wicked Servant (Matt 24:45–51; Luke 12:45–48). But what is interesting is Eusebius' thought that perhaps the word of rebuke was originally uttered against the man who made huge profits.

Additional problems arise when we consider the Lucan form of the parable (Luke 19:11–27), the so-called parable of the Pounds (or Minas). Not only is the man (called a "nobleman") harsh and demanding, but he is hated by his subjects who do not want him to reign as king over them (Luke 19:14). After his return, he settles with his servants, much as in the Matthean version. But he appears even more harsh, for he demands that those who did not want him to be king be brought before him and be slain in his very presence (Luke 19:27). The traditional interpretation of this form of the parable is not unlike the interpretation of the Matthean version (e.g., J. A. Fitzmyer, 2.1232–33; C. A. Evans, 284–87). The evangelist Luke, as the evangelist Matthew, probably understood the parable along the lines that modern commentators interpret it.

There is a second problem with the Lucan version. It appears that the unique parts of the parable, that of the nobleman's quest to receive a kingdom and the citizens' sending a delegation in the hope of frustrating this goal, are based upon the experience of the hated Archelaus not too many years before. (He ruled Judea from 4 B.C.E. to 6 C.E.) This is suggested by the numerous parallels between the parable's nobleman and Archelaus (whose experience is recounted in Josephus): The nobleman went to a far country (v. 12), just as Archelaus went to Rome (*Ant.* 17.9.3 §219); the nobleman hoped to receive a kingdom *(basileia)* and to return (v. 12), just as Archelaus hoped (*Ant.* 17.9.3 §220: *basileia*); the nobleman left household instructions to his servants (v. 13), just as Archelaus did (*Ant.* 17.9.3 §219, 223); the nobleman's citizens hated *(misein)* him (v. 14), just as Archelaus' subjects hated him (*Ant.* 17.9.4 §227: *misos*); an embassy *(presbeia)* is sent after the nobleman (v. 14), as one was sent after Archelaus (*Ant.* 17.11.1 §300: *presbeia*); the citizens petitioned the foreign country against the nobleman's rule (v. 14), just as the envoys petitioned against Archelaus (*Ant.* 17.11.1 §302); the nobleman slaughtered *(katasphazein)* his citizens who opposed him (v. 27), just as Archelaus had done before his journey (*Ant.* 17.9.5 §237, 239: *sphazein*); when the nobleman returned as ruler, he collected his revenues (vv. 15–19), just as Josephus notes that Archelaus was to receive 600 talents as his yearly tribute (*Ant.* 17.11.4 §320); and finally, when the nobleman returned, he settled accounts with those who had opposed him (v. 27), which parallels Archelaus' settling with Joazar the high priest for having supported the rebels (*Ant.* 17.13.1 §339). Since Herod Antipas also traveled to Rome to press his claim to the throne, and was also opposed, his experience loosely fits the experience of the parable's nobleman. But it is Archelaus who offers the closest match.

Why would Jesus tell a parable whose hero is supposed to be law-breaking, despised tyrant? In what sense does such a man model Jesus? In what sense are the servants who work for this man and assist him in his oppressive activities models for Jesus' followers? But perhaps this is not what Jesus originally intended. Following the lead of Eusebius' discussion of the form of the parable in the Gospel of the Nazoreans, it is possible, if not probable, that Jesus originally told his parable(s) to illustrate how *not* to be a master and how *not* to be servants. This idea coheres with his teaching elsewhere (Mark 10:42–44):

> You know that those who are supposed to rule over the Gentiles lord it over them, and their great men exercise authority over them. But it shall not be so among you; but whoever would be great among you must be your servant, and whoever would be first among you must be slave of all.

In its original context, the parable may have presented a contrast between Jesus' style of kingship and that of the Herodian dynasty. The latter was known for its oppression and ruthlessness. But Jesus wished to present a new way and expected his followers to practice it as well.

It is easy to see how the original point of the parable(s) came to be confused with teaching concerned with stewardship and responsibility (cf. Matt 24:45–47; Luke 12:35–38; 17:7–10). The servant that is wise and faithful, doing what he is expected to do, such as treating the members of the master's household properly (not profiteering at his neighbors' expense) will be rewarded. It is possible, then, that the theme of reward drew these parables together, so that the servants of the oppressive master and nobleman came to be interpreted much as the servants of the other parables. But whereas the latter were held up as worthy models, the former were not.

Bibliography: C. A. Evans, *Luke* (NIBC 3; Peabody: Hendrickson, 1990); J. A. Fitzmyer, *The Gospel According to Luke X–XXIV* (AB 28A; Garden City: Doubleday, 1985); R. H. Gundry, *Matthew: A Commentary on His Literary and Theological Art* (Grand Rapids: Eerdmans, 1982); D. E. Oakman, *Jesus and the Economic Questions of His Day* (Queenston: Mellen, 1986); R. Rohrbaugh, "A Peasant Reading of the Parable of the Talents/Pounds: A Text of Terror?" a paper read in New Orleans at the 1990 annual SBL meeting.

THE PARABLE OF THE WICKED VINEYARD TENANTS

The parable of the Wicked Tenants (Mark 12:1–11=Matt. 21:33–46=Luke 20:9–19) is clearly based on Isaiah's Song [or Parable] of the Vineyard (Isa 5:1–7, esp. 5:1–2; cf. Mark 12:1). Whereas Isaiah's parable is directed against the "house of Israel and the men of Judah" (Isa 5:7), Jesus' parable is directed against the religious authorities: "they perceived that he had told the parable against them" (Mark 12:12). How could the chief priests (cf. Mark 11:27) so readily perceive that the parable was directed against them? If Isaiah's parable was aimed against the people as a whole, why should Jesus' allusion to it be perceived as a threat against one particular group within Jewish society? The explanation is suggested by the *Isaiah Targum*, which inserts "sanctuary" and "altar" in place of tower and wine vat. This would seem to indicate that in the time of Jesus (for the *Isaiah Targum* clearly contains traditions that derive from the first century) Isaiah's Song of the Vineyard had come to be understood as directed against the temple establishment. Tosefta's explicit identification of the tower with the temple, and the wine vat with the altar (cf. *t. Me'il.* 1.16 and *t. Sukk.* 3.15) shows that this interpretation was not limited to the synagogue, where the targum evolved, but seems to have been known in the rabbinic academies as well.

The targum plays a further role when Jesus quotes Ps 118:22: "The stone which the builders rejected has become the head of the corner." According to the targum the builders rejected "the son" (or child). If this was how Ps 118:22 was understood, then the association of this verse with the rejected son of the parable becomes understandable. When we note further that the religious authorities referred to themselves as "builders" (cf. *y. Yoma* 3.5; *b. Šabb.* 114a; *b. Ber.* 64a; *Exod. Rab.* 23.10 [on 15:1]; *Song Rab.* 1.5 §3; cf. Paul's usage in 1 Cor 3:10), and in fact were called "builders of a rickety wall" by their critics (cf. CD 4:19; 8:12, 18), then the appropriateness of Ps 118:22 for this context becomes even clearer.

The realism of the parable is demonstrated when one makes comparison with Cicero's account of one Marcus Brutus, a landlord, who had difficulty collecting a debt from his tenants (cf. Cicero *Ad Atticum* 5.21; 6.1). The authenticity of the parable, moreover, is not undermined by its appearance in the Coptic *Gospel of Thomas* (see log. §65 and §66). It has sometimes been asserted that the quotation of Ps 118:22 represents a later, inauthentic addition to the parable. Thomas, it is believed, supports this view. On the contrary, the fact that the parable (log. §65) is followed immediately by the quotation of Ps 118:22 (log. §66) could just as easily argue that the quotation was an original component of the parable. In any case, *Thomas'* habit of introducing statements with "he said" or "Jesus said" (within logia and not just at the beginning) does not provide conclusive grounds for making certain judgments. Note that Matthew, who has probably followed Mark, inserts "Jesus said" (Matt 21:42), which is without parallel in Mark. *Thomas'* reading may reflect Matthew's redaction and not an earlier tradition which contained the parable minus the OT quotation.

Bibliography: B. D. Chilton, *A Galilean Rabbi and His Bible: Jesus' Use of the Interpreted Scripture of His Time* (GNS 8; Wilmington: Glazier, 1984) 111–14; C. A. Evans, "On the Vineyard Parables of Isaiah 5 and Mark 12," *BZ* 28 (1984) 82–86; K. R. Snodgrass, *The Parable of the Wicked Tenants: An Inquiry into Parable Interpretation* (WUNT 27; Tübingen: Mohr [Siebeck], 1983).

"I SAID, 'YOU ARE GODS' "

When Jesus claims that he and the Father are "one" (John 10:3), his countrymen are ready to put him to death (John 10:31). Jesus then defends his extraordinary claim by appealing to his good works. For which of these will they stone him? His accusers retort:

> "It is not for a good work that we stone you but for blasphemy; because you, being a man, make yourself God." Jesus answered them, "Is it not written in your law, 'I said, you are gods' [Ps 82:6]? If he called them gods to whom the word of God came . . . do you say of him whom the Father consecrated and sent into the world, 'You are blaspheming,' because I said, 'I am the Son of God'?" (John 10:33–36).

This remarkable passage raises several questions. First, how did Jesus understand Ps 82:6 and, therefore, how did he imagine that by appealing to it he had answered his critics? Second, how was Ps 82:6 interpreted in late antiquity? Third, what is meant by "gods"? Fourth, what did Jesus mean by being "one" with the Father? By claiming this did he make himself God?

The fourth question can be answered easily. When Jesus claimed that he was "one" with the Father he was in fact claiming to be equal to God (John 5:18). In many places Jesus claims the prerogatives normally associated with God himself. Jesus will raise and judge the dead (5:28–29). He is able to grant eternal life (5:21; 10:28). No one but God can do these things. Accordingly, when Jesus says, "I and the Father are one," he surely means that he is equal to God. His accusers, therefore, are at least partially correct; Jesus has made himself God.

The first three questions cannot be understood until we have studied the ancient interpretations and applications of Ps 82:6. Recently Jerome Neyrey has undertaken this task. He finds Ps 82:6 interpreted in several Jewish midrashim: *Mek.* on Exod 20:18–19 (*Bahodeš* 9); *b. ʾAbod. Zar.* 5a; *Sipre Deut.* §320 (on Deut 32:20); and *Num. Rab.* 16.24 (on Num 14:11). Neyrey observes that Ps 82:6 is applied to passages which discuss Sinai, when Israel received the law. On that occasion they were immortal, as Adam had been. Hence, they could be called "gods," because like God, they were immortal. But when they sinned (the golden calf), they were subject to death, just as Adam's sin led to his mortality. Therefore, though once called "gods" (because the Word of God came to them), they nevertheless died like mere men.

How then has Jesus applied the passage to himself. Because he has been consecrated, that is, made holy, he too is immortal. Who can convict him of sin (John 8:46)? Because of his sinlessness he will not die. Because of his immortality, he has every right to claim divinity, just as Psalm 82 had called the generation of the exodus "gods."

Bibliography: J. H. Neyrey, "I Said 'You Are Gods': Psalm 82:6 and John 10," *JBL* 108 (1989) 647–63.

"THE WORD IS NEAR YOU"

In Rom 10:5–10 Paul contrasts righteousness based on law with righteousness based on faith. To make his case he paraphrases parts of Deut 30:11–14. In applying Deuteronomy 30, which speaks of the law, to Christ, Paul is doing something similar to what has been done before. This same OT passage had been applied earlier to personified Wisdom: "Who has gone up into heaven, and taken her, and brought her down from the clouds? Who has gone over the sea and found her . . . ?" (Bar 3:29–30). For Paul, of course, Christ is the "wisdom of God" (cf. 1 Cor 1:24). Baruch provides the bridge between speaking of the law and speaking of Christ.

But Paul's paraphrase of Deut 30:12–13 is at variance with both Greek and Hebrew versions of the OT. His paraphrase and commentary read as follows:

> Do not say in your heart, "Who will ascend into heaven?" (that is, to bring Christ down) or "Who will descend into the abyss?" (that is, to bring Christ up from the dead). But what does it say? The word is near you. . . .

The relevant lines of the Masoretic Text read this way:

> "Who will go up for us to heaven, and bring it to us . . . ?"
>
> "Who will go over the sea for us, and bring it to us . . . ?"

The relevant lines of the LXX read this way:

> "Who will ascend into heaven for us and receive it for us . . . ?"
>
> "Who will cross for us to the other side of the sea and receive it for us . . . ?"

In contrast to the Greek and Hebrew versions, Paul's paraphrase speaks of descending into the sea, not of crossing it. He prefers this reading, of course, in order to complement the picture of Jesus descending into the grave and being raised up. But did this variant reading originate with Paul? No, probably not. It is likely that it reflects an Aramaic paraphrase of the synagogue, since a similar reading is found in *Targum Neofiti*. The relevant lines read as follows:

> "Would that we had one like the prophet Moses, who would ascend to heaven and fetch it for us. . . ."
>
> "Would that we had one like the prophet Jonah, who would descend into the depths of the Great Sea and bring it up for us. . . ."

The point of Deut 30:11–14 is that the law has been given once and for all. There is no need for a prophet to ascend to heaven or to traverse the sea to obtain it. The Aramaic paraphrase illustrates this with two biblical characters whose experiences roughly match the language of the passage. Moses, it was believed, had ascended to heaven when he received the law from God. For example, in *Tg. Ps.-J.* Deut 34:5 we are told that Moses "brought it [the law] from heaven"; and in *Pesiq. R.* 4.2 we read: "Moses went up to heaven" (see also Pseudo-Philo, *Bib. Ant.* 15:6; 2 Esdr 3:17–18). These traditions are based on Exod 19:3 and 20, where God summons Moses to meet him on the mountain. The reference to the sea, of course, provides the link to Jonah. In fact, the targum's "descend into the depths" draws the OT passage into closer alignment with Jonah's experience, for the prophet did not go *across* the sea, but *down into* it (see the reference to "abyss" in Jonah 2:3).

In the NT, of course, Christ is compared to both Moses and Jonah, specifically at points that are relevant to the traditions just reviewed. Like Moses, Jesus brought a new law from heaven (Mark 9:2–8; John 1:17; 3:13–14); like Jonah, Jesus descended into the abyss (Matt 12:39–40; 16:4; Luke 11:29–30).

Bibliography: M. McNamara, *The New Testament and the Palestinian Targum to the Pentateuch* (2d ed.; AnBib 27A; Rome: Pontifical Biblical Institute, 1978) 70–78.

ASCENDING AND DESCENDING WITH A SHOUT

By way of consolation to the bereaved of the church at Thessalonica Paul repeats a tradition "by the word of the Lord" (1 Thess 4:15–17a):

> . . . we who are alive and remain until the coming of the Lord will not precede those who sleep; because the Lord himself will descend from heaven with a shout, with the voice of the archangel, and with the trumpet of God, and the dead in Christ will rise first. . . .

The apocalyptic elements in this passage and its context echo many texts, both in the NT (Matt 24:31; 1 Cor 15:51–52) and outside it (Isa 27:13; Zech 9:14; Joel 2:1). Although these passages and others like them parallel various details of 1 Thess 4:16, none can be said specifically to lie behind Paul's "word of the Lord."

A few years ago C. F. D. Moule suggested that Paul's statement might be an echo of Ps 47:5 (47:6 in the MT; 46:6 in the LXX). The suggestion has merit. The reading of the LXX compares as follows:

LXX Ps 46:6	1 Thess 4:16
God has ascended [*anabainein*] with a shout, the Lord with the sound of a trumpet	The Lord himself with a shout with the sound of an archangel and with the trumpet of God will descend [*katabainein*] from heaven.

Seven of the LXX's (Greek) words appear in 1 Thess 4:16. The major difference, however, is that whereas the LXX speaks of the Lord's ascent, Paul speaks of the Lord's descent. But could the passages be related, nonetheless? And, if 1 Thess 4:16 is based on Ps 46:6 [LXX], what does that tell us about Paul's "word of the Lord"?

Patristic interpretation of Ps 47:5 proves to be very interesting. Justin Martyr (*Dialogue with Trypho* 37), John Chrysostom (*Expositions in the Psalms* on Ps 47:5 [46:6 LXX]), Eusebius (*Commentaries on the Psalms* on Ps 47:5 [46:6 LXX]), and other Fathers interpret Ps 47:5 as fulfilled in Christ's ascension. In fact, they often cite Acts 1:11, noting that Jesus will return the same way that he departed. The most crucial exegesis for our purposes comes from Origen (*Selections on the Psalms* on Ps 47:5 [46:6 LXX]):

> "God went up with a shout, etc." Even as the Lord will come "with the voice of an angel, and with the trumpet of God he will descend from heaven," so "God went up with a shout." But the Lord "with the sound of a trumpet" (went up) meaning possibly with the shout of all the nations clapping their hands, shouting to God with the sound of rejoicing. To these ones I expect God to ascend. But if some one should praise him with the sound of a trumpet, even the one who ascends will himself ascend with the sound of a trumpet.

Not only has Origen interpreted Ps 47:5 [46:6 LXX] in terms of the ascension of Christ, something that several Greek and Latin Fathers did, but he explicitly relates the verse from the psalm to 1 Thess 4:16: "Even as the Lord . . . 'will descend [*katabainein*] from heaven,' so 'God ascended [*anabainein*] with a shout.' " Apparently what has drawn the two passages together is their common language, especially *anabainein/katabainein.*

Is it possible that early patristic exegesis has preserved an interpretive tradition presupposed by Paul, but only partially presented? Just as "God ascended with a shout," so Jesus "will descend with a shout." Or, as Acts 1:11 promises, "This Jesus, who was taken up from you into heaven, will come in the same way as you saw him go into heaven."

Jewish interpretation coheres with the eschatological interpretation that Paul and the Fathers have given Ps 47:5. This is an important point to observe, for in its original ancient setting Psalm 47 was not understood in an eschatological sense. Several Tannaic and Amoraic rabbis believe that the passage will be fulfilled in the day of judgment (cf. *Mek.* on Exod 19:19 [*Bahodeš* §4]; *Lev. Rab.* 29.3 [on Lev 23:24]; *Pesiq. R.* 40.5; *Pesiq. Rab Kah.* 1.4). In one midrash Ps 47:5 may even be related to the Messiah (cf. *Num. Rab.* 15.13 [on 10:1]).

If we are correct in concluding that lying behind the words of 1 Thess 4:16 is Ps 47:5, we are left with a striking implication. This NT passage has applied to Christ an OT verse that speaks of God. What we could have here is a fragment of early, but remarkably advanced Christology. Consider this very different rabbinic interpretation of Ps 47:5: " 'Who has ascended into heaven (and descended?)' [Prov 30:4] alludes to the Holy One, blessed be he, of whom it is [also] written, 'God has ascended with a shout' [Ps 47:5]" (*Num. Rab.* 12.11 [on 7:1]). Psalm 47 speaks of *God* ascending, as this rabbinic interpretation understands. The early Christian interpretation of 1 Thessalonians has applied the text to the risen and returning *Christ*.

Bibliography: F. F. Bruce, *1 & 2 Thessalonians* (WBC 45; Dallas: Word, 1982) 101; C. A. Evans, "Ascending and Descending with a Shout: Psalm 47.6 and 1 Thessalonians 4.16," in Evans and J. A. Sanders, eds., *Paul and the Scriptures of Israel* (JSNTSup; Sheffield: JSOT, forthcoming); C. F. D. Moule, *The Origin of Christology* (Cambridge: Cambridge University, 1977) 42.

APPENDIX ONE

CANONS OF SCRIPTURE THAT INCLUDE THE APOCRYPHA

Apocrypha	Roman Catholic	Greek Orthodox	Russian Orthodox	Coptic
1 Esdras		1 Esdras	1 Esdras	
2 Esdras			2 Esdras	
Tobit	Tobit	Tobit	Tobit	Tobit
Judith	Judith	Judith	Judith	Judith
Add Esther	Add Esther	Add Esther	Add Esther	Add Esther
Wisdom	Wisdom	Wisdom	Wisdom	Wisdom
Sirach	Sirach	Sirach	Sirach	Sirach
Baruch	Baruch	Baruch	Baruch	Baruch
Ep Jeremiah	Ep Jeremiah	Ep Jeremiah	Ep Jeremiah	Ep Jeremiah
Song of Three	Song of Three	Song of Three	Song of Three	Song of Three
Susanna	Susanna	Susanna	Susanna	Susanna
Bel	Bel	Bel	Bel	Bel
Pr Man		Pr Man	Pr Man	
1 Macc	1 Macc	1 Macc	1 Macc	1 Macc
2 Macc	2 Macc	2 Macc	2 Macc	2 Macc
3 Macc		3 Macc	3 Macc	
4 Macc		4 Macc*		
Psalm 151		Psalm 151	Psalm 151	

*Contained in an appendix

Third and Fourth Maccabees and Psalm 151 are usually included among the Pseudepigrapha.

Numerous Eastern groups, such as the Syrians, Nestorians, Melchites, Armenians, and Jacobites, accept most, if not all, of the apocryphal books (and in some cases more besides). The Apocrypha is viewed as having semi-canonical status in the Anglican Church.

Even with regard to the canon of the NT, there is some diversity. The Coptic Church includes the *Apostolic Constitutions* and *1 and 2 Clement*. The Armenian Church accepts an apocryphal letter *to* the Corinthians and two others *from* the Corinthians. The Nestorians, however, exclude the four smaller catholic epistles (2 Peter, 2 and 3 John, Jude), part of the "anti-legomena."

APPENDIX TWO

QUOTATIONS, ALLUSIONS, AND PARALLELS TO THE NEW TESTAMENT

This appendix contains a list of NT passages that quote, allude to, or contain ideas that closely parallel the OT and/or the writings surveyed in this book. This list is not comprehensive; it is illustrative only. For an index of OT passages in the Dead Sea Scrolls see J. A. Fitzmyer, *The Dead Sea Scrolls: Major Publications and Tools for Study* (SBLRBS 20; rev. ed.; Atlanta: Scholars, 1990) 205–37.

Matthew

Matt 1:11	1 Esdr 1:32
Matt 1:23	LXX Isa 7:14
Matt 2:2	Jer 23:5; Num 24:17; Philo *On Rewards and Punishments* 16 §95; Josephus *J.W.* 6.5.4 §§312–313; cf. 3.8.9 §§400–402; 4QTest 9–13; CD 7:18–21; *Tgs.* Num 24:17; *Aristobulus* frg. 4:5; *Orphica* 31
Matt 2:5–6	Mic 5:2; *Tg.* Mic 5:1–3
Matt 2:15	Hos 11:1; cf. LXX Num 24:7–8a; *Frg. Tg.* Num 24:7
Matt 2:18	Jer 31:15
Matt 2:23	Isa 11:1; Isa 4:2; Jer 23:5; 33:15; Zech 3:8; 6:12; cf. Judg 13:5–7; *Tg.* Isa 11:1; *Tg.* Zech 3:8; 6:12
Matt 3:12 = Luke 3:17	*Tg.* Isa 33:11–12
Matt 3:16	*2 Apoc. Bar.* 22:2
Matt 4:2	*Life of Adam and Eve (Vita)* 6:3
Matt 4:4–10 = Luke 4:4–12	Deut 8:3; 6:16, 13
Matt 4:4	Wis 16:26
Matt 4:15–16	Isa 9:1–2; cf. *Tg.* Isa 9:1–6
Matt 4:15	1 Macc 5:15
Matt 5:2–3	Sir 25:7–12
Matt 5:5	Ps 37:11; 4QpPs 37 (frg. 1) 1:8–10; *Tg.* Ps 37:11; *1 Enoch* 5:7; *m. Qidd.* 1:10
Matt 5:6	*4 Bar.* 9:21
Matt 5:8	*4 Ezra* 7:98; *2 Enoch* 45:3
Matt 5:9	*2 Enoch* 52:9; *m. Pe'a* 1:1; *'Abot* 1:12
Matt 5:12	*Tg.* Isa 28:11

Matt 5:15	Bar 4:1
Matt 5:21	Exod 20:13; Deut 5:17; *t. Šebu.* 3.6
Matt 5:22	*2 Enoch*
Matt 5:25–26	*Ahiqar 142*; Sir 8:1
Matt 5:27	Exod 20:14; Deut 5:18; *t. Šebu.* 3.6
Matt 5:28	Sir 9:8
Matt 5:29–30	*1 Enoch 27:2*
Matt 5:31	Deut 24:1–4; *m. Soṭa* 6:3; *m. Giṭ.* 3:2; 9:10; *t. Soṭa* 5.9; *t. Giṭ.* 2.4–10
Matt 5:33	Lev 19:12
Matt 5:34–35	Isa 66:1; *2 Enoch 49:1*; *m. 'Abot* 6:10; *Barn.* 16:2
Matt 5:35	Ps 48:2; *m. Tamid* 7:4
Matt 5:38	Exod 21:23–25; Lev 24:19–20; Deut 19:21; *m. Mak.* 1:6
Matt 5:43	Lev 19:17–18; *m. Ned.* 9:4; *t. Šebu.* 3.8
Matt 5:48	Deut 18:13
Matt 6:7	Sir 7:14
Matt 6:9	Sir 23:1, 4
Matt 6:10	1 Macc 3:60
Matt 6:12	Sir 28:2
Matt 6:13	Sir 23:1; 33:1
Matt 6:19–20	*2 Apoc. Bar.* 14:13
Matt 6:20–21	*T. Levi* 13:5
Matt 6:20	Sir 29:10–11
Matt 6:22	*T. Iss.* 4:6
Matt 6:23	Sir 14:10
Matt 6:24	*Tg.* Isa 5:23
Matt 6:26	*Pss. Sol.* 5:9–11
Matt 6:33	Wis 7:11
Matt 7:2	*T. Zeb.* 8:3; *2 Enoch 44:4*; *Ps.-Phocylides 11*; *Tg.* Isa 27:8; cf. *b. Šabb.* 127b; *b. Meg.* 28a; *b. Roš Haš.* 16b
Matt 7:12	Tob 4:15; Sir 31:15
Matt 7:13	*2 Apoc. Bar.* 85:13
Matt 7:16	Sir 27:6
Matt 7:23 = Luke 13:27	Ps 6:8
Matt 8:4	Lev 14:2–20; *m. Neg.* 3:1
Matt 8:11	Ps 107:3; Bar 4:37; 4 Macc 13:17
Matt 8:17	Isa 53:4; *Tg.* Isa 52:13–53:12
Matt 8:21	Tob 4:3
Matt 8:23–27	Ps 65:5–8
Matt 8:29	*1 Enoch 16:1*
Matt 9:13	Hos 6:6; *'Abot R. Nat.* §4
Matt 9:36	Num 27:16–17; 1 Kgs 22:17; Zech 10:2; Jdt 11:19
Matt 9:38	1 Macc 12:17
Matt 10:16	Sir 13:17
Matt 10:21	Mic 7:6; *m. Soṭa* 9:15; *3 Apoc. Bar.* 4:17
Matt 10:34–36 = Luke 12:51–53	Mic 7:6; *m. Soṭa* 9:15; *3 Apoc. Bar.* 4:17
Matt 10:28	4 Macc 13:14–15
Matt 10:42	*2 Apoc. Bar.* 48:19
Matt 11:5 = Luke 7:22	Isa 35:5–6; 61:1; *Apoc. Elijah* 3:9
Matt 11:10 = Luke 7:27	Mal 3:1; 4:5; *m. 'Ed.* 8:7
Matt 11:14	Sir 48:10

Matt 11:22	Jdt 16:17
Matt 11:23 = Luke 10:15	Isa 14:13, 15; *Pss. Sol.* 1:5; *t. Soṭa* 3.19
Matt 11:25	Tob 7:17; Sir 51:1
Matt 11:28–29	Sir 24:19; 51:23–27; Jer 6:16; *m. Ber.* 2:2
Matt 11:29	Sir 6:24–29; *2 Enoch* 34:1
Matt 12:1	Deut 23:25
Matt 12:2	Exod 20:10; Deut 5:14
Matt 12:3–4	1 Sam 21:1–6
Matt 12:4	2 Macc 10:3
Matt 12:7	Hos 6:6; *'Abot R. Nat.* §4
Matt 12:18–21	Isa 42:1–4; *Tg.* Isa 42:1–6; 1QH 13:18–19; *Barn.* 14:7
Matt 12:40	*T. Zeb.* 4:4
Matt 12:41	Jonah 3:5
Matt 12:42	1 Kgs 10:1–13; Sir 47:17
Matt 13:5	Sir 40:15
Matt 13:6	*Pss. Sol.* 18:6–7
Matt 13:17	*2 Apoc. Bar.* 85:2; *Tg.* Isa 48:6
Matt 13:32	Dan 4:20–22
Matt 13:35	Ps 78:2
Matt 13:39	*1 Enoch* 16:1
Matt 13:43	Dan 12:3 *T. Levi* 4:2; *4 Ezra* 7:97; *2 Enoch* 22:10; 65:8, 11
Matt 13:44	Sir 20:30–31
Matt 14:19–20	*4 Bar.* 9:21
Matt 14:27	*2 Enoch* 1:7
Matt 16:18	Wis 7:11; 16:13
Matt 16:22	1 Macc 2:21
Matt 16:26	*2 Apoc. Bar.* 51:16
Matt 16:27	Ps 62:12; cf. Prov 24:12; Sir 35:19, 22
Matt 17:2	*2 Apoc. Bar.* 51:3
Matt 17:5	*2 Enoch* 14:8; *2 Apoc. Bar.* 22:2
Matt 17:11	Sir 48:10
Matt 18:6, 10	*2 Apoc. Bar.* 48:19; *Pr. Joseph* frg. A
Matt 18:10	Tob 12:15
Matt 18:15	Lev 19:16–17; CD 9:6–8
Matt 18:16	Deut 19:15; CD 9:16–10:3; *m. Soṭa* 6:3; *t. Šeb.* 3.8; 5.4
Matt 19:5	Gen 2:24; CD 4:19–5:2
Matt 19:28–30	*T. Benj.* 10:7; *Pss. Sol.* 26:29
Matt 20:2	Tob 4:6; 5:15
Matt 21:5	Isa 62:11; Zech 9:9
Matt 21:12	*Pss. Sol.* 17:30
Matt 21:16	LXX Ps 8:3 (8:2)
Matt 22:13	Wis 17:2
Matt 22:32	4 Macc 7:19; 16:25
Matt 23:35	Gen 4:8; 2 Chr 24:20–21; *Lives of Prophets* 23:1; Zech 1:1
Matt 23:37 = Luke 13:34	Isa 31:5
Matt 23:38 = Luke 13:35	Jer 12:7; 22:5; Tob 14:4
Matt 23:39 = Luke 13:35	Ps 118:26
Matt 24:1	*4 Ezra* 5:2
Matt 24:4	*Apoc. Elijah* 1:14
Matt 24:5	*Apoc. Elijah* 3:1
Matt 24:6–7	*Sib. Or.* 3:636–37

Matt 24:6	*2 Apoc. Bar.* 48:34, 37
Matt 24:7	4 Ezra 13:31; 15:15; *2 Enoch* 70:23; *2 Apoc. Bar.* 27:9
Matt 24:8	*2 Apoc. Bar.* 27:3
Matt 24:11	*2 Apoc. Bar.* 48:34
Matt 24:15	1 Macc 1:54; 6:7; 2 Macc 8:17; *2 Apoc. Bar.* 28:1
Matt 24:16	1 Macc 2:28
Matt 24:17	*2 Apoc. Bar.* 53:9
Matt 24:19	*2 Apoc. Bar.* 10:14
Matt 24:21	*T. Mos.* 8:1
Matt 24:24	*2 Apoc. Bar.* 48:34
Matt 24:27	*Apoc. Elijah* 3:4
Matt 24:29	*Apoc. Elijah* 3:6
Matt 24:30	*2 Apoc. Bar.* 25:3
Matt 24:31	*1 Enoch* 22:3; *Life of Adam and Eve (Apoc.)* 22:3
Matt 24:38	Gen 7:6–10
Matt 24:40–41	*Apoc. Zeph.* 2:2
Matt 25:14–30	*Ahiqar* 192
Matt 25:23	*3 Apoc. Bar.* 15:4
Matt 25:31–46	*T. Jos.* 1:5
Matt 25:31	*1 Enoch* 61:8; 62:2–3; 69:27
Matt 25:34	*2 Enoch* 9:1; 23:5; 42:3
Matt 25:35	Tob 4:17; *T. Isaac* 6:21; *2 Enoch* 9:1
Matt 25:36	Sir 7:32–35
Matt 25:41	*1 Enoch* 10:13; *2 Enoch* 10:4
Matt 25:46	Dan 12:2
Matt 26:13	*1 Enoch* 103:4
Matt 26:15	Zech 11:12–13; LXX Exod 9:12; Jer 18:1–3; 19:11; 32:6–15
Matt 26:24	*1 Enoch* 38:2; *2 Apoc. Bar.* 10:6
Matt 26:38	Sir 37:2
Matt 26:39	*Sib. Or.* 3:655
Matt 26:52	*Tg.* Isa 50:11
Matt 26:64	*1 Enoch* 69:27
Matt 27:3–8	Zech 11:12–13; LXX Exod 9:12; Jer 18:1–3; 19:11; 32:6–15
Matt 27:9–10	Zech 11:12–13; Jer 18:2–3; 32:6–15
Matt 27:24–25	*T. Levi* 16:3
Matt 27:24	Sus 44, 46
Matt 27:43	Ps 22:8; Wis 2:13, 18–20
Matt 27:55–56	Ps 38:11
Matt 27:60	Josh 10:18, 27

Mark

Mark 1:2–3	Mal 3:1; Exod 23:20; LXX Isa 40:3; 1QS 8:12–14; 9:19–20; Bar 5:7; *Barn.* 9:3
Mark 1:4–5	*Sib. Or.* 4:165
Mark 1:10	*T. Jud.* 24:2; cf. *T. Levi* 18:6–7; Mal 3:10
Mark 1:11	Ps 2:7; cf. Gen 22:2; Isa 42:1; 2 Esdr 7:28–29; 1QSa 2:11–12; 4QFlor 1:10–12 (on 2 Sam 7:11–16); *b. Sukk.* 52a; *Midr. Ps.* 2.9 (on 2:7); *Tg.* Isa 41:8–9; 42:1; 43:10
Mark 1:15	Tob 14:5
Mark 2:27	*Mek.* on Exod 31:12–17 (*Šabb.* 1.25–28)
Mark 3:22	*Jub.* 10:7
Mark 3:27	*Pss. Sol.* 5:3

Mark 4:5	Sir 40:15
Mark 4:11–12	*Tg.* Isa 6:9–10; *Mek.* on Exod 19:2; *b. Roš Haš.* 17b; *b. Meg.* 17b; *y. Ber.* 2:3; *S. Elijah Rab.* 16 (§§82–83); *Gen. Rab.* 81.6 (on 42:1); *Ap. John* 22:25–29; *Testim. Truth* 48:8–13; *Ap. Jas.* 7:1–10
Mark 4:11	Wis 2:22
Mark 4:24	*Tg.* Isa 27:8; cf. *b. Šabb.* 127b; *b. Meg.* 28a; *b. Roš Haš.* 16b
Mark 4:29	LXX Joel 3:13
Mark 5:34	Jdt 8:35
Mark 6:11	*2 Apoc. Bar.* 13:4
Mark 6:18	Lev 18:16; 20:21; *m. Yeb.* 3:10
Mark 6:34	Num 27:17; cf. 1 Kgs 22:17; Ezek 34:5; Jdt 11:19
Mark 6:35–42	2 Kgs 4:42–44
Mark 6:48	*Apoc. Elijah* 3:8
Mark 6:49	Wis 17:15
Mark 7:3–5	*m. Yad.* 1:1–2:3
Mark 7:11–12	*m. Ned.* 1:2–2:2, 5; 3:2, 5; 9:7; 11:5; *m. Nazir* 2:1–3
Mark 7:6–7	LXX Isa 29:13; PEger2 §3; *2 Clem.* 3:5
Mark 7:10–11	Exod 20:12; 21:17; Lev 20:9; Deut 5:16
Mark 7:15	*Ps.-Phocylides* 228
Mark 8:18	Jer 5:21; cf. Isa 6:9–10; Ezek 12:2
Mark 8:29	*1 Enoch* 46:10
Mark 8:37	Sir 26:14
Mark 9:7	Ps 2:7; Gen 22:2; Deut 18:15
Mark 9:31	Ep Jer 2:18
Mark 9:48	*Tg.* Isa 66:24; *t. Ber.* 5.31; *t. Sanh.* 13.5; *Pesiq. R. Kah.* 10:4; *Midr. Ps.* 12.5 (on 12:8); *2 Clem.* 7:6; 17:5; Jdt 16:17
Mark 9:49	*T. Levi* 9:14
Mark 10:4	Deut 24:1–4
Mark 10:6	Gen 1:27; CD 4:20–5:2; *m. Yebam.* 6:6
Mark 10:7–8	Gen 2:24
Mark 10:19	Exod 20:12–16; Deut 5:16–20; *m. Mak.* 1:3
Mark 10:20	*2 Apoc. Bar.* 38:4
Mark 11:9–10	Ps 118:25–26; *Midr. Ps.* 118.22 (on 118:24–29)
Mark 11:17	Isa 56:7; Jer 7:11; cf. *Tg.* Jer 7:11
Mark 11:18	*T. Levi* 16:3
Mark 12:1	Isa 5:1–2; *Tg.* Isa 5:1–7; *t. Me'il.* 1.16; *Sukk.* 3.15; *Sipre Deut.* §312 (on 32:9)
Mark 12:10–11	Ps 118:22–23; cf. *Tg.* Ps 118:22
Mark 12:19	Gen 38:8; Deut 25:5–6; *m. Yebam.* 3:9
Mark 12:25	*1 Enoch* 15:6–7; 51:4
Mark 12:26–27	4 Macc 16:25
Mark 12:26	Exod 3:6; 4 Macc 7:19
Mark 12:29–30	Deut 6:4–5; *m. Ber.* 2:2; 9:5; *m. Soṭa* 7:8; *t. Roš Haš.* 2.13; *t. Soṭa* 7.17
Mark 12:31	Lev 19:18; *m. Ned.* 9:4; *t. Soṭa* 5.11; *t. Sanh.* 9.11
Mark 12:36	Ps 110:1; *Midr. Ps.* 110.4 (on 110:1); *b. Sanh.* 38b; *Gen. Rab.* 85.9 (on 38:18); *Num. Rab.* 18.23 (on 17:21); cf. *Apoc. Elijah* 4:28; *Barn.* 12:10–11
Mark 13:2	2 Sam 17:13; cf. Ezek 26:12
Mark 13:4	*2 Apoc. Bar.* 25:3

Mark 13:5	*Apoc. Elijah* 1:14
Mark 13:7	*Apoc. Elijah* 2:2
Mark 13:8	2 Chr 15:6; Isa 19:2; *2 Apoc. Bar.* 27:9; *Sib. Or.* 3:363–64
Mark 13:9	*2 Apoc. Bar.* 13:4
Mark 13:11	*Ahiqar* 114
Mark 13:12	*3 Apoc. Bar.* 4:17
Mark 13:14	Dan 9:27; 11:31; 12:11; 1 Macc 1:54
Mark 13:19	Dan 12:1
Mark 13:22	Deut 13:1–3
Mark 13:24–25	Isa 13:10; 34:4
Mark 13:26	Dan 7:13–14; *b. Sanh.* 96b–97a, 98a; *Num. Rab.* 13.14 (on 7:13); *Midr. Ps.* 21.5 (on 21:7); 93.1 (on 93:1); *Frg. Tg.* Exod 12:42
Mark 14:1	*T. Levi* 16:3
Mark 14:24	Jer 31:31; Zech 9:11; cf. Exod 24:8
Mark 14:27	Zech 13:7; CD 19:5–11
Mark 14:34	Sir 37:2
Mark 14:58	*2 Apoc. Bar.* 4:2
Mark 14:62	Ps 110:1; Dan 7:13 (cf. Mark 13:26 above)
Mark 14:63–64	Lev 24:16
Mark 15:24	Ps 22:18
Mark 15:29	Ps 22:7; Wis 2:17–18
Mark 15:34	Ps 22:1
Mark 15:36	Ps 69:2
Mark 15:42–46	Deut 21:22–23; *t. Sanh.* 9.7

Luke

Luke 1:6	*2 Enoch* 9:1; *Apoc. Zeph* 3:4
Luke 1:7–23	Judg 13:2–21
Luke 1:13	Gen 17:19
Luke 1:15	Num 6:3; Judg 13:4; *m. Nazir* 9:5
Luke 1:17	Mal 4:5–6; Sir 48:10; 3 Macc 48:10; *m. 'Ed.* 8:7
Luke 1:19	Tob 12:15
Luke 1:31	Isa 7:14
Luke 1:32–33	2 Sam 7:12, 13, 16; Isa 9:6–7; *Tg.* Isa 9:6–7; Mic 4:7; Dan 2:44; 7:14; 4QFlor 1:1–13; 4QpsDan ar[a] 1:7–9; 2:1–4; 4QPBless 1–2
Luke 1:18	Gen 15:8
Luke 1:34–38	*T. Isaac* 3:17
Luke 1:42	Jdt 13:18; *2 Apoc. Bar.* 54:11
Luke 1:46–55	1 Sam 2:1–10
Luke 1:47	Hab 3:18
Luke 1:48	LXX 1 Sam 1:11; Ps 113:5–6
Luke 1:49	Deut 10:21; Ps 111:9
Luke 1:50	Ps 103:17
Luke 1:51	Ps 89:11
Luke 1:52	1 Sam 2:4, 7; Sir 10:14
Luke 1:53	Ps 107:9; 1 Sam 2:5; Job 22:9
Luke 1:54–55	Isa 41:8–9; Ps 98:3; Gen 12:1–3; 17:6–8; Mic 7:20
Luke 1:59	Lev 12:3
Luke 1:68	Pss 41:3; 111:9
Luke 1:69	Pss 18:2; 132:17

Luke 1:71	Ps 18:71; 2 Sam 22:18; Ps 106:10
Luke 1:72	Gen 24:12; Mic 7:2; Pss 105:8; 106:45
Luke 1:73	Gen 26:3; Jer 11:5
Luke 1:75	Josh 24:14; Isa 38:20
Luke 1:76	Mal 3:1; Isa 40:3
Luke 1:79	Ps 107:10; Isa 9:2; 59:8
Luke 2:11	*Pss. Sol.* 17:32
Luke 2:14	*Pss. Sol.* 18:10
Luke 2:19	*Life of Adam and Eve (Apoc.)* 3:3
Luke 2:22	Lev 12:6; *m. Ker.* 6:9
Luke 2:23	Exod 13:2, 12, 15
Luke 2:24	Lev 12:8
Luke 2:25	Isa 40:1; 49:13; *2 Apoc. Bar.* 44:8
Luke 2:29	Tob 11:9
Luke 2:30	Isa 40:5
Luke 2:31	Isa 52:10
Luke 2:32	Isa 42:6; 49:6; *1 Enoch* 48:4; *Tg.* Isa 42:6; cf. Isa 40:5; LXX Isa 46:13; *Barn.* 14:8
Luke 2:34	Isa 8:14
Luke 2:37	Jdt 8:6
Luke 2:51	*Life of Adam and Eve (Apoc.)* 3:3
Luke 2:52	1 Sam 2:26; Prov 3:4
Luke 3:3–4	*Sib. Or.* 4:165
Luke 3:4–6	Exod 40:3–5
Luke 3:36	*Jub.* 8:2
Luke 4:13	*Life of Adam and Eve (Vita)* 17:2
Luke 4:18–19	LXX Isa 61:1–2; 58:6; cf. LXX Lev 25:10–13; 11QMelch 9–16
Luke 6:12	4 Macc 3:13–19
Luke 6:24	*1 Enoch* 94:8
Luke 6:35	Wis 15:1
Luke 6:36	*Tg. Ps.-J.* Lev 22:28
Luke 6:38	*2 Enoch* 44:4; 50:5; *Ps.-Phocylides* 12–13
Luke 7:22	Isa 35:5; 61:1; Sir 48:5
Luke 9:8	Sir 48:10
Luke 9:51	LXX Ezek 21:1–3
Luke 9:54	LXX 2 Kgs 1:10, 12
Luke 9:61–62	1 Kgs 19:20
Luke 10:17	Tob 7:17
Luke 10:18	*Tg.* Isa 14:12; *Life of Adam and Eve (Vita)* 12:1
Luke 10:19–20	Ps 91:13; *T. Levi* 18:12
Luke 10:19	Sir 11:19
Luke 10:21	Sir 51:51
Luke 10:27	Deut 6:5; Lev 19:18; *T. Iss.* 5:2
Luke 11:21–22	*Pss. Sol.* 5:4
Luke 11:25	*2 Apoc. Bar.* 25:3
Luke 12:11–12	*Ahiqar* 114
Luke 12:13–21	*Ahiqar* 137
Luke 12:19–20	Sir 11:19
Luke 12:19	Tob 7:10; *1 Enoch* 97:8–10
Luke 12:20	Wis 15:8
Luke 13:27	1 Macc 3:6

Luke 13:28–29	*2 Enoch* 42:5
Luke 13:29	Bar 4:37
Luke 13:35	Tob 14:4
Luke 14:14	*2 Enoch* 50:5
Luke 14:16	*2 Enoch* 42:5
Luke 15:12	Tob 3:17; 1 Macc 10:29–30
Luke 15:20	Tob 11:9
Luke 16:3	*Ps.-Phocylides* 158
Luke 16:9, 11	*1 Enoch* 39:4; 63:10; *Tg.* Isa 5:23; 33:15; *Tg.* 1 Sam 12:3; *Tg.* Ezek 22:27; *Tg.* Hos 5:11
Luke 16:23, 26	4 Ezra 7:36; 4 Macc 13:15; *1 Enoch* 22:9–11
Luke 17:28–29	Gen 7:6–23; 18:20–21; 19:1–14
Luke 17:24	*Apoc. Elijah* 3:4
Luke 17:34–35	*Apoc. Zeph.* 2:2
Luke 18:7	Sir 35:22
Luke 18:21	*2 Apoc. Bar.* 38:4
Luke 18:22	Sir 29:11
Luke 19:12–27	*Ahiqar* 193; Josephus *Ant.* 17.9.3–11.4 §§219–320; *J.W.* 2.2.1–6.3 §§14–100 (on Archelaus' bid for kingship)
Luke 19:40	4 Ezra 5:5
Luke 19:41	Jer 8:23 (9:1)
Luke 19:42	Jer 6:8; cf. Isa 48:18
Luke 19:43	2 Kgs 20:17; cf. Jer 7:32; Jer 6:6; Ezek 4:2; Isa 29:3
Luke 19:44	Hos 10:14; cf. 2 Kgs 8:12; 2 Sam 17:13; Wis 3:7
Luke 20:36	*2 Apoc. Bar.* 51:9
Luke 20:37	4 Macc 7:19; 16:25
Luke 21:7	*2 Apoc. Bar.* 25:3
Luke 21:10	*Sib. Or.* 636–37
Luke 21:11	*2 Apoc. Bar.* 27:9
Luke 21:19	*2 Enoch* 50:2
Luke 21:20	LXX Jer 41:1 (34:1); Dan 12:11
Luke 21:21	Jer 50:8; 51:6, 45; cf. Eusebius *Eccl. Hist.* 3.5.3; Epiphanius *Panarion* 29.7.8; *Treatise on Weights and Measures* §15
Luke 21:22	Hos 9:7; LXX Jer 28:6 (51:6)
Luke 21:23	2 Kgs 8:12; Zeph 1:15–16
Luke 21:24	Sir 28:18; Deut 28:41; Jer 15:2; Tob 1:10; LXX Ezra 9:7; Zech 12:3; *Pss. Sol.* 17:22, 25; 1 Macc 3:45, 51; Dan 12:7; Tob 14:5
Luke 21:25–26	*2 Apoc. Bar.* 25:4
Luke 21:25	Wis 5:22
Luke 21:28	*1 Enoch* 51:2
Luke 21:34–35	Isa 24:17; CD 4:12–19
Luke 22:27	*T. Jos.* 17:8
Luke 22:37	Isa 53:12; cf. *Tg.* Isa 52:13–53:12; *Pss. Sol.* 16:5
Luke 23:28	Jer 9:20
Luke 23:29	*2 Apoc. Bar.* 10:14; *Apoc. Elijah* 2:38
Luke 23:29	2 Kgs 20:17; Jer 7:32; Isa 54:1
Luke 23:30	Hos 10:8; cf. Rev 6:16; Jer 7:32; 16:14; *Apoc. Elijah* 2:34
Luke 23:39–43	*Ruth Rab.* 3.3 (on 1:17)
Luke 23:46	Ps 31:5; cf. *Num. Rab.* 20.20 (on 23:24); *Midr. Ps.* 25.2 (on 25:1); *b. Ber.* 5a; *Life of Adam and Eve (Apoc.)* 42:8

Luke 24:4	2 Macc 3:26
Luke 24:31	2 Macc 3:34
Luke 24:44	4QMMT frg. 3.17 ("the Book of Moses, and the words of the Prophets, and David")
Luke 24:46	Isaiah 53; Hos 6:2
Luke 24:50	Sir 50:20–21
Luke 24:53	Sir 50:22

John

John 1:1–2	Gen 1:1; *Tg. Neof.* Gen 1:1; Prov 8:23, 27, 30; Wis 18:15; Philo *On the Confusion of the Languages* 14 §§62–63; 28 §§146–147; *On Dreams* 1.39 §§228–230
John 1:1	*2 Enoch* 33:4
John 1:3	Wis 9:1–2; LXX Ps 32:6 (33:6); 1QS 11:11; Philo *On the Cherubim* 35 §127
John 1:5	Gen 1:2–5, 15; *Tg. Neof.* Exod 12:24; *Frg. Tg.* Gen 1:3; Philo, *On the Creation of the World* 9 §§33–34
John 1:8	*2 Enoch* 46:3
John 1:9	Sir 24:27, 32; *2 Apoc. Bar.* 18:2
John 1:14–18	Exod 33:18–34:6; Philo *On the Confusion of the Languages* 28 §146; Wis 1:4; Sir 1:10
John 1:14	Sir 24:8; *Pss. Sol.* 7:6; *Pr. Joseph* frg. A; *Jub.* 7:6
John 1:18	Sir 43:31; Prov 8:30; *'Abot R. Nat.* A §31; *Gen. Rab.* 8.2 (on 1:26)
John 1:23	Isa 40:3 (see Mark 1:3 above)
John 1:26	*Tg.* Mic 4:8; cf. *Tg.* Zech 4:7; 6:12
John 1:29	*2 Enoch* 64:5
John 1:51	Gen 28:12; *Frg. Tg.* Gen 28:12
John 2:17	Ps 69:9
John 3:8	Sir 16:21
John 3:12	Wis 9:16; 18:15–16
John 3:13	Prov 30:4; Bar 3:29; *4 Ezra* 4:8
John 3:17	*Apoc. Elijah* 1:6
John 3:19–21	*2 Enoch* 46:3
John 3:19	*2 Apoc. Bar.* 18:2
John 3:21	Tob 4:6
John 3:27	*Jub.* 5:3–4
John 3:29	1 Macc 9:39
John 4:9	Sir 50:25
John 4:10, 14	*Memar Marqah* 2:1–2; 6:3
John 4:12–13	*Frg. Tg.* Gen 28:10
John 4:48	Wis 8:8
John 5:18	Wis 2:16
John 5:22	*Jub.* 69:27; *1 Enoch* 69:27
John 5:35	*2 Apoc. Bar.* 18:2; *2 Enoch* 46:3
John 6:12	Sir 24:19
John 6:31	Ps 78:24; cf. Exod 16:4, 15; Neh 9:15; *t. Soṭa* 4.3
John 6:35, 53	Sir 24:21–22
John 6:38	*Sib. Or.* 3:655; *Pr. Joseph* frg. A
John 6:45	LXX Isa 54:13; cf. Jer 31:33–34
John 7:38	Prov 18:4; Zech 14:8; Isa 55:1; 58:11; Sir 24:40, 43; cf. *m. 'Abot* 6:1

John 7:42	*Jub.* 17:21
John 8:12; 9:5	*b. B. Bat.* 4a; *Deut. Rab.* 7.3 (on 28:1); *2 Enoch* 46:3
John 8:33	*Tg.* Isa 34:12; *m. B. Qam.* 8:6
John 8:44	Wis 2:24
John 8:53	Sir 44:19
John 8:56	*Gen. Rab.* 14.22 (on Gen 15:10–11); cf. *Pirqe R. Eliezer* §28
John 8:58	*Pr. Joseph* frg. A
John 9:22	*b. Ber.* 28b–29a; *Amidah* §12; cf. John 12:42; 16:2
John 10:20	Wis 5:4
John 10:22	1 Macc 4:59; *m. Mo'ed Qa.* 3:9
John 10:34	Ps 82:6; *Exod. Rab.* 32.1, 7 (on Exod 23:20); *Lev. Rab.* 4.1 (on Lev 4:2); 11.3 (on Lev 9:1); *Num. Rab.* 7.4 (on Num 5:2); 16.24 (on Num 14:11); *Deut. Rab.* 7.12 (on Deut 29:5 [4]); *Song Rab.* 1.2 §5; *Eccl. Rab.* 3.16 §1
John 12:26	4 Macc 17:20
John 12:31	*Life of Adam and Eve (Vita)* 12:1
John 12:34	Ps 89:36 (LXX 88:37); 89:4–5; 110:4; Isa 9:7; Ezek 37:25; Dan 7:13–14
John 12:38	LXX Isa 53:1
John 12:40	Isa 6:10 (see Mark 4:12 above)
John 13:18	Ps 41:9; *Ahiqar* 139
John 14:2	*2 Apoc. Bar.* 48:6; *2 Enoch* 61:2
John 14:15	Wis 6:18
John 14:17	*Jub.* 25:14
John 14:23	*1 Enoch* 45:3
John 15:1–5	Sir 24:16–17
John 15:1	LXX Jer 2:21; *2 Apoc. Bar.* 39:7
John 15:9–10	Wis 3:9
John 15:25	Ps 69:4; cf. Ps 35:19; *Jub.* 7:1
John 16:7–13	*T. Jud.* 20:5
John 17:3	Wis 15:3
John 17:12	*Apoc. Elijah* 2:40
John 17:22	*T. Jud.* 25:3
John 19:30	*Life of Adam and Eve (Vita)* 45:3
John 19:36	Exod 12:46; cf. Num 9:12; Ps 34:20; cf. *m. Pesaḥ* 7:10, 11
John 19:37	Zech 12:10
John 20:22	Wis 15:11

Acts of the Apostles

Acts 1:8	*Pss. Sol.* 8:15
Acts 1:9	*2 Enoch* 3:1
Acts 1:10	2 Macc 3:26
Acts 1:11–12	*4 Bar.* 9:20
Acts 1:18	Wis 3:17
Acts 1:20	Ps 69:25; 109:8
Acts 2:4	Sir 48:12
Acts 2:11	Sir 36:7; *2 Enoch* 54:1
Acts 2:15	*2 Enoch* 51:5
Acts 2:17–21	LXX Joel 3:1–5 = ET 2:28–32; Num 11:29; *Midr. Ps.* 14.6 (on 14:7); *Num. Rab.* 15.25 (on 11:17)

Acts 2:25–28, 31	LXX Ps 15:8–11 (16:8–11); *Midr. Ps.* 16.4, 10–11 (on 16:4, 9–10)
Acts 2:30	Ps 132:11; Ps 89:3–4; 2 Sam 7:12–13; *Tg.* Ps 132:10–18, esp. v. 17
Acts 2:34–35	Ps 110:1 (see Mark 12:36 above)
Acts 2:39	Sir 24:32
Acts 3:1	*2 Enoch* 51:5
Acts 3:13, 26	*2 Apoc. Bar.* 70:10; Pr Man 1
Acts 3:22–23	Deut 18:15–16, 19; Lev 23:29; cf. 1 Macc 4:46; 14:41; *T. Benj.* 9:2; *T. Levi* 8:15; 1QS 9:11; 4QTest 5–8; Josephus *Ant.* 18.4.1 §§85–86
Acts 3:25	Gen 22:18; cf. Gen 12:3; 17:4, 5; 18:18; 26:4; 28:14
Acts 4:11	Ps 118:22 (see Mark 12:10 above)
Acts 4:24	Jdt 9:12
Acts 4:25–26	Ps 2:1–2; 4QFlor 1:18–19; *Midr. Ps.* 2.2–3 (on 2:1–2); *b. Ber.* 7b; *'Abod. Zar.* 3b
Acts 4:27	*2 Apoc. Bar.* 70:10
Acts 5:2	2 Macc 4:32
Acts 5:7	3 Macc 4:17
Acts 5:21	1 Macc 12:6; 2 Macc 1:10
Acts 5:39	Wis 12:13–14; 2 Macc 7:19
Acts 7:2	LXX Gen 12:7; 1QapGen 22:27 (on Gen 15:1); *Apoc. Elijah* 1:5
Acts 7:3	Gen 12:1
Acts 7:4	Gen 11:26–12:4; SP Gen 11:32
Acts 7:5	Gen 17:8; Deut 2:5
Acts 7:6–7	Gen 15:13–14; Exod 2:22; 3:12
Acts 7:8	Gen 17:10–14; 21:4
Acts 7:9	Gen 37:11, 28; 39:21
Acts 7:10	Gen 41:37–39, 40–44; LXX Ps 104:21 (105:21)
Acts 7:11	Gen 41:54–57; 42:5; LXX Ps 36:19 (37:19)
Acts 7:12	Gen 42:1–2
Acts 7:13	Gen 45:3–4, 16
Acts 7:14	Gen 45:9–11, 18–19; LXX 46:27; cf. LXX Exod 1:4–5; 4QExod[a]
Acts 7:15–16	*Jub.* 46:10
Acts 7:15	Gen 46:5–6; 49:33; Exod 1:6
Acts 7:16	Gen 23:16–17
Acts 7:17–18	LXX Exod 1:7–8
Acts 7:19	Exod 1:10–11, 22
Acts 7:20–28	Exod 2:2–14; Sir 45:3
Acts 7:23	*Jub.* 47:10
Acts 7:29	Exod 2:15, 21–22; 18:3–4
Acts 7:30–34	Exod 3:2–10
Acts 7:30	*Jub.* 48:2
Acts 7:35	Exod 2:14; 3:2
Acts 7:36–41	*T. Mos.* 3:11
Acts 7:36	Exod 7:3; 14:21; Num 14:33; *T. Mos.* 3:11
Acts 7:37	LXX Deut 18:15 (see Acts 3:22–23 above)
Acts 7:38	Exod 19:1–6; 20:1–17; Deut 5:4–22; 9:10
Acts 7:39	Num 14:3
Acts 7:40	Exod 32:1, 23

Acts 7:41	Exod 32:4–6; cf. Wis 13:10; Ep Jer 50
Acts 7:42–43	LXX Jer 7:18; Amos 5:25–27
Acts 7:44	Exod 27:21; Num 1:50; Exod 25:9, 40; *Sib. Or.* 4:10
Acts 7:45	Josh 3:14–17; 18:1; 23:9; 24:18
Acts 7:45–46	2 Sam 7:2–16; 1 Kgs 8:17–18
Acts 7:47	1 Kgs 6:1, 14; 8:19–20
Acts 7:48–49	*Sib. Or.* 4:8
Acts 7:49–50	Isa 66:1–2; *m. 'Abot* 6:10; *Barn.* 16:2
Acts 7:51	Exod 32:9; 33:3, 5; Lev 26:41; Jer 9:26; 6:10; Isa 63:10; *m. Ned.* 3:11
Acts 7:53	*Jub.* 1:28
Acts 7:55	*Life of Adam and Eve (Apoc.)* 33:1
Acts 7:57	*2 Apoc. Bar.* 22:1
Acts 7:58	*m. Sanh.* 6:1–6; 7:4–5
Acts 8:10	*Tg.* SP Gen 17:1
Acts 8:32–33	LXX Isa 53:7–8; *Tg.* Isa 52:13–53:12; *Barn.* 5:2
Acts 8:38	*2 Apoc. Bar.* 6:4
Acts 9:1–29	2 Macc 3:24–40; 4 Macc 4:1–14
Acts 9:2	1 Macc 15:21
Acts 9:7	Wis 18:1
Acts 10:2	Tob 12:8
Acts 10:9	*2 Enoch* 51:5
Acts 10:13–14	*m. Ḥul.* 1:1–2:3
Acts 10:22	1 Macc 10:25; 11:30, 33
Acts 10:26	Wis 7:1
Acts 10:30	2 Macc 11:8
Acts 10:34	Sir 35:12–13
Acts 10:36	Wis 8:3
Acts 11:18	Wis 12:19
Acts 12:5	Jdt 4:9
Acts 12:10	Sir 19:26
Acts 12:23	1 Macc 7:41; 2 Macc 9:9; Jdt 16:17; Sir 28:7; *m. Soṭa* 7:8; *t. Soṭa* 7.16; cf. *m. Bik.* 3:4
Acts 13:10	Sir 1:30
Acts 13:17	Wis 19:10
Acts 13:33	LXX Ps 2:7 (see Mark 1:11 above)
Acts 13:34	LXX Isa 55:3
Acts 13:35	LXX Ps 15:10 (16:10) (see Acts 2:25–28 above)
Acts 13:41	LXX Hab 1:5
Acts 13:47	LXX Isa 49:6 (see Luke 2:32 above)
Acts 14:14	Jdt 14:16–17
Acts 14:15	4 Macc 12:13; Wis 3:17
Acts 15:4	Jdt 8:26
Acts 15:16–18	LXX Amos 9:11–12; Isa 45:21; Jer 12:15; 4QFlor 1:11–13; CD 7:13–21; *Tg.* Amos 9:11; *b. Sanh.* 96b–97a; *Midr. Ps.* 76.3 (on 76:3, and 1); *Gen. Rab.* 88.7 (on 40:23)
Acts 15:29	4 Macc 5:2
Acts 15:20	*1 Enoch* 7:5; *m. Yoma* 5:6; *m. Mak.* 3:2; *m. Ḥul.* 1:1; 2:1, 4; 3:1–4; 8:3; *m. Ker.* 1:1; 5:1; *m. Ṭohor.* 1:1
Acts 16:14	2 Macc 1:4
Acts 16:23, 25	*T. Jos.* 8:5
Acts 17:23	Wis 14:20; 15:17

Acts 17:24–25	Wis 9:1
Acts 17:24	Wis 9:9; Tob 7:17
Acts 17:26	Wis 7:18
Acts 17:27	Wis 13:6
Acts 17:28	Aratus *Phaenomena* 5; Cleanthes; *Aristobulus* frg. 4:6
Acts 17:29	Wis 13:10
Acts 17:30	Sir 28:7
Acts 17:31	Ps 9:8; cf. 96:13; 98:9
Acts 19:19	*Ps.-Phocylides* 149
Acts 19:27	Wis 3:17
Acts 19:28	Bel 18, 41
Acts 20:26	Sus 46
Acts 20:32	Wis 5:5
Acts 20:35	Sir 4:31
Acts 21:26	1 Macc 3:49
Acts 22:9	Wis 18:1
Acts 23:11	*2 Enoch* 1:7
Acts 24:2	2 Macc 4:6
Acts 24:14	4 Macc 12:17
Acts 26:18	Wis 5:5
Acts 26:23	Isa 42:6; 49:6 (see Luke 2:32 above)
Acts 26:25	Jdt 10:13
Acts 28:26–27	LXX Isa 6:9–10
Acts 28:28	LXX Ps 66:3 (67:2)

Romans

Rom 1:4	*T. Levi* 18:7
Rom 1:7	*2 Apoc. Bar.* 78:3
Rom 1:9	*2 Apoc. Bar.* 86:1
Rom 1:17	Hab 2:4; 1QpHab 7:17–8:3; 8HevXIIgr 17:30; *Tg.* Hab 2:4; *Tg.* Zech 2:17 (MS Parma 555); *b. Mak.* 24a; *2 Apoc. Bar.* 54:17
Rom 1:18	*1 Enoch* 91:7
Rom 1:19–32	Wisdom 13–15
Rom 1:19	*2 Apoc. Bar.* 54:17–18
Rom 1:20–23	*m. Sanh.* 7:6; *m. 'Abod. Zar.* 4:7
Rom 1:20–21	*2 Apoc. Bar.* 54:18
Rom 1:21	4 Ezra 8:60; Wis 13:1; *1 Enoch* 99:8
Rom 1:23	Wis 11:15; 12:12
Rom 1:25	*T. Mos.* 5:4
Rom 1:26	*T. Jos.* 7:8; *Sib. Or.* 3:185
Rom 1:28	2 Macc 6:4; 3 Macc 4:16
Rom 1:29–31	4 Macc 1:26; 2:15
Rom 1:29	*Ps.-Phocylides* 71
Rom 1:32	*2 Enoch* 10:4
Rom 2:3	*Jub.* 15:8
Rom 2:4	Wis 11:23
Rom 2:5	*Jub.* 9:5; *T. Levi* 3:2; *Apoc. Elijah* 1:19
Rom 2:6	Sir 16:14
Rom 2:11	Sir 35:12–13
Rom 2:14–15	*2 Apoc. Bar.* 48:40
Rom 2:15	*T. Reub.* 4:3; Wis 17:11; *2 Apoc. Bar.* 57:2

Rom 2:17	*Jub.* 17:1; *2 Apoc. Bar.* 48:22
Rom 2:22	*T. Levi* 14:4
Rom 2:24	Isa 52:5; Ezek 36:20; Ign. *Rom.* 8:2; Pol. *Phil.* 10:3; *2 Clem.* 13:2
Rom 2:29	*Jub.* 1:23
Rom 3:1	*2 Apoc. Bar.* 14:4
Rom 3:3	*Jub.* 8:28
Rom 3:4	LXX Ps 115:2 (116:11); Ps 50:6 (51:4)
Rom 3:10–18	LXX Ps 13:2–3 (14:1–3); LXX 52:2–6 (53:1–3); Eccl 7:20; LXX Ps 5:9–10 (5:9); LXX 139:4 (140:3); LXX 9:28 (10:7); Isa 59:7–8; Prov 1:16; Ps LXX 35:2 (36:1)
Rom 3:20	LXX Ps 142:2 (143:2)
Rom 4:3, 9, 22	Gen 15:6; *1 Clem.* 10:6; *Barn.* 13:7
Rom 4:7–8	Ps 32:1–2
Rom 4:10–11	Gen 17:10; *t. Ned.* 2.5
Rom 4:13	Sir 44:21; *Jub.* 19:21; *2 Apoc. Bar.* 14:13; 51:3
Rom 4:15	*2 Apoc. Bar.* 15:2; *Jub.* 33:16
Rom 4:17	Gen 17:5; *2 Apoc. Bar.* 21:5; 48:8; *t. Ber.* 1.12–14
Rom 4:18	Isa 48:13; Gen 15:5
Rom 5:3	*T. Jos.* 10:1
Rom 5:5	Sir 18:11
Rom 5:12–21	*Life of Adam and Eve (Apoc.)* 14:2
Rom 5:12	Wis 2:24; 4 Ezra 3:21–22, 26; *2 Apoc. Bar.* 17:3; 23:4; 54:15; *1 Clem.* 3:4
Rom 5:16	4 Ezra 7:118–19
Rom 6:10	4 Macc 7:19
Rom 6:23	*2 Enoch* 30:16
Rom 7:7	Exod 20:17; Deut 5:21; 4 Macc 2:5–6; *Life of Adam and Eve (Apoc.)* 19:3
Rom 7:12	4 Ezra 9:37
Rom 7:23	4 Ezra 7:72
Rom 8:18	*2 Apoc. Bar.* 15:8; 32:6
Rom 8:19	4 Ezra 7:11, 75
Rom 8:22	4 Ezra 10:9
Rom 8:28	*Pss. Sol.* 4:25
Rom 8:35	*2 Enoch* 66:6
Rom 8:36	LXX Ps 43:23 (44:22)
Rom 8:38	*Life of Adam and Eve (Vita)* 28:2
Rom 9:4	Sir 44:12, 18; 2 Macc 6:23
Rom 9:7	Gen 21:12; *t. Soṭa* 5.12
Rom 9:9	Gen 18:10, 14
Rom 9:12	Gen 25:23
Rom 9:13	Mal 1:2–3
Rom 9:14	Deut 32:4
Rom 9:15	Exod 33:19
Rom 9:16	*T. Mos.* 12:7
Rom 9:17	Exod 9:16
Rom 9:18	Exod 4:21; 7:3; 9:12; 14:4, 17
Rom 9:19	Wis 12:12; *2 Apoc. Bar.* 3:7
Rom 9:20	Isa 29:16; 45:9; Wis 12:12
Rom 9:21	Jer 18:6; Wis 15:7
Rom 9:22	Jer 50:25; *2 Apoc. Bar.* 24:2; 59:6

Rom 9:24	*Jub.* 2:19
Rom 9:25	Hos 2:23
Rom 9:26	Hos 1:10
Rom 9:27–28	Isa 10:22–23; Hos 1:10
Rom 9:29	Isa 1:9
Rom 9:31	Wis 2:11; Sir 27:8
Rom 9:32	Isa 8:14; 28:16
Rom 10:5	Lev 18:5; *2 Apoc. Bar.* 67:6; *m. Mak.* 3:15; *t. Šabb.* 15.17
Rom 10:6–8	Deut 9:4; 30:12–14; Bar 3:29–30; 4 Ezra 4:8; *Frg. Tg.*, *Tg. Neof.* Deut 30:12–14
Rom 10:7	Wis 16:13
Rom 10:11	Isa 28:16
Rom 10:13	Joel 3:5 (ET 2:32)
Rom 10:15	Isa 52:7; Nah 1:15; 11QMelch 9–16
Rom 10:16	Isa 53:1
Rom 10:18	LXX Ps 18:5 (19:4)
Rom 10:19	Deut 32:21; *3 Apoc. Bar.* 16:3
Rom 10:20	Isa 65:1
Rom 10:21	Isa 65:2
Rom 11:2	1 Sam 12:22; LXX Ps 93:14 (94:14)
Rom 11:3	1 Kgs 19:10, 14
Rom 11:4	1 Kgs 19:18; 2 Macc 2:4
Rom 11:8	Deut 29:3 (4); Isa 29:10
Rom 11:9–10	Ps 68:23–24 (69:22–23); 34:8 (35:8)
Rom 11:15	Sir 10:20–21
Rom 11:16	Num 15:17–21; Neh 10:37; Ezek 44:30
Rom 11:21	*2 Apoc. Bar.* 13:10
Rom 11:25	4 Ezra 4:35–36; *T. Zeb.* 9; *2 Apoc. Bar.* 23:5
Rom 11:26–27	Isa 59:20; LXX Ps 13:7 (14:7); Isa 27:9; Jer 31:33–34; *T. Benj.* 10:11
Rom 11:33	Isa 45:15; 55:8; Wis 17:1; *2 Apoc. Bar.* 14:8–10
Rom 11:34–35	Isa 40:13; Job 15:8; Jer 23:18; Job 41:11
Rom 11:34	*2 Enoch* 33:4
Rom 12:1	*T. Levi* 3:6
Rom 12:9	Amos 5:15
Rom 12:15	Sir 7:34
Rom 12:17	LXX Prov 3:4
Rom 12:19	Deut 32:35; *T. Gad* 6:6; *2 Enoch* 50:4
Rom 12:20	Prov 25:21–22
Rom 12:21	*T. Benj.* 4:3–4
Rom 13:1	*T. Benj.* 4:27; Wis 6:3–4
Rom 13:9	Exod 20:13–15, 17; Deut 5:17–19, 21; Lev 19:18; 4 Macc 2:6; *t. Šebu.* 3.7
Rom 13:10	Wis 6:18
Rom 13:13, 16–18	*Ps.-Phocylides* 69
Rom 14:8	4 Macc 7:19
Rom 14:11	Isa 49:18; 45:23
Rom 15:3	LXX Ps 68:10 (69:9)
Rom 15:4	1 Macc 12:9
Rom 15:8	Mic 7:20; Sir 36:20
Rom 15:9	LXX Ps 17:50 (18:49); 2 Sam 22:50
Rom 15:10	Deut 32:43

Rom 15:11	LXX Ps 116:1 (117:1)
Rom 15:12	Isa 11:10
Rom 15:21	Isa 52:15
Rom 15:33	*T. Dan* 5:2
Rom 16:20	Gen 3:15; *Frg. Tg., Tg. Ps.-J.* Gen 3:15; cf. *T. Levi* 18:12
Rom 16:27	4 Macc 18:24; *Ps.-Phocylides* 54

1 Corinthians

1 Cor 1:3	*2 Apoc. Bar.* 78:3
1 Cor 1:19	Isa 29:14
1 Cor 1:30	Jer 23:5–6
1 Cor 1:31	Jer 9:24; *1 Clem.* 13:1
1 Cor 2:9	Isa 52:15; 64:4; 65:17; Sir 1:10; Ps.-Philo *Bib. Ant.* 26:13; 4 Ezra 7:15; *1 Clem.* 34:8; *2 Clem.* 11:7; 14:5
1 Cor 2:11	Prov 20:27
1 Cor 2:16	Isa 40:13
1 Cor 3:11	Isa 28:16
1 Cor 3:14	4 Ezra 7:99
1 Cor 3:19	Job 5:13
1 Cor 3:20	LXX Ps 93:11 (94:11)
1 Cor 4:4	Ps 143:2
1 Cor 4:5	*2 Apoc. Bar.* 83:3
1 Cor 4:9	4 Macc 17:14
1 Cor 4:12	Ps 109:28
1 Cor 4:13	Lam 3:45
1 Cor 5:1	Lev 18:7–8; Deut 22:30; 27:20; *Ps.-Phocylides* 179
1 Cor 5:11	*Ps.-Phocylides* 69
1 Cor 5:12–13	Deut 17:7; 19:19; 22:21, 24; 24:7; *m. Sanh.* 11:2
1 Cor 6:2	Dan 7:22; Wis 3:8
1 Cor 6:3	*1 Enoch* 14:3
1 Cor 6:9–10	*Sib. Or.* 3:185
1 Cor 6:10	*Ps.-Phocylides* 69
1 Cor 6:12	Sir 37:28
1 Cor 6:16	Gen 2:24
1 Cor 8:4	Deut 6:4
1 Cor 9:9	Deut 25:4
1 Cor 9:25	*2 Apoc. Bar.* 15:8
1 Cor 10:7	Exod 32:6
1 Cor 10:8	Num 25:1, 9
1 Cor 10:9	Num 25:5–6
1 Cor 10:10	Num 14:2, 36; 16:41–49; Ps 106:25–27
1 Cor 10:20	Deut 32:17; Ps 106:37; Bar 4:7
1 Cor 10:26	LXX Ps 23:1 (24:1)
1 Cor 11:7	Gen 1:27; 5:1; Wis 2:23; *T. Naph.* 2:5
1 Cor 11:8	Gen 2:21–23
1 Cor 11:9	Gen 2:18
1 Cor 11:14	*Ps.-Phocylides* 212
1 Cor 11:25	Exod 24:8; Jer 31:31; 32:40; Exod 24:6–8; Zech 9:11
1 Cor 12:2	Hab 2:18–19
1 Cor 14:5	Num 11:29 (see Acts 2:17–21 above)
1 Cor 14:21	Isa 28:11–12; Deut 28:49

1 Cor 14:25	Isa 45:14; Dan 2:47; Zech 8:23; *Tg.* Isa 45:14; *2 Apoc. Bar.* 83:3
1 Cor 15:3	Isa 53:8–9; *Tg.* Isa 52:13–53:12
1 Cor 15:4	Ps 16:10; Hos 6:2; Jonah 1:17
1 Cor 15:9	*2 Apoc. Bar.* 21:13
1 Cor 15:21	Gen 3:17–19; *2 Apoc. Bar.* 17:3
1 Cor 15:24–25	*2 Apoc. Bar.* 73:1
1 Cor 15:24	Dan 2:44
1 Cor 15:25	Ps 110:1
1 Cor 15:27	LXX Ps 8:7 (8:6)
1 Cor 15:32	Isa 22:13; 56:12
1 Cor 15:33	Menander *Thais* §218
1 Cor 15:38	Gen 1:11; *Apoc. Zeph* 10:14
1 Cor 15:41	*2 Apoc. Bar.* 51:1
1 Cor 15:45, 47	Gen 2:7; Philo *On the Virtues* 37 §§203–204; *On the Confusion of the Languages* 14 §§62–63; 28 §§146–147; *Questions and Answers on Genesis* 1.4 (on Gen 2:7)
1 Cor 15:49	Gen 5:3
1 Cor 15:51	*T. Benj.* 10:8; *2 Apoc. Bar.* 49:3; 51:1
1 Cor 15:52	4 Ezra 6:23; *2 Apoc. Bar.* 30:2; *Life of Adam and Eve (Apoc.)* 22:3
1 Cor 15:54	Isa 25:8; *Tg.* Isa 25:8
1 Cor 15:55	Hos 13:14

2 Corinthians

2 Cor 1:2	*2 Apoc. Bar.* 78:3
2 Cor 3:3	Exod 24:12; 31:18; 34:1; Deut 9:10, 11; Prov 3:3; 7:3; Jer 31:33; Ezek 11:19; 36:26
2 Cor 3:6	Exod 24:8; Jer 31:31; 32:40
2 Cor 3:7, 10	Exod 34:29–30
2 Cor 3:9	Deut 27:26
2 Cor 3:13	Exod 34:33, 35
2 Cor 3:16	Exod 34:34
2 Cor 3:18	Exod 16:7; 24:17
2 Cor 4:6	Gen 1:3; Isa 9:2
2 Cor 4:13	Ps 116:10
2 Cor 4:17	*2 Apoc. Bar.* 15:8; 48:50
2 Cor 5:1–5	*Life of Adam and Eve (Apoc.)* 31:1
2 Cor 5:1–2	*2 Apoc. Bar.* 48:6
2 Cor 5:1	Job 4:19
2 Cor 5:3–4	*2 Enoch* 22:8
2 Cor 5:4	4 Ezra 14:15
2 Cor 5:17	Isa 43:18
2 Cor 5:20	Isa 52:7
2 Cor 6:2	Isa 49:8
2 Cor 6:14	*2 Enoch* 34:1
2 Cor 6:16	Lev 26:12; Jer 32:38; Ezek 37:27
2 Cor 6:17	Isa 52:11; Ezek 20:34, 41
2 Cor 6:18	2 Sam 7:8, 14; Isa 43:6; Jer 31:9; LXX Amos 3:13; 4:13
2 Cor 7:6	Isa 49:13
2 Cor 7:10	3 Macc 38:18
2 Cor 7:10	Sir 38:18

2 Cor 8:12	Prov 3:27–28
2 Cor 8:15	Exod 16:18
2 Cor 8:21	LXX Prov 3:4
2 Cor 9:6	Prov 11:24; 22:9
2 Cor 9:7	LXX Prov 22:8; *2 Enoch 61:5*
2 Cor 9:9	LXX Ps 111:9 (112:9)
2 Cor 9:10	LXX Hos 10:12
2 Cor 10:17	Jer 9:24
2 Cor 11:3	*2 Enoch 31:6; Life of Adam and Eve (Apoc.)* 14:2
2 Cor 11:14	*Life of Adam and Eve (Apoc.)* 17:1; *(Vita)* 9:1
2 Cor 11:27	*2 Enoch 66:6*
2 Cor 12:2	*2 Enoch 8:1; 42:3; Life of Adam and Eve (Apoc.)* 37:5
2 Cor 12:4	*2 Apoc. Bar. 4:7; 2 Enoch 8:1*
2 Cor 13:1	Deut 19:15

Galatians

Gal 1:5	4 Macc 18:24
Gal 1:15	Isa 49:1; Jer 1:5
Gal 2:6	Deut 10:17; Sir 35:13
Gal 2:15	*Jub.* 23:24
Gal 2:16	Ps 143:2
Gal 2:19	4 Macc 7:19
Gal 3:8	Gen 12:3; 18:18; Sir 44:21; 3 Macc 44:21
Gal 3:10	Deut 27:26; 4 Macc 5:20
Gal 3:11	Hab 2:4 (see Rom 1:17 above)
Gal 3:12	Lev 18:5
Gal 3:13	Deut 21:23; *t. Sanh.* 9.7
Gal 3:16	Gen 12:7; 13:15; 17:7; 24:7
Gal 3:17	Exod 12:40
Gal 3:19	*Jub.* 1:28
Gal 4:4	Tob 14:5; *2 Apoc. Bar.* 40:4
Gal 4:8	2 Chr 13:9; Isa 37:19; Jer 2:11; Ep Jer 16, 23, 29, 40, 44, 56, 65, 69
Gal 4:10	*1 Enoch* 72–82
Gal 4:16	Amos 5:10
Gal 4:22	Gen 16:15; 21:2
Gal 4:26	4 Ezra 10:7; *4 Bar.* 5:35
Gal 4:27	Isa 54:1
Gal 4:29	Gen 21:9
Gal 4:30	Gen 21:10
Gal 5:14	Lev 19:18
Gal 5:19–20	*Ps.-Phocylides* 71
Gal 6:1	Wis 17:17
Gal 6:7–8	*T. Levi* 13:6
Gal 6:6	*2 Enoch 42:11*
Gal 6:16	LXX Ps 124:5 (125:5); 127:6 (128:6)
Gal 6:17	3 Macc 2:29

Ephesians

Eph 1:6	Sir 45:1; 46:13
Eph 1:17	Isa 11:2; Wis 7:7
Eph 1:20	Ps 110:1

Eph 1:21	*Pr. Joseph* frg. A
Eph 1:22	Ps 8:6
Eph 2:2	*2 Enoch* 29:4; *4 Bar.* 9:17
Eph 2:3	*Life of Adam and Eve (Apoc.)* 3:2
Eph 2:12	*Apoc. Elijah* 1:14
Eph 2:13	Isa 57:19
Eph 2:14	*2 Apoc. Bar.* 54:5
Eph 2:17	Isa 57:19; 52:7; Zech 9:10
Eph 2:20	Isa 28:16
Eph 3:9	3 Macc 2:3
Eph 4:4–6	*2 Apoc. Bar.* 48:24
Eph 4:4	*T. Jud.* 25:3
Eph 4:8	LXX Ps 67:19 (68:18); *Apoc. Elijah* 1:4
Eph 4:9–10	*Pr. Joseph* frg. A
Eph 4:14	Sir 5:9
Eph 4:24	Gen 1:26; Wis 9:3
Eph 4:25	Zech 8:16; *2 Enoch* 42:12; *Ps.-Phocylides* 6–7
Eph 4:26	LXX Ps 4:5 (4:4)
Eph 4:30	Isa 63:10
Eph 5:2	LXX Ps 39:7 (40:6)
Eph 5:5	*T. Jud.* 19:1
Eph 5:12	*2 Enoch* 34:1
Eph 5:14	Isa 26:19; 51:17; 52:1; 60:1
Eph 5:18	LXX Prov 23:31; *T. Jud.* 14:1
Eph 5:31	Gen 2:24
Eph 6:2–3	Exod 20:12; Deut 5:16
Eph 6:4	Deut 6:7, 20–25; *Ps.-Phocylides* 207
Eph 6:5	*2 Enoch* 66:2
Eph 6:9	Deut 10:17; 2 Chr 19:17
Eph 6:10–20	*Life of Adam and Eve (Apoc.)* 20:2
Eph 6:12	*T. Levi* 3:10; *Life of Adam and Eve (Apoc.)* 28:2
Eph 6:13	*T. Levi* 8:2; Wis 5:17
Eph 6:14	Isa 11:5; 59:17; Wis 5:18
Eph 6:15	Isa 52:7; Nah 1:17
Eph 6:16	LXX Ps 7:14 (7:13); Wis 5:19, 21
Eph 6:17	Isa 59:17; 11:4; 49:2; Hos 6:5

Philippians

Phil 1:19	Job 13:16
Phil 2:6–8	*Apoc. Elijah* 1:6
Phil 2:9	*Pr. Joseph* frg. A
Phil 2:10–11	Isa 45:23
Phil 2:12	Ps 2:11; *2 Enoch* 66:2
Phil 2:15	Deut 32:5
Phil 2:16	Isa 49:4; 65:23
Phil 3:6	*2 Apoc. Bar.* 67:6
Phil 3:19	*Apoc. Elijah* 1:13; *Ps.-Phocylides* 69
Phil 3:21	*2 Apoc. Bar.* 51:3
Phil 4:3	Dan 12:1
Phil 4:5	Wis 2:19
Phil 4:13	Wis 7:23
Phil 4:18	Gen 8:21; Exod 29:18; Ezek 20:41; Sir 35:6

Colossians

Col 1:15	*Pr. Joseph* frg. A
Col 1:16	*T. Levi* 3:8; *Apoc. Elijah* 1:8; 4:10; *2 Enoch* 20:1
Col 1:17	*Pr. Joseph* frg. A
Col 1:22	*1 Enoch* 102:5
Col 2:3	Isa 45:3; Sir 1:24–25; *1 Enoch* 46:3; Prov 2:3–4
Col 2:22	Isa 29:13
Col 3:1	Ps 110:1
Col 3:5	*T. Jud.* 19:1
Col 3:10	Gen 1:26–27
Col 3:21	*Ps.-Phocylides* 207
Col 4:1	Lev 25:43, 53
Col 4:16	*2 Apoc. Bar.* 86:1

1 Thessalonians

1 Thess 1:3	4 Macc 17:4
1 Thess 1:8	4 Macc 16:12
1 Thess 2:4	Jer 11:20
1 Thess 2:16	*T. Levi* 6:11
1 Thess 3:11	Jdt 12:8
1 Thess 3:13	Zech 14:5
1 Thess 4:5	Ps 79:6; Jer 10:25
1 Thess 4:6	Ps 94:1; Sir 5:3; *2 Enoch* 60:1
1 Thess 4:8	Ezek 36:27; 37:14
1 Thess 4:9	Jer 31:33–34
1 Thess 4:13	Wis 3:18
1 Thess 4:16	LXX Ps 46:6 (47:5); 4 Ezra 6:23; *Life of Adam and Eve (Apoc.)* 22:3
1 Thess 5:1	Wis 8:8
1 Thess 5:2–3	*Apoc. Elijah* 2:40
1 Thess 5:2	Wis 18:14–15
1 Thess 5:3	Jer 6:14; 8:11; Ezek 13:10; *1 Enoch* 62:4; Wis 17:14
1 Thess 5:8	Isa 59:17; Wis 5:18; *Apoc. Elijah* 4:31
1 Thess 5:15	Prov 20:22
1 Thess 5:22	Job 1:1, 8; 2:3
1 Thess 5:23	*T. Dan* 5:2

2 Thessalonians

2 Thess 1:7	Zech 14:5; *Apoc. Elijah* 3:3
2 Thess 1:8	Ps 79:6; Isa 66:15; Jer 10:25
2 Thess 1:9	Isa 2:10, 19, 21
2 Thess 1:10	LXX Ps 67:36
2 Thess 1:12	Isa 24:15; 66:5; Mal 1:11
2 Thess 2:1	2 Macc 2:7
2 Thess 2:3	*Jub.* 10:3; *Sib. Or.* 3:570–71; *Apoc. Elijah* 1:10; 2:40
2 Thess 2:4	Dan 11:36; Ezek 28:2
2 Thess 2:8	Job 4:9; Isa 11:4; *Apoc. Elijah* 2:41
2 Thess 2:13	Deut 33:12
2 Thess 3:10	*Ps.-Phocylides* 153

1 Timothy

1 Tim 1:17	Tob 13:7, 11
1 Tim 2:2	2 Macc 3:11; Bar 1:11–12
1 Tim 2:4	Ezek 18:23
1 Tim 2:14	Gen 3:6, 13; *2 Enoch* 30:17
1 Tim 3:16	4 Macc 6:31; 7:16; 16:1
1 Tim 4:3	Gen 9:3
1 Tim 4:4	Gen 1:31
1 Tim 5:1	Lev 19:32
1 Tim 5:5	Jer 49:11
1 Tim 5:18	Deut 25:4
1 Tim 5:19	Deut 17:6; 19:15
1 Tim 6:7	Eccl 5:15; Job 1:21; *Ps.-Phocylides* 110–11
1 Tim 6:8	Prov 30:8
1 Tim 6:9	Prov 23:4; 28:22
1 Tim 6:10	*Ahiqar* 137
1 Tim 6:15	Deut 10:17; 2 Macc 12:15; 13:4; 3 Macc 5:35; Sir 46:5
1 Tim 6:16	Ps 104:2; Exod 33:20
1 Tim 6:17	*Ps.-Phocylides* 62

2 Timothy

2 Tim 2:13	Num 23:19
2 Tim 2:19	Num 16:5, 26; Sir 23:10; 35:3
2 Tim 3:1–5	*T. Dan* 5:4
2 Tim 3:8–9	Exod 7:11, 22; *Tg. Ps.-J.* Exod 7:11; 1:15; Num 22:22
2 Tim 3:11	Ps 34:19; *Pss. Sol.* 4:23
2 Tim 4:1–5	*Apoc. Elijah* 1:13
2 Tim 4:5	*2 Enoch* 50:3–4
2 Tim 4:8	Wis 5:16; *2 Apoc. Bar.* 15:8
2 Tim 4:14	2 Sam 3:39; Ps 28:4; 62:12; Prov 24:12
2 Tim 4:17	Ps 22:21; Dan 6:21; 1 Macc 2:60

Titus

Titus 1:12	Epimenides *De Oraculis*
Titus 2:11	2 Macc 3:30; 3 Macc 6:9
Titus 2:12	*Aristobulus* frg. 4:8
Titus 2:14	Ps 130:8; Exod 19:5; Deut 4:20; 7:6; 14:2; Ezek 37:23
Titus 3:4	Wis 1:6
Titus 3:6	Joel 3:1 (2:28)

Hebrews

Heb 1:3	Ps 110:1; Wis 7:25–26
Heb 1:4	*Pr. Joseph* frg. A
Heb 1:5	LXX Ps 2:7; 2 Sam 7:14; 1 Chr 17:13
Heb 1:6	LXX Deut 32:43; LXX Ps 96:7 (97:7)
Heb 1:7	LXX Ps 103:4 (104:4); 4 Ezra 8:22; *2 Enoch* 29:1
Heb 1:8–9	LXX Ps 44:7–8 (45:6–7)
Heb 1:10–12	LXX 101:26–28 (102:25–26)
Heb 1:13	LXX Ps 109:1 (110:1)
Heb 1:14	Ps 34:8; 91:11
Heb 2:5	Sir 17:17

Heb 2:6–8	LXX Ps 8:5–7
Heb 2:9	LXX Ps 8:6
Heb 2:12	LXX Ps 21:23 (22:22)
Heb 2:13	LXX Isa 8:17; LXX 2 Sam 22:3; Isa 12:2
Heb 2:13	LXX Isa 8:18
Heb 2:16	Isa 41:8–9
Heb 3:2, 5	Num 12:7
Heb 3:7–11	LXX Ps 94:7–11 (95:7–11)
Heb 3:11	Num 14:21–23
Heb 3:12	Exod 17:7; Num 20:2–5
Heb 3:15	LXX Ps 94:7–8 (95:7–8)
Heb 3:16–18	Num 14:1–35
Heb 3:17	Num 14:29
Heb 3:18	Num 14:22–23; LXX Ps 94:11 (95:11)
Heb 4:3	LXX Ps 94:11 (95:11); *2 Apoc. Bar.* 73:1; *2 Enoch* 53:3
Heb 4:4	Gen 2:2
Heb 4:5	LXX Ps 94:11 (95:11)
Heb 4:7	LXX Ps 94:7–8 (95:7–8)
Heb 4:8	Deut 31:7; Josh 22:4
Heb 4:10	Gen 2:2
Heb 4:12	Isa 49:2; Wis 7:22–30; 18:15–16; *2 Apoc. Bar.* 83:3; *Ps.-Phocylides* 124
Heb 4:13	*1 Enoch* 9:5
Heb 4:15	*Pss. Sol.* 17:36
Heb 5:3	Lev 9:7; 16:6
Heb 5:4	Exod 28:1
Heb 5:5	LXX Ps 2:7
Heb 5:6	LXX Ps 109:4 (110:4); 1 Macc 14:41
Heb 5:9	Isa 45:17
Heb 5:10	LXX Ps 109:4 (110:4)
Heb 5:12	*1 Enoch* 61:7
Heb 6:8	Gen 3:17–18
Heb 6:12	*Pss. Sol.* 12:6
Heb 6:13–18	*T. Mos.* 3:9
Heb 6:13	Gen 22:16
Heb 6:14	Gen 22:17; Sir 44:21; 3 Macc 44:21
Heb 6:16	Exod 22:11
Heb 6:18	Num 23:19; 1 Sam 15:29
Heb 6:19	Lev 16:2–3, 12, 15
Heb 6:20	LXX Ps 109:4 (110:4)
Heb 7:1–2	Gen 14:17–20
Heb 7:3	LXX Ps 109:4 (110:4)
Heb 7:5	Num 18:21
Heb 7:14	Gen 49:10; Isa 11:1; 4QpIsa (on 11:1–5); *Tgs.* Gen 49:10; *Tg.* Isa 11:1
Heb 7:17, 21	LXX Ps 109:4 (110:4)
Heb 7:22	Sir 29:14–16
Heb 7:27	Lev 9:7; 16:6, 15
Heb 8:1–5	*Sib. Or.* 4:10
Heb 8:1	LXX Ps 109:1 (110:1)
Heb 8:2	LXX Num 24:6
Heb 8:5	Exod 25:40; *2 Apoc. Bar.* 59:3

Heb 8:8–12	Jer 31:31–34
Heb 9:2	Exod 26:1–30; 25:31–40, 23–30
Heb 9:3	Exod 26:31–33
Heb 9:4–5	Exod 30:1–6; 25:10–16; 16:33; Num 17:8–10; Exod 25:16; Deut 10:3–5; Exod 25:18–22
Heb 9:6	Num 18:2–6
Heb 9:7	Exod 30:10; Lev 16:2, 14, 15
Heb 9:10	Lev 11:2, 25; 15:18; Num 19:13
Heb 9:11–12	*Sib. Or.* 4:10
Heb 9:13	Lev 16:3, 14, 15; Num 19:9, 17–19
Heb 9:19	Exod 24:3, 6–8; Lev 14:4; Num 19:6
Heb 9:20	Exod 24:8; *t. Ned.* 2.6
Heb 9:21	Lev 8:15, 19
Heb 9:22	Lev 17:11
Heb 9:26	*T. Levi* 18:9
Heb 9:27	Gen 3:19
Heb 9:28	Isa 53:12
Heb 10:4	Lev 16:15, 21
Heb 10:5–7, 8–9	LXX Ps 39:7–9 (40:6–8)
Heb 10:11	Exod 29:38
Heb 10:12, 13	LXX Ps 109:1 (110:1)
Heb 10:16, 17	Jer 31:33, 34
Heb 10:22	Ezek 36:25
Heb 10:27	Isa 26:11
Heb 10:28	Deut 17:6; 19:15
Heb 10:29	Exod 24:8
Heb 10:30	Deut 32:35, 36; LXX Ps 134:14 (135:14); *2 Enoch* 50:4
Heb 10:32	*2 Enoch* 50:3–4
Heb 10:37–38	LXX Hab 2:3–4 (see Rom 1:17 above); LXX Isa 26:20
Heb 10:38	*2 Apoc. Bar.* 54:17
Heb 11:3	Gen 1:1; LXX Ps 32:6, 9 (33:6, 9); *2 Apoc. Bar.* 14:17; *2 Enoch* 24:2; 25:1; 48:5
Heb 11:4	Gen 4:3–10
Heb 11:5	Gen 5:24; Wis 4:10; Sir 44:16; 3 Macc 44:16; *1 Enoch* 70:1–4
Heb 11:6	Wis 10:17
Heb 11:7	Gen 6:13–22; 7:1
Heb 11:8	Gen 12:1–5; *1 Clem.* 10:3
Heb 11:9	Gen 23:4; 26:3; 35:12, 27; *T. Abr.* (A) 8:6
Heb 11:10	4 Ezra 10:27; 2 Macc 4:1; Wis 13:1
Heb 11:11	Gen 17:19; 18:11–14; 21:2
Heb 11:12	Gen 15:5–6; 22:17; 32:12; Exod 32:13; Deut 1:10; 10:22; LXX Dan 3:36; Sir 44:21; 3 Macc 44:21
Heb 11:13	Gen 23:4; 47:9; 1 Chr 29:15; LXX Ps 38:13 (39:12)
Heb 11:16	Exod 3:6, 15; 4:5
Heb 11:17	Gen 22:1–10; 1 Macc 2:52
Heb 11:18	Gen 21:12
Heb 11:20	Gen 27:27–29, 39–40
Heb 11:21	Gen 48:15–16; Exod 1:22
Heb 11:24	Exod 2:10–12
Heb 11:25	4 Macc 15:2, 8
Heb 11:27	Exod 2:15; 12:51; Sir 2:2

Heb 11:28	Exod 12:21–30; Wis 18:25
Heb 11:29	Exod 14:21–31
Heb 11:30	Josh 6:12–21
Heb 11:31	Josh 2:11–12; 6:21–25
Heb 11:33	Judg 14:6–7; 1 Sam 17:34–36; Dan 6:1–27
Heb 11:34	Dan 3:23–25
Heb 11:35	1 Kgs 17:17–24; 2 Kgs 4:25–37; 2 Macc 6:18–7:42
Heb 11:36	1 Kgs 22:26–27; 2 Chr 18:25–26; Jer 20:2; 37:15; 38:6
Heb 11:37	2 Chr 24:21; *Asc. Isa.* 5:11–14
Heb 12:1	4 Macc 16:16; 17:10–15
Heb 12:2	Lxx Ps 109:1 (110:1)
Heb 12:4–11	*2 Apoc. Bar.* 13:10
Heb 12:5–6	Prov 3:11–12
Heb 12:7	Deut 8:5; 2 Sam 7:14; *Pss. Sol.* 10:2; 14:1
Heb 12:9	Num 16:22; 27:16; 2 Macc 3:24
Heb 12:12	Isa 35:3; Sir 25:23
Heb 12:13	Lxx Prov 4:26
Heb 12:14	Lxx Ps 33:15 (34:14)
Heb 12:15	Lxx Deut 29:27
Heb 12:16	Gen 25:33–34
Heb 12:17	Gen 27:30–40; Wis 12:10
Heb 12:18–19	Exod 19:16–22; 20:18–21; Deut 4:11–12; 5:22–27
Heb 12:20	Exod 19:12–13
Heb 12:21	Deut 9:19; 1 Macc 13:2
Heb 12:22	*4 Bar.* 5:35
Heb 12:23	Gen 18:25; Lxx Ps 49:6 (50:6)
Heb 12:24	Gen 4:10
Heb 12:26	Exod 19:18; Judg 5:4; Lxx Ps 67:9 (68:8); Hag 2:6
Heb 12:29	Deut 4:24; 9:3; Isa 33:14
Heb 13:2	Gen 18:1–8; 19:1–3; *Ps.-Phocylides* 24–25
Heb 13:5	Deut 31:6; cf. Gen 28:15; Deut 31:8; Josh 1:5; *Ps.-Phocylides* 6–7
Heb 13:6	Lxx Ps 117:6–7 (118:6)
Heb 13:7	Sir 33:19; Wis 2:17
Heb 13:11	Lev 16:27
Heb 13:15	2 Chr 29:31; Lxx Ps 49:14, 23 (50:14, 23); Hos 14:2; *Pss. Sol.* 15:2–3
Heb 13:17	Isa 62:6; Ezek 3:17
Heb 13:20	Isa 63:11; Zech 9:11; Isa 55:3; Jer 32:40; Ezek 37:26; *T. Dan* 5:2
Heb 13:22	*2 Apoc. Bar.* 81:1

James

Jas 1:1	2 Macc 1:27
Jas 1:2	Sir 2:1; Wis 3:4–5
Jas 1:3	4 Macc 1:11
Jas 1:4	4 Macc 15:7
Jas 1:5	Prov 2:3–6
Jas 1:10–11	Ps 102:4, 11; Isa 40:6–7
Jas 1:12	*2 Apoc. Bar.* 15:8; *2 Enoch* 50:3–4; *Apoc. Elijah* 1:8, 14
Jas 1:13	Sir 15:11–13; 16:12
Jas 1:14	*1 Enoch* 98:4

Jas 1:15	*Life of Adam and Eve (Apoc.)* 19:3
Jas 1:17	*2 Enoch* 33:4
Jas 1:19	Sir 5:11; Eccl 7:9; *Ps.-Phocylides* 57
Jas 1:21	Sir 3:17
Jas 1:22	*Apoc. Zeph.* 10:8
Jas 1:26	Ps 34:13; 39:1; 141:3
Jas 2:1	Job 34:19
Jas 2:5	*Apoc. Elijah* 1:14
Jas 2:8	Lev 19:18
Jas 2:9	Deut 1:17
Jas 2:10	4 Macc 5:20
Jas 2:11	Exod 20:14; Deut 5:18; Exod 20:13; Deut 5:17
Jas 2:13	Tob 4:10
Jas 2:21	Gen 22:9, 12
Jas 2:23	Gen 15:6; 2 Chr 20:7; Isa 41:8; Wis 7:27; *Jub.* 19:9; *Apoc. Abr.* 9:7; *Apoc. Zeph.* 9:5
Jas 2:25	Josh 2:4, 15; 6:17
Jas 3:2	Sir 14:1
Jas 3:6, 10	Sir 5:13
Jas 3:6	*1 Enoch* 48:7
Jas 3:8	Ps 140:3
Jas 3:9	Gen 1:26, 27; Sir 23:1, 4; *2 Enoch* 44:1
Jas 3:10	Sir 28:12
Jas 3:13	Sir 3:17
Jas 3:18	Isa 32:17
Jas 4:1	*Apoc. Elijah* 1:16
Jas 4:2	1 Macc 8:16
Jas 4:5	Exod 20:5
Jas 4:6	LXX Prov 3:34
Jas 4:7	*T. Naph.* 8:4
Jas 4:8	Zech 1:3; Mal 3:7; Isa 1:16; *T. Dan* 4:8
Jas 4:10	Job 5:11
Jas 4:11	Wis 1:11
Jas 4:13–14	Prov 27:1
Jas 4:13	*1 Enoch* 97:8–10
Jas 4:14	*2 Apoc. Bar.* 14:10
Jas 5:1	*1 Enoch* 94:8
Jas 5:3	Ps 21:9; Jdt 16:17; Sir 29:10; *2 Apoc. Bar.* 23:7
Jas 5:4	Deut 24:14–15; Mal 3:5; Gen 4:10; Ps 18:6; Isa 5:9; Tob 4:14; *Ps.-Phocylides* 19–21
Jas 5:5	Jer 12:3; 25:34
Jas 5:6	Wis 2:10, 12, 19
Jas 5:7	Deut 11:14; Jer 5:24; Joel 2:23
Jas 5:10	4 Macc 9:8
Jas 5:11	Dan 12:12; Exod 34:6; Ps 103:8; 111:4; *T. Job* 1:5
Jas 5:12	*2 Enoch* 49:1
Jas 5:13	*Pss. Sol.* 3:2
Jas 5:17	1 Kgs 17:1
Jas 5:18	1 Kgs 18:42–45
Jas 5:20	Prov 10:12

1 Peter

1 Pet 1:3	Sir 16:12
1 Pet 1:7	Job 23:10; Ps 66:10; Prov 17:3; Isa 48:10; Zech 13:9; Mal 3:3; Sir 2:5
1 Pet 1:11	Psalm 22; Isaiah 53
1 Pet 1:12	*1 Enoch* 1:2; 16:3; *2 Enoch* 24:3
1 Pet 1:16	Lev 11:44, 45; 19:2; 20:7
1 Pet 1:17	Ps 89:26; Isa 64:8; Jer 3:19; Wis 14:3; Sir 23:4; 2 Chr 19:7; Ps 28:4; 62:12; Prov 24:12; Isa 59:18; Jer 17:10
1 Pet 1:23	Dan 6:26
1 Pet 1:24–25	Isa 40:6–8
1 Pet 2:3	LXX Ps 33:9 (34:8)
1 Pet 2:4–8	LXX Ps 117:22 (118:22); Isa 28:16; 8:14
1 Pet 2:5	Exod 19:6; Isa 61:6
1 Pet 2:9	Isa 43:20; Exod 19:5–6; LXX 23:22; Isa 43:21; Deut 4:20; 7:6; 14:2; Isa 43:21; 9:2; *Jub.* 16:19
1 Pet 2:10	Hos 2:23
1 Pet 2:11	Ps 39:12; *Apoc. Elijah* 1:17
1 Pet 2:12	Isa 10:3
1 Pet 2:17	Prov 24:21
1 Pet 2:19	*2 Enoch* 50:3–4; 51:3
1 Pet 2:22	Isa 53:9
1 Pet 2:23	Isa 53:7
1 Pet 2:24	Isa 53:4, 12, 5
1 Pet 2:25	Isa 53:6; Ezek 34:5–6; Wis 1:6
1 Pet 3:6	Gen 18:12
1 Pet 3:10–12	LXX Ps 33:13–17 (34:12–16)
1 Pet 3:14–15	Isa 8:12–13
1 Pet 3:14	*2 Enoch* 51:3
1 Pet 3:19	*1 Enoch* 9:10; 10:11–15
1 Pet 3:20	Genesis 6–7
1 Pet 4:7	*2 Apoc. Bar.* 23:7
1 Pet 4:8	Prov 10:12
1 Pet 4:14	Ps 89:50–51; Isa 11:2
1 Pet 4:17	Jer 25:29; Ezek 9:6
1 Pet 4:18	LXX Prov 11:31
1 Pet 4:19	Ps 31:5; 2 Macc 1:27
1 Pet 5:4	*2 Apoc. Bar.* 15:8; *Apoc. Elijah* 2:7
1 Pet 5:5	LXX Prov 3:34
1 Pet 5:6	Job 22:29
1 Pet 5:7	Ps 55:22; Wis 12:13

2 Peter

2 Pet 1:19	4 Ezra 12:43
2 Pet 2:2	Isa 52:5; Wis 5:6
2 Pet 2:4	*1 Enoch* 10:4–5, 11–14; 91:15; *2 Enoch* 7:1; *Life of Adam and Eve (Vita)* 12:2
2 Pet 2:5	Gen 8:18; *Jub.* 7:35
2 Pet 2:6	Gen 19:24
2 Pet 2:7	Gen 19:1–16; Wis 10:6; 3 Macc 2:13
2 Pet 2:15	Num 22:7

2 Pet 2:16	Num 22:28
2 Pet 2:22	Prov 26:11
2 Pet 3:3	*T. Dan* 5:4; *1 Enoch* 72:2
2 Pet 3:5	Gen 1:6–9; *2 Enoch* 33:4; 47:4
2 Pet 3:6	Gen 7:11–21; *1 Enoch* 83:3–5
2 Pet 3:8	Ps 90:4; *Jub.* 4:30
2 Pet 3:9	Hab 2:3; Sir 35:19; *2 Apoc. Bar.* 21:21; 48:40
2 Pet 3:13	Isa 65:17; 66:22; 60:21; *Jub.* 1:29; *1 Enoch* 72:2
2 Pet 3:18	Sir 18:10

1 John

1 John 1:1	Gen 1:1; *Tg. Ps.-J.* Gen 3:24
1 John 1:7	Isa 2:5
1 John 1:9	Ps 32:5; Prov 28:13
1 John 2:10	Ps 119:165
1 John 2:12	Ps 25:11
1 John 2:15	*Apoc. Elijah* 1:2
1 John 2:16	27:20
1 John 2:17	Wis 5:15
1 John 2:27	Jer 31:34
1 John 3:5	Isa 53:9
1 John 3:12	Gen 4:8
1 John 3:17	Deut 15:7–8
1 John 4:6	*Jub.* 8:14
1 John 5:3	Deut 30:11
1 John 5:16–17	*T. Iss.* 7:1
1 John 5:16	*Jub.* 21:22
1 John 5:21	Ep Jer 72

3 John

3 John 11	*Ps.-Phocylides* 77

Jude

Jude 3	*1 Enoch* 10:4
Jude 4	*1 Enoch* 48:10
Jude 5	Exod 12:51; Num 14:29–30, 35
Jude 6	*1 Enoch* 10:6, 12; 12:4; 22:11; *2 Enoch* 7:1
Jude 7	Gen 19:4–25; *T. Naph.* 3:4
Jude 9	*As. Mos.* (according to Clement, Origen, and Didymus); Dan 10:13, 21; 12:1; Zech 3:2; *Life of Adam and Eve (Vita)* 15:3
Jude 11	Gen 4:3–8; Num 22:7; 31:16; 16:19–35
Jude 12	Ezek 34:8
Jude 13	Isa 57:20; Wis 14:1; *1 Enoch* 18:15–16; 21:5–6; *2 Enoch* 40:13
Jude 14–16	*Life of Adam and Eve (Vita)* 51:9
Jude 14–15	*1 Enoch* 1:9
Jude 14	*1 Enoch* 60:8; 93:3; Deut 33:2; Zech 14:5; *Jub.* 7:39
Jude 16	*1 Enoch* 5:4
Jude 22–23	*T. Naph.* 3:3
Jude 23	Amos 4:11; Zech 3:2

Revelation

Rev 1:1	Dan 2:28, 29, 45; *2 Apoc. Bar.* 10:3
Rev 1:4, 8	Exod 3:14; Isa 41:4
Rev 1:5	Ps 89:27; Ps 130:8; Isa 40:2
Rev 1:6	Exod 19:6; Isa 61:6
Rev 1:7	Dan 7:13; Zech 12:10, 12, 14
Rev 1:8	LXX Amos 3:13; 4:13; *2 Apoc. Bar.* 21:9; *T. Isaac* 6:34; *Orphica* 39; *Aristobulus* frg. 4:5
Rev 1:13–15	*Apoc. Zeph.* 6:12
Rev 1:13	Dan 7:13; LXX Ezek 9:2, 11; Dan 10:5
Rev 1:14–15	Dan 10:6
Rev 1:14	Dan 7:9; *2 Enoch* 1:5; *Apoc. Abr.* 11:3
Rev 1:15	Ezek 1:24; 43:2
Rev 1:16	Isa 49:2; *2 Enoch* 1:5
Rev 1:17	Isa 44:6; 48:12; *4 Ezra* 10:30
Rev 1:18	Sir 18:1
Rev 1:19	LXX Isa 48:6; Dan 2:28, 29, 45; *2 Enoch* 39:2
Rev 2:7	Gen 2:9; LXX Gen 2:8; LXX Ezek 28:13; 31:8, 9; *4 Ezra* 8:52; *2 Apoc. Bar.* 4:7; *1 Enoch* 25:5; *2 Enoch* 8:3
Rev 2:10	2 Macc 13:14; *2 Apoc. Bar.* 15:8
Rev 2:12	Wis 18:15–16
Rev 2:17	2 Macc 2:4–8; *2 Apoc. Bar.* 29:8
Rev 2:18	*Apoc. Zeph.* 6:13
Rev 2:26–27	Ps 2:8, 9; *Pss. Sol.* 17:23–24
Rev 3:4–5	*2 Enoch* 22:9
Rev 3:7	Isa 22:22; Job 12:14
Rev 3:12	*Apoc. Elijah* 1:9
Rev 3:18	*Pss. Sol.* 17:43; *2 Enoch* 22:9
Rev 4:1–11	*T. Levi* 3:9
Rev 4:1–2	*2 Enoch* 20:1
Rev 4:1	*2 Apoc. Bar.* 10:3; 22:2; 23:7
Rev 4:2, 9, 10	1 Kgs 22:19; Isa 6:1; Ezek 1:26–27; Sir 1:8
Rev 4:2	*2 Enoch* 20:3
Rev 4:2–3	*1 Enoch* 14:18
Rev 4:4	*2 Enoch* 4:1; 22:9; *Apoc. Elijah* 4:10
Rev 4:6–7	Ezek 1:5–10, 22; 10:14
Rev 4:6	*2 Enoch* 3:3
Rev 4:7	*T. Naph.* 5:6
Rev 4:8	Isa 6:2; Ezek 1:18; 10:12; Isa 6:3; LXX Amos 3:13; Isa 41:4; Exod 3:14; *Apoc. Elijah* 5:2
Rev 4:11	3 Macc 2:3; Wis 1:14; Sir 18:1
Rev 5:1, 7	1 Kgs 22:19; Isa 6:1; Ezek 1:26–27; Sir 1:8
Rev 5:1	*2 Enoch* 20:3; *4 Bar.* 3:10
Rev 5:7	Sir 1:8
Rev 5:11	Dan 7:10; *1 Enoch* 14:22; 40:1; *Apoc. Zeph.* 4:1–2
Rev 5:13	1 Kgs 22:19; Isa 6:1; Ezek 1:26–27; Sir 1:8
Rev 5:20	*Jub.* 16:19
Rev 6:10	*Sib. Or.* 3:313
Rev 6:11	*2 Apoc. Bar.* 23:5; *2 Enoch* 22:9
Rev 6:12	*Apoc. Elijah* 3:8; *Ap. Ezek.* frg. 2
Rev 6:14	*Sib. Or.* 3:82

Rev 6:16	Hos 10:8; 1 Kgs 22:19; Isa 6:1; Ezek 1:26–27; Sir 1:8; *Apoc. Elijah* 2:34
Rev 6:17	*Apoc. Zeph.* 12:6
Rev 7:3, 13, 14	*Apoc. Elijah* 1:9
Rev 7:3	Ezek 9:4; CD 19:12–13; *Pss. Sol.* 15:6
Rev 7:9	2 Macc 10:7; *2 Enoch* 22:9
Rev 7:10	1 Kgs 22:19; Isa 6:1; Ezek 1:26–27; Sir 1:8
Rev 7:15	1 Kgs 22:19; Isa 6:1; Ezek 1:26–27; Sir 1:8
Rev 7:16	Isa 49:10; *Apoc. Elijah* 5:6
Rev 7:17	Ps 23:1; Ezek 34:23; Ps 23:2; Isa 49:10; Jer 2:13; Isa 25:8
Rev 8:1	Wis 18:14
Rev 8:2	Tob 12:15; *Life of Adam and Eve (Apoc.)* 22:3
Rev 8:3	Tob 12:12
Rev 8:7	Exod 9:23–25; Ezek 38:22; Wis 16:22; Sir 39:29
Rev 8:8	*1 Enoch* 18:13; 21:3
Rev 8:10	*1 Enoch* 86:1; *Sib. Or.* 5:155
Rev 8:12	*Life of Adam and Eve (Apoc.)* 36:3
Rev 9:1	*Sib. Or.* 5:155; *2 Enoch* 42:1
Rev 9:2	4 Ezra 7:36
Rev 9:3	Exod 10:12, 15; Wis 1:14; 16:9
Rev 9:4	Ezek 9:4; CD 19:12–13; *Pss. Sol.* 15:6
Rev 9:6	*Apoc. Elijah* 2:5, 32
Rev 9:13–18	*Sib. Or.* 5:93–94
Rev 9:20	Ps 115:4–7; 135:15–17; Dan 5:23
Rev 10:5–6	Deut 32:40; Dan 12:7; Gen 14:19, 22; Exod 20:11
Rev 11:8	*Apoc. Elijah* 4:13
Rev 11:15	*2 Enoch* 1:5
Rev 11:19	2 Macc 2:4–8
Rev 12:1–3	*2 Apoc. Bar.* 24:4
Rev 12:1	*T. Naph.* 5:1
Rev 12:5	Isa 7:14; 66:7; Ps 2:9
Rev 12:7–12	*Life of Adam and Eve (Vita)* 14:1
Rev 12:9	*Lives of Prophets* 12:13; *Life of Adam and Eve (Vita)* 12:1
Rev 12:11	*T. Jud.* 25:4
Rev 12:17	*Lives of Prophets* 12:13
Rev 13:1	4 Ezra 11:1
Rev 13:10	Jer 15:2; 43:11
Rev 13:14	*1 Enoch* 54:6
Rev 14:1	Ezek 9:4; CD 19:12–13; *Pss. Sol.* 15:6; *Apoc. Elijah* 1:9
Rev 14:10	Gen 19:24; Ps 11:6; Ezek 38:22; 3 Macc 2:5
Rev 14:15	*1 Enoch* 10:13
Rev 15:1	*2 Apoc. Bar.* 27:4
Rev 15:2	*2 Enoch* 3:3
Rev 15:3	Jer 10:10 (Theodotion); Tob 13:7, 11; *1 Enoch* 9:4; 25:5; 27:3
Rev 16:5	*1 Enoch* 66:2; *2 Enoch* 19:4
Rev 16:16	4 Ezra 13:34
Rev 17:9	*1 Enoch* 21:3
Rev 17:14	Deut 10:17; Dan 2:47; 2 Macc 13:4; 3 Macc 5:35; *1 Enoch* 9:4
Rev 18:2	Isa 13:21; 34:11; Jer 50:39; Bar 4:35
Rev 18:11	*Apoc. Elijah* 2:31
Rev 19:1	Tob 13:18; *Pss. Sol.* 8:2

Rev 19:4	1 Kgs 22:19; Isa 6:1; Ezek 1:26–27; Sir 1:8; *2 Enoch* 20:3
Rev 19:10	*Apoc. Zeph.* 6:15
Rev 19:11	2 Macc 3:25; 11:8
Rev 19:12	*2 Enoch* 1:5
Rev 19:15	Ps 2:9
Rev 19:16	Deut 10:17; Dan 2:47; 2 Macc 13:4; 3 Macc 5:35; *1 Enoch* 9:4
Rev 19:19	4 Ezra 13:43
Rev 19:20	*1 Enoch* 10:6; *2 Enoch* 10:2; *Apoc. Zeph.* 6:2
Rev 20:1	*2 Enoch* 42:1
Rev 20:2	*T. Jud.* 25:3
Rev 20:3	*1 Enoch* 18:16; 21:6
Rev 20:4	*T. Jud.* 25:4; *Apoc. Elijah* 1:9; 5:39
Rev 20:7–10	*Sib. Or.* 3:319
Rev 20:8	Ezek 38:2
Rev 20:10–15	*2 Enoch* 10:2
Rev 20:10	Gen 19:24; Ps 11:6; Ezek 38:22; 3 Macc 2:5; *1 Enoch* 10:13
Rev 20:11–12	Dan 7:9–10
Rev 20:12–13	Ps 28:4; 62:12; Prov 24:12; Isa 59:18; Jer 17:10; Sir 16:12
Rev 20:12	4 Ezra 6:20; *2 Apoc. Bar.* 24:1
Rev 20:13	*1 Enoch* 51:1; 61:5
Rev 20:14	*T. Jud.* 25:3
Rev 21:1	*1 Enoch* 72:3; *Apoc. Elijah* 5:38
Rev 21:3	Lev 26:11–12; 2 Chr 6:18; Ezek 37:27; Zech 2:10; *2 Enoch* 20:3; *Pr. Joseph* frg. A
Rev 21:4	Isa 25:8; *2 Apoc. Bar.* 73:2–3; *2 Enoch* 65:9
Rev 21:5–22:5	*T. Levi* 5:1
Rev 21:5	1 Kgs 22:19; Isa 6:1; Ezek 1:26–27; Sir 1:8
Rev 21:6	Isa 44:6; 48:12; 55:1; Ps 36:9; Jer 2:13
Rev 21:7	2 Sam 7:14
Rev 21:8	Gen 19:24; Ps 11:6; Ezek 38:22; 3 Macc 2:5; *2 Enoch* 10:2, 5
Rev 21:9–21	4 Ezra 10:27
Rev 21:12–13	Exod 28:21; Ezek 48:30–35
Rev 21:15	Ezek 40:3, 5
Rev 21:16–17	Ezek 48:16, 17
Rev 21:19–20	Tob 13:17
Rev 21:24	Isa 60:3, 5; *Pss. Sol.* 17:34
Rev 21:26	Ps 72:10–11; *Pss. Sol.* 17:34
Rev 22:1	*1 Enoch* 14:19
Rev 22:2, 14, 19	Gen 2:9; 3:22; Ezek 47:12
Rev 22:2	*T. Levi* 18:11; 4 Ezra 8:52; *Pss. Sol.* 14:3; *1 Enoch* 25:5; *2 Enoch* 8:2; *Life of Adam and Eve (Apoc.)* 9:3
Rev 22:4	*T. Levi* 18:11; 4 Ezra 7:98
Rev 22:6	Dan 2:28, 29, 45
Rev 22:8–9	*Apoc. Zeph.* 6:15
Rev 22:12	4 Ezra 7:99
Rev 22:13	Isa 44:6; 48:12
Rev 22:14	*1 Enoch* 25:5
Rev 22:16	Isa 11:1, 10; Num 24:17; *Tgs.* Num 24:17
Rev 22:18–19	Deut 4:2; 12:32; *2 Enoch* 48:7
Rev 22:19	*T. Levi* 18:11

APPENDIX THREE

PARALLELS BETWEEN NEW TESTAMENT GOSPELS AND PSEUDEPIGRAPHAL GOSPELS

This appendix lists parallels between the four NT Gospels and a select number of the pseudepigraphal gospels.

Mark

Mark 1:4–6	*Gos. Eb.* §2 (Epiphanius *Against Heresies* 30.13.4–5)
Mark 1:9–11	*Gos. Eb.* §4 (Epiphanius *Against Heresies* 30.13.7–8; cf. Matt 3:14–15; Luke 3:22); GHeb §2 (Jerome *Comm. Isaiah* 4 [on Isa 11:2]); *Gos. Naz.* 2 (Jerome *Against the Pelagians* 3.2)
Mark 1:16–20	*Gos. Eb.* §1 (Epiphanius *Against Heresies* 30.13.2–3)
Mark 1:40–45	PEger2 §2
Mark 2:15–17	POxy1224 §1; Justin Martyr *Apology* 1.15.8
Mark 2:18–10	*Gos. Thom.* §27, §104
Mark 2:21–22	*Gos. Thom.* §47
Mark 3:1–6	*Gos. Naz.* §10 (Jerome *Comm. Matthew* 2 [on Matt 12:13])
Mark 3:23–27	*Gos. Thom.* §35
Mark 3:28–30	*Gos. Thom.* §44
Mark 3:31–35	*Gos. Thom.* §99; *Gos. Eb.* §5 (Epiphanius *Against Heresies* 30.13.5)
Mark 4:2–9	*Gos. Thom.* §9
Mark 4:10–12	*Ap. Jas.* 7:1–10
Mark 4:13–20	*Ap. Jas.* 8:10–17
Mark 4:21	*Gos. Thom.* §33
Mark 4:22	POxy654 §5; *Gos. Thom.* §5, §6
Mark 4:24–25	*Gos. Thom.* §41
Mark 4:26–29	*Gos. Thom.* §21; *Ap. Jas.* 12:20–31
Mark 4:30–32	*Gos. Thom.* §20
Mark 6:4	POxy1 §6; *Gos. Thom.* §31
Mark 7:6–8	PEger2 §3
Mark 7:14–15	*Gos. Thom.* §14
Mark 8:27–30	*Gos. Thom.* §13
Mark 8:31–33	*Ap. Jas.* 5:31–6:11

Mark 8:34	*Gos. Thom.* §55, §101
Mark 9:40	POxy1224 §2
Mark 10:13–16	*Gos. Thom.* §22
Mark 10:17–22	*Gos. Naz.* §16 (Origen *Comm. Matthew* 15.14 [on Matt 19:16–30])
Mark 10:28–30	*Ap. Jas.* 4:22–37
Mark 10:31	POxy654 §4; *Gos. Thom.* §4
Mark 11:22–23	*Gos. Thom.* §48, §106
Mark 12:1–12	*Gos. Thom.* §§65–66
Mark 12:13–17	*Gos. Thom.* §100; PEger2 §3; *Gos. Thom.* §100
Mark 12:31	*Gos. Thom.* §25
Mark 12:34	*Gos. Thom.* §82
Mark 13:21	*Gos. Thom.* §113
Mark 14:12	*Gos. Eb.* §7 (Epiphanius *Against Heresies* 30.22.4)
Mark 14:27–30	Fayyum Fragment
Mark 14:58	*Gos. Thom.* §71
Mark 14:65	*Gos. Pet.* 3 §9
Mark 15:1–5	*Acts Pil.* 3:2
Mark 15:6–15	*Acts Pil.* 4:4–5; 9:4–5
Mark 15:7	*Gos. Naz.* §20 (Jerome *Comm. Matthew* 4 [on Matt 27:16])
Mark 15:16–20	*Gos. Pet.* 2 §5–3 §9; *Acts Pil.* 10:1
Mark 15:22–32	*Acts Pil.* 10:1
Mark 15:33–39	*Gos. Pet.* 5 §§15–20; *Acts Pil.* 11:1
Mark 15:38	*Gos. Naz.* §21 (Jerome *Epistle to the Hedybiam* 120.8)
Mark 15:40–41	*Acts Pil.* 11:2–3a
Mark 15:42–47	*Gos. Pet.* 2 §3–5; 6 §§21–24; *Acts Pil.* 11:3b
Mark 16:1–8	*Gos. Pet.* 9 §35—13 §57; *Acts Pil.* 13:1–3
Mark 16:14–18	*Acts Pil.* 14:1

Q (Luke/Matthew)

Luke 3:7–9 = Matt 3:7–10	*Ap. Jas.* 9:24–10:6
Luke 4:5 = Matt 4:8	*Gos. Heb.* §3 (Origen *Comm. John* 2.12.87 [on John 1:3])
Luke 6:20 = Matt 5:3	*Gos. Thom.* §54
Luke 6:21 = Matt 5:6	*Gos. Thom.* §69b
Luke 6:22 = Matt 5:11	*Gos. Thom.* §68
Luke 6:27–28 = Matt 5:44	POxy1224 §2
Luke 6:30 = Matt 5:42	*Gos. Thom.* §95
Luke 6:31 = Matt 7:12	POxy654 §6; *Gos. Thom.* §6; cf. Tob 4:15
Luke 6:35 = Matt 5:44	POxy1224 §2
Luke 6:39 = Matt 15:14	*Gos. Thom.* §34
Luke 6:41–42 = Matt 7:1–5	POxy1 §1; *Gos. Thom.* §26
Luke 6:43–45 = Matt 7:16; 12:33–35	*Gos. Thom.* §45, §43
Luke 7:24–25 = Matt 11:7–8	*Gos. Thom.* §78
Luke 7:28 = Matt 11:11	*Gos. Thom.* §46
Luke 8:16–17; 12:2 = Matt 10:26	POxy654 §5; *Gos. Thom.* §5, §6
Luke 9:58 = Matt 8:20	*Gos. Thom.* §86
Luke 10:2 = Matt 9:37–38	*Gos. Thom.* §73

Luke 10:3 = Matt 10:16	POxy655 §2; *Gos. Thom.* §39; *Gos. Eg.* [?] frg. 3
Luke 10:7–8 =	*Gos. Thom.* §14b
Matt 10:10b–11	
Luke 10:21 = Matt 11:25	POxy654 §3; *Gos. Thom.* §4
Luke 11:3 = Matt 6:11	*Gos. Naz.* §5 (Jerome *Comm. Matthew* 1 [on Matt 6:11]);
	Gos. Heb. §4
Luke 11:9–13 =	
Matt 7:7–11	POxy654 §2; *Gos. Thom.* §2, §92, §94
Luke 11:33 = Matt 5:15	*Gos. Thom.* §33
Luke 11:34–36 =	*Gos. Thom.* §24
Matt 6:22–23	
Luke 11:39–40 =	
Matt 23:25–26	*Gos. Thom.* §89
Luke 12:3 = Matt 10:27	POxy1 §8; *Gos. Thom.* §33
Luke 12:12–31 =	POxy655 §1a; *Gos. Thom.* §36
Matt 6:25–34	
Luke 12:33 =	*Gos. Thom.* §76
Matt 6:19–20	
Luke 12:39–40 =	*Gos. Thom.* §21, §103
Matt 24:43–44	
Luke 12:49–53; 14:25–27	*Gos. Thom.* §10, §16, §55, §101
= Matt 10:34–38	
Luke 12:54–56 =	*Gos. Thom.* §91
Matt 16:2–3	
Luke 13:20–21 =	*Gos. Thom.* §96
Matt 13:33	
Luke 13:24 =	*T. Abr.* (A) 11:1–12
Matt 7:13–14	
Luke 14:15–24 =	*Gos. Thom.* §64
Matt 22:1–14	
Luke 15:3–7 =	*Gos. Thom.* §107
Matt 18:12–14	
Luke 16:13 = Matt 6:24	*Gos. Thom.* §47
Luke 16:17 = Matt 5:18	*Gos. Thom.* §11
Luke 17:3–4 = Matt 18:15	*Gos. Naz.* §15 (Jerome *Against the Pelagians* 3.2)
Luke 17:34–35 =	*Gos. Thom.* §61a
Matt 24:40–41	
Luke 19:11–27 =	*Gos. Naz.* §18 (Eusebius *Theophania* 22 [on Matt
Matt 25:14–30	25:14–15])

"M" (Material special to Matthew)

Matt 1:18–25	*Prot. Jas.* 14:1–2
Matt 2:1–12	*Prot. Jas.* 21:1–4
Mat 2:13	PCairo §1 §2
Matt 2:15	*Gos. Naz.* (Jerome *On Men of Distinction* 3)
Matt 2:16–18	*Prot. Jas.* 22:1–2
Matt 2:23	*Gos. Naz.* (Jerome *On Men of Distinction* 3)
Matt 5:10	*Gos. Thom.* §69a
Matt 5:14	POxy1 §7; *Gos. Thom.* §32
Matt 5:17	*Gos. Eb.* §6 (Epiphanius *Against Heresies* 30.16.4–5)
Matt 6:2–4	POxy654 §6; *Gos. Thom.* §6, §14
Matt 6:3	*Gos. Thom.* §62

Matt 7:6	*Gos. Thom.* §93
Matt 11:30	*Gos. Thom.* §90
Matt 13:24–30	*Gos. Thom.* §57
Matt 13:44	*Gos. Thom.* §109
Matt 13:45–46	*Gos. Thom.* §76
Matt 13:47–50	*Gos. Thom.* §8
Matt 15:13	*Gos. Thom.* §40
Matt 18:20	POxy1 §5; *Gos. Thom.* §30
Matt 23:13	POxy655 §2; *Gos. Thom.* §39, §102
Matt 27:16	*Gos. Naz.* §20 (Jerome *Comm. Matthew* 4 [on Matt 27:16])
Matt 27:24–25	*Gos. Pet.* 1 §1–2; *Acts Pil.* 9:4–5
Matt 27:62–66	*Gos. Pet.* 8 §28—9 §34

"L" (Material special to Luke)

Luke 1:5–7	*Gos. Eb.* §3 (Epiphanius *Against Heresies* 30.13.6)
Luke 1:8–11	*Prot. Jas.* 8:3
Luke 1:20	*Prot. Jas.* 10:2
Luke 1:21	*Prot. Jas.* 23:1–24:2
Luke 1:26–38	*Prot. Jas.* 11:1–3
Luke 1:36	PCairo §2
Luke 1:39–56	*Prot. Jas.* 12:2–3
Luke 1:80	*Infan. Thom.* 19:5b
Luke 2:1–6	*Prot. Jas.* 17:1–3
Luke 2:7	*Prot. Jas.* 22:2
Luke 2:19	*Infan. Thom.* 11:2c
Luke 2:26	*Prot. Jas.* 24:4
Luke 2:46–52	*Infan. Thom.* 19:1–5
Luke 6:46	PEger2 §3
Luke 11:27–28	*Gos. Thom.* §79
Luke 12:13–14	*Gos. Thom.* §72
Luke 12:16–21	*Gos. Thom.* §63
Luke 17:4	*Gos. Naz.* §15 (Jerome *Against the Pelagians* 3.2)
Luke 17:21	POxy654 §3; *Gos. Thom.* §3
Luke 22:43–44	*Gos. Naz.* §32 (Hennecke-Schneemelcher, 1.152)
Luke 23:34	*Acts Pil.* 10:1b; *Gos. Naz.* §24 (Haimo of Auxerre *Comm. Isaias* [on Isa 53:2]); *Gos. Naz.* §35 (Hennecke-Schneemelcher, 1.153)
Luke 23:39–43	*Gos. Pet.* 4 §§10–14; *Acts Pil.* 10:2
Luke 23:46–48	*Acts Pil.* 11:1
Luke 23:48	*Gos. Pet.* 7 §25
Luke 24:30–31	*Gos. Heb.* §7 (Jerome *On Men of Distinction* 2)

John

John 1:9	POxy655 §24; *Gos. Thom.* §24
John 1:14	POxy1 §28; *Gos. Thom.* §28
John 4:13–15	*Gos. Thom.* §13
John 7:32–36	POxy655 §38; *Gos. Thom.* §38
John 8:12; 9:5	*Gos. Thom.* §77
John 18:31	*Acts Pil.* 4:4
John 18:33–38	*Acts Pil.* 3:2
John 19:12	*Acts Pil.* 9:1b

John 19:20   Acts Pil. 10:1b
John 20:5, 11–12   Gos. Pet. 13 §55
John 20:29   Ap. Jas. 8:3

SOURCES AND BIBLIOGRAPHY

Acts Pil.   Acts of Pilate
Composed in the second or third century, it claims to have been written in Hebrew by Nicodemus. Eventually it was incorporated into the *Gospel of Nicodemus*. It is extant in Greek. Cameron, 163–65; Hennecke-Schneemelcher, 1.444–70.

Ap. Jas.   Apocryphon of James
The *Apocryphon of James* was found at Nag Hammadi as the second tractate in Codex I (NHC I,2). It comprises a series of sayings of the risen Jesus, which, it claims, James wrote down in Hebrew. It was composed in Greek, probably in the second century. Koester, 2.224–25; Cameron, 55–57; Robinson, 29–37; Williams, 13–53.

Fayyum Fragment
This document is a third-century Greek fragment. It is so brief (fewer than twenty legible words) that its derivation is uncertain (an apocryphal gospel?). Hennecke-Schneemelcher, 1.115–16.

Gos. Eb.   Gospel of the Ebionites
Epiphanius (fourth century) preserves several fragments of a gospel in circulation among Greek-speaking Jewish Christians (second and third century). Epiphanius erroneously calls it the Hebrew Gospel. It may have originated as early as the second century. Koester, 2.202–3; Cameron, 103–4; Hennecke-Schneemelcher, 1.153–58.

Gos. Eg.   Gospel of the Egyptians
There is one Latin fragment from Ps.-Titum that reads: "The Lord himself said, 'Hear me, you whom I have chosen as lambs, and fear not the wolves.' " This *Gospel of the Egyptians* is not to be confused with the Coptic Gnostic *Gospel of the Egyptians* (NHC III,2 and IV,2). Kloppenborg, 67, 239.

Gos. Heb.   Gospel of the Hebrews
The Gospel of the Hebrews was composed in the second half of the first century or the first half of the second. Only fragments are extant in the church fathers. Koester, 2.223–24; Cameron, 83–85; Hennecke-Schneemelcher, 1.158–65.

Gos. Naz.   Gospel of the Nazoreans
The *Gospel of the Nazoreans* is an expansion of the Gospel of Matthew. Fragments are preserved in the church fathers and in the margins of NT MSS. Koester, 2.201–2; Cameron, 97–98; Hennecke-Schneemelcher, 1.139–53.

Gos. Pet.   Gospel of Peter

The *Gospel of Peter* has survived as a large Greek fragment dating to the eighth century. Other fragments found at Oxyrhynchus, which date to the second or third century, may be related to this apocryphal gospel. The writing has been versified in two ways: chaps. 1–14 and vv. 1–60. Accordingly, chap. 1 begins with v. 1, but chap. 2 begins with v. 3, chap. 4 with v. 10, etc. Koester, 2.162–63; Cameron, 76–78; Hennecke-Schneemelcher, 1.179–87.

Gos. Thom.   Gospel of Thomas

The *Gospel of Thomas* comprises 114 sayings. It was originally written in Greek, perhaps as early as the late first century. Other than fragments from Oxyrhynchus (POxy 1, 654, 655) the work survives in the fourth-century Coptic Gnostic library found at Nag Hammadi (NHC II,2). Koester, 2.150–54; Cameron, 23–25; Robinson, 124–38; Hennecke-Schneemelcher, 1.278–307.

Infan. Thom.   Infancy Gospel of Thomas

The *Infancy Gospel* tells several imaginative tales of Jesus' boyhood. It may have been written as early as the second century. It is extant in a sixth-century Syriac MS and in several Greek MSS dating from the fourteenth to the sixteenth centuries. It has affinities with the Gospel of Luke. Cameron, 122–24; Hennecke-Schneemelcher, 1.388–401.

PCairo   Papyrus Cairensis 10 735

This fragment, perhaps originally part of a gospel, describes the flight of the holy family to Egypt. Only a few sentences can be restored with any confidence. Hennecke-Schneemelcher, 1.114–15.

PEger2   Papyrus Egerton 2

This papyrus contains a fragment of an unknown gospel, perhaps dating to the early second century. Koester, 2.181–83; Hennecke-Schneemelcher, 1.94–97.

POxy1   Oxyrhynchus Papyrus 1

POxy 1 dates to the end of the second century and contains sayings of Jesus that approximate *Gos. Thom.* §§26–33 and a portion of §77; Hennecke-Schneemelcher, 1.104–10.

POxy654   Oxyrhynchus Papyrus 654

POxy 654 dates to the third century and contains sayings of Jesus that approximate *Gos. Thom.* §1–5. Hennecke-Schneemelcher, 1.97–104.

POxy655   Oxyrhynchus Papyrus 655

POxy 655 dates to the first half of the third century and contains sayings of Jesus that approximate *Gos. Thom.* §§36–40. Hennecke-Schneemelcher, 1.110–13.

POxy1224   *Oxyrhynchus Papyrus 1224*

POxy 1224 dates to the beginning of the fourth century. It consists of fragments of an unknown apocryphal gospel. Hennecke-Schneemelcher, 1.113–14.

Prot. Jas.   *Protevangelium of James*

The *Protevangelium*, dating from late second century or early third, is an infancy gospel that tells the story of the birth of Mary and the birth of Jesus. It is called "protevangelium" implying that it is the first part of the gospel, the part that precedes the canonical gospel story. Cameron, 107–9; Hennecke-Schneemelcher, 1.370–88.

Sec. Gos. Mark   *Secret Gospel of Mark*

The *Secret Gospel of Mark* appears only in a fragment of a letter of Clement of Alexandria, discovered by Morton Smith in 1958. In the fragment Clement charges that the Carpocratians are misusing and "falsifying" what has been entrusted only to those being perfected. Scholars debate the provenance of the fragment; some think it may be early second century (e.g., Cameron), but others disagree: "It is possible that Clement's letter, along with the quotations of the Secret Gospel of Mark, which it contains, is a forgery, perhaps even [being written by] a twentieth-century forger" (see Quesnell).

T. Abr.   *Testament of Abraham*

The *Testament of Abraham* is not one of the pseudepigraphal gospels; rather, it is part of the OT Pseudepigrapha. Abraham's vision of the narrow and broad ways parallels Jesus' saying in Q (Luke 13:24 = Matt 7:13–14) so closely that it seemed appropriate to note it. Kloppenborg, 153.

GENERAL BIBLIOGRAPHY: R. E. Brown, "The Relation of 'the Secret Gospel of Mark' to the Fourth Gospel," *CBQ* 36 (1974) 466–85; R. Cameron, *The Other Gospels: Non-Canonical Gospel Texts* (Philadelphia: Westminster, 1982); R. W. Funk, *New Gospel Parallels: Volume One, the Synoptic Gospels* (Philadelphia: Fortress, 1985); idem, *New Gospel Parallels: Volume Two, John and the Other Gospels* (Philadelphia: Fortress, 1985); E. Hennecke and W. Schneemelcher, *The New Testament Apocrypha*, vol. 1: *Gospels and Related Writings* (Philadelphia: Westminster, 1963); J. S. Kloppenborg, *Q Parallels* (Sonoma: Polebridge, 1987) [ET and original languages]; H. Koester, *Introduction to the New Testament* (2 vols.; Philadelphia: Fortress, 1982); Q. Quesnell, "The Mar Saba Clementine: A Question of Evidence," *CBQ* 37 (1975) 48–67; J. M. Robinson, ed., *The Nag Hammadi Library in English* (San Francisco: Harper & Row, 1977; 3d ed. 1988); F. E. Williams, "NHC I,2: The Apocryphon of James," in H. W. Attridge, ed., *Nag Hammadi Codex I (The Jung Codex): Introduction, Texts, Translations, Indices* (NHS 22; Leiden: Brill, 1985) 13–53.

APPENDIX FOUR

JESUS' PARABLES AND THE PARABLES OF THE RABBIS

H. K. McArthur and R. M. Johnston have identified more than two dozen parables of Jesus that closely parallel rabbinic parables (most are tannaic). With some modification and expansion they are as follows:

1. The Sower [or the Four Soils] (Mark 4:3–8; Matt 13:3–8; Luke 8:5–8)
   The Four Types of Students (*m. 'Abot* 5:15) [anonymous]
2. The Mustard Seed (Mark 4:30–32; Matt 13:31–32; Luke 13:18–19)
   The Seed under Hard Ground (*b. Ta'an.* 4a) [anonymous]
3. The Wicked Tenants (Mark 12:1–11; Matt 21:33–44; Luke 20:9–18)
   The Unworthy Tenants (*Sipre Deut.* §312 [on Deut 32:9]) [anonymous]
4. Paying a Debt and Settling a Dispute (Matt 5:25–26; Luke 12:57–59)
   Paying a Debt and Settling a Dispute (*Pesiq. Rab Kah.* 18.6) [anonymous]
5. Wise Builder and Foolish Builder (Matt 7:24–27; Luke 6:47–49)
   Wise Builder and Foolish Builder (*'Abot R. Nat.* A 24:1–4) [R. Elisha ben Abuyah, ca. 120 C.E.]
   The Builder with or without Tools (*'Abot R. Nat.* A 22) [R. Yohanan ben Zakkai, ca. 80 C.E.]
6. The Lost Sheep (Matt 18:10–14; Luke 15:3–7)
   On Who Will Seek the Lost Sheep (*Midr. Ps.* 119.3 [on 119:1]; cf. *Exod. Rab.* 2.2 [on Exod 3:1]: "he placed the lamb on his shoulder"; *Gen. Rab.* 86.4 [on Gen 39:2]) [R. Haggai ben Eleazar, ca. 350 C.E.]
7. The Wise and Foolish Maidens (Matt 25:1–13; cf. Matt 22:1–10; Luke 14:15–24)
   The Wise and Foolish Servants (*b. Šabb.* 153a; cf. *Qoh. Rab.* 9.8 §1) [R. Yohanan ben Zakkai, ca. 70–80 C.E.]
8. The Faithful and Unfaithful Servants (Matt 24:45–51; Luke 12:42–46)
   The Wise and Foolish Servants (*Qoh. Rab.* 9.8 §1; cf. *b. Šabb.* 153a) [anonymous, based on parable by R. Yohanan ben Zakkai, ca. 70–80 C.E.]
   The King's Ungrateful Servants (*S. Elijah Rab.* §12 [55]) [anonymous]
9. The Watchful Householder (Matt 24:42–44; Luke 12:39–40)

The Wise and Foolish Servants (*b. Šabb.* 153a) [R. Yohanan ben Zakkai, ca. 70–80 C.E.]

10. The Talents and the Servants' Stewardship (Matt 25:14–30; Luke 19:21–27)
    The Wife's Stewardship (*Song Rab.* 7.14 §1) [anonymous]
    The King' Steward (*'Abot R. Nat.* A 14:6) [R. Eleazar ben Arak, ca. 90 C.E.]
    The Two Administrators (*Mek.* on Exod 20:2 [*Bahodeš* §§5.81–92])
    [R. Simon ben Eleazar, ca. 170 C.E.]
    The King's Daughters (*Song Rab.* 4:12 §1) [R. Joshua ben Levi, ca. 220–240 C.E.]

11. The Tares in the Wheat (Matt 13:24–30)
    The Trees of Life and the Trees of Death (*Gen. Rab.* 61.6 [on Gen 25:5]; cf. 83.5 [on 36:39]) [anonymous]

12. The Pearl of Great Price (Matt 13:45–56)
    The Precious Pearl (*Midr. Ps.* 28.6 [on 28:7]; cf. Luke 11:5–8; 18:1–8)
    [R. Simon, ca. 325 C.E.]

13. The Hidden Treasure (Matt 13:44)
    The Cheaply Sold Field (*Mek.* on Exod 14:5 [*Bešallaḥ* 2.142–48]) [R. Yose the Galilean, ca. 120 C.E.]
    The Cheaply Sold Estate (*Mek.* on Exod 14:5 [*Bešallaḥ* 2.149–55]; cf. *Pesiq. Rab Kah.* 11.7; *Song Rab.* 4.12 §1; *Exod. Rab.* 20.2, 5 [on Exod 13:17]) [R. Simeon ben Yohai, ca. 140 C.E.]

14. The Drag Net (Matt 13:47–50)
    Four Types of Fish (*'Abot R. Nat.* A 40:9) [R. Gamaliel the Elder, ca. 40–50 C.E.]

15. The Unmerciful Servant (Matt 18:23–35)
    The Forgetful Debtor (*Exod. Rab.* 31.1 [on Exod 22:25]) [anonymous]

16. The Generous Employer (Matt 20:1–16)
    The Exceptional Laborer (*Sipra Lev.* §262 [on 26:9]; *Pirqe R. El.* §53)
    [anonymous]
    The Laborer Paid a Full Day's Wage (*Song Rab.* 6.2 §6; *y. Ber.* 2.8)
    [R. Zeira, ca. 360–370 C.E.]

17. The Two Sons (Matt 21:28–32)
    The Two Workers (*Exod. Rab.* 27.9 [on Exod 18:1]) [anonymous]
    The Two Tenants (*Deut. Rab.* 7.4 [on Deut 28:1]) [anonymous]

18. The Guest without a Wedding Garment (Matt 22:11–14)
    The Unprepared Guests (*b. Šabb.* 153b; cf. *Qoh. Rab.* 3.9 §1) [R. Yohanan ben Zakkai, ca. 70–80 C.E.]

19. The Friend at Midnight (Luke 11:5–8)
    The Brazen Daughter and the Polite Daughter (*y. Ta'an.* 3.4; cf. *Midr. Ps.* 28.6 [on 28:7]) [R. Aqiba, ca. 95 C.E.]

20. The Insistent Widow (Luke 18:1–8)
    The Brazen Daughter and the Polite Daughter (*y. Ta'an.* 3.4; cf. *Midr. Ps.* 28.6 [on 28:7]) [R. Aqiba, ca. 95 C.E.]

21. The Rich Fool (Luke 12:16–21)
    The Rich Hoarder (*Pesiq. Rab Kah.* 10.3; cf. Sir 11:18–19) [anonymous]

22. The Fruitless Fig Tree (Luke 13:6–9)
    The Fruitless Vineyard (*Exod. Rab.* 43.9 [on Exod 32:11]) [R. Simeon ben Yehozadak, ca. 220–230 C.E.]

23. The Closed Door (Luke 13:24–30)
    The Closed Door (*Midr. Ps.* 10.2 [on 10:1]) [R. Hanina (ben Hama), ca. 220–230 C.E.]
24. Choosing the Right Place at the Table (Luke 14:7–11)
    Choosing the Right Place at the Table (*Lev. Rab.* 1.5 [on Lev 1:1], commenting on Prov 25:6–7 and Ps 113:5–6; cf. Sir 3:17–20) [R. Aqiba and R. Simeon ben Azzai, ca. 120 C.E.]
25. Building a Tower (Luke 14:28–30)
    Counting the Cost of *not* being Reconciled to God (*Pesiq. Rab Kah.*, Supplement 7.3) [R. Jonathan, ca. 270 C.E.]
26. The King Going to War (Luke 14:31–33)
    Counting the Cost of *not* being Reconciled to God (*Pesiq. Rab Kah.*, Supplement 7.3) [R. Jonathan, ca. 270 C.E.]
27. The Lost Coin (Luke 15:8–10)
    The Lost Coin (*Song Rab.* 1.1 §9) [R. Phineas ben Yair, ca. 165–175 C.E.]
28. The Prodigal Son (Luke 15:11–32)
    The Errant Son (*Deut. Rab.* 2.24 [on Deut 4:30]) [R. Meir, ca. 150 C.E.]
    The Repatriated Prince (*Sipre Deut.* §345 [on Deut 33:4]) [anonymous]
    The Returning Prince (*Pesiq. R.* 44.9) [anonymous]
    The Favored Son (*Sipre Deut.* §352 [on Deut 33:12]) [anonymous]
29. The Rich Man and Lazarus (Luke 16:19–31)
    The Fate of the Two Men (*Ruth Rab.* 3.3 [on Ruth 1:17], commenting on Eccl 1:15; *Qoh. Rab.* 1.15 §1) [anonymous]
    The Two Pious Men and the Tax Collector (*y. Sanh.* 6.23; *y. Ḥag.* 2.27) [anonymous]
30. The Servants Who Have Done Their Duty (Luke 17:7–10)
    Servants Who Labor for the Fear of Heaven (*m. 'Abot* 1:3) [Antigonus of Soko, ca. 200? B.C.E.]
    Work Claims No Merit (*m. 'Abot* 2:8) [R. Yohanan ben Zakkai, ca. 80 C.E.]
31. The Log and the Speck (Matt 7:3–5; Luke 6:41–42)
    The Log and the Splinter (*b. 'Arak.* 16b) [R. Tarfon, ca. 120 C.E.]
32. The Two Gates (Matt 7:13–14; cf. Luke 13:24)
    The Two Ways (*Sipre Deut.* §53 [on Deut 11:26]; *Midr. Haggadol* on Deut 11:26) [anonymous]

Other tannaic parables that resemble the parables of Jesus (in theme, style, or details) include the following (principally based on McArthur and Johnston, 18–24):

1. The Throne and the Footstool (*Gen. Rab.* 1.15 [on Gen 1:1]) [Bet Shammai, ca. 40 C.E.]
2. The Palace (*Gen. Rab.* 1.15 [on Gen 1:1]) [Bet Hillel, ca. 40 C.E.]
3. The Ill-Treated Cupbearer (*m. Sukk.* 2:9) [anonymous]
4. The Well-Rooted Tree (*m. 'Abot* 3:18; cf. *'Abot R. Nat.* A 22:2) [R. Eleazar ben Azariah, ca. 90 C.E.]
5. Ink on Paper (*m. 'Abot* 4:20; cf. *'Abot R. Nat.* A 23:3) [Elisha ben Abuyah, ca. 120 C.E.]
6. The Eater of Ripe Grapes (*m. 'Abot* 4:20; cf. *'Abot R. Nat.* A 23:3 [see Mark 2:22]) [R. Yose ben Judah of Kefar ha-Babli, ca. 190 C.E.]

7. The Inept Servant (*t. Ber.* 6.18) [anonymous]
8. The Lamp Removed (*t. Sukk.* 2.6) [anonymous]
9. The Road between Fire and Snow (*t. Ḥag.* 2.5; cf. *'Abot R. Nat.* A 28:10) [anonymous]
10. The Unfortunate Fugitive (*t. Soṭa* 15.7) [anonymous]
11. The Protected Vineyard (*t. Qidd.* 1.11) [R. Gamaliel II, ca. 80 C.E.]
12. The Married Woman (*t. Qidd.* 1.11) [R. Gamaliel II, ca. 80 C.E.]
13. The Fenced Vineyard (*t. Qidd.* 1.11) [R. Gamaliel II, ca. 80 C.E.]
14. The Two Men Who Planned a Wedding Feast (*t. B. Qam.* 7.2) [R. Gamaliel II, ca. 80 C.E.]
15. The Wife Sent Back to Her Father (*t. B. Qam.* 7.3) [R. Yohanan ben Zakkai, ca. 70 C.E.]
16. The King Engaged to a Woman (*t. B. Qam.* 7.4) [R. Yohanan ben Zakkai, ca. 70 C.E.]
17. The Villager Who Smashed Glassware (*Gen. Rab.* 19.6 [on Gen 3:7]) [R. Yohanan ben Zakkai, ca. 70–80 C.E., or R. Aqiba, ca. 120 C.E.]
18. The King's Twin Who Was Executed (*t. Sanh.* 9.7) [R. Meir, ca. 140 C.E.]
19. The Man with a Fine Beard (*b. Ber.* 11a) [R. Eleazar ben Azariah, ca. 80 C.E.]
20. The Fox and the Fishes (*b. Ber.* 61b) [R. Aqiba, ca. 135 C.E.]
21. The King Who Did Not Exempt Himself from Taxes (*b. Sukk.* 30a) [R. Simeon ben Yohai, ca. 140 C.E.]
22. The King Who Forgave a Debt (*b. Roš Haš.* 17b–18a) [R. Yose the Priest, ca. 90 C.E.]
23. Giving Promptly and Slowly (*b. Taʿan.* 25b) [R. Samuel the Younger, ca. 90 C.E.]
24. The Trees with Overhanging Boughs (*b. Qidd.* 40b) [R. Eleazar ben Zadok, ca. 90 C.E.]
25. The Retracted Betrothal (*'Abot R. Nat.* A 2:3) [R. Yose the Galilean, ca. 130 C.E.]
26. The Inferior Field (*'Abot R. Nat.* A 16:3) [R. Simeon ben Yohai, ca. 140 C.E.]
27. Wise and Foolish Guests at the King's Banquet (*Ṣem.* 8.10) [R. Meir, ca. 140 C.E.]
28. The Proud Father (*Mek.* on Exod 13:2 [*Pisha* 16.62–67]) [R. Eleazar ben Azariah, ca. 80 C.E.]
29. The King and His Guards (*Mek.* on Exod 15:2 [*Širata* 3.28–39]) [R. Eliezer (ben Hyrcanus?), ca. 90 C.E.]
30. The King Going Out to War (*Mek.* on Exod 20:5 [*Bahodeš* §§6.103–124]) [R. Gamaliel II, ca. 80 C.E.]
31. The King's Images (*Mek.* on Exod 20:16 [*Bahodeš* §§8.69–77]) [R. Hanina ben Gamaliel, ca. 85 C.E.]
32. The Foolish Centurion (*Sipre Num.* §131) [R. Aqiba, ca. 130 C.E.]
33. The King Who Repented His Intention to Divorce (*Sipre Num.* §131) [R. Aqiba, ca. 130 C.E.]
34. The Unwise Suitor (*Sipre Deut.* §37 [on Deut 11:10]) [R. Simeon ben Yohai, ca. 140 C.E.]

35. The King Who Enforced His Will (*Sipre Deut.* §40 [on Deut 11:12])
    [R. Simeon ben Yohai, ca. 140 C.E.]
36. The King's Bird (*Sipre Deut.* §48 [on Deut 11:22]) [R. Simeon ben Yohai,
    ca. 140 C.E.]
37. The Frugal Brother and the Wasteful Brother (*Sipre Deut.* §48 [on Deut
    11:22]) [R. Simeon ben Yohai, ca. 140 C.E.]
38. The Two Wrestlers (*Gen. Rab.* 22.9 [on Gen 4:10]) [R. Simeon ben Yohai,
    ca. 140 C.E.]
39. The King Who Found His Lost Pearl (*Gen. Rab.* 39.10 [on Gen 12:1]; cf.
    Ruth Rab. 8.1 [on Ruth 4:20]) [R. Nehemiah, ca. 150 C.E.]
40. The Foolish Shipmate (*Lev. Rab.* 4.6 [on Lev 4:2]) [R. Simeon ben Yohai,
    ca. 140 C.E.]

Jewish parables from non-rabbinic sources:
1. The Trees and the Bramble (Judg 9:7–21)
2. The Poor Man's Ewe Lamb (2 Sam 12:1–4)
3. The Two Brothers and the Avengers of Blood (2 Sam 14:1–11)
4. The Escaped Prisoner (1 Kgs 20:35–40)
5. The Thistle and the Cedar (2 Kgs 14:9)
6. The Fruitless Vineyard (Isa 5:1–7)
7. The Eagles and the Vine (Ezek 17:3–10)
8. The Lion Whelps (Ezek 19:2–9)
9. The Vine (Ezek 19:10–14)
10. The Forest Fire (Ezek 21:1–5)
11. The Seething Pot (Ezek 24:3–5)
12. The Lame Man and the Blind Man (*Apoc. Ezek.* frg. 1, cited by Epiphanius
    Against Heresies 64.70.5–17).

Manson (pp. 61–64) classifies the first and fifth examples above as "fables"
rather than parables.

Bibliography: A. Feldman, *Parables and Similes of the Rabbis: Agricultural and Pastoral* (Cambridge: Cambridge University, 1927); D. Flusser, *Die rabbinischen Gleichnisse und der Gleichniserzähler Jesus* (Bern: Peter Lang, 1981); T. W. Manson, *The Teaching of Jesus: Studies of Its Form and Content* (Cambridge: Cambridge University, 1948); H. K. McArthur and R. M. Johnston, *They Also Taught in Parables: Rabbinic Parables from the First Centuries of the Christian Era* (Grand Rapids: Zondervan, 1990); W. O. E. Oesterley, *The Gospel Parables in the Light of Their Jewish Background* (London: Macmillan, 1936); D. Stern, *Parables in Midrash: Narrative and Exegesis in Rabbinic Literature* (Cambridge: Harvard University, 1991); B. H. Young, *Jesus and His Jewish Parables* (New York: Paulist, 1989).

APPENDIX FIVE

JESUS AND JEWISH MIRACLE STORIES

THE HOLY MEN

Honi ha-Me'aggel (first century B.C.E.)
Abba Hilkiah, grandson of Honi (late first century B.C.E., early first century C.E.)
Hanin ha-Nehba, grandson of Honi (late first century B.C.E., early first century C.E.)
Hanina ben Dosa (first century C.E.)
Eleazar the Exorcist (first century C.E.)
Phineas ben Yair (mid-second century C.E.)
An Anonymous Hasid (first or second century C.E.)

There were several Jewish holy men in the time of Jesus who were well known for mighty acts and remarkable answers to prayer. The lives and activities of seven of them compare in various ways to the life and ministry of Jesus. The principal features of what is known of them will be briefly reviewed, and where appropriate a few comparisons with Jesus have been drawn.

HONI HA-ME'AGGEL

In the rabbinic literature Honi is called ha-Me'aggel ("the circle drawer"). Josephus refers to him as "Onias, a righteous man beloved by God." He was remembered for praying for rain during a time of severe drought. When his prayer initially went unheeded, he drew a circle on the ground and told God that he would not leave it until rain came (perhaps following the example of Habakkuk; Hab 2:1). Soon it did rain.

The story is found in the Mishna (*m. Ta'an.* 3:8; cf. *b. Ta'an.* 23a) and is alluded to by Josephus (*Ant.* 14.2.1 §22). A certain Simeon ben Shetah expressed disapprobation over Honi's familiarity with heaven: "Had you not been Honi, I would have pronounced a ban against you! For were these years like those concerning which Elijah said no rain should fall—for the keys to rainfall were in his hands—would not the result of your action have been the desecration of God's name? But what can I do with you, since you importune God and he performs your will, like a son that importunes his father and he performs his will." Simeon's complaint implies comparison between Elijah and Honi. In another tradition the comparison is explicit: "No man has existed comparable to Elijah and Honi the Circle-Drawer, causing mankind to serve God" (*Gen. Rab.* 13.7 [on 2:5]; however, some MSS omit either Elijah or Honi). According to Josephus, Honi was stoned (ca. 65 B.C.E.) when he refused to pronounce a curse on Aristobulus and his supporters (*Ant.* 14.2.1 §§23–24).

Honi's life and activities present a few points of comparison with the life and ministry of Jesus. Honi's persistence in praying for rain parallels Jesus' similar teaching, as seen in the parables of the Persistent Friend (Luke 11:5–8) and the Importunate Widow (Luke 18:1–8). Honi's filial relationship with God is also interesting. Jesus taught his disciples to pray to God as "Father" (Matt 6:9; Mark 14:36). Moreover, Jesus was regarded as God's Son (Mark 1:11; more on this below). Since there are other examples of the weather's being affected through the prayers of the Jewish holy men, this aspect will be discussed below.

ABBA HILKIAH, GRANDSON OF HONI

Abba Hilkiah, grandson of Honi (son of Honi's son), a very pious and poor man (worked for hire, wore a borrowed coat, insufficient food for guests), was requested by the rabbis to pray for rain. He and his wife went upstairs and, from opposite corners, prayed. Soon clouds began to form (*b. Ta'an.* 23a–23b).

Poverty is a feature common to most of the traditions of the holy men. Jesus' lifestyle was also one of poverty: "Foxes have holes, and birds of the air have nests; but the Son of man has nowhere to lay his head" (Matt 8:20; Luke 9:58).

HANIN HA-NEHBA

Hanin ha-Nehba (i.e., "the hidden"), grandson of Honi (son of Honi's daughter), was a modest man who used to hide from public view. When the country needed rain the rabbis would send children to him. On one occasion they came to him and said, "Father, give us rain!" Hanin then prayed to God, "Master of the Universe, give rain for the sake of these children who do not even know enough to distinguish between a Father who gives rain and a father who does not" (*b. Ta'an.* 23b).

HANINA BEN DOSA

Hanina, one of the "men of [great] deeds" (*m. Soṭa* 9:15), lived in the town of Arab, a small Galilean village about ten miles north of Nazareth. He was famous for his prayers that resulted in healing (*m. Ber.* 5:5). On one occasion he prayed for the son of Gamaliel II (or possibly Gamaliel the Elder). Because the words of his prayer in this instance came fluently, he knew he had been answered. Gamaliel's disciples noted the time and returned to their master to discover that the boy had indeed recovered at the very hour Hanina had spoken (*b. Ber.* 34b). On another occasion he prayed for the son of Yohanan ben Zakkai, Hanina's teacher. The son recovered (*b. Ber.* 34b).

Once Hanina was walking at night alone, when he met the "queen of the demons." She claimed that had he not enjoyed heaven's protection, she would have harmed him. Hanina then banned her from passing through inhabited places (*b. Pesaḥ.* 112b).

Once while praying, Hanina was bitten by a poisonous snake (or lizard). The snake was later found dead at the opening of its hole. Hanina, however, was unharmed. This gave rise to the saying, "Woe to the man bitten by a snake, but woe to the snake which has bitten Rabbi Hanina ben Dosa" (*t. Ber.* 3.20; *b. Ber.* 33a). This episode may be alluded to in the Mishna: "Even if a snake was twisted around his heel he may not interrupt his prayer" (*m. Ber.* 5:1). There is also a parallel account where Hanina offers his heel to a poisonous lizard that has been injuring people. The lizard bites Hanina's heel and dies. Then Hanina pronounces: "See, my sons, it is not the lizard that kills, it is sin that kills!" (*b. Ber.* 33a).

Through prayer Hanina caused the rain to stop and later continue (*b. Ta'an.* 24b; *b. Yoma* 53b). So impressed with this story Rabbi Joseph commented: "How could the prayer of even the high priest be compared to that of Rabbi Hanina ben Dosa?" The parallels with the Elijah/Elisha stories (1 Kgs 17:1 [drought]; 18:45 [rain]) should be noted.

Once a neighbor woman was building a house. After erecting the walls she discovered that the beams for the roof were too short. She went to Hanina for help. Playing on her name, Hanina said, "May your beams reach!" One Polemo, supposedly an eyewitness, said: "I saw that house and its beams projected one cubit on either side, and people told me, 'This is the house which Rabbi Hanina ben Dosa covered with beams, through his prayer' " (*b. Ta'an.* 25a).

According to Rab: "Each day a heavenly voice came [from Mount Horeb] and said: 'The whole universe is sustained on account of my son, Hanina' " (*b. Ta'an.* 24b; *b. Ber.* 17b; *b. Ḥul.* 86a). Elsewhere Rab views Ahab (Elijah's contemporary and foe) as representative of evil, while Hanina is representative of good (*b. Ber.* 61b). Such an analogy implies a comparison between Hanina and Elijah. Indeed, it may even suggest that Hanina was thought to have superseded Elijah. Another tradition calls Hanina a "man of rank" (cf. Isa 3:3), who enjoyed the favor of heaven (*b. Ḥag.* 14a).

Hanina's life and activities parallel those of Jesus at many points. In the disputed passage in Josephus (*Ant.* 18.3.3 §63), Jesus is called a "wise man [*sophos anēr*]" and a "doer of amazing deeds [*paradoxon ergon poiētēs*]." Even R. Eisler (*The Messiah Jesus and John the Baptist* [trans. A. H. Krappe; New York: Dial, 1931] 62), who suspects that the passage has been tampered with, accepts the latter phrase as original, but with a different sense ("astonishing tricks"). Recall that Hanina was called a "man of doing [or deeds]."

The healing of Gamaliel's son at the very "hour" that Hanina announced to the disciples that he would recover parallels the Jesus tradition: "The father knew that was the hour when Jesus had said to him, 'Your son will live' " (John 4:46–53; cf. Matt 8:5–13; Luke 7:1–10).

Hanina's encounter with the queen of demons is somewhat analogous to Jesus' encounter with the Gerasene demoniac, who ran up and declared that he knew who Jesus was (Mark 5:1–20). The demoniac recognized that he was no match for God's "holy one." Elsewhere Jesus has encounters with Satan: the temptations (Matt 4:1–11; Luke 4:1–13), the vision of Satan falling from heaven (Luke 10:17–20), and Satan's demand to have Peter to sift like wheat and Jesus' prayer in Peter's behalf (Luke 22:31–32). More will be said on Jesus' exorcisms below.

The stories about Hanina's encounters with poisonous snakes and lizards parallel canonical and noncanonical stories about Jesus. In one place Jesus says: "Behold, I have given you authority to tread upon serpents and scorpions . . . and nothing shall hurt you" (Luke 10:19; cf. Mark 16:18; Acts 28:3–6). Hanina's dictum, "See, my sons, it is not the lizard that kills, it is sin that kills!" coheres with Jesus' forgiving sin as either a prerequisite or at least as a corollary of healing (e.g., Mark 2:1–11). The *Infancy Gospel of Thomas* offers an amusing parallel (Greek *Thomas* A 16:1–2; Latin *Thomas* 14:1). On one occasion Jesus' younger brother James was bitten by a poisonous viper. Just as he was about to die, Jesus approached and breathed upon the bite. Immediately James recovered and the viper burst.

Because of their miracles and mighty works Honi and Hanina were compared to Elijah, the venerated prophet famous for his mighty deeds (Sir 48:1–16). Jesus was also compared to Elijah (Mark 6:15; 8:28) and may himself have compared his ministry to outcasts and the disenfranchised to the similar ministries of Elijah and Elisha (Luke 4:25–27). On the Mount of Transfiguration he was in Elijah's company (Mark 9:4–5).

The *Infancy Gospel of Thomas* also parallels the story of the stretched beams (Greek *Thomas* A 13:1–2; Greek *Thomas* B 11:1–3; Latin *Thomas* 11:1–2). It seems that Joseph, the father of Jesus, failed to cut two beams precisely the same length. Jesus had him take hold of the short beam and then he stretched it to the proper length.

Just as the heavenly voiced declared Hanina to be "my son," so the heavenly voice spoke at the baptism and transfiguration of Jesus: "You are my beloved Son" (Mark 1:11; 9:7; cf. John 12:28).

ELEAZAR THE EXORCIST

According to Josephus (*Ant.* 8.2.5 §§46–49), a certain Eleazar, who followed the incantations of Solomon, could draw out demons through a person's nostrils, through use of the Baaras root (further described in *J.W.* 7.6.3 §§180–185). Solomon "composed incantations by which illnesses are relieved, and left behind forms of exorcisms with which those possessed by demons drive them out, never to return" (*Ant.* 8.2.5 §45). The tradition of Solomon as exorcist par excellence was widespread in late antiquity. The tradition begins in the Bible itself where Solomon is described as unsurpassed in knowledge (1 Kgs 4:29–34). His knowledge of proverbs and plants (1 Kgs 4:32–33) contributed to later speculation that he had mastered the secrets of herbs and spells. And with his knowledge of herbs and spells the king had power over spirits. According to the Wisdom of Solomon God gave the monarch knowledge of "the powers of spirits and the reasonings of men, the varieties of plants and the virtues of roots; [he] learned what is both secret and what is manifest" (Wis 7:17–21). Solomon's power over demonic forces was appealed to for protection, as has been shown by Aramaic and Hebrew incantations dating from the early centuries of the Common Era. It is to this tradition that Josephus refers in mentioning Eleazar. The tradition was well known in Christian circles. Origen refers to those who attempted exorcisms according to the spells written by Solomon (*Comm. Matthew* 33 [on Matt 26:63]). The pseudepigraphal *Testament of Solomon*, probably written by a Greek-speaking Christian in the second or third century, is wholly dedicated to this theme.

All of this may have an important bearing on Jesus' ministry and self-understanding.

> Then a blind and dumb demoniac was brought to him, and he healed him, so that he saw. And all the people were amazed, and said, "Can this be the son of David?" But when the Pharisees heard it they said, "It is only by Beelzebul, the prince of demons, that this man casts out demons." . . . [Jesus

replied,] "if Satan casts out Satan, he is divided against himself; how then will his kingdom stand? And if I cast out demons by Beelzebul, by whom do your sons cast them out?" . . . Then some of the scribes and Pharisees said to him, "Teacher, we wish to see a sign from you." But he answered them, "An evil and adulterous generation seeks for a sign; but no sign shall be given it except the sign of Jonah. . . . The queen of the South will arise at the judgment with this generation and condemn it; for she came from the ends of the earth to hear the wisdom of Solomon, and behold, something greater than Solomon is here. When the unclean spirit has gone out of a man, he passes through waterless places seeking rest, but he finds none. Then he says, 'I return to my house from which I came.' And when he comes he finds it empty, swept, and put in order. Then he goes and brings with him seven other spirits more evil than himself, and they enter and dwell there; and the last state of that man becomes worse than the first. So shall it be also with this evil generation" (Matt 12:22–45; cf. Luke 11:29–32, 24–26).

When Jesus healed a demonized man the crowd thought of him as the son of David, i.e., one like Solomon. This is evidence of the close association of exorcism and Solomon. It may also indicate that a messianic figure should possess the powers of David's famous son. The religious leaders, however, cast doubt on this inference by suggesting that Jesus is in league with Satan himself (Beelzebul). Jesus replies pointing out how this is illogical. His reference to the exorcisms of their "sons" (as opposed to David's "son"?) and the demons that could return may suggest that Jesus did not think that these exorcisms were entirely successful. In other words, they were not up to standards associated with Solomon, the son of David. Nor were they, by implication, up to the standards of Jesus who was one "greater than Solomon."

PHINEAS BEN YAIR

Phineas ben Yair, son-in-law of R. Simeon ben Yohai and a pious ascetic, lived in the second century. Although later than Hanina ben Dosa, he was compared to his famous predecessor. After the story of Hanina's remarkable donkey, who had outwitted bandits and had safely returned home, Raba ben Zemuna [or Abba ben Zevina] commented: "If the sages of former times were like angels, then we are like men. And if they were like men, then we are like donkeys—but not like the donkey of Rabbi Hanina ben Dosa nor like the donkey of Phineas ben Yair, but like ordinary donkeys" (b. Šabb. 112b; y. Dem. 1.3; 'Abot R. Nat. A §8).

AN ANONYMOUS HASID

The prayer of a certain pious hasid brought on a flood (t. Ta'an. 3.1). To some extent this parallels Honi's prayer for rain. When the rain began as a drizzle, he asked for abundant rain. Then it began to pour with the danger of flooding. Honi's continued petitioning resulted in reducing the rain to moderation.

Five of the seven Jewish holy men considered here were remembered to have had their prayers for rain answered. Hanina's request that the rain stop is particularly noteworthy. In no case does Jesus pray for rain. But on at least one occasion he commands a storm to stop (Mark 4:35–41; cf. 6:47–52; John 6:16–21).

LATER TRADITIONS ABOUT FAMOUS RABBIS

There are later traditions about several of the better known rabbis. It is said (anonymously) that both Eliezer (late first, early second century C.E.) and Aqiba (late first, early second century C.E.) were successful in praying for rain, though apparently the latter enjoyed greater success than the former (b. Ta'an. 25b). Joshua ben Levi (early third century C.E.) also apparently had his prayers for rain answered (b. Ta'an. 25a). Evidently there was a tradition of requesting major figures and authorities to pray for rain during periods of drought. According to Rabbi Samuel bar Nahmani (ca. 300 C.E.): "When Israel sins and does evil deeds, the rains are withheld. When they bring an elder, such as Rabbi Yose the Galilean [ca. 130–140 C.E.], to intercede for them, the rains fall again" (y. Ber. 5.2; cf. Meg. Ta'an. [on Adar §7]: "On the 20th [of Adar] the people fasted for rain, and it was granted to them"). There may have been other traditions of mighty deeds accomplished through Yose the Galilean. Abba Silver cites a tenth-century prayer of a sick man: "Rabbi Yose the Galilean, heal me!" Such a prayer is evidence of belief that healing could be had through Yose's intercession. Such an idea likely had its origin in some remarkable deeds in Yose's lifetime, or in some remarkable legends in the years following his death.

GENERAL BIBLIOGRAPHY: C. Brown, "Synoptic Miracle Stories: A Jewish Religious and Social Setting," Forum 2/4 (1986) 55–76; A. Guttmann, "The Significance of Miracles for Talmudic Judaism," HUCA 20 (1947) 363–406; H. van der Loos, The Miracles of Jesus (NovTSup 9; Leiden: Brill, 1965) 139–50; J. Nadich, Jewish Legends of the Second Commonwealth (Philadelphia: JPS, 1983) 194–200, 255–59, 296, n. 93, 396, n. 149; J. Neusner, A Life of Yohanan ben Zakkai (Leiden: Brill, 1970); S. Safrai, "The Teaching of the Pietists in Mishnaic Literature," JJS 16 (1965) 15–33; A. H. Silver, A History of Messianic Speculation in Israel (Gloucester: Peter Smith, 1978); 22–23; G. Vermes, "Hanina ben Dosa," in Vermes, Post-Biblical Jewish Studies (SJLA 8; Leiden: Brill, 1975) 178–214; idem, Jesus the Jew: A Historian's Reading of the Gospels (London: Collins, 1973) 58–82.

APPENDIX SIX

MESSIANIC CLAIMANTS OF THE FIRST AND SECOND CENTURIES

In the first and second centuries of the Common Era several persons claimed some form of messianic status. Review of the claims and activities of these claimants helps clarify the "messianic context" of the time and place in which Jesus lived and the later interpretive backgrounds against which the New Testament authors wrote. The usefulness of the writings of Josephus and others will become readily apparent.

Outline
1. Biblical and Historical Precedents
2. Messianic Kings
3. Messianic Prophets
4. Messianic Priests
5. Later Messianic Claimants

1. Biblical and Historical Precedents. Although "messiah" (i.e., "anointed one," from Heb. *māšaḥ*/Gk. *chriein*) is often understood in terms of the royal "son of David," in reality messianic concepts in late antiquity were quite diverse. If we understand "messiah" to mean one who believes himself to be anointed by God in order to play a leading role in the restoration of Israel, a restoration which may or may not involve the Davidic monarchy, then it is correct to speak of anointed kings, anointed prophets, and anointed priests. There is evidence that several individuals in the period of time under consideration qualify for inclusion in one or more of these three categories. All of these categories are rooted in biblical and historical precedents.

Kings. The concept of the "anointed" king derives from early biblical history. Saul was anointed king (1 Sam 15:1); later David was anointed (1 Sam 16:13). David, of course, became the archetype of the anointed king (Pss 18:50; 89:20; 132:17) and the basis for future hope (Isa 9:2–7;

11:1–10; cf. v. 2 in the Targum: "And a king shall come forth from the sons of Jesse, and a Messiah"). Kings were sometimes prophets as well. The spirit of prophecy came upon King Saul (1 Sam 10:6–13; 19:23–24). King David also was able to prophesy (1 Sam 16:13; 2 Sam 23:1–7; cf. Josephus *Ant.* 6.8.2 §166 [where he also casts out demons]; Acts 2:29–30). At the end of 11QPsalms[a] we are told that "All these [psalms and songs] he [David] spoke through prophecy which was given him from before the Most High." Kings apparently also functioned as priests (1 Sam 14:35 [Saul]; 2 Sam 6:12–19 [David]; 2 Sam 8:18 [David's sons]; 1 Kgs 3:15 [Solomon]; cf. Ps 110:1–4).

The hopes pinned on Zerubbabel may very well have been the earliest instance of post-Davidic messianism (Neh 7:7; 12:1, 47; Hag 1:14; 2:20–23; Zech 3:8; 4:6–10; 6:12–14; Sir 49:11–12). Probably of great influence was the portrait of the expected Messiah in *Psalms of Solomon* 17–18, where he is described as a warrior, a wise ruler, and one who will purge Jerusalem. Herod the Great, who had been appointed King of the Jews by the Roman Senate in 40 B.C.E., and whose marriage three years later to Mariamne I, of the Hasmonean family, which was probably intended to strengthen his claim to the throne, may very well have thought of himself as some sort of messiah (Josephus *J.W.* 1.17.4 §331: "[considered] a man of divine favor"; see also *b. B. Bat.* 3b–4a). The account of Herod's attempt to destroy Jesus may imply that the Matthean evangelist regarded the former as some sort of messianic rival of the latter (Matt 2:1–18).

Prophets. Prophets, as well as kings, were "anointed." This is seen in a variety of texts, biblical and post-biblical: God told Elijah to anoint Hazael as king of Syria, Jehu as king of Israel, and Elisha "to be prophet" in Elijah's place (1 Kgs 19:15–16). It is significant that the anointing of Elisha is parallel to the anointing of the two kings. With reference to the wandering patriarchs God warned gentile kings: "Touch not my anointed ones, do my prophets no harm!" (1 Chr 16:22 = Ps 105:15; cf. Gen 20:7). A particularly instructive example comes from Isa 61:1–2: "The Spirit of the Lord God is upon me, because the Lord has anointed me to bring good tidings to the afflicted." According to the targum, the anointed one is none other than the prophet himself: "The prophet said: 'The spirit of prophecy is upon me. . . .' " In *Mek.* on Exod 20:21 (*Bahodeš* §9.103) the passage is applied to Moses. At Qumran (11QMelch 4–20; 1QH 17:14) and in the NT (Luke 4:18–19; 7:22 = Matt 11:5) Isa 61:1–2 seems to have been understood in prophetic/messianic terms.

Another central idea was the "prophet-like-Moses" theme, for this idea was as kingly as it was prophetic (Meeks, 1967). At many points in rabbinic tradition Moses was compared with Messiah. Like Messiah (*Pesiq. R.* 33.6; *Frg. Tg.* Exod 12:42), so Moses was thought to have come into existence prior to the creation of the universe (*T. Mos.* 1:14; cf.

Pesiq. R. 15.10; and the comparison between the Exodus and Israel's eschatological restoration in *Pesiq. Rab Kah.* 5.8; *Sipre Deut.* §130 [on Deut 16:3]; *Tg.* Lam 2:22). Comparisons between Moses and David may also imply comparison between Moses and Messiah: "You find that whatever Moses did, David did. . . . As Moses became king in Israel and in Judah . . . so David became king in Israel and in Judah" (*Midr. Ps.* 1.2 [on Ps 1:1]). Both Moses and David "gave their lives for Israel" (*Sipre Deut.* §344 [on Deut 33:3]). Although these traditions are late, they probably represent embellishments of earlier comparisons between Moses and Messiah. Christians, of course, made their own comparisons (John 1:14–18; Acts 3:22–23; 7:37; Heb 3:1–6; 8:5–6; *Sib. Or.* 8:250: "Moses prefigured [Christ]").

Undoubtedly the most influential prophetic figure in Jesus' lifetime was his contemporary John the Baptist. His baptizing activity around the Jordan, his disciples, the crowds, his eventual arrest and execution, all suggest that he should be included among the other charismatic prophets of this period (Mark 1:2–9; 6:14–29; Matt 3:7b–12; Luke 3:7b–9, 16–17; John 1:19–28; Acts 19:1–7; Josephus *Ant.* 18.5.2 §§116–119).

Priests. In very old tradition priests appear as kings. Melchizedek, priest-king of Salem, is an obvious example (Gen 14:18; cf. Ps 110:1–4). As were kings, priests also were anointed. Aaron, the brother of Moses was anointed *and crowned* (cf. Exod 29:6–7; cf. Ps.-Philo *Bib. Ant.* 13:1). All priests were to be anointed (Lev 16:32). Zadok, the founder of a high-priestly line, was anointed (1 Chr 29:22; cf. 2 Chr 31:10). After the collapse of the Davidic dynasty, the high priest was often the highest Jewish authority. High priest Onias III ruled Jerusalem (2 Macc 3–4). Jason the priest attempted to gain control of Jerusalem when he thought Antiochus IV had died (2 Macc 5:5–7). After the successful Maccabean revolt, the Hasmonean family not only served as high priests, thus usurping the Zadokite succession, but even regarded themselves as kings (Aristobulus I [104–103 B.C.E.]; cf. Josephus *J.W.* 1.3.1 §70; *Ant.* 13.11.1 §301; and Janneus [103–76 B.C.E.]; cf. Josephus *Ant.* 13.12.1 §320; *b. Sanh.* 107b). Reflecting the Hasmonean period, the *Testaments of the Twelve Patriarchs* anticipated a priestly ruler, as well as kingly ruler (*T. Sim.* 7:2; *T. Jud.* 21:2; *T. Jos.* 19:6). Qumran looked for an "anointed [priest] of Aaron," who would serve alongside the "anointed of Israel" (CD 12:23–13:1, 21; 14:19; 1QS 9:11). Christians believed that Jesus was not only prophet and king, but was also the heavenly high priest (Heb 5:1–6), whose death ended the need for a priesthood or for further sacrifice (Heb 7:27–28; 9:23–26).

Even in later rabbinic tradition the anointed priest plays a part in the messianic era. Commenting on Zech 4:14 ("There are the two anointed ones who stand by the Lord"): "This is in reference to Aaron and the Messiah" ('*Abot R. Nat.* A §34). In *Ps.-J.* Num 25:12, enriched with phrases from Isa 61:1 and Mal 3:1, Eleazar, Aaron's son, is told that he will be made "the messenger of the covenant . . . to announce redemption at the end of days."

2. *Messianic Kings.* Our best historical source for the Herodian-Roman period is Josephus. Unfortunately, because of his bias, it is not always easy to distinguish bona fide messianic claimants from those who were truly no more than criminals. Josephus tended to denigrate these claimants as deceivers, impostors, and brigands. For example, he says: "Judea was filled with brigandage. Anyone might make himself a king [*basileus*] . . . causing trouble to few Romans . . . but bringing the greatest slaughter upon their own people" (*Ant.* 17.10.8 §285). This comment certainly betrays Josephus' cynical attitude toward the liberation movements of the first century. But despite this pejorative assessment, several of these aspirants in all probability were messianic claimants whose goal was the liberation of Israel (R. Horsley and J. Hanson, *Bandits*, 88–134; B. Witherington, *Christology*, 84–85). The following figures sought to rule Israel and bring about political, if not religious, restoration.

Judas (of Sepphoris, Galilee) son of Hezekiah the "brigand chief." In the wake of Herod's death (4 B.C.E.) Judas plundered the royal arsenals and attacked other kingly aspirants (*Ant.* 17.10.5 §§271–272; *J.W.* 2.4.1 §56). According to Josephus, this man "became a terror to all men by plundering those he came across in his desire for great possessions and in his ambition for royal honor [*zēlosei basileiou timēs*]." Although Josephus does not say explicitly, presumably Judas, as well as many of the other insurrectionists of this period of time, was subdued by Varus, the Roman governor of Syria, who quelled rebellion in Galilee, Samaria, Judea, Jerusalem, and Idumea (cf. *Ant.* 17.10.9–10 §§286–298; *J.W.* 2.5.1–3 §§66–79).

Simon of Perea, a former royal servant. Evidently this Simon was another opportunist who arose after Herod's death. According to Josephus, he was a handsome man of great size and strength, who "was bold enough to place the diadem on his head [*diadēma tē etolmēse perithēsthai*], and having got together a body of men, he was himself also proclaimed king [*autos basileus anangeltheis*] by them in their madness, and he rated himself worthy of this beyond anyone else. After burning the royal palace in Jericho, he plundered and carried off the things seized there. He also set fire to many other royal residences . . ." (*Ant.* 17.10.6 §§273–276; *J.W.* 2.4.2 §§57–59: "he placed the diadem on himself [*peritithēsin men heautou diadēma*]"). His claim to kingship was even noted by Tacitus (*Histories* 5.9: "After the death of Herod . . . a certain Simon seized the title king"). Simon was eventually slain by Gratus (4 B.C.E.).

Athronges the shepherd of Judea. According to Josephus, one Athronges, "remarkable for his great stature and feats of strength," though a mere shepherd of no special ancestry or character, "dared to (gain) a kingdom [*etolmēsen epi basileia*]." "Having put on the diadem [*ho de diadēma perithēmenos*]," he began giving orders, exercising and retaining "power for a long while [4–2 B.C.E.], for he was called king [*basilei tē keklēmeno*]" (*Ant.* 17.10.7 §§278–284; *J.W.* 2.4.3 §§60–65: "He himself, like a king [*autos de kathaper basileus*], handled matters of graver importance. It was then that he placed the diadem on himself [*heauto peritithēsin diadēma*]"). He and his brothers eventually surrendered to Archelaus.

Judas (of Gamala) the Galilean. Judas the Galilean is regarded as one of the anointed kings, and not simply a bandit, because of his "bid for independence" (*Ant.* 18.1.1 §4) and because of his mention in Acts 5:37, thus putting him in the company of Jesus and Theudas, both prophets and probably both messianic claimants. Furthermore, the fact that Judas' son Menahem claimed to be a messiah could suggest that he had inherited his kingly aspirations from his father (which may be hinted at by Josephus himself in *J.W.* 2.17.8 §§433–434). Probably not the same person as Judas son of Hezekiah, this Judas called on his countrymen not to submit to the census administered by Quirinius, the Roman governor who had replaced the deposed Archelaus (*Ant.* 18.1.1 §4–10; *J.W.* 2.8.1 §118). According to Acts, the Pharisee Gamaliel said that "Judas the Galilean arose in the days of the census and drew away some of the people after him; he also perished, and all who followed him were scattered" (5:37). (This passage is problematic, especially if the "Theudas" of Acts 5:36 is the Theudas of 45 C.E.) It is significant that a parallel is drawn between Judas and Theudas (who will be considered below), at least in that both movements ended in the deaths of their leaders. (Josephus does not tell us what became of Judas.) Josephus describes Judas' movement as a "rebellion" and as a "a bid for (national) independence," as well as a "fourth philosophy." It is perhaps significant that at the mention of Judas' call for civil disobedience Josephus goes on to summarize the disturbances of the first century and to suggest that it was this sort of thinking that led to violence and bloodshed that ultimately culminated in the catastrophe of 66–70 C.E. (*Ant.* 18.1.1 §10: "My reason for giving this brief account of [the events that led up to the war] is chiefly that the zeal which Judas and Saddok inspired in the younger element meant the ruin of our cause"). Therefore, although Judas' personal role seems to have been principally that of a teacher, the effect of his teaching warrants regarding him as yet another founder of a movement that opposed foreign domination and, by implication, that advocated the establishment of an independent kingdom of Israel. The crucifixion of his sons Jacob and Simon under Governor Tiberius Alexander (46–48 C.E.) may also have had something to do with rebellion (*Ant.* 20.5.2 §102).

Menahem (grand)son of Judas the Galilean. Josephus tells us that Menahem (ca. 66 C.E.), either the son or the grandson of Judas the Galilean, plundered Herod's armory at Masada, arming his followers as well as other "brigands," and then "returned like a king [*basileus*] to

Jerusalem, became the leader of the revolution, and directed the siege of the palace." His followers occupied the Roman barracks and eventually caught and killed Ananias the high priest. As a result of Menahem's accomplishments, Josephus tells us, Menahem, believing himself unrivalled, became an "insufferable tyrant [*tyrannos*]." Finally, insurgents loyal to Eleazar son of Ananias the high priest rose up against him. Menahem, "arrayed in royal [*basilikē*] apparel," was attacked while in the temple. Although he initially managed to escape and hide, he was eventually caught, dragged out into the open, tortured, and put to death (*J.W.* 2.17.8–10 §§433–448). It is possible, but I think improbable, that he is the Menahem referred to in a tradition that tells of the birth of King Messiah, whose name is Menahem son of Hezekiah, born on the day that the temple was destroyed (*y. Ber.* 2.4; cf. *b. Sanh.* 98b).

John of Gischala son of Levi. Initially John of Gischala was commander of the rebel forces in Gischala (*J.W.* 2.20.6 §575). He later became part of the zealot coalition (*J.W.* 4.1.1–5 §§121–146; 5.3.1 §§104–105; 5.6.1 §§250–251) that, having been forced to retreat into Jerusalem, gained control of most of the city and installed a high priest of its own choosing (*J.W.* 4.3.6 §§147–150; 4.3.8 §§155–161). Although Josephus describes him as little more than a power-hungry brigand (*J.W.* 2.21.1 §§585–589), apparently John did have kingly aspirations. Josephus tells us that he aspired to "tyrannical power [*tyrannionti*]," "issued despotic [*despotikoteron*] orders," and began "laying claim to absolute sovereignty [*monarchias*]" (*J.W.* 4.7.1 §§389–393). Fearing the possibility that John might achieve "monarchical rule [*monarchias*]," many of the zealots opposed him (*J.W.* 4.7.1 §§393–394; see also 4.9.11 §566, where the Idumeans turn against the "tyrant"). When the city was finally overrun, John surrendered and was imprisoned for life (*J.W.* 6.9.4 §433). Later in his account of the Jewish war Josephus evaluates John much in the same terms as he does Simon bar Giora (*J.W.* 7.8.1 §§263–266; in 4.9.10 §§564–565 they are compared as the tyrants "within" and "without" Jerusalem; in 6.9.4 §§433–434 Josephus also compares their respective surrenders). One of John's worst crimes was his "impiety towards God. For he had unlawful food served at his table and abandoned the established rules of purity of our forefathers" (*J.W.* 7.8.1 §264). What apparently was so reprehensible to Josephus the Pharisee, of priestly descent, was probably no more than different halakot, ones which were evidently more lenient and more popular. The disgust that Josephus shows is reminiscent of reactions that Jesus' table manners sometimes evoked (cf. Mark 2:15–17; 7:2; Luke 15:1–2).

Simon bar Giora of Gerasa. The most important leader of the rebellion was Simon bar Giora (Aramaic = "son of the proselyte"), a man from Gerasa (or Jerash). Simon distinguished himself with military prowess and cunning (*J.W.* 2.19.2 §521; 4.6.1 §353; 4.9.4 §510; 4.9.5 §§514–520). He drew a large following by "proclaiming liberty for slaves and rewards

for the free" (*J.W.* 4.9.3 §508; 4.9.7 §534 ["forty thousand followers"]).
His army was "subservient to his command as to a king [*basilea*]" (*J.W.*
4.9.4 §510). Josephus avers that early in his career Simon had shown
signs of being tyrannical (*J.W.* 2.22.2 §652 [*tyrannein*]; 4.9.3 §508 [*ho de
tyrannion*]; 5.1.3 §11; 7.2.2 §32 [*etyrannesen*]; 7.8.1 §265 [*tyrannon*]). Simon
subjugated the whole of Idumea (*J.W.* 4.9.6 §§521–528). The ruling
priests, in consultation with the Idumeans and many of the inhabitants
of the city, decided to invite Simon into Jerusalem to protect the city from
John of Gischala (*J.W.* 4.9.11 §§570–576). Simon entered the city and took
command in the spring of 69 C.E. (*J.W.* 4.9.12 §577). Among the leaders
of the rebellion "Simon in particular was regarded with reverence and
awe . . . each was quite prepared to take his very own life had he given
the order" (*J.W.* 5.7.3 §309). Finally defeated and for a time in hiding,
Simon, dressed in white tunics and a purple mantle, made a dramatic
appearance before the Romans on the very spot where the temple had
stood (*J.W.* 7.1.2 §29). He was placed in chains (*J.W.* 7.2.2 §36), sent to
Italy (*J.W.* 7.5.3 §118), put on display as part of the victory celebration in
Rome (*J.W.* 7.5.6 §154), and was finally executed (*J.W.* 7.5.6 §155).

Lukuas of Cyrene. During the reign of Trajan the Jewish inhabitants
of Judea, Egypt, and Cyrene revolted (114 or 115 C.E.). According to
Eusebius they rallied to one Lukuas, "their king" (*Eccl. Hist.* 4.2.1–4). Dio
Cassius mentions this revolt, but calls the Jewish leader Andreas (*Roman
History* 68.32; 69.12–13). Eusebius says that General Marcius Turbo
"waged war vigorously against [the Jews] in many battles for a considerable time and killed many thousands" (*Eccl. Hist.* 4.2.4). Although Dio's
claim that hundreds of thousands perished is probably an exaggeration,
the papyri and archaeological evidence confirm that the revolt was
widespread and very destructive (see E. Schürer, *History*, 1.530–33).

Simon ben Kosiba. Apparently Simon, either the son of a man named
Kosiba or from a village (or valley) by that name, was the principal leader
of the second Jewish rebellion against Rome (132–135 C.E.). (The rabbis
often spell his name with the letter *z* to make a word play with "lie.")
According to rabbinic tradition, Rabbi Aqiba, contrary to other rabbis,
regarded Simon as the Messiah (*y. Ta'an.* 4.5). Another tradition adds:
"Bar Koziba reigned two and a half years, and then said to the rabbis, 'I
am the Messiah.' They answered, 'Of Messiah it is written that he smells
[instead of sees] and judges: let us see if he [Bar Koziba] can do so"
(*b. Sanh.* 93b). Administering justice by smelling, instead of seeing, is an
allusion to Isa 11:3–5 ("He shall not judge by what his eyes see, or decide
by what his ears hear; but with righteousness he shall judge the poor,
and decide with equity for the meek of the earth . . ."). The talmudic
passage goes on to say that Simon failed and so was slain. According to
y. Ta'an. 4.5 (cf. *m. Ta'an.* 4:6; *b. Giṭ.* 57a–b; *Lam. Rab.* 2.2 §4) Simon was
defeated at Bether because of arrogance against heaven ("Lord of the

Universe, neither help us nor hinder us!") and violence against Rabbi Eleazar, one of Israel's revered teachers.

No doubt because of his ultimate defeat and the disastrous consequences for Israel, the rabbis were very critical of Simon. The evidence suggests, however, that initially he was quite successful. Legends such as his catching and throwing back Roman siege stones may be remnants of popular stories in which Simon had been depicted in a much more favorable light. (According to Jerome [*Against Rufinus* 3.31], Simon deceived the people with fraudulent miracles.) Obviously Aqiba found something appealing about him. In fact, it was Simon's military success, the tradition tells us, that led the famous rabbi to recognize Simon as the Messiah (*Lam. Rab.* 2.2 §4). According to Moses Maimonides, "Rabbi Aqiba, the greatest of the sages of the Mishna, was a supporter of King Ben Kozeba, saying of him that he was King Messiah. He *and all the contemporary sages* regarded him as the King Messiah, until he was killed for sins which he had committed" (*Mishneh Torah, Melakhim* 11:3, my emphasis). For these reasons, as well as the fact that the Romans subdued Judea only with great difficulty, it is probable that Simon enjoyed widespread popularity and support. It is quite possible that the persecution against Christians described by Justin Martyr had to do with their refusal to acknowledge the messiahship of Simon: "During the Jewish war Bar Kochebas, the leader of the Jewish rebellion, commanded Christians to be led away to terrible punishment, unless they denied Jesus as the Messiah and blasphemed" (*Apology* 31.6). According to Eusebius, "Bar Kochebas . . . claimed to be a luminary who had come down to them from heaven" (*Eccl. Hist.* 4.6.2).

Simon became known as "Bar Kochba" because of a word-play between his name and the star of Num 24:17–19, a passage widely regarded as messianic: "A star [*kôkāb*] shall come out of Jacob, and a scepter shall rise out of Israel; it shall crush the forehead of Moab, and break down all the sons of Sheth. Edom [= Rome] shall be dispossessed. . . ." The earliest messianic interpretation of this verse is apparently found in the *Testament of Judah*: "And after this there shall arise for you a Star from Jacob. . . . This is the Shoot of God. . . . Then he will illumine the scepter of my kingdom, and from your root will arise the Shoot, and through it will arise the rod of righteousness for the nations, to judge and to save all that call on the Lord" (24:1–6).

Not only are there allusions to Numbers 24, there are allusions to Isa 11:1–5 as well. At Qumran Num 24:17–19 seems to have been understood in a messianic sense: "Yours is the battle! From [you] comes the power . . . as you declared to us in former times, 'A star has journeyed from Jacob, a scepter has arisen from Israel. . . .' And by the hand of your Anointed Ones . . . you have announced to us the times of the battles . . . " (1QM 11:4–9); "And the Star [alluding to Amos 9:11 in line 15] is the Seeker of the Law who came to Damascus; as it is written, 'A star has journeyed out of Jacob and a scepter is risen out of Israel.' The scepter is the Prince of all the congregation, and at his coming 'he will break down all the sons of Seth'" (CD 7:18–21; cf. 1QSb 5:27–28; 4QTest 9–13). In the targums the messianic interpretation of Num 24:17 is explicit: ". . . a king shall arise out of Jacob and be anointed the Messiah out of Israel" (Onqelos); ". . . a mighty king of the house of Jacob shall reign, and shall be anointed Messiah, wielding the mighty scepter of Israel" (Ps.-Jonathan); "A king is destined to arise from the house of Jacob, a redeemer and ruler from the house of Israel, who shall slay the mighty ones . . . who shall destroy all that remains of the guilty city, which is Rome" (Frg. Tg. 24:17–19). This messianic interpretation of Numbers 24 is likely what lies behind Matt 2:1–12: the magi have seen the Messiah's "star" and have concluded that the "king of the Jews" has been born. Philo alluded to the passage: "For 'there shall come a man,' says the oracle, and leading his host to war he will subdue great and populous nations, because God has sent to his aid the reinforcement which befits the godly" (On Rewards and Punishments 16 §95). It may also be the passage to which Josephus alluded a generation later: "But what more than all else incited [the Jews] to [the first] war was an ambiguous oracle, likewise found in their sacred scriptures, to the effect that at that time one from their country would become ruler of the world. This they understood to mean someone of their own race, and many of their wise men went astray in their interpretation of it. The oracle, however, in reality signified the sovereignty of Vespasian, who was proclaimed emperor on Jewish soil" (J.W. 6.5.4 §§312–313; cf. 3.8.9 §§400–402). (The report that a Jewish oracle had spoken of Vespasian's accession to the throne was known to Tacitus [Histories 1.10; 5.13], Suetonius [Vespasian 4–5], Dio Cassius [Roman History 66.1], and Appian [Roman History 22, according to Zonaras Annals 11.16].)

But the messianic kingdom that Simon hoped to establish was crushed by the Romans. In the wake of this defeat Aqiba undoubtedly reassessed his view of Simon, as would be seen in J. Neusner's translation of y. Ta'an. 4.5: "A disappointment shall come forth out of Jacob" (Messiah, 95). Aqiba's retraction of his earlier messianic interpretation of Dan 7:9, and possibly the length of the messianic reign, may also have had something to do with Simon's defeat. For Aqiba and many other rabbis the defeat proved costly. The edict of Hadrian forbade Jews to enter Jerusalem and from possessing or teaching Torah. The period is referred to as the "age of the edict" (b. Šabb. 60a; m. Ta'an. 4:6; Mek. on Exod 20:6 [Bahodeš §§6.136–143]; see also Dio Cassius Roman History 69.12.2; Eusebius Eccl. Hist. 4.6.4: "Hadrian then commanded that by a legal decree and ordinances the whole nation should be absolutely prevented from entering from thenceforth even the district around Jerusalem"; Demonstration of the Gospel 6.18.10). Jerusalem's name was changed to Aeilia Capitolina (cf. Dio Cassius *Roman History* 69.12.1). Aqiba violated the edict, was imprisoned (*t. Sanh.* 2.8; cf. *t. Ber.* 2.13; *b. 'Erub.* 21b; *b. Yebam.* 105b, 108b; *y. Yebam.* 12.5), and was cruelly tortured and put to death (*b. Yebam.* 62b; *Lev. Rab.* 13.5 [on 11:4–7]; *Song Rab.* 2.7 §1; *b. Ber.* 61b; *b. Menaḥ.* 29b).

3. *Messianic Prophets.* Even those who claimed to be prophets had intentions not too different from the kingly aspirants. They too wished to liberate Israel and consequently provoked violent response from the Romans. Although their respective understandings of leadership, or messiahship, may have differed from those who attempted to wear the diadem (in that they may have expected a little more of Heaven's aid), their attempts at modeling their leadership after Moses strongly suggest that they too were part of the struggle to restore Israel. Part of Moses typology was the "wilderness summons," an idea probably related to Isa 40:3 ("In the wilderness prepare the way of the Lord"), a passage cited in Christian writings (Mark 1:2–3), Qumran (1QS 8:12–14; 9:19–20), and other (Bar 5:7; *T. Mos.* 10:1–5) sources. In the case of Christians (at least with regard to John the Baptist) and Essenes, the passage was acted upon quite literally: they went out into the wilderness to prepare the way of the Lord. Synoptic warnings about not heeding a summons to the wilderness (cf. Matt 24:26) and various claims of false Christs (cf. Mark 13:21–22 par.) surely have in mind the people of whom Josephus wrote. At many points there are suggestive parallels (Mark 13:21–22; Matt 24:26; Luke 17:20–23; 21:8; cf. Josephus *Ant.* 17.10.7 §§278–284; 20.8.6 §168; 20.8.10 §188; *J.W.* 2.13.5 §§261–263; 6.5.4 §315).

The Anonymous Samaritan. Josephus tells us that during the administration of Pontius Pilate (26–36 C.E.) a certain Samaritan (36 C.E.), whom he calls a liar and demagogue, convinced many of his people to follow him to Mount Gerizim where he would show them the place where their sacred temple vessels were buried. (The Samaritan temple on Mount Gerizim had been destroyed by John Hyrcanus in 128 B.C.E. [Josephus *Ant.* 13.9.1 §256].) Pilate sent a detachment of troops, which routed the pilgrims before they could ascend the mountain (*Ant.* 18.4.1 §§85–87). This episode, although not a Jewish affair, parallels the type of thinking found in Jewish regions (i.e., Galilee and Judea). This Samaritan "uprising" probably had to do with the Samaritan hope for the appearance of the *Taheb*, the "restorer," whose coming was expected in keeping with the promise of Deut 18:15–18 (cf. *Memar Marqah* 4:12; John 4:20, 25: "Our [Samaritan] fathers worshiped on this mountain [i.e., Mount Gerizim]. . . I know that Messiah is coming . . . when he comes, he will show us all things"). As such, it is another example of the messianic fervor and unrest of the region in this period of time.

Theudas. During the administration of Fadus (44–46 C.E.), Josephus tells us that "a certain impostor named Theudas persuaded the majority of the populace to take up their possessions and follow him to the Jordan

River. He stated that he was a prophet and that at his command the river would be parted and would provide easy passage. With this talk he deceived many" (*Ant.* 20.5.1 §§97–98). The Roman governor dispatched the cavalry, which scattered Theudas' following. The would-be prophet was himself decapitated and his head put on display in Jerusalem. Acts 5:36 tells us that he had a following of about four hundred men. Although he regarded himself as a "prophet [*prophētēs*]," Josephus calls Theudas an "impostor [*goēs*]" who "deceived many." (Note the similar description in 2 Tim 3:13: "evil men and impostors will go from bad to worse, deceivers and deceived." Judging by Philo's usage [*On Special Laws* 1.58 §315], a *goēs* was the precise opposite of the genuine *prophētēs*.) Theudas' claim to be able to part the Jordan River is an unmistakable allusion either to the crossing of the Red Sea (Exod 14:21–22) or to the crossing of the Jordan River (Josh 3:14–17), part of the imagery associated with Israel's redemption (cf. Isa 11:15; 43:16; 51:10; 63:11). In either case, it is probable that Theudas was claiming to be the prophet "like Moses" (Deut 18:15–19; cf. 1 Macc 4:45–46; 9:27; 14:41). As such, he was claiming to be more than a mere prophet; he was claiming to be a messianic figure. Indeed, it is possible that Theudas may have had even more ideas about himself. O. Betz (*Jesus,* 22–23) has suggested that Theudas' claim "to be someone" (*einai tina*; Acts 5:36) may allude to a claim to be the "son of man" (*bar 'enāš*) of Dan 7:13, an expression which was understood in a messianic sense in the *Similitudes of Enoch* (*1 Enoch* 37–71), material that likely dates from the first half of the first century (cf. 48:10; 52:4). His suggestion is based on the fact that the Aramaic expression, "son of man," is often the equivalent of the indefinite pronoun "someone," which in Greek is *tis*. If Betz is correct, then we have evidence of another first-century messianic claimant who understood himself as Daniel's "son of man."

The Anonymous Egyptian (Jew). At the outset of the section in which he speaks of the Egyptian, Josephus tells us that "impostors and deceitful men persuaded the crowd to follow them into the wilderness. For they said that they would show them unmistakable wonders and signs according to God's foreknowledge." They and many of their following "were brought before (Governor) Felix" and "were punished" (*Ant.* 20.8.6 §168). Felix's response suggests that the proclamations and activities of these men were not viewed as politically innocent. Indeed, Josephus tells us that these "madmen" promised their followers "signs of freedom" (*J.W.* 2.13.4 §259). Felix himself regarded these actions as "preliminary to insurrection" (*J.W.* 2.13.4 §260). In this the governor was probably correct. As to the Egyptian, Josephus reports: "At this time [ca. 56 C.E.] there came to Jerusalem from Egypt a man who said that he was a prophet [*prophētēs*] and advised the masses of the common people to go out with him to the mountain called the Mount of Olives, which lies opposite the city. . . . For he asserted that he wished to demonstrate from there that at his command Jerusalem's walls would fall down, through which he promised to provide them an entrance into the city" (*Ant.* 20.8.6 §§169–170). Felix promptly dispatched the cavalry, which routed and dispersed the following. However, the Egyptian himself escaped.

In the parallel account in *Jewish War* Josephus calls the Egyptian a "false prophet" and "impostor" who, with a following of thirty thousand, "proposed to force an entrance into Jerusalem and, after overpowering the Roman garrison, to set himself up as tyrant [*tyrannein*] over the people" (*J. W.* 2.13.5 §§261–263). The hoped-for sign of the walls falling down was probably inspired by the story of Israel's conquest of Jericho, led by Joshua the successor of Moses (Josh 6:20). This Egyptian is mentioned in other sources as well. According to Acts 21:38 a Roman tribune asked Paul: "Are you not the Egyptian, then, who recently stirred up a revolt and led the four thousand men of the Assassins out into the wilderness?"

It is possible that the rabbis may have confused Jesus, also thought to have spent time in Egypt where he acquired knowledge of magic (*b. Sanh.* 107b; cf. Origen *Against Celsus* 1.38), with the Egyptian. It is interesting to note that according to the accounts in Acts and in *Jewish War,* the Egyptian summoned people "out into the wilderness." This wilderness summons, as well as the Joshua-like sign of the walls falling down, is very likely part of the prophet-like-Moses theme, or some variation of it, that evidently lay behind much of the messianic speculation of the first century. Moreover, the fact that this Jewish man was known as the man from Egypt might also have had to do with some sort of association with Moses.

Anonymous "Impostor." In a context in which he described the troubles brought on by the *sicarii*, Josephus reports that "Festus [ca. 61 C.E.] also sent a force of cavalry and infantry against those deceived by a certain impostor who had promised them salvation [*sōtērian*] and rest [*paula*] from troubles, if they chose to follow him into the wilderness [*eremias*]. Those whom Festus sent destroyed that deceiver and those who had followed him" (*Ant.* 20.8.10 §188). It is likely that this "impostor" was another messianic prophet, probably in keeping with the prophet-like-Moses theme (as the wilderness summons would seem to indicate). The impostor's promise of rest, moreover, may have had something to do with Ps 95:7b–11, a passage warning Israelites not to put God to the test, as they did at Meribah and Massah "in the wilderness [*eremo*]," and consequently fail to enter God's "rest [*katapausin*]" (cf. Exod 17:1–7; Num 20:1–13). Although the parallel is not precise, it is worth noting that this passage is cited and commented upon in Hebrews (3:7–4:13), a writing in which Jewish Christians are exhorted not to neglect their "salvation [*sōtērias*]" (2:3) but to "strive to enter that rest [*katapausin*]" (4:11).

Jonathan the refugee. Following the Roman victory over Israel, one Jonathan fled to Cyrene. According to Josephus, this man, by trade a weaver, was one of the sicarii. He persuaded many of the poorer Jews to follow him out into the desert, "promising to show them signs and apparitions" (*J.W.* 7.11.1 §§437–438; *Life* 76 §§424–425). Catullus the Roman governor dispatched troops who routed Jonathan's following and eventually captured the leader himself (*J.W.* 7.11.1 §§439–442). Although Josephus does not describe Jonathan as a (false) prophet, it is likely that this is how the man viewed himself, as the desert summons would imply.

4. *Messianic Priests.* Although there were eschatological ideas that envisioned the appearance of messianic priests, some based on the Hasmonean model (*T. Reub.* 6:10–12; *T. Jud.* 21:2–3), others based on Melchizedek (Heb 5, 7–8; perhaps 11QMelch), there are no clear examples of messianic priestly claimants in the period under consideration. It is possible that the Samaritan (see §3 above), who hoped to find the sacred vessels of the Samaritan temple, had some priestly ideas. And possibly the zealots thought that they were installing an anointed high priest (one "Phanni," possibly of Zadokite lineage) on the threshold of the restoration of the kingdom (Josephus *J.W.* 4.3.8 §§155–157). But this is doubtful, since Phanni, described by Josephus as clownish, incompetent, and reluctant, was probably no more than a pawn in the hands of the rebels. Thus, it would appear that although there were many who made kingly and prophetic claims, evidently none attempted to fulfill the restorative ideas associated with the anointed high priest.

5. *Later Messianic Claimants.* Following the defeat of Simon in 132 C.E. it would be three centuries before the reappearance of messianic fervor. Based on various calculations it was believed that Messiah would come either in 440 C.E. (cf. *b. Sanh.* 97b) or in 471 C.E. (cf. *b. 'Abod. Zar.* 9b). (Other dates were suggested.) Answering this expectation, one "Moses of Crete" (ca. 448 C.E.) promised to lead the Jewish people through the sea, dry-shod, from Crete to Palestine. At his command many of his followers threw themselves into the Mediterranean. Some drowned; others were rescued. Moses himself disappeared (cf. Socrates Scholasticus *Historia Ecclesiastica* 7.38; 12.33). Evidently Moses typology had continued to play an important role in shaping restoration hopes.

A variety of other pseudo-messiahs appeared in the Islamic period (especially in the eighth century), during the later crusades (especially in the twelfth and thirteenth centuries), and even as late as the sixteenth, seventeenth, and eighteenth centuries (cf. *JewEnc* 10.252–55).

GENERAL BIBLIOGRAPHY: E. Bammel and C. F. D. Moule, eds., *Jesus and the Politics of His Day* (Cambridge: Cambridge University, 1984); O. Betz, *Jesus und das Danielbuch* (Frankfurt am Main: Peter Lang, 1985); M. Black, "Judas of Galilee and Josephus' 'Fourth Philosophy,'" in O. Betz, L. Haacker, and M. Hengel, eds., *Josephus Studien* (Göttingen: Vandenhoeck & Ruprecht, 1974) 45–54; S. G. F.

Brandon, *Jesus and the Zealots* (Manchester: Manchester University, 1967); J. D. Crossan, *Jesus and the Revolutionaries* (New York: Harper & Row, 1970); S. Freyne, *Galilee from Alexander the Great to Hadrian* (Notre Dame: University of Notre Dame, 1980); M. Hengel, *Die Zeloten* (2d ed.; Leiden: Brill, 1976); D. Hill, "Jesus and Josephus' 'Messianic Prophets,' " in E. Best and R. McL. Wilson, eds., *Text and Interpretation: Studies Presented to Matthew Black* (Cambridge and New York: Cambridge University, 1979) 143–54; R. A. Horsley and J. S. Hanson, *Bandits, Prophets, and Messiahs: Popular Movements at the Time of Jesus* (Minneapolis: Winston, 1985); M. de Jonge, "The Use of the Word 'Anointed' in the Time of Jesus," *NovT* 8 (1966) 132–48; A. Fuks, "Aspects of the Jewish Revolt in A.D. 115–117," *JRS* 15 (1961) 98–104; H. P. Kingdon, "Who were the Zealots and their Leaders in A.D. 66?" *NTS* 17 (1970–71) 68–72; W. Klassen, "Jesus and Phineas: A Rejected Role Model," in SBLSP (Atlanta: Scholars, 1986) 490–500; J. Klausner, *The Messianic Idea in Israel* (New York: Macmillan, 1955); W. A. Meeks, *The Prophet-King: Moses Traditions and the Johannine Christology* (NovTSup 14; Leiden: Brill, 1967); J. Neusner, W. S. Green, and E. Frerichs, eds., *Judaisms and Their Messiahs at the Turn of the Christian Era* (Cambridge: Cambridge University, 1987); J. Neusner, *Messiah in Context* (Philadelphia: Fortress, 1984); J. Reiling, "The Use of ψευδοπροφήτης in the Septuagint, Philo and Josephus," *NovT* 13 (1971) 147–56; D. M. Rhoads, *Israel in Revolution* (Philadelphia: Fortress, 1976); A. J. Saldarini, "Political and Social Roles of the Pharisees and the Scribes in Galilee," in SBLSP (Atlanta: Scholars, 1988) 200–209; E. Schürer, *The History of the Jewish People in the Age of Jesus Christ* (rev. and ed. by G. Vermes and F. Millar; vol. 1; Edinburgh: T. & T. Clark, 1973); E. M. Smallwood, *The Jews under Roman Rule from Pompey to Diocletian* (Leiden: Brill, 1976); M. Smith, "Zealots and Sicarii, Their Origins and Relation," *HTR* 64 (1971) 1–19; B. Witherington, *The Christology of Jesus* (Minneapolis: Fortress, 1990) 81–96.

INDEX OF MODERN AUTHORS

INDEX OF ANCIENT WRITINGS AND WRITERS

This index enables the reader to find quickly the name of an ancient author or title. Titles are listed according to the normal form (e.g., *Testament of Levi*) and also according to the name of the ancient worthy (e.g., *Levi, Testament of*). The appropriate chapter where the author or title is discussed in the present volume is noted in parentheses.

2 Baruch (2)
3 Baruch (2)
4 Baruch (2)
Bee, Book of (2)
Bel and the Dragon (1)
Benjamin, Testament of (2)
Berešit Rabbati (7)
Birth of Mary (8)
Book of Elchasai (8)
Book of Jasher (2)
Book of John (8)
Book of the Bee (2)
Book of the Resurrection of Christ by
    Bartholomew (8)
Book of the Rolls (2)

Cairo Genizah (3, 4, 6)
Cassiodorus (9)
Cave of Treasures (2)
CD (Damascus Document) (3)
Celsus (11)
Cherubim (On the Cherubim) (5)
Christ, Letter of, from Heaven (8)
Christ, Letters of, and Abgarus (8)
Chronicle of Jerahmeel (7)
Chronicles, Samaritan (11)
Claudius, Pilate's Letter to (8)
Clement of Alexandria (9)
1 Clement (or Clemens Romanus) (9)
2 Clement (9)
Cleodemus Malchus (2)
Commodian (9)
Concept of Our Great Power (10)
Conflict of Adam and Eve with Satan (2)
Confusione Linguarum (On the Confusion of the
    Languages) (5)
Congressu quaerendae Eruditionis gratia (On the
    Preliminary Studies) (5)
Consumption of Thomas (8)
Contra Celsum (9)
Coptic Lives of the Virgin (8)
Coptic Narratives of the Ministry and the
    Passion (8)
Corinthians, Paul's Third Epistle to the (8)
Corpus Hermeticum (11)
Correspondence between Seneca and Paul (8)
Cyprian (9)
Cyril of Jerusalem (9)

Dan, Testament of (2)
Daniel, Apocalypse of (2)
Daniel, Vision of (2)
David Kimhi (7)

Death of Abraham (2)
Death of Pilate (8)
Decalogo (On the Decalogue) (5)
Defter (11)
Demetrius the Chronographer (2)
Demonstratio Evangelica (9)
Derek Ereṣ Rabba (7)
Derek Ereṣ Zuṭa (7)
Deuteronomy Rabbah (7)
Dialogue of the Savior (10)
Dialogue of Timothy and Aquila (8)
Dialogue with Trypho the Jew (9)
Diatessaron (9)
Didache (9)
Diognetus (9)
Discourse on the Eighth and Ninth (10)
Dositheus, Dositheans (11)
Durran (11)

Ebionites, Gospel of the (8)
Ebrietate (On Drunkenness) (5)
Ecclesiastes Rabbah (7)
Ecclesiasticus (1)
Egyptians, Gospel of the (8, 10)
Elchasai, Book of (8)
Eldad and Modad (2)
Eliezer, Pirqe de Rabbi (7)
Elijah, Apocalypse of (2)
Elijah, Hebrew Apocalypse of (2)
1 Enoch (2)
2 Enoch (2)
3 Enoch (2)
Epiphanius (9)
Epistle of Barnabas
Epistle of Jeremiah (1)
Epistle of Paul to the Alexandrians (8)
Epistle of the Apostles (8)
1 Esdras (1)
2 Esdras (1)
Esther Rabbah (7)
Esther, Additions of (1)
Eugnostos the Blessed (10)
Eupolemus (2)
Eusebius (9)
Eve (see Life of Adam and Eve)
Eve with Satan, Conflict of Adam and (2)
Eve, Gospel of (8)
Exegesis of the Soul (10)
Exodus Rabbah (7)
Ezekiel the Tragedian (2)
Ezekiel, Apocryphon of (2)
4 Ezra (Fourth Book of = 2 Esdr 3–14) (2)
Ezra, Greek Apocalypse of (2)

INDEX OF ANCIENT SOURCES

Note: This index includes references from all parts of the book except Appendixes 2 and 3.

Church Fathers